Table of Contents

KU-536-551

Preface

As we began to plan this book, we worried that it would become lost in the hundreds—no, thousands—of volumes that have been written on "Web design," HTML, Java, XML, or any of the myriad technologies that must be understood to build successful Web-based systems and applications (WebApps). To our surprise, we found that one crucial topic—the *process* through which each of the other technologies is applied—has received relatively little coverage. We call the process *Web engineering,* and we believe people who apply it have a higher likelihood of building WebApps that satisfy users' needs and provide real benefit to their clients' businesses or organizations.

It has become a cliché to state that WebApps can be pivotal to the success of virtually all businesses and organizations. And yet, many WebApps continue to be built in an ad hoc manner with little regard to the fundamental principles of problem analysis, effective design, solid testing, and change management. As a consequence, many WebApps fail to meet the needs of their users and the objectives of the business that has commissioned them.

Today, we're making the transition from an old-school approach to Web engineering in order to meet the challenges posed by the next generation of Web-based systems and applications. The industry is moving toward a more pragmatic Web engineering process—one that exhibits agility and adaptability. At the same time, the process must deliver the integrity of a disciplined approach.

Web Engineering: A Practitioner's Approach has been written to provide you with a solid understanding of a pragmatic process for engineering Web-based systems and applications. The content is presented in an informal, conversational style, using a question-and-answer format to mentor the reader in this new engineering discipline.

Throughout the book, we emphasize an agile process and simple, practical methods that have been proven in industry application. At the same time, we have purposely deemphasized our treatment of specific Web-based tools and technologies. This is not because we think they are unimportant, but because there are literally thousands of books, papers, and Web-based resources that address them and surprisingly few that consider Web engineering issues in a cohesive manner. For that reason, our focus is unapologetically on Web engineering. Our intent is to provide a book that can be used by industry practitioners and by students at the undergraduate or first-year graduate level.

The Web engineering process emphasizes an agile approach and presents simple, yet effective methods for gathering and analyzing problem requirements, designing an effective solution, and then building and testing a high-quality WebApp.

But the process is not just about technology. We also present proven techniques for project management, change and content management, and quality assurance. Throughout the book, we present a case study designed to provide examples of the methods and techniques we present. A website, **www.SafeHomeAssured.com**, complements the case study with additional in-depth detail, as well as providing extra supporting information.

Our work on this book has been facilitated by many print and Web-based resources that discuss principles and techniques for building high-quality WebApps. Our thanks to the authors of each source referenced within these pages and to hundreds of other colleagues and authors who have shaped our thinking over the years. Special thanks also go to Didar Zowghi, Norazlin Yusop, Xiaoying Kong, and Rachatrin Tongrungrojana.

Throughout this book, we have used text excerpts, selected figures, and the *SafeHome* case study from Roger Pressman's *Software Engineering: A Practitioner's Approach* (sixth edition). In some cases, we have used these materials as is, but in many others, we have adapted them to meet the special needs of Web engineers. In every case, these materials are used with permission.

We each have families of four and want to express special thanks for their support during this endeavor. Our wonderful wives—Barbara and Catherine—have graciously tolerated the many hours of writing, revision, and travel that come with the production of a book. Roger's sons—Mathew and Michael—are grown, have businesses of their own, and use the Internet and Web every day. David's sons—Oliver and Dominic—are young, have their whole future ahead of them, and will surely spend much of their professional lives navigating the Web of tomorrow. We hope that the ideas presented in this book will make their journey easier.

Roger Pressman
Boca Raton, Florida, USA

David Lowe
Sydney, Australia

CHAPTER 1

WEB-BASED SYSTEMS

Let's go back in time and revisit the early decades of computer software development. During the 1950s and 1960s few people appreciated the importance of computer-based systems, and virtually no one foresaw the global impact that computer hardware and software would have on every aspect of society in the late twentieth and early twenty-first centuries. Most people who worked with computers during the early days stumbled into the business, creating computer programs using a combination of informality, urgency, intuition, and art. When things worked out well, this approach lead to important advances in computing. But things didn't always work out well. Computer-based systems often failed to do what they were supposed to do; were delivered late or not at all; and were difficult and sometimes impossible to correct, adapt, and enhance in any reasonable time frame. The old-school approach was, regrettably, a hit-or-miss proposition.

But old-school thinking established a culture that quickly became entrenched. Informality, urgency, intuition, and art were the driving forces behind the activities of most computer-based system developers. After all, *informality* leads to an easy work environment—one in which you can do your own thing. *Urgency* leads to action and rapid decision making. Intuition is an intangible quality that enables you to "feel" your way through complex situations. And *art* leads to aesthetic form and function—to something that pleases those who encounter it. And what, you might ask, is wrong with any of that?

As we change our focus from the past to the present, you'll find that the answer to this question has much to do with *Web engineering*, the topic that we'll discuss throughout this book.

The Web

Today, we're living in the formative years of the Internet era. So much has already been said about this exciting time that it's impossible to discuss the impact of the Internet and the World Wide Web without lapsing into a cliché-ridden dialogue. You already know the Web is *big*, very big. But we don't mean "big" in the typical sense (e.g., number of Web pages and sites, number of users, amount of information flowing across the network), although the size of the Web and its projected growth rate are staggering. We mean *big* in a societal and cultural sense.

1

The Web has become an indispensable technology for business, commerce, communication, education, engineering, entertainment, finance, government, industry, media, medicine, politics, science, and transportation—to name just a few areas that impact your life. But being an "indispensable technology" only scratches the surface of the Web's impact on each of us. It has changed the ways in which we buy products (e-commerce), meet people (online dating), understand the world (portals), acquire our news (online media), voice our opinions (blogs), entertain ourselves (everything from music downloads to online casinos), and go to school (online learning).

All of these impacts have one thing in common—they need a delivery vehicle that takes raw information associated with the area of interest; structures it in a way that is meaningful; builds a packaged presentation that is organized, aesthetic, ergonomic, and interactive (where required); and delivers it to your Web browser in a manner that initiates a *conversation*.

The conversation between you and a Web application can be passive or active. In a *passive conversation,* you select the information that is to be presented, but have no direct control over its volume, type, or structure. In an *active conversation,* you provide input so that the information that is presented is customized to meet your needs specifically.

The vehicle that acquires information, structures it, builds a packaged presentation, and delivers it is called a *Web application* (WebApp). When a WebApp is combined with client and server hardware, operating systems, network software, and browsers, a *Web-based system* emerges.

Web Applications

In the early days of the World Wide Web (circa 1990 to 1995), "websites" consisted of little more than a set of linked hypertext files that presented information using text and limited graphics. As time passed, Hypertext Markup Language (HTML) was augmented by development tools and technologies [e.g., Extensible Markup Language (XML), Java] that enabled Web engineers to provide both client-side and server-side computing capability along with content. Web-based systems and applications[1] were born. Today, WebApps have evolved into sophisticated computing tools that not only provide stand-alone functionality to the end user, but also have been integrated with corporate and governmental databases and applications.

---

1   In the context of this book, the term *Web application* (WebApp) encompasses everything from a simple Web page that might help a consumer compute an automobile lease payment to a comprehensive website that provides complete travel services for business people and vacationers. Included within this category are complete websites, specialized functionality within websites, and information-processing applications that reside on the Internet or on an Intranet or Extranet.

Let's Introduce a Case Study

You've been approached by CPI Corporation, a (fictional) company that builds, markets, sells, and monitors security systems for homes and small businesses. CPI has no Web presence and wants to roll out a "significant" website that will coincide with the introduction of a new line of security sensors and a set of radically new Web-based services. They want your help in the development of the WebApp, which is called **SafeHomeAssured.com,** and at the same time for you to assist them as they create new Web services that will increase their market share.

You have been asked to attend a meeting in which basic ideas are discussed. During the meeting you learn that CPI has engineered a compact, wireless sensor-controller that will become the core element in a new line of commercial and residential security systems that it intends to call *SafeHome*. A snippet of conversation from the meeting is depicted in the sidebar.

SAFEHOME

A Project Begins

The scene: Meeting room at CPI Corporation, a (fictional) company that makes consumer products for home and commercial use

The players: A senior business manager; a product development manager; a marketing manager; an engineering manager; and you, the Web engineering expert

The conversation:

Business manager (to product manager): Okay, what's this I hear about your folks developing a what? A generic universal wireless box?

Product manager: It's pretty cool . . . about the size of a small matchbook . . . we can attach it to sensors of all kinds, a digital camera, just about anything using an IEEE wireless protocol. It allows us to access the device without wires. We think it'll lead to a whole new generation of products.

Business manager (looking at the marketing manager): You agree?

Marketing manager: I do. In fact, with sales as flat as they've been this year, we need something new. We've been doing a little market research, and we think we've got a line of products and services that could be big.

Business manager: How big . . . bottom line big?

Marketing manager: It's a whole new generation of what we call "home management products." We call 'em *SafeHome*. They use the new wireless interface, provide homeowners or small-business people with a system that's controlled by their PC via the Internet—home security, home surveillance, appliance and device control—you know, turn down the home air conditioner while you're driving home, that sort of thing. We're also thinking about video monitoring and control within a house or business. Just as important, we intend to vertically integrate the product into our monitoring services, allowing customers to access their account via the Web and determine things like when the system is armed or disarmed, what "events" have occurred over a defined time period . . . things like that. We also intend to do most of our maintenance diagnostics via the Web.

Product manager: Engineering's done a technical feasibility study of these ideas. They're doable at relatively low cost. Most hardware is off-the-shelf. Software for the Web is an issue, but it's nothing that we can't get done. We already registered a domain . . . **SafeHomeAssured.com.**

[All CPI managers look directly at you and smile.]

Business manager: Interesting. Now, I asked about the bottom line.

(continued)

SafeHome (CONTINUED)

Marketing manager: PCs have penetrated a huge percentage of all households in the United States. If we could price this thing right, it could be a killer-App. Nobody else has our wireless box . . . it's proprietary. We'll have a 2-year jump on the competition.

Revenue? Maybe as much as $30 to $40 million in the second year.

Business manager (smiling broadly): Let's take this to the next level. I'm interested.

And so, a project begins. You'll notice that there are few details at this stage. Many things need to be defined, specified, and then implemented. The internal perception of the product will change, along with the Web-based system that will support it. But that really doesn't matter at this early stage. *SafeHome* has the support of senior management (who see significant profit potential), and you have an opportunity to be one of the team that will get the job done.

We'll return to *SafeHome* and the **SafeHomeAssured.com** WebApp repeatedly throughout this book, using the project as a case study for describing many aspects of Web engineering. But for now, let's return to our introductory discussion of WebApps and examine their similarity to conventional computer software.

Are WebApps Really Computer Software?

There's really no debate here—WebApps are computer software in the sense that they are a collection of executable instructions and data that provide both information and functionality for end users. The implication, therefore, is that it's reasonable to expect that we can develop WebApps by heeding some, if not all, of the lessons we've learned during the many decades we've built conventional computer-based systems. It's also reasonable to assume that we'll encounter many, if not all, of the problems (both cultural and technical) that we experienced during the earlier era. But more on all that later in this book.

Are the Attributes of WebApps Different from the Attributes of Conventional Software?

There is some debate about the correct answer to this question. Some people argue that a WebApp is nothing more than a client-server application with a heavy emphasis on both aesthetic presentation (e.g., layout, graphics, audio and video elements) and functionality and that both WebApps and conventional client-server applications have the same attributes. But others (including us, the authors of this book) think that when considered in their totality, a complete set of WebApp characteristics do differentiate Web-based systems from more conventional computer-based systems. The following attributes are encountered in the vast majority of WebApps.

Network intensiveness. Every WebApp resides on a network and must serve the needs of a diverse community of clients. In the case of the *Safe-Home* Product,[2] many of the new features to be implemented by CPI will be initiated, controlled, and/or monitored via the Web. The network will enable communication between client-based features of the **SafeHomeAssured.com** WebApp and the servers established by CPI.

Concurrency. A large number of users may access the WebApp at one time. In many cases, the patterns of usage among end users will vary greatly. In some cases, the actions of one user or one set of users may have an impact on the actions of other users or the information presented to other users. In the case of **SafeHomeAssured.com,** tens of thousands of homes will be monitored concurrently, hundreds or thousands of customers may access the WebApp at any given time, and dozens of service technicians may also be online.

Unpredictable load. The number of users of the WebApp may vary by orders of magnitude from day to day. In the case of **SafeHomeAssured.com,** the number of homes and businesses that are monitored will change slowly. But the WebApp must be capable of handling an indeterminate number of events simultaneously (e.g., burglar alarm, fire detection, carbon monoxide detection). On Monday, 10 events might be reported per hour. On Tuesday, 100 events might be recorded, and on Wednesday (after a region suffers a major power outage) thousands of events may be reported per minute.

Performance. If a WebApp user must wait too long (for access, for server-side processing, for client-side formatting and display), he or she may decide to go elsewhere. In the case of **SafeHomeAssured.com,** performance is critical since human life may be at stake. If the WebApp responds too slowly to an event, litigation may result.

Availability. Although an expectation of 100 percent availability is unreasonable, users of popular WebApps often demand access on a "24/7/365" basis. In the case of **SafeHomeAssured.com,** availability of 100 percent is the goal and—given that the system is about home security—the WebApp must be designed to achieve this ideal (or something very close to it).

---

2 *SafeHome* is a security system supported by a Web-based system that was introduced earlier in this chapter. It will be used as a running case study throughout this book.

Data driven. The primary function of many WebApps is to use hypermedia to present text, graphics, audio, and video content to the end user. In addition, WebApps are commonly used to access information that exists on databases that are not an integral part of the Web-based environment (e.g., e-commerce or financial applications). In the case of **SafeHomeAssured.com,** all of these attributes will be evident. In addition, the WebApp must access a database that contains information about each customer; the system configuration the customer has; and the monitoring requirements for that system, an event log, and a maintenance log.

Content sensitive. The quality and aesthetic nature of content remains an important determinant of the quality of a WebApp. In the case of **SafeHomeAssured.com,** an important user class for the WebApp will be "civilians," that is, nontechnical people who demand simple, yet meaningful content presentation.

Continuous evolution. Unlike conventional application software that evolves over a series of planned, chronologically spaced releases, WebApps evolve continuously. It is not unusual for some WebApps (specifically, their content) to be updated on a minute-by-minute schedule or for content to be independently computed for each request. As we'll see later in the book, the **SafeHomeAssured.com** WebApp will evolve as the perception of the system changes over time. The evolution of the WebApp will demand an "incremental" approach to its development.

Immediacy. Although *immediacy*—the compelling need to get software to market quickly—is a characteristic of many application domains, WebApps often exhibit a time-to-market that can be a matter of a few days or weeks.[3] Web engineers must use methods for planning, analysis, design, implementation, and testing that have been adapted to the compressed time schedules required for WebApp development. In the case of **SafeHomeAssured.com,** CPI management is focused on a revenue boost in the short term and significant revenue in the medium term. When this occurs, the WebApp is needed "yesterday."

Security. Because WebApps are available via network access, it is difficult, if not impossible, to limit the population of end users who may access the application. In order to protect sensitive content and provide secure modes of data transmission, strong security measures must be implemented throughout the infrastructure that supports a WebApp and within the application itself. In the case of **SafeHomeAssured.com,** information is flowing into

---

3   With modern tools, sophisticated Web pages can be produced in only a few hours.

and out of people's homes and businesses, making the WebApp a perfect target for those with criminal intent. It had better be secure!

Aesthetics. An undeniable part of the appeal of a WebApp is its look and feel. When an application has been designed to market or sell products or ideas or provide services that generate revenue, aesthetics may have as much to do with success as technical design. In the case of **SafeHomeAssured.com,** the multiplicity of content and functions that the WebApp will provide (to be discussed in Chapter 4) demands that their presentation be both simple and elegant. Aesthetics is a key element for the acceptance of the system.

What Categories Are Encountered as a WebApp Evolves?

You continue your meetings with the folks at CPI, gaining a better understanding of the current perception of **SafeHomeAssured.com** from the managers who have product responsibility and the technical people who will be working with you directly. It becomes apparent that the **SafeHomeAssured.com** WebApp will be fairly significant. There have been no firm commitments as yet, but it appears that the following features (content and function) will be implemented:

- Information about CPI and its products and people
- Specifications for all security hardware components, including pictures, technical descriptions, installation instructions, pricing, and other pertinent information
- Security system design assistance that enables a customer to specify a living or business space (e.g., rooms, doors, windows) and then get semiautomated layout assistance for a security system
- e-Commerce capability that enables a customer to order security hardware and monitoring services. This capability will be coupled to backroom systems that support a customer purchase.
- Customer monitoring via the Internet that enables a homeowner or businessperson to use video to monitor a space in real time
- Customer account access capability
- Customer service access capability including specialized in-house functionality
- Technical service staff access capability including specialized in-house functionality

In addition, CPI wants to abandon a brick-and-mortar sales strategy (i.e., salespeople, store fronts) and move toward a twenty-first century paradigm. The company wants to sell exclusively via the Web.

But CPI has no meaningful Web presence, not to mention written requirements for what the **SafeHomeAssured.com** WebApp is to be, and it doesn't yet have a particularly sophisticated understanding of the true capabilities of the Web. For example, the people at CPI look at you blankly when you mention the possibility of eventually—in a year or two—having an interface to clients' security systems through a virtual world containing three-dimensional (3D) renditions of their homes (like Second Life[4]). You decide to provide them with a quick example website, if only to get started. The actual **SafeHomeAssured.com** WebApp will evolve in stages that we'll call WebApp *increments.* As the WebApp evolves, it will take on the characteristics of the categories[5] that follow:

Informational WebApps. You decide to build a home page and a few supplementary pages that describe CPI and its products and services. What you've done is to create an *informational WebApp*—one that contains read-only content with simple navigation and links.

Download WebApps. A few weeks later, you begin to add content that describes *SafeHome* sensors and other security system hardware. CPI provides you with PDF (Portable Document Format) specification files describing each. You add a capability that allows visitors to the **SafeHomeAssured.com** WebApp to download the product specs. The WebApp now incorporates informational and *download* capability.

Customizable WebApps. As you learn more from CPI stakeholders, it becomes apparent that you have four kinds of potential end users: homeowners, small-business owners, CPI customer service staff, and CPI technical service staff. You want to tailor the content presented at the website to the specific needs of each customer type, using jargon and presenting content that will meet their needs. You do a major overhaul of your initial WebApp and create a new one that is *customizable* for each user.

Interaction WebApps. Traffic increases rapidly, and before long you have hundreds of visitors each day (after all, people worry about effective solutions for home and business security). You want to create a feeling of community among your visitors—a place where people can chat, ask and answer questions, provide product testimonials, and the like. You decide to implement an extension to **SafeHomeAssured.com** that supports a chat room feature. You've now provided an interactive component for your WebApp.

User Input WebApps. CPI management wants to move away from e-mail and telephone calls requesting quotes for specific security products. You

---

4   See **http://secondlife.com/**.
5   The WebApp categories that follow have been adapted from [Dar99].

implement forms-based input so that every request for a quote is organized in a predictable manner. You still develop the quotes using other automation, but at least you don't have to transcribe a variety of disparate inputs and sources of information.

Transaction-Oriented WebApps. The forms-based input for quotes works well, but CPI management quickly realizes that the entire quotation process can be automated. They provide you with a series of algorithms for computing hardware and monitoring pricing based on forms-based input. The user is now provided with an instant quote based on the input provided via the forms. A *transaction* between the user and the WebApp occurs.

Service-Oriented WebApps. You're now ready to provide a comprehensive design assistance capability. The user inputs a description of a space graphically and is then assisted in the design of a security system for that space. This *service* can lead directly to sales revenue. In addition, it emphasizes the overall sophistication of CPI and *SafeHome* products.

Portals. Time passes, and your dedicated hard work pays off with thousands of visitors each day. CPI staff members receive hundreds of security-related questions each day. They don't have the time to answer each. To help solve the problem you begin providing links to appropriate websites that do have answers. Before long, a portion of your site channels users to a wide variety of useful information sources. The **SafeHomeAssured.com** WebApp now has attributes of a *portal*.

Database Access. Your product line and customer base grow dramatically, and it becomes necessary to build three new databases: (1) all *SafeHome* products as well as technical specifications, pricing (for customer category), installation guidelines, and delivery and availability information, (2) all customer-related information, and (3) all monitoring related information. These databases can be queried using aspects of the user input elements of the WebApp.

Data Warehousing. CPI is rapidly becoming a major international supplier of security products. To meet the needs of many countries, you must tap information about local building regulations, suppliers, installers, and the like. You need to gain access to multiple databases and extract information that will be useful for your customers. You begin to build a large-scale *data warehousing* component for the **SafeHomeAssured.com** WebApp.

The **SafeHomeAssured.com** WebApp will evolve through each of these categories. As we move further into the book, we'll take a much more detailed look at the requirements

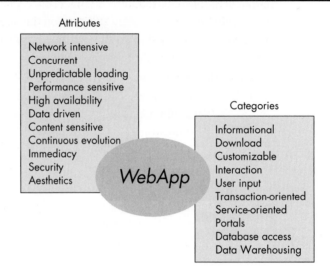

Attributes

Network intensive
Concurrent
Unpredictable loading
Performance sensitive
High availability
Data driven
Content sensitive
Continuous evolution
Immediacy
Security
Aesthetics

WebApp

Categories

Informational
Download
Customizable
Interaction
User input
Transaction-oriented
Service-oriented
Portals
Database access
Data Warehousing

that will lead to the evolution of **SafeHomeAssured.com.** WebApp attributes and categories are summarized in Figure 1.1.

WebApps—A Philosophical View

Earlier we noted that the Web is *big,* both physically and culturally. But its impact goes beyond bigness. It is reasonable to assert that the Web represents a *global consciousness*—a vast sea of data, information, knowledge, and even wisdom—that includes the collective "thinking" of disparate entities (people, institutions, cultures, and nations).

Some elements of the new global consciousness are relatively mundane. We can apply simple data-mining techniques to merge information from seemingly unrelated Web sources, thereby creating a new way of looking at the world (applications of this nature are often referred to as *mashups*). For example, information acquired from **maps.google.com** can be combined with information from the **SafeHomeAssured.com** database to create a city map that shows the location of every *SafeHome*-monitored house in a city.

Other aspects of global consciousness are intriguing but much more difficult to achieve. For example, it might be possible for advanced search engines to examine the universe of Web sources (e.g., blogs, online media, chat rooms, business data sources, online technical journals, entertainment sites) in an effort to extract trends (for business, entertainment, politics) that could not be discerned from one or two Web sources alone. CPI Corporation could use Web-based data-mining techniques to collect crime-related statistics by neighborhood in cities across the country, then use Web-based demographic data to target households in those neighborhoods that are potential purchasers of *SafeHome,* and, finally, develop a targeted marketing campaign that focuses on those households.

Today, this Internet sea washes over each of us. We surf (it's interesting that this term is used) looking for data, information, and knowledge. But we almost never get a glimpse at the consciousness that seethes beneath the surface. As time passes and we move further into the twenty-first century, *Web engineers* will begin to create systems that will enable all of us to extract data, information, and knowledge in novel ways—to do more than skim across the surface.

Most of this book is about a philosophy, but one of a more pragmatic kind. In the chapters that follow, we'll discuss *Web engineering*—a framework that enables the creation of WebApps that may ultimately guide us along the journey toward a global consciousness.

Reference

[Dar00] Dart, S., *Configuration Management: The Missing Link in Web Engineering,* Artech House, 2000.

WEB ENGINEERING

So, you want to build a WebApp? You could, of course, use the old-school approach that we discussed at the beginning of Chapter 1—crafting a WebApp using a combination of informality, urgency, intuition, and art. If things work out well, you and your colleagues will be heroes and a meaningful WebApp will be born.

But things don't always work out well, particularly if your approach relies solely on informality, urgency, intuition, and art. And when that happens, the "hero" will crash and burn. The WebApp may not do what it was supposed to do; it may be delivered late or not at all; or it may be difficult or impossible to correct, adapt, and enhance in a time frame that is acceptable in the hurry-up world of the Web.

You'll be taking a big risk if you adopt the old-school WebApp development philosophy. If it's just about you, go ahead and be a risk taker—roll the dice. We have no problem with that. But it's rarely just about you. Your customers want a WebApp that will meet their needs, one that will be reliable, extensible, and functional. Your management (if you work for a business, an educational institution, or government) has probably built the existence of the WebApp into a broader business strategy. Your coworkers are relying on the timely delivery of the WebApp to coincide with systems and processes that they are developing. A community of people needs a WebApp that works. They don't want big risks.

There is an alternative to the old-school approach—one that reduces (but does not eliminate) risk and has a higher likelihood of success when industry-quality WebApps are to be built. The alternative is *Web engineering* (WebE).

What Is Web Engineering?

Let's answer the question posed in the heading of this section in a succinct manner: *Web engineering proposes an agile, yet disciplined framework for building industry-quality WebApps.* This seems simple enough, but it's very important that you understand two key words in our answer: *agile* and *framework*.

What Is Meant by Agile?

Web engineers must understand that modern business demands adaptation, business strategies and rules change rapidly, management demands near-instantaneous responsiveness (even when such demands are completely unreasonable), and stakeholders[1] keep changing their minds even as they demand rapid delivery. Customers care about a WebApp that's delivered when they need it, not about the work that goes into creating a deliverable WebApp. With all this in mind, a WebE team must emphasize *agility*. Ivar Jacobson [Jac02] provides a useful discussion of the concept:

> An agile team is a nimble team able to appropriately respond to changes. Change is what software development is very much about. Changes in the software being built, changes to the team members, changes because of new technology, changes of all kinds that may have an impact on the product they build or the project that creates the product. Support for changes should be built-in everything we do in software, something we embrace because it is the heart and soul of software. An agile team recognizes that software is developed by individuals working in teams and that the skills of these people, their ability to collaborate is at the core for the success of the project.

In Jacobson's view, the pervasiveness of change is the primary driver for agility. Web engineers must be quick on their feet if they are to accommodate the rapid changes that Jacobson describes.

What Is a WebE Framework?

A *framework*[2] establishes the foundation for a complete Web engineering process by identifying a small number of *framework activities* that are applicable to *all* WebApp projects, regardless of their size or complexity. In addition, the framework encompasses a set of *umbrella activities* that are applicable across the entire WebE process.

Referring to Figure 2.1, each framework activity is populated by a set of *Web engineering actions*—a collection of related tasks that produces a work product (e.g., design is a WebE action). Each action is populated with individual *work tasks* that accomplish some part of the work implied by the action.

The following WebE activities are part of a *generic framework* and are applicable to the vast majority of WebApp projects:

Communication. Involves heavy interaction and collaboration with the customer (and other stakeholders) and encompasses requirements gathering and other related activities.

Planning, Establishes an incremental plan[3] for the WebE work. It describes the WebE actions that will occur, the technical tasks to be conducted, the

---

1 A *stakeholder* is anyone who has a stake in the successful outcome of the project—business managers, end users, Web engineers, support people, and the like. Rob Thomsett jokes that "a stakeholder is a person holding a large and sharp stake . . . If you don't look after your stakeholders, you know where the stake will end up."
2 The phrases *process, process model,* and *process framework* are also used in this context.
3 An incremental plan assumes that the WebApp is to be delivered in a series of "increments" that provide successively more robust sets of requirements with each delivery.

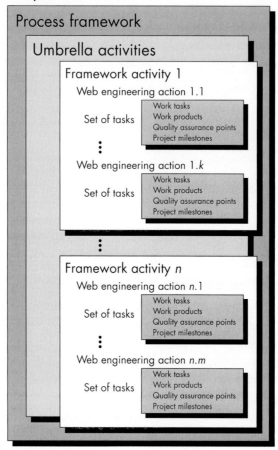

WebE process

risks that are likely, the resources that will be required, the work products to be produced, and a work schedule.

Modeling. Encompasses the creation of models that assist the developer and the customer to better understand WebApp requirements and the design that will achieve those requirements.

Construction. Combines both the generation of HTML, XML, Java, and similar code with testing that is required to uncover errors in the code.

Deployment. Delivers a WebApp increment[4] to the customer who evaluates it and provides feedback based on the evaluation.

---

4   A WebApp increment delivers selected content and functionality to the end user. Later increments expand on the content and functionality delivered until the completed WebApp is deployed.

These five generic framework activities can be used during the development of WebApps of all sizes and complexity. The details of the framework can be quite different in each case, but the framework activities remain the same.

Referring again to Figure 2.1, each Web engineering action is represented by a set of tasks—each a collection of Web engineering work tasks, related work products, quality assurance points, and project milestones. The set of tasks that best accommodates the needs of the project and the characteristics of the team is chosen. This implies that a Web engineering action (e.g., requirements gathering) can be adapted to the specific needs of the WebApp project and the characteristics of the project team.

Umbrella activities (e.g., risk management, quality assurance, content management) are applied throughout the WebE process and are discussed in detail later in this book.

Intelligent application of any framework must recognize that adaptation (to the problem, to the project, to the team, and to the organizational culture) is essential for success. Adaptation affects each of the following framework characteristics:

- Overall flow of activities, actions, and tasks and the interdependencies among them
- Degree to which work tasks are defined within each framework activity
- Degree to which work products are identified and required
- Manner in which quality assurance activities are applied
- Manner in which project tracking and control activities are applied
- Overall degree of detail and rigor with which the process is described
- Degree to which customers and other stakeholders are involved with the project
- Level of autonomy given to the software project team
- Degree to which team organization and roles are prescribed

What Principles Should You Follow as You Adapt the Framework?

The adapted framework for WebE should emphasize project agility and follow a set of 12 agility principles adopted by the Agile Alliance [Agi03]:

- Our highest priority is to satisfy the customer through early and continuous delivery of valuable software.
- Welcome changing requirements, even late in development. Agile processes harness change for the customer's competitive advantage.
- Deliver working software frequently, from a couple of weeks to a couple of months, with a preference to the shorter timescale.

- Business people and developers must work together daily throughout the project.

- Build projects around motivated individuals. Give them the environment and support they need, and trust them to get the job done.

- The most efficient and effective method of conveying information to and within a development team is face-to-face conversation.

- Working software is the primary measure of progress.

- Agile processes promote sustainable development. The sponsors, developers, and users should be able to maintain a constant pace indefinitely.

- Continuous attention to technical excellence and good design enhances agility.

- Simplicity—the art of maximizing the amount of work not done—is essential.

- The best architectures, requirements, and designs emerge from self-organizing teams.

- At regular intervals, the team reflects on how to become more effective, then tunes and adjusts its behavior accordingly.

Is There Any Merit in an Old-School Approach?

It's reasonable to ask whether informality, urgency, intuition, and art have any role to play in Web engineering. The answer is an unqualified "yes." But each of these forces should be moderated by a philosophy that works to reduce risk while at the same time improving the likelihood of success.

Agility encourages informality and at the same time recognizes that there is a sense of urgency associated with the development of every industry-quality WebApp. Each WebE team should adapt the generic framework to best fit the problem at hand and, at the same time, rely on intuition as well as past experience to guide the manner in which the adaptation occurs. The WebE actions and tasks that are performed as part of any adapted framework adopt defined technical methods (for requirements analysis, design, code generation, and testing). However, these methods will succeed only if the technology (delivered by the methods) is coupled with the art that every skilled Web engineer brings to the work that is performed.

The Components of Web Engineering

The implication of our discussion earlier in this chapter is that Web engineering encompasses the entire landscape of *software engineering* practices and process flow but does so in a manner that adapts and distills the process and each practice to the special attributes and characteristics of WebApps.

Hopefully, you already have some familiarity with software engineering practices and process flow, but in case you don't, let's spend a moment discussing them.

How Does Software Engineering Come into Play?

In a virtual round table published in *IEEE Software* [Pre98], Roger staked out a position that couples Web engineering and software engineering:

> It seems to me that just about any important product or system is worth engineering. Before you start building it, you'd better understand the problem, design a workable solution, implement it in a solid way, and test it thoroughly. You should probably also control changes to it as you work and have some mechanism for ensuring the end result's quality. Many Web developers don't argue with this; they just think their world is really different and that conventional software engineering approaches simply don't apply.

His argument was that software engineering principles, concepts, and methods can be applied to Web development, but their application requires a somewhat different approach than their use during the development of conventional software-based systems.

Software engineering[5] is a philosophy, incorporating a process, a collection of methods, and a tool set, that has been adopted wherever software is built. And yet, software engineering continues to have a public relations problem with at least some (often vocal) software developers. Some developers think that software engineering is ponderous and slow. They believe that it is about generating documents—lots of documents. They argue that it overburdens a software team with planning and places unfair management restrictions on the team. The problem is: *they're wrong*. If software engineering is applied incorrectly, it can be the things that some people worry about, but if it is applied in an agile manner, it can only serve to improve the quality and speed the delivery of each system that is built using it.

Software engineering is a layered technology. Referring to Figure 2.2, its foundation is an organizational commitment to quality[6]—a promise to foster a continuous process improvement culture. It is this culture that ultimately leads to the development of increasingly more effective approaches to software engineering.

The *process* layer is the glue that holds the technology layers together and enables rational and timely development of computer software. It forms the basis for management control of software projects and establishes the context in which technical methods are applied, work products (e.g., models and documents) are produced, milestones are established, quality is ensured, and change is properly managed.

---

5 For a reasonably comprehensive discussion of software engineering, we recommend that you examine *Software Engineering: A Practitioner's Approach* [Pre09].
6 *Total quality management, Six Sigma,* and *ISO 9001* are typical of corporate programs that foster a quality culture.

FIGURE 2.2

Software
engineering
layers.

Software engineering *methods* provide the technical how-to's for building software. Methods encompass a broad array of actions and tasks that include communication, requirements analysis, design modeling, program construction, testing, and support. These methods rely on a set of basic principles that govern each area of the technology and include modeling activities and other descriptive techniques.

Software engineering *tools* provide automated or semiautomated support for the process and the methods. When tools are integrated so that information created by one tool can be used by another, an automated environment for the support of software engineering is established.

Why Is WebE Process Agility So Important?

We have already noted that a WebE process model (we referred to this as a *framework* earlier in this chapter) should be agile. This implies a *lean* engineering approach that incorporates rapid development cycles. Each cycle results in the deployment of a WebApp increment. Aoyama [Aoy98] describes the motivation for the agile approach in the following manner:

> The Internet changed software development's top priority from *what* to *when*. Reduced time-to-market has become the competitive edge that leading companies strive for. Thus, reducing the development cycle is now one of software engineering's most important missions.

Even when rapid cycle times dominate development thinking, it is important to recognize that the WebE framework must be defined within a process that: (1) embraces change, (2) encourages the creativity and independence of development staff and strong interaction with WebApp stakeholders, (3) builds systems using small development teams, and (4) emphasizes incremental development using short development cycles.

In Chapter 3 we'll discuss the details of a process framework that can work well for many WebE projects. For now, you should recognize that agility will be the underlying philosophy for our Web engineering work. But you should also understand that an emphasis on agile development in no way mitigates the need for a disciplined engineering approach.

What WebE Methods Reside within the Process Framework?

The WebE methods landscape encompasses a set of technical tasks that enable a Web engineer to understand, characterize, and then build a high-quality WebApp. WebE methods (discussed in detail in Chapters 6 through 15) can be categorized in the following manner:

Communication methods. Define the approach used to facilitate communication between Web engineers and all other WebApp stakeholders (e.g., end users, business clients, problem domain experts, content designers, team leaders, project managers). Communication techniques are particularly important during requirements gathering and whenever a WebApp increment is to be evaluated.

Requirements analysis methods. Provide a basis for understanding the content to be delivered by a WebApp, the functions to be provided for the end user, and the modes of interaction that each class of user will require as navigation through the WebApp occurs.

Design methods. Encompass a series of design techniques that address WebApp content, application and information architecture, interface design, and navigation structure.

Construction methods. Apply a broad set of languages, tools, and related technology to the creation of WebApp content and functionality.

Testing methods. Incorporate technical reviews of both the content and design model and a wide array of testing techniques that address component-level and architectural issues, navigation testing, usability testing, security testing, and configuration testing.

In addition to the technical methods that have just been outlined, a series of umbrella activities (with associated methods) are essential for successful Web engineering. These include project management techniques (e.g., estimation, scheduling, risk analysis), software configuration management techniques, and review techniques.[7]

Isn't Web Engineering All about Tools and Technology?

Tools and technology amplify a technologist's ability to build computer-based systems. When used properly, good tools allow us to work faster and to create a higher-quality end product. And that's why every generation of technologists falls in love with tools and technology. The developers of WebApps have been no exception.

---

7   These techniques, referred to as umbrella activities, are discussed in Chapters 4 and 16.

But tools and technology cannot be used in a vacuum. If you don't really understand the problem, if you have no way of accommodating changes that will invariably occur, if you haven't spent some time laying out a viable solution, if you have no intention of ensuring the "solution" that you've generated (using powerful tools) meets the needs of your stakeholders, then you're working in a vacuum. And that's a recipe for disaster!

What we're trying to say is this: *Tools and technology are very important, but they'll work well only if they're used within the context of an agile framework for Web engineering and in conjunction with proven methods for understanding the problem, designing a solution, and testing it thoroughly.*

A vast array of tools and technology has evolved over the past decade as WebApps have become more sophisticated and pervasive. These technologies encompass a wide range of content description and modeling languages [e.g., HTML, virtual reality modeling language (VRML), XML], programming languages (e.g., Java), component-based development resources [e.g., Common Object Request Broker Architecture (CORBA), Component Object Model (COM) architecture, ActiveX, .NET], browsers, multimedia tools, site authoring tools, database connectivity tools, security tools, servers and server utilities, and site management and analysis tools.

An overview of some of the more important tools and technology for Web engineering is presented in Chapter 14. For a more comprehensive discussion, you should visit one or more of the following websites: Web Developer's Virtual Library (**www.wdvl.com**), WebDeveloper (**www.webdeveloper.com**), Developer Shed (**www. devshed.com**), Webknowhow.net (**www.webknowhow.net**), or WebReference (**www. webreference.com**).

SafeHome

Agreeing on a Process

The scene: Meeting room for the Web engineering group at CPI Corporation prior to the initiation of the project

The players: Technical manager, WebE team members

The conversation:

Technical manager (to the team): So, let's recapitulate. We've been tapped to build *SafeHome Assured.com*. It's the biggest and certainly the most visible WebApp we've ever tried to construct. No doubt, we've got a lot of work to do to simply define

the thing, but I'd like you guys to begin thinking about how you're going to approach the engineering part of this project.

Team member 1: Seems like we've been pretty disorganized in our approach to Web projects in the past.

Team member 2: I don't agree; we always got product out the door.

Technical manager: True, but not without a lot of grief, and this project looks like it's bigger and more complex than anything we've done in the past.

Team member 3: Doesn't look that hard, but I agree . . . our ad hoc approach to past projects might not work here, particularly if we have a very tight time line.

Technical manager (smiling): I want to be a bit more professional in our approach. I went to a short course last week and learned a lot about Web engineering . . . good stuff. We need a process here.

Team member 2 (with a frown): Process? My job is to build WebApps, not push paper around.

Technical manager: Give it a chance before you go negative on me. Here's what I mean. [He proceeds to describe the process framework described in this chapter and the agile Web engineering philosophy

presented to this point.] So anyway, it seems to me that it's possible to implement an agile process with straightforward activities that won't result in "pushing a lot of paper around."

Team member 1: Yeah, agility sounds good, and the five steps, er, activities, you mentioned are just common sense.

Team member 2: I agree, they're common sense. That's why I don't think we need to implement a process.

Team member 3 (laughing): Yeah, but common sense isn't always so common. Why don't we give this a chance?

Web Engineering Best Practices

Before we proceed into the core chapters of this book, some plain talk is in order. We recognize that you may choose not to use the WebE process framework and methods that we'll discuss in detail throughout the remainder of this book. We know that Web engineering teams are sometimes under enormous time pressure and will try to take shortcuts (even if these are ill advised and result in *more* development effort, not less). We also accept the fact that some WebE teams want to keep things very informal and reject the notion of a process framework and defined methods as a matter of philosophy. We think that kind of reasoning is erroneous, but it's your call.

What we do hope is that you spend enough time in the remaining chapters to assess each of the practices that we describe, accepting those that seem applicable and rejecting those that don't. As an absolute minimum, we hope that you and your colleagues will adopt the following best practices whenever you build industry-quality WebApps:

1. **Take the time to understand business needs and product objectives, even if the details of the WebApp are vague.** Many WebApp developers erroneously believe that vague requirements (which are quite common) relieve them from the need to be sure that the system they are about to engineer has a legitimate business purpose. The end result is (too often) good technical work that results in the wrong system being built for the wrong reasons and for the wrong audience. If stakeholders cannot enunciate a business need for the WebApp, proceed with extreme caution.

If stakeholders struggle to identify a set of clear objectives for the product (WebApp), do not proceed until they can. See Chapters 4 and 5 for details.

2. **Describe how users will interact with the WebApp using a scenario-based approach.** Stakeholders should be convinced to develop scenarios (Chapters 4, 5, and 7) that reflect how various users will interact with the WebApp. These scenarios can then be used: (1) for project planning and tracking, (2) to guide analysis and design modeling, and (3) as important input for the design of tests.

3. **Develop a project plan, even if it's very brief.** Base the plan (Chapter 5) on a process framework (Chapter 3) that is acceptable to all stakeholders. Because project time lines are very short, use a "fine" granularity for your schedule; i.e., in many instances, the project should be scheduled and tracked on a daily basis.

4. **Spend some time modeling what it is that you're going to build.** Generally, comprehensive analysis and design documentation is *not* developed as a part of Web engineering work. However, well-targeted graphical models (Chapters 6 through 12) can and do illuminate important engineering issues.

5. **Review the models for consistency and quality.** Pair walkthroughs and other types of reviews (Chapter 5) should be conducted throughout a WebE project. The time spent on reviews pays important dividends because it often eliminates rework and results in a high-quality WebApp—thereby increasing customer satisfaction.

6. **Use tools and technology that enable you to construct the system with as many reusable components as possible.** A wide array of WebApp tools is available for virtually every aspect of the WebApp construction (Chapter 14). Many of these tools enable a Web engineer to build significant portions of the application using reusable components.

7. **Don't reinvent when you can reuse.** A wide range of design patterns have been developed for WebApps. These patterns allow a WebE team to develop architectural, navigation, and component-level details quickly using proven templates. See Chapter 13 for a detailed discussion.

8. **Don't rely on early users to debug the WebApp—design comprehensive tests and execute them before releasing the system.** Users of a WebApp will often give it one chance. If it fails to perform, they move elsewhere—never to return. It is for this reason that "test first, then deploy" should be an overriding philosophy, even if deadlines must be stretched. See Chapter 15 for details.

Where We've Been . . . Where We're Going

As we begin our consideration of Web engineering and the process framework that acts as its foundation, agility becomes a very important concept. As a Web engineer, you have to be quick on your feet. Your job is to build high-quality WebApps—quickly. But as you do this, you have to accommodate a system that continues to evolve as work is conducted. You have to adapt a generic framework for each WebApp increment and integrate a collection of WebE methods and tools into the framework. You have to follow a set of agility principles and a collection of best practices that guide the team toward success.

As we move into Chapter 3, you'll learn more about the WebE process framework. More importantly, we suggest a set of WebE actions and tasks that can serve as a basis for adapting the framework to the very specific needs of the problem, the people, and the project.

References

[Agi03]   The Agile Alliance Home Page, **www.agilealliance.org/home** (accessed July 24, 2007).

[Aoy98]   Aoyama, M., "Web-based Agile Software Development," *IEEE Computer,* November/December 1998, pp. 56–65.

[Fow01]   Fowler, M., and J. Highsmith, "The Agile Manifesto," *Software Development Magazine,* August 2001, **www.sdmagazine.com/documents/s=844/sdm0108a/0108a.htm** (accessed July 24, 2007).

[Jac02]   Jacobson, I., "A Resounding 'Yes' to Agile Processes—But Also More," *Cutter IT Journal,* vol. 15, no. 1, January 2002, pp. 18–24.

[Pre98]   Pressman, R. S. (moderator), "Can Internet-Based Applications Be Engineered?" *IEEE Software,* September 1998, pp. 104–110.

[Pre09]   Pressman, R. S., *Software Engineering: A Practitioner's Approach,* 7th ed., McGraw-Hill, 2009.

3

A WEB ENGINEERING PROCESS

Some people believe that an organization can fully define a process for WebApp development before the fact; put it on the shelf (metaphorically); and then take it down, dust it off, and apply it as is when a new Web engineering project appears. Sadly, that's not how things work.

It is true that you and your colleagues can develop an effective WebE process framework and apply it to each WebApp project that comes along. But as we noted in Chapter 2, the framework must be adapted to the specific characteristics of the problem, the project, and the people who will specify the need and do the work.

A generic WebE process framework provides you with the ability to gain an understanding of what the problem is (both in terms of business context and technology). Armed with this fundamental understanding, you work to refine or adapt the basic process to meet the specific needs of the problem at hand. You consider the culture of the team that will do the work, the desires of your customers, the degree of stability in the problem requirements, and the demands of your managers (for oversight, time-to-market, quality).

As work begins, you continuously adapt the process to be sure that: (1) it does not get in the way of agility, (2) that it truly does accommodate the needs of WebE team members, (3) that it produces only those intermediate work products that enable you to move rapidly toward the delivery of a planned WebApp increment, (4) that it allows you to continually assess the quality of your work, and (5) that it enables you to accommodate the changes that have already begun to impact your work schedule and approach.

In essence, the framework remains the same, but the way you apply it will change with every project and every project team. The framework is applied iteratively as each WebApp increment is created.

Defining the Framework

Before we define a process framework for WebE, we must reiterate a few realities that are encountered in most WebApp projects:

1. **Requirements evolve over time.** When you begin a WebApp project, there may be uncertainty about some elements of the business strategy, the content and functionality to be delivered, interoperability issues, and many other facets of the problem.

2. **Changes will occur frequently.** Because uncertainty is an inherent part of most WebApp projects, changes to requirements are common. In addition, user feedback (based on an assessment of delivered increments) and changing business conditions may drive change.

3. **Time lines are short.** This mitigates against the creation of voluminous engineering documentation, but it does not preclude the simple reality that problem analysis, design, and testing must be documented in some manner.

Because of these realities, *WebApps are often delivered incrementally.* That is, framework activities will occur repeatedly as each WebApp increment is engineered and delivered (Figure 3.1). In addition, the agility principles described in Chapter 2 should be applied. However, these principles should not be applied dogmatically, and it is sometimes reasonable to adopt them in spirit without necessarily building each into the process framework that you've chosen.

FIGURE 3.1

A WebApp delivered in four increments.

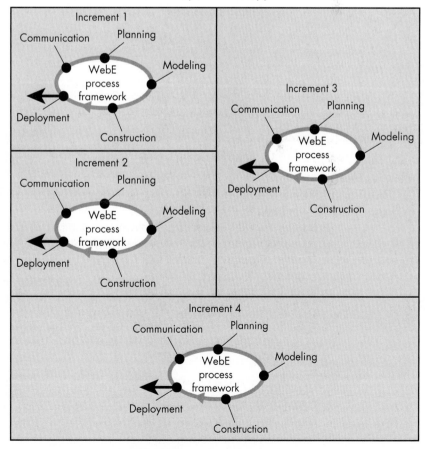

FIGURE 3.2

Process flow with
WebE actions.

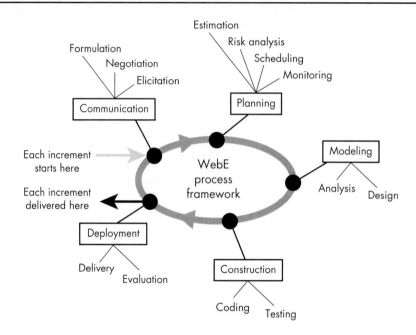

With these issues in mind and referring to Figure 3.2, we expand our discussion of the WebE process framework presented in Chapter 2.

Communication. Within the WebE process, communication is characterized by three WebE actions: formulation, elicitation, and negotiation. *Formulation* defines the business and organizational context for the WebApp. In addition, stakeholders are identified; potential changes in the business environment or requirements are predicted; and integration between the WebApp and other business applications, databases, and functions are defined. *Elicitation* is a requirements-gathering activity involving all stakeholders.[1] The intent is to describe the problem that the WebApp is to solve (along with basic requirements for the WebApp) using the best information available. In addition, an attempt is made to identify areas of uncertainty and where potential changes will occur. Finally, *negotiation* is often required to reconcile differences between various stakeholders for the project.

---

1   As we've noted in Chapter 2, a stakeholder is any person who has a vested interest in the WebApp. A stakeholder may be actively involved in defining requirements (e.g., marketing people), managing the business aspects of a project (e.g., business managers), using the WebApp (e.g., end users), or developing the WebApp itself (e.g., the WebE team).

Planning. The overall number of WebApp increments is identified[2] and a brief project plan (Chapter 5) for the next WebApp increment to be deployed is created. Resources are estimated for the increment, risks are considered, tasks are selected and scheduled, and project tracking and monitoring commence. In most cases, the planning work product consists of a task definition and a time line schedule for the time period (usually measured in weeks) projected for the development of the WebApp increment.

Modeling. Conventional software engineering analysis and design tasks are adapted to WebApp development, merged, and then melded into the WebE modeling activity (Chapters 6 through 13). The intent is to develop agile analysis and design models that define requirements and at the same time represent a WebApp that will satisfy them.

Construction. WebE tools and technology (Chapter 14) are applied to construct the WebApp that has been modeled. Once the WebApp increment has been constructed, a series of rapid tests are conducted to ensure that errors in design (e.g., errors in content, architecture, interface, and navigation) are uncovered. Additional testing addresses other WebApp characteristics.

Deployment. The WebApp is configured for its operational environment. It is then delivered to end users, and an evaluation period commences. Evaluation feedback is presented to the WebE team, and the increment is modified as required.

These five WebE framework activities (with actions superimposed) are applied using the incremental process flow illustrated in Figure 3.2.

Incremental Process Flow

In Chapter 1, we introduced you to the CPI Corporation and its *SafeHome* security products and **SafeHomeAssured.com**—a comprehensive WebApp that will serve as the hub for product marketing and sales, as well as the focus for a new generation of security monitoring services. At the moment, nothing exists but a broad strategy and a few good ideas.

You've been chartered with the job of building a WebE team that will create the WebApp. The need is immediate, and a Web presence must be up and running as soon as possible. It's obvious that you have to be agile. It's also obvious that things will change (probably drastically) as you begin to engineer the WebApp.

You decide to use the activities defined for the generic process framework—communication, planning, modeling, construction, and deployment—and that the

---

2   The number of increments to be delivered may change as feedback from the deployment of early increments is received.

only reasonable way to deliver the WebApp is in increments. What might those increments be?

In Chapter 4, we'll discuss a specific technique for defining deliverable WebApp increments. For now, we'll only note that these increments are identified as part of the first iteration through the communication activity. The list of increments may be further refined with every subsequent iteration.

How Are Framework Activities Conducted?

Referring once again to Figures 3.1 and 3.2, the iterative process flow will be applied to each increment. The very first iteration focuses primarily on defining overall WebApp requirements and identifying the increments to be deployed in subsequent iterations.

The first iteration.   The first communication activity is initiated. The intent is to define business context, establish overall requirements, create a set of usage scenarios, negotiate conflicting needs among stakeholders, and then from this information derive the set of WebApp increments that is to be delivered. Detailed guidelines for conducting these tasks are presented in Chapters 4 and 5. For now, we'll assume that the first increment to be deployed is an informational WebApp that introduces the CPI Corporation and its products. Stakeholders indicate that this informational WebApp must be deployed in one week!

The second iteration.   Even though time is very short, you commit yourself to the WebE process framework. The next morning you initiate the communication activity for the first increment by conducting a 1-hour meeting with stakeholders. You get a reasonably good picture of what is required for the increment. You learn (much to your relief) that all content necessary for the increment is available in preexisting files and an in-house graphic artist is already at work designing the aesthetic look that CPI wants. After the meeting, you review your notes:

Logo and graphics—need aesthetic design.
One- or two-paragraph introduction.
      CPI mission statement (file exists)
      A word to visitors (someone will write this tomorrow)
Basic navigation bar will look like . . .
      About the company
      Our offerings
         Home security products (hierarchical at next level)
         Monitoring services (a list)
      Our Technology (the new sensor)
      Contact us
Other issues:
      Informational content will change over time.

> This "home page" will be the navigation starting point for content and functions required for subsequent increments.

The requirements for the first **SafeHomeAssured.com** increment are straightforward.

Because you've decided to follow the WebE process framework, your next activity is planning. Since all content exists and no functionality is to be implemented at this stage, you decide to do the work yourself (while thinking about assembling a small WebE team for subsequent increments). Over the next half-hour, you create a simple time line:

Day 1: Create a prototype layout (a model) of the WebApp.
Collect and review all existing CPI content and graphics.
Get stakeholder feedback on prototype, if possible.
Day 2: Using the prototype as a guide, begin construction of the increment.
Build navigation bar.
Lay out content areas.
Integrate graphics, links, etc.
Test all links for validity.
Review all content for completeness and correctness.
Day 3: FTP all files to (an existing) domain.
Perform navigation tests.
Deployment: Inform selected stakeholders that the increment is available.
Day 4: Poll stakeholders for feedback.
Make modifications based on stakeholder feedback.

The plan for the first **SafeHomeAssured.com** WebApp increment is complete. Modeling, construction, and deployment follow over the next 3 to 4 days.

The next iteration.   As soon as deployment (for the first increment) is complete, you're ready to initiate the next iteration of the WebE process. For **SafeHome Assured.com,** the *communication* activity during this second iteration will identify the requirements (including content and functionality) for the second increment.[3] So you restart the process flow at the beginning, performing the communication activity for this increment. The tasks you select to populate each framework activity for the increment may differ from the tasks performed for the preceding increment, but the overall process flow remains the same.

As increments become more complex, the number of work tasks required for each framework activity, and often the complexity of those tasks, is likely to grow. The implication is clear: your approach to a given framework activity for a particular increment may not be the same as your approach for the same activity

---

3   For the purposes of this discussion, we'll assume that the second increment delivers the capability to select and download product specifications and related information.

in the next increment. With each iteration, framework activities must be adapted and refined.

As you move through each iteration, *agility* should be your watchword. You and your stakeholders are a team, and teammates talk to one another—communicate as part of each increment flow. You and your colleagues should plan, but only to the extent that it provides a route to the end result and a way to track progress. You should model, but only when the increment to be built is complex or the requirements or design approach are not as clear as you'd like. You'll construct the increment with an eye toward testing and perform tests before you deploy the increment. You'll listen to end-user feedback, using it to correct problems with the deployed increment, but also to guide your work as you move forward to other increments. You'll also conduct umbrella activities[4] so that quality is ensured, change is controlled, risk is managed, and the project is supervised.

How Is the Framework Refined?

The Web engineering actions and tasks required to refine each framework activity are left to the discretion of the Web engineering team. In some cases, a framework activity is conducted informally. In others, a distinct set of actions will be defined and conducted by team members. When an action is complex (e.g., design), it may be further refined into a set of Web engineering tasks (e.g., aesthetic design, content design, architecture design, navigation design, and component design).

But how do you decide which WebE tasks should be applied? To answer this question, the scope of the framework activity for a specific increment must be understood. For example, *communication* is a framework activity that is applied in all Web engineering projects. Consider the refinement of *communication* for two different increments to be delivered as part of the **SafeHomeAssured.com** WebApp.

For the first deliverable increment—an informational WebApp—you must understand the content that is to be presented, the overall aesthetic (e.g., color scheme, layout, menu format, typefaces, and styles) that is desired for the website, the number of distinct categories of information to be presented, and related information. Because your overriding philosophy stresses agility, you want to determine this information as quickly as possible (after all, you have only 5 days to deploy the WebApp increment). Hence, communication involves only a single action: *meet with the customer.*

Recalling our discussion earlier in the chapter, no formal work product is produced, and the time required to ask and answer the questions implied by these tasks is relatively short.

---

4   Umbrella activities are discussed later in this chapter.

Now consider the *communication* activity for the third deliverable **SafeHome-Assured.com** increment. For the purposes of this discussion, let's assume the third increment enables e-commerce functionality. For this increment, the communication activity is more complex. Three actions, formulation, elicitation, and negotiation, will be conducted. Work tasks will be defined for each action.

You must understand the business context (formulation), identify a specific set of content and functional requirements (elicitation) for e-commerce (e.g., forms-based processing requirements, product pricing requirements, shipping costs, taxes, special orders), and reconcile differences among stakeholders (negotiation). You'll also have to identify constraints and performance requirements.

You still have to meet with the stakeholders, but the duration of the meeting(s) and the number of WebE tasks that must be performed will both grow. It's likely that you'll produce a few formal work products (e.g., usage scenarios for various user categories, a sketch of the order entry form) and spend more time reviewing them with your stakeholders. Alternatively, it may be possible to use a preexisting e-commerce template (we would recommend this approach, see Chapter 13) that will enable you to present a prototype to your stakeholders, thereby expediting the communication task.

SafeHome

Refining the WebE Process for Each WebApp Increment

The scene: Meeting room for the Web engineering group as work on the first increment—an informational WebApp for **SafeHome**—ends

The players: Technical manager, WebE team members

The conversation:

Technical manager (to the team): Looks like we'll get the first increment online on Wednesday.

Team member 2: It was a piece of cake. But the next increment looks a bit more complex and the ones after that . . .

Team member 1: There's something I don't understand. Getting the requirements for the first increment was easy—simple conversation and then accessing existing content. But the other stuff is more complicated, and we don't have the requirements yet.

Team member 3: True. We have to begin work on Thursday, and there's a lot that's unclear.

Technical manager: That's why we begin the next increment with communication, again.

Team member 1: But what's the process for the communication activity? For the first increment it was nothing but a quick conversation.

Technical manager: Like we decided. We tune the process—and that means the communication activity as well as others—to the increment at hand. This time we'll have to be a bit more formal and define specific communication tasks.

Team member 2: And we'll use those for every remaining increment?

Technical manager: Nope, every time we begin a new increment, we'll look at its complexity and decide on the "task set" that seems appropriate.

Team member 3 (smiling): Agile and adaptable.

Technical manager: That's us!

Generic Actions and Tasks for the WebE Framework

Although it's necessary to adapt your own set of Web engineering actions and tasks, you have to start somewhere. For this reason we've provided an overview of the generic actions and tasks that can serve as a starting point as you and your team refine each framework activity for the WebApp increment that is to be delivered. It is important to note that each of the activities presented here is considered in much greater detail in later chapters.

How Should the Communication Activity Be Refined?

If you don't know your destination, then it is extremely difficult to get where you need to go and to know when you might have gotten there. That's common sense, and yet many Web developers start their journey toward the development of a WebApp with little or no idea where they're going. They may ultimately reach an acceptable destination, but they'll take many wrong turns and arrive at numerous dead ends as they travel. As a result, they'll be late. Sometimes, they never arrive. At other times they get there, but don't know when to stop, and so keep going unnecessarily.

Communication is the activity that establishes the "destination" for a WebApp project. For a simple destination, there are a relatively small number of informal actions and tasks required to be sure you know where you're going. If the destination is more difficult to describe, you'll need to refine the communication activity with more care. The following tasks and related questions should get you started:

- **Identify business stakeholders.** Exactly who is the "customer" for the WebApp? What businesspeople can serve as experts and representative end users? Who will serve as an active member of the team? What is the degree of consensus among stakeholders? Who is the final arbiter when disputes between stakeholders arise?

- **Identify user categories.** How many different types of users will interact with the WebApp? What is the background and sophistication of each user category? Who will identify special needs for each user category, and what are those needs? What special content and functionality are required by each user category?

- **Formulate the business context.** How does the WebApp fit into a broader business strategy? Is the strategy well established, and are existing business rules well understood?

- **Define key business goals and objectives for the WebApp.** How is the success of the WebApp to be measured in both qualitative and quantitative terms? If there are multiple objectives, what are their priorities? Do different stakeholders have different goals and objectives? Are all goals and objectives consistent with one another?

- **Identify the problem.** What specific problem does the WebApp solve? What information is produced for the end user? What information is input by the end user? What functionality is required to manipulate data? What stored information does the WebApp use? Which existing systems will interoperate with the WebApp?

- **Define informational and applicative goals.** What classes of content are to be provided to end users? What is the status of this content? How dynamic is the content; that is, how often does it change? What functions and user tasks are to be accomplished when using the WebApp? How stable are the required functions?

- **Gather requirements.** What user tasks will be supported by the WebApp increment? What content is to be developed? What interaction metaphor will be used? What computational functions will be provided by the WebApp? How will the WebApp be configured for network utilization? What navigation schema is desired? What constraints exist for the increment? What special performance requirements must be considered?

- **Develop usage scenarios.** Have all categories of users who will interact with the increment been considered? Are usage scenarios complete and consistent with increment requirements? Do usage scenarios require further refinement?

As we noted earlier, if the destination is relatively simple, each of the communication tasks (and the questions noted) can be accomplished informally by meeting with appropriate stakeholders and taking notes. However, if the destination is more complex, a more structured approach to each of the tasks may have to be implemented. We'll discuss this approach in more detail in Chapter 4.

What Tasks Are Required to Develop an Increment Plan?

The communication activity has provided you with a destination, and now you're ready to plan the journey. Your route may be reasonably complex. Therefore, you decide to plan the route in stages by defining *way points* that will ensure that you're heading in the right direction and making step-by-step progress toward your ultimate goal.

In actuality, the first iteration of the communication activity establishes the way points (WebApp increments), but it is the planning activity that defines the resources that will be required to achieve each way point and estimates the time that will be required to get there. The following tasks and related questions should help you as you develop an incremental plan:

- **Refine your description of the WebApp increment to be delivered.** Do requested changes (by any stakeholder) require a modification in the number or definition of increments that remain to be delivered? If modifications are required, what changes in content and functionality are necessary? How much effort is likely to be expended on each increment that remains to be delivered? How much calendar time will be expended on each increment? What is the estimated deployment date for each increment?

- **Select the WebApp increment to be delivered now.** Is there enough information about the increment to begin other framework activities? Do you have a clear understanding of the content and functionality to be delivered by the increment? Are constraints and performance issues clearly understood? Are all necessary usage scenarios available and complete?

- **Estimate the effort and time required to deploy the increment.** How much effort (person-days) and time (calendar days) will be required to model, construct, and deploy the increment? What resources (people, hardware, software) will be required to do the work?

- **Assess risks associated with the delivery of the increment.** What risks should be addressed during the development of this increment? How will high-probability, high-impact risks be mitigated? What long-range risks should be considered?

- **Define the development schedule for the increment.** How will tasks be allocated along the time line for the increment? What intermediate milestones will be established?

- **Establish work products to be produced as a consequence of each framework activity.** What work products (e.g., written scenarios, sketches, models, documents) will be developed as work on the increment proceeds?

- **Define your approach to change control.** How will changes to content and functionality be requested, evaluated, and executed within the context of other development activities?

- **Establish your quality assurance approach.** How will the team assess quality as the increment is modeled, constructed, and deployed? What, if any, reviews will be conducted? What, if any, metrics will be used?

Since increments are often developed in weeks, not months, it's reasonable to ask whether planning is justified for Web engineering. It's always a good idea to establish the route to your destination, but it's foolhardy to spend so much time planning the route that you have little time left to get there. We advocate *agile planning* for each increment—a single, team-oriented meeting in which all WebE team members assist in planning. We also advocate *adaptive planning*. Things happen, and as a consequence, the plan may have to be modified as the WebApp increment is engineered.

What Is Modeling?

In the context of this Web engineering process framework, *modeling* is an activity that creates one or more conceptual representations of some aspect of the WebApp to be built. A *conceptual representation* encompasses one or more of the following forms: written documents, sketches, schematic diagrams, graphical models, written scenarios, paper or executable prototypes, and executable code.[5] Two Web engineering actions occur during modeling: *analysis* and *design*.

What Analysis Modeling Tasks Can Be Applied?

Analysis examines stakeholder requirements using information gathered during the communication activity as a starting point. In many instances, the information gathered during communication is sufficient as a basis for building an increment, and there is no need for analysis modeling. However, when the requirements for an increment are complex, it is sometimes a good idea to create a model that refines your understanding of the WebApp. In general the analysis model focuses on WebApp content, modes of interaction (including navigation), functionality, and the technical configuration[6] of the WebApp. The following tasks and related questions should help determine whether to develop an analysis model:

- **Decide whether a requirements model is needed.** Does existing information (gathered during the communication activity) provide sufficient detail about: (1) WebApp content, (2) required modes of interaction, (3) required functionality, and (4) technical configuration issues? Have usage scenarios been developed in sufficient detail to guide the design and construction activities? If this information exists and is complete, there is no need for analysis modeling for the increment. If the information is incomplete or implies a degree of complexity that demands further examination, proceed to the analysis modeling tasks that follow.

- **Represent WebApp content.** What content is to be presented? What is its origin? Who is responsible for acquiring and developing it? Is it advisable to organize content into a collection of classes? Are the relationships between content classes complex? Which content classes are static (do not change

---

5   These conceptual representations are discussed in more detail in Chapters 6 through 13.
6   In this context, the technical configuration refers to the hardware and software environment in which the WebApp will reside.

based on user type or input), and which are dynamic (generated based on user type or input)?

- **Identify content relationships.** How is one class of content related to others classes? What is the form and style of each content class?

- **Refine and extend user scenarios.** What user tasks are performed as part of this increment? How does the user perform the task? What information does the user need to perform a task? What information does the user provide to perform a task? What steps are required, and specifically how does the user interact with the WebApp? What functions must exist to enable the user to perform the task?

- **Review usage scenarios.** Are there inconsistencies or omissions in a scenario? Is each scenario detailed enough? Does the scenario conform to the content and function that is to be implemented within the WebApp increment?

- **Create an interaction model for complex scenarios.** If the sequence of actions specified in a scenario is complex, what is the relationship between user tasks and the content that is required for each task? What externally observable states[7] can be identified? What user actions cause transition from one state to another?

- **Refine interface requirements.** Does the look and feel of the WebApp interface accommodate the user scenarios that have been defined? Are modifications required for menus, the layout, or navigation?

- **Identify functions.** What functions will the WebApp perform for the user? What data will the user provide to invoke the function? Is the algorithm implied by each function well understood?

- **Define constraints and performance requirements.** Have constraints and performance requirements (defined as part of the communication activity) been presented in sufficient detail? What privacy policies are to be implemented?

- **Identify database requirements.** What database(s) will be accessed? Is the interface protocol for the database(s) well defined? What content classes will be involved?

A number of useful WebE methods and notations can be applied as analysis modeling tasks are conducted. These are discussed in Chapter 7.

---

7   A *state* is an externally observable mode of behavior. In the context of a WebApp, a mode of behavior might be a significant change in on-screen display content, the initiation of a computational function, or a particular condition within a workflow. See Chapters 7 and 9.

What Are the Elements of a Design Model?

Design is a core Web engineering activity. In the early 1990s Mitch Kapor[8] presented a "design manifesto" in *Dr. Dobbs Journal* [Kap91]. We have taken the liberty of adapting his discussion of software design to the world of Web engineering:

> What is design? It's where you stand with a foot in two worlds—the world of technology and the world of people and human purposes—and you try to bring the two together . . . The Roman architecture critic Vitruvius advanced the notion that well-designed buildings were those which exhibited firmness, commodity, and delight. The same might be said of good [WebApps]. *Firmness:* A [WebApp] should not have any bugs that inhibit its function. *Commodity:* A [WebApp] should be suitable for the purposes for which it was intended. *Delight:* The experience of using the [WebApp] should be a pleasurable one. Here we have the beginnings of a theory of design for [Web engineering].

The goal of design for Web engineering is to produce a model or representation that exhibits firmness, commodity, and delight.

Do we always create a design model when we engineer a WebApp increment? The answer is "yes," but the manifestation of the model may be different for each increment. If the increment is well understood and very easy to construct, the only design model might be a simple sketch. If, on the other hand, the increment is more complex, a more detailed design model may be created. The model can consider some or all of the following aspects of WebApp design:

- **Interface design.** Describes the structure and organization of the user interface. Includes a representation of screen layout, a definition of the modes of interaction, and a description of navigation mechanisms.

- **Aesthetic design.** Also called graphic design, describes the "look and feel" of the WebApp. Includes color schemes, geometric layout, text size, font and placement, the use of graphics, and related aesthetic decisions.

- **Content design.** Defines the layout, structure, and outline for all content that is presented as part of the WebApp. Establishes the relationships among content objects.

- **Navigation design.** Represents the navigational flow among content objects and for all WebApp functions.

- **Architecture design.** Identifies the overall hypermedia structure for the WebApp.

---

8   Mitch Kapor is a well-known software developer and entrepreneur who developed Lotus 1-2-3, the first truly sophisticated spreadsheet App. His more recent work as founder of an Internet WebApp start-up is the subject of the book *Dreaming in Code* (Crown Publishers, 2007) by Scott Rosenberg.

- **Component design.** Develops the detailed processing logic required to implement functional components that implement a complete WebApp function.

SafeHome

Is Modeling Really Necessary?

The scene: Conversation in the Web engineering developers' area

The players: Two WebE team members

The conversation:

Team member 2: Doug [the project manager] is insisting that we have to model the second increment, and I just don't think it's necessary.

Team member 1: Well, what he really said was we should model those aspects of the increment that are especially complex or where marketing has been vague about what the requirements are.

Team member 2: Maybe, but it seems like a waste of time . . . besides we'll have to learn a new modeling notation, what do they call it, UML? It's just extra paperwork, if you ask me.

Team member 1: But what if it helps us to solidify requirements or helps us find some flaws in our design?

Team member 2: We'd find that anyway after we coded the WebApp.

Team member 1: I'm not so sure that's true. What if we didn't model and because of that we got requirements wrong? We code the wrong solution and then marketing [the customer] screams. We've got to go back and do it again. That's rework, and that takes time.

Team member 2: More time than modeling?

Team member 1 (smiling): Yeah, more time than modeling.

What Design Modeling Tasks Can Be Applied?

The degree to which a design model addresses each of the aspects noted in the preceding section depends on the complexity of the WebApp increment that is to be built.[9] The following tasks and related questions should help when you consider how to develop a design model:

- **Design the interface (Chapter 9).** How are interaction tasks and subtasks to be represented as part of the interface? What interface control mechanisms (e.g., links, buttons, menus) are required? How are control mechanisms positioned on a Web page? Does the design accommodate every usage scenario?

- **Design the aesthetic for the WebApp (Chapter 9).**[10] How will the page layout be implemented? Will color and form vary depending on context?

---

9   In most cases, a design model incorporates some, but not necessarily all, of the design aspects discussed.

10 It's worth noting that aesthetic design for industry-quality WebApps should be left to professionals (e.g., graphic artists).

How will navigation mechanisms be positioned and represented? Are all logos, graphics, images, and backgrounds implemented and available? Is the aesthetic design consistent across increments?

- **Design the navigation scheme (Chapter 10).** What navigation links and nodes are required? What navigation conventions and aids are to be used? Is the overall navigational flow defined? Do navigation mechanisms correspond to the interface requirements and design? Has navigation been optimized for different user categories? Do navigation semantics agree with each usage scenario?

- **Design the WebApp architecture (Chapter 10).** What architectural style(s) will be used for the content and function?

- **Design the content and the structure that supports it (Chapter 10).** What content must be designed as part of the WebApp increment? What large data structures and databases are required to implement functionality or to display content? Are interfaces to existing databases defined at the design level?

- **Design functional components (Chapter 11).** What components must be developed? Have all algorithms been defined? Is appropriate content available when processing is required?

- **Select appropriate design patterns (Chapter 13).** What architectural patterns are appropriate for the information space? Can the navigational design problems use existing patterns? Can interaction patterns be used as part of the interface design? Are existing presentation patterns appropriate for content? Can workflows, behaviors, processing, and communications be achieved via functional patterns?

- **Design appropriate security and privacy mechanisms.** What level of security is required for user access to the system? What level of security and privacy protection is required to protect server-side and client-side functionality and content from unauthorized access?

- **Review the design.** Does the design conform to customer requirements? Can the design be implemented according to the increment deployment schedule?

In many instances, design is conducted using the same tools that will be used for construction (Chapter 14). These tools allow a Web engineer to: lay out architectural and navigational structure, position and specify content; lay out forms-level input; and prototype the WebApp aesthetic. Using this approach, the transition from design to construction becomes almost seamless.

What Construction Tasks Should Be Applied?

If all framework activities have gone well, you've identified what stakeholders require for the WebApp increment. You've also developed a design that will serve as the basis for the construction activity. As construction proceeds, you'll perform two WebE actions: *code generation* and *testing.* The following tasks and related questions should help you plan the code generation action (Chapter 14):

- **Build and/or acquire all content, and integrate the content into the WebApp architecture.** What WebE technology and tools are to be applied to build content and functional components? What existing forms, templates, and patterns can be used during construction?

- **Select the appropriate tool set for the generation of HTML code.** Can the tool set be used exclusively? Must specialized capabilities be hand coded?

- **Implement each page layout, function, form, and navigation capability.** Is all content available for integration into each Web page for the increment? Have links to all functions been implemented? What linking mechanisms have been activated?

- **Implement all computation functions.** What forms, scripts, and database interfaces must be implemented? Have computational algorithms been adequately designed? Is functionality deployed on the client side or server side?

- **Address configuration issues.** What browsers, plug-ins, and operating system environments will be supported on both the client and server sides?

Once the WebApp has been constructed, it must be tested. Testing begins with a relatively narrow focus and then continues to exercise a broader view of the WebApp. The following tasks and related questions should help you plan the testing action (Chapter 15):

- **Test all WebApp components (content and function).** What components are to be tested within the context of user tasks? Have tests been designed to fully exercise functionality?

- **Test navigation.** What links are to be tested within the context of user tasks? What user scenarios are applicable to the WebApp increment to develop appropriate navigation tests? Have tests been designed to fully exercise the navigational structure?

- **Test usability.** What interactive mechanisms must be tested for ease of use? What user scenarios are applicable to the WebApp increment to develop appropriate usability tests? Have tests been designed to ensure that each usage scenario is supported?

- **Test security (as required) and performance.** How do we exercise all security filters and test the overall performance of the increment? Have tests been designed to ensure that both client-side and server-side capabilities are secure?

- **Test the WebApp increment for different configurations.** Has a list of all technical configurations been developed? Have tests been designed to exercise the WebApp increment within all operational configurations?

It's likely that most, if not all, of these construction tasks will be applied for every increment that you develop. However, a WebE team could combine or streamline tasks (or add additional tasks) if the situation warrants.

How Is a WebApp Increment Deployed?

You've completed the WebApp increment,[11] and now you're ready to deliver it to end users. Your intent is to: (1) provide functionality to one or more user categories, (2) gain feedback from end users to determine whether requirements for the increment have been met, and (3) establish a base for modification that will invariably occur as a consequence of deployment. The following tasks and related questions should help you deploy the WebApp increment:

- **Deliver the WebApp increment to a server at a predefined domain.** Have all file and directory naming and link reference conventions been followed? Have users been provided with access information? Are appropriate security elements (e.g., password checks) in place and operational?

- **Establish an online feedback mechanism for end users.** Has an online feedback form been implemented along with the delivery of the first WebApp increment? Is the feedback free-form, or does it have a list of specific multiple-choice questions? Is it possible to evaluate the feedback form quantitatively?

- **Evaluate end-user interaction?** How does the user interact with the system? What problem areas are encountered? What parts of the interaction are unclear, ambiguous, or missing? What content or functionality is incorrect or missing?

---

11 Unless this increment is the last one to be delivered, you have *not* completed the WebApp. The process flow will continue in an iterative fashion.

- **Assess lessons learned and consider all end-user feedback.** What changes are required based on user feedback? Should changes be made immediately or as part of the next increment to be engineered?
- **Make modifications to the WebApp increment as required.** What modifications must be made to this increment? What changes (to requirements and design) must be made to subsequent increments?

The framework activities, actions, and tasks discussed in these sections are supported by a broad collection of WebE principles, guidelines, and methods (encompassing planning, analysis, design, construction, and testing). These are discussed in more detail throughout the remainder of this book.

Umbrella Activities

As the framework activities discussed in the preceding sections are applied to each WebApp increment, a collection of *umbrella activities* occurs in the background. Because these activities are equally important to the success of a project, a WebE team should consider them explicitly.

Although many umbrella activities can be defined, only four are crucial for a successful Web engineering project:

- **Change management.** Manages the effects of change as each increment is engineered, integrating tools that assist in the management of all WebApp content
- **Quality assurance.** Defines and conducts those tasks that help ensure that each work product and the deployed increment exhibits quality
- **Risk management.** Considers project and technical risks as an increment is engineered
- **Project management.** Tracks and monitors progress as an increment is engineered

Each will be examined in detail later in this book. For now, we'll consider a few important questions about umbrella activities.

How Should a WebE Team Manage Change?

Change can create chaos on any technology project. It disrupts the normal flow of the process (e.g., the team is ready to deploy a WebApp increment, but now, it must delay to accommodate a change); it saps resources (people respond to the change, causing normal work tasks to be temporarily abandoned); and it blurs a team's focus (the destination is now unclear). And yet, change is inevitable and often constructive. What to do?

The incremental strategy that we advocate for Web engineering helps a team to manage change. Change requests (from stakeholders and Web engineers) can occur at any time, but once work on a WebApp increment is under way, changes are queued for assessment and action *after the increment is deployed.* This reduces the disruptive nature of a change request, allows a team to proceed with its work, and still allows changes to be evaluated relatively quickly (recall that work on an increment typically spans weeks, not months).

There is, of course, considerably more to this important umbrella activity. We consider change management in detail in Chapter 16.

How Is the Quality of an Increment Ensured?

Every WebE team strives to produce a high-quality WebApp. But what is "quality" in this context, and what guidelines and specific tasks are available for achieving it?

WebApp quality is achieved through solid design, and the goals of solid design are "firmness, commodity, and delight."[12] The first attribute of quality—*firmness*—is achieved when a WebApp is reliable and presents both content and function without error. The second attribute of quality—*commodity*—is achieved when the WebApp meets the needs of all stakeholders. The third attribute of quality—*delight*—occurs when a WebApp exceeds both user and technical expectations.

As an umbrella activity for Web engineering, quality assurance focuses on each work product that is produced as an increment is built. The focus is to ensure that firmness, commodity, and delight will be the outcome when the increment is deployed. Techniques that help you to evaluate and achieve these attributes are discussed throughout the remainder of this book.

How Is Risk Managed?

What can go wrong? It's such an obvious question that we sometimes forget to ask it. Answering this question is what risk management is all about. Risks are events or circumstances that can cause a WebE project to go wrong. You need to identify risks and then manage them.

Risk identification occurs throughout the WebE process. Whenever any stakeholder (Web engineers *are* stakeholders) identifies something that might go wrong, it is recorded for discussion and (if required) action. The potential risk is described, and its potential impact is noted.

High-impact risks should be managed, and there are two ways to accomplish this: reactive management and proactive management. Reactive risk strategies have been laughingly called the "Indiana Jones school of risk management" [Tho92]. In the movies that have carried his name, Indiana Jones, when faced with

---

12 Recall our earlier reference to Mitch Kapor's discussion of design.

overwhelming difficulty, would invariably say, "Don't worry, I'll think of something!" Never worrying about problems until they happened, Indy would react in some heroic way.

Sadly, the average Web engineer is not Indiana Jones. Yet, the majority of WebE teams rely solely on reactive risk strategies—hoping that when something goes wrong someone will be able to be a hero. At best, a reactive strategy monitors the project for likely risks. Resources are set aside to deal with them should they become actual problems. More commonly, the team does nothing about risks until something goes wrong.

A considerably more intelligent strategy for risk management is to be proactive. Potential risks are identified, their probability and impact are assessed, and they are ranked by importance. Then, the WebE team establishes a plan for managing each risk. We discuss proactive risk management in Chapter 5.

How Should the Work Be Managed?

In the best of all circumstances, a WebE team manages itself. Each team member commits to the tasks to be performed and works diligently to accomplish them within the time allotted. In essence, the team is self-organizing and self-supervising.

However, as the complexity of an increment grows, the interdependencies among work tasks often demand tracking and control by a team leader or manager. After all, it's important to know if things are falling behind and to act quickly to remedy the situation.

Project management is an umbrella activity that occurs as a consequence of planning. It encompasses change management, quality assurance, and risk management, and at the same time, assesses progress by examining the outcome of each framework activity as an increment is built. Techniques for project management are discussed in Chapter 5.

Where We've Been . . . Where We're Going

The WebE process framework is an agile, adaptable, iterative road map for building Web applications. The framework incorporates five activities—communication, planning, modeling, construction, and deployment—and a set of umbrella activities that are available to every WebE team for any industry-quality Web application. Framework activities are adapted to accommodate the specific characteristics of the problem, the project, and the people who will specify the need and do the work.

Each framework activity integrates WebE actions and tasks. An action includes a number of tasks and is applied as part of the broader framework activity. A task represents a unit of work that can be tracked as part of the WebApp plan. It is the job of the WebE team to select and adapt the actions and tasks that are appropriate to the increment that is to be deployed next.

A complete WebApp is delivered incrementally. That is, content and functionality are segmented into deliverable components, called increments. As each increment is planned and deployed, an increasingly more complete version of the WebApp is available to end users.

Up to this point in the book, we've discussed WebE activities in general terms. It's now time to become more specific. In Chapter 4 you'll learn how to communicate with stakeholders in an effective manner and to establish a foundation for the planning, modeling, and construction activities that follow.

References

[Kap91]   Kapor, M., "A Software Design Manifesto," *Dr. Dobbs' Journal,* January, no. 172, 1991, pp. 62–68.

[Tho92]   Thomsett, R., "The Indiana Jones School of Risk Management," *American Programmer,* vol. 5, no. 7, September 1992, pp. 10–18.

4

COMMUNICATION

During the roaring 1990s, the Internet boom generated more hubris than any other event in the history of computers. WebApp developers at hundreds of young dotcom companies argued that a new paradigm for system development had arisen, that old rules no longer applied, and that time-to-market trumped all other concerns. They laughed at the notion that careful problem formulation should occur before construction commenced.[1] And who could argue? Money was everywhere; 24-year-olds became multimillionaires (on paper, at least)—maybe things really had changed. And then the bottom fell out.

It became painfully apparent that a "build it and they will come" philosophy just doesn't work, that problem formulation is essential to ensure that a WebApp is really needed, and that requirements elicitation is essential if the WebApp is to meet the needs of end users. Constantine and Lockwood [Con02] note this situation when they write:

> Despite breathless declarations that the Web represents a new paradigm defined by new rules, professional developers are realizing that lessons learned in the pre-Internet days of software development still apply. Web pages are user interfaces, HTML programming is programming, and browser-deployed applications are software systems that can benefit from basic software engineering principles.

Among the most fundamental principles of software engineering is: *understand the problem before you begin to solve it, and be sure that the solution you conceive is one that people really want.* It's reasonable to suggest that this principle should become a cornerstone of Web engineering as well.

The communication activity provides the WebE team with an organized way of eliciting requirements from stakeholders. In essence, it establishes the team's destination as each WebApp increment is built.

The Communication Activity

The WebE process begins with the communication activity. Referring to Figure 4.1, *communication* serves as the entry point for the process flow. It is the place where Web engineers and stakeholders engage in a series

---

1 Few bothered to plan or model; after all, there was a "gold rush" going on, wasn't there? If you bothered to stop and plan, then you risked missing out on the gold! Or so they thought.

FIGURE 4.1

Communication
in the WebE
process flow.

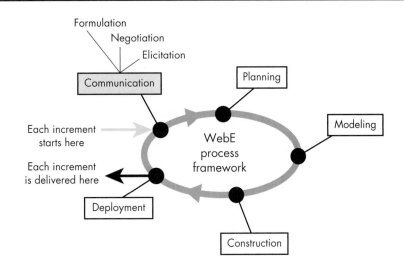

of WebE actions that: (1) ask and answer a set of fundamental questions about the WebApp and its business context, (2) elicit requirements that will serve as the basis for all activities that follow, and (3) negotiate needs against the realities of time, resources, and technology. These actions are called *formulation, elicitation* (also called *requirements gathering*), and *negotiation,* respectively.

With these actions in mind, let's set the stage for the very first iteration of the process framework for **SafeHomeAssured.com**.

The communication activity during the first iteration will begin by identifying the business context, goals, and objectives for the WebApp as a whole.[2] This formulation action is as important for the stakeholders (to ensure that everyone is on the same page) as it is for the WebE team (to ensure that there is a business need for the WebApp to be built). The information developed during formulation, coupled with the requirements gathered during elicitation, will serve as the basis for identifying the increments that are to be delivered in subsequent iterations.

Formulation

Formulation is a WebE action that begins with the identification of a business need, moves into a description of WebApp objectives, defines major WebApp features, and establishes a basis for the elicitation action that follows. Formulation allows stakeholders and the WebE team to establish a common set of goals and objectives for the creation of each WebApp increment. It also identifies the scope of the development effort and provides a means for determining a successful outcome.

---

2   Later iterations through the communication activity will focus on individual increments that are defined during the first iteration.

Before we consider formulation in more detail, it's reasonable to ask where formulation stops and elicitation begins. There is no easy answer to this question. Formulation focuses on the big picture—on business needs and objectives and related information. However, stakeholders and Web engineers also enumerate specific features, define required content, discuss specific functionality, and identify the manner in which end users will interact with the WebApp. When the level of abstraction moves from big-picture business issues (associated with the WebApp) to more specific WebApp-oriented requirements, the transition from formulation to elicitation has occurred.

Who Should You Communicate With?

Before you worry about the formulation questions to ask, you must identify who the target of the questions will be. You'll need to identify stakeholders. A *stakeholder* can be defined as "anyone who benefits in a direct or indirect way from the system which is being developed" [Som97].

In the best of all worlds, one person will be the focus of your questions. This individual will have appropriate business experience, good technical knowledge, and the authority to negotiate needs in terms of delivery time and resources. More likely, however, you'll deal with a number of different stakeholders, each with a different point of view, sometimes diverging needs, and substantially different business and technical knowledge. In general, stakeholders are drawn from the following categories: business managers, product managers, marketing people, internal and external customers, end users, consultants, product engineers, Web engineers, and support and maintenance staff.

What Techniques Can You Use for Communication?

Unless the WebApp is quite simple and the end-user profile is predictable, it is not advisable to use information gathered from just one or two people as the basis for formulation or analysis. More people (and more opinions and points of view) should be considered.

Communication can be accomplished using one or more of the following mechanisms [Fuc98]:

- **Traditional focus group.** A trained moderator meets with a small (usually fewer than 10 people) group of representative end users (or internal stakeholders playing the role of end users). The intent is to discuss the WebApp to be developed and, out of the discussion, to better understand requirements for the system.

- **Electronic focus group.** A moderated electronic discussion conducted with a group of representative end users and stakeholders. The number of people who participate can be larger. Because all users can participate at the same time, more information can be collected in a shorter time period. Since all discussion is text based, a contemporaneous record is automatic.

- **Iterative surveys.** A series of brief surveys, addressed to representative users and requesting answers to specific questions about the WebApp, is conducted via a website or e-mail. Responses are analyzed and used to fine-tune the next survey.

- **Exploratory survey.** A Web-based survey is tied to one or more WebApps that have users who are similar to the ones who will use the WebApp to be developed. Users link to the survey and respond to a series of questions (usually receiving some reward for participation).

- **Scenario building**. Selected end users (or other internal stakeholders who play the role of end users) are asked to create usage scenarios that describe specific interactions with the WebApp.

Won't There Be Different Viewpoints?

Every stakeholder has a different view of the WebApp, achieves different benefits when the WebApp is successfully deployed, and is open to different risks if the development effort should fail. For example, business managers are interested in the feature set that will result in sales growth and improved revenue for the company. The marketing group is interested in features that will excite the potential market, leading to new customers and increased sales. The product manager wants a WebApp that can be built within budget and that will be ready to meet defined market windows. End users may want features that are already familiar to them and that are easy to learn and use. Web engineers may be concerned with functions that are invisible to nontechnical stakeholders but that enable the infrastructure that supports more marketable features. Support engineers may focus on the maintainability and extensibility of the WebApp.

As information from multiple viewpoints is collected, emerging requirements may be inconsistent or may conflict with one another. Your job during formulation and elicitation is to categorize all stakeholder information (including inconsistent and conflicting requirements) in a way that will set the stage for the last WebE action, *negotiation*.

What Questions Should We Ask?

It's time to meet with CPI Corporation stakeholders and begin the communication activity. Representatives from business management, marketing, product engineering, customer service, sales, and product support are present. Your intent is to formulate a view of the business context for **SafeHomeAssured.com**.

After pleasantries, you discuss the answers to three fundamental questions [Pow98]:

1. What is the main motivation (business need) for the WebApp?
2. What are the objectives that the WebApp must fulfill?
3. Who will use the WebApp?

After some discussion, the group agrees on the following simple statement of motivation:

SafeHomeAssured.com will allow customers to evaluate, configure, and purchase security system products and monitoring services.

It is important to note that detail is not provided in this statement. The objective here is to bound the overall intent of the WebApp and to place it within a legitimate business context.

After additional discussion with various stakeholders, an answer to the second question is stated:

SafeHomeAssured.com will allow us to sell directly to consumers, thereby eliminating middleman costs and improving our profit margins. It will also allow us to increase sales by a projected 25 percent over current annual sales and will allow us to penetrate geographic regions where we currently do not have sales outlets. It will reduce the need for expanding our customer service call center by providing features that allow a customer to access monitoring information directly.

Finally, the third question (Who will use the WebApp?) is addressed and user characteristics are defined for the WebApp:

Projected end users (the primary demographic) of SafeHomeAssured.com are homeowners and owners of small businesses. However, the application will also be used by CPI sales and service staff.

This primary demographic is assumed to have limited knowledge of security systems technology and to possess nontechnical computer skills.

These answers imply a set of specific goals for the **SafeHomeAssured.com** WebApp. In general, two categories of goals [Gna99] are identified: *informational goals* that indicate an intention to provide specific content and/or information for the end user, and *applicative goals* that indicate the ability to perform some task within the WebApp.

In the context of the **SafeHomeAssured.com** WebApp, a list of informational goals is developed:

- To allow the user to learn about CPI Corporation, its people, and products
- To provide users with detailed product specifications, including technical descriptions, installation instructions, and pricing information
- To display the security configuration (including all hardware) for the facility (house or business) that the end user defines

- To enable a user to obtain a quote for product cost
- To create an account database that provides account information for customers

Among the applicative goals for **SafeHomeAssured.com** are the following:

- To provide tools that will enable a user to represent the layout of a "space" (i.e., house, office/retail space) that is to be protected
- To make customized recommendations about security and monitoring products that can be used within the user space
- To integrate forms-based **SafeHomeAssured.com** input with CPI's existing customer and order entry database
- To allow users to place an order for security hardware
- To allow users to control monitoring equipment (e.g., cameras, microphones) within their space
- To enable users to sign up for monitoring services
- To allow monitoring customers to query the monitoring database about their account activity

Once all informational and applicative goals have been identified, a user profile is developed. The *user profile* captures "relevant features related to potential users including their background, knowledge, preferences and even more" [Gna99].

In the case of **SafeHomeAssured.com**, a user profile would identify the characteristics of a typical purchaser of security systems (this information would be supplied by the marketing department).

Once the WebApp objective, goals, and user profiles have been developed, the formulation activity focuses on a *statement of scope* for the WebApp. In many cases, informational and applicative goals provide sufficient information to identify the scope of the problem.

How Do We Encourage Collaboration?

If five stakeholders are involved in a WebApp project, you may have five (or more) different opinions about the proper set of requirements. Stakeholders should collaborate among themselves (avoiding petty turf battles) and with Web engineers if a successful system is to result. But how is this collaboration accomplished?

Your job is to act as a consultant during formulation and elicitation—to identify areas of commonality (i.e., requirements on which all stakeholders agree) and areas of conflict or inconsistency (i.e., requirements that are desired by one stakeholder but conflict with the needs of another stakeholder). It is, of course, the latter category that presents a challenge.

One way of resolving conflicting requirements and at the same time achieving a better understanding of the relative importance of all requirements is to use a voting scheme based on *priority points.* All stakeholders are provided with some number of priority points that can be "spent" on one or more requirements (at this stage represented by informational and applicative goals) in different amounts.

A list of requirements is presented, and each stakeholder indicates the relative importance of each (from his or her viewpoint) by spending one or more priority points on it. Points spent cannot be reused. Once a stakeholder's priority points are exhausted, no further action on requirements can be taken by that person. The total points spent on each requirement by all stakeholders provide an indication of the overall importance of the requirement.

SAFEHOME

Prioritizing WebApp Goals (Top-Level Requirements)

The scene: Meeting room at CPI Corporation

The players: All stakeholders for the **SafeHome-Assured.com** WebApp who are meeting to prioritize top-level project requirements. A facilitator (you) is leading the meeting.

The conversation:

Facilitator: As you all know, we've met with each of the constituencies represented here to define the basic project-level requirements for *SafeHome*. The handouts I've just given you list five informational goals and seven applicative, er, functional goals for the WebApp.

Team leader: These are pretty vague, I think we've got to provide some detail, for example, the requirement that . . .

Facilitator (interrupting): We'll elaborate on these soon, but right now the focus is on establishing some top-level priorities.

Marketing person: From what I can see, they're all important, so . . .

Facilitator (again interrupting): I understand, but it's important that we establish priorities so that

we can begin to think about the order in which the content and function will be delivered for online use.

Business manager: You mean it won't all be delivered at once?

Team leader: We're going to deliver the WebApp in stages that we call "increments." That'll allow us to get things up and running much more quickly.

Business manager (suspicious): How quickly?

Team leader: We'll have something up—albeit simple—in a week. More content up within 2 weeks or so. It's the right approach.

Marketing person (nodding): We agree.

[The business manager shrugs in a way that indicates acceptance.]

Facilitator: Understand that the increments we define may very well combine some of these requirements [looks at the handout], so . . .

Marketing person (interrupting): But we haven't defined any increments yet.

Facilitator: We'll begin to do that once we've established priorities. Here's how we're going to do it. [Explains priority points.]

Collaboration does not necessarily mean that the committee defines the requirements. In many cases, stakeholders collaborate by individually prioritizing WebApp requirements. The final decision about which requirements make the cut can then be made by a strong "project champion" (e.g., a business manager or a senior technologist).

Elicitation

Many different approaches to collaborative requirements gathering have been proposed. Each makes use of a slightly different scenario, but all apply some variation on the following basic guidelines:

- A meeting[3] is conducted and attended by all stakeholders.
- Rules for preparation and participation are established.
- An agenda is suggested that is formal enough to cover all important points but informal enough to encourage the free flow of ideas.
- A facilitator (can be a customer, a Web engineer, or an outsider) controls the meeting.
- A definition mechanism (can be work sheets, flip charts, wall stickers, an electronic bulletin board, chat room, or virtual forum) is used.

The goal is to identify a set of requirements that address WebApp content, function, user interaction, and interoperability with existing business systems and databases.

To better understand the flow of events as they occur, we present a brief scenario that outlines the events that lead up to the requirements gathering meeting, the events that occur during the meeting, and the tasks that should follow the meeting.

What Happens Before an Elicitation Session?

During formulation, basic questions and answers establish the WebApp scope and provide some insight into WebApp features. If the scope indicates a relatively significant development effort, preparation is advisable before any requirements gathering (elicitation) is conducted. If time permits, you might consider writing a one-page WebApp description that will serve as the basis for requirements gathering. The WebApp description is assembled using the information already derived from the formulation meeting. For the **SafeHomeAssured.com** WebApp, the description might look like:

SafeHomeAssured.com will allow CPI Corporation to market and sell security products and monitoring services directly to consumers, thereby eliminating middleman costs and improving our profit margins. To accomplish this goal, the WebApp will incorporate both content and functions that implement the following product-related features:

- End users can examine the *SafeHome* product line and request product specs.
- Users can configure a security system by representing the layout of a "space" (i.e., house, office/retail space) and then initiating functions within **SafeHomeAssured.com** to make

---

3   The "meeting" can be either physical or virtual.

      customized recommendations about security and monitoring products that can be used within the space.

- Users can request an instant quote for product and/or system pricing.
- Users can place an order for sensors, controllers, audio, and video hardware and related infrastructure.

The WebApp will incorporate both content and functions that implement the following monitoring-related features:

- Users can sign up for monitoring services, order installation of a *SafeHome* system, and coordinate all other setup activities that will lead to a purchase of security products, their installation, and the execution of a monitoring contract with CPI.
- Contract customers can control security and monitoring equipment (e.g., cameras, microphones) within their space and use the **SafeHomeAssured.com** WebApp to acquire the output of security devices and display them for their own customers.
- Customers can query the CPI monitoring database about their account activity.

      The **SafeHomeAssured.com** WebApp must be implemented so that usage is intuitive. It must have very strong security features and be available 24/7/365.

      The **SafeHomeAssured.com** WebApp will also have specialized features for in-house CPI staff. These features will provide enhanced customer support and security system technical support and maintenance.

There is a tendency to try and write a "perfect" WebApp description, but this simply isn't possible at this stage (if indeed it ever is). Ambiguity will be present, omissions are likely, and errors may occur. Your intent is to establish a point of departure.

    A meeting place, time, and date are selected, and a meeting facilitator (that's probably *you*) is chosen. All stakeholders are invited to attend. The WebApp description is distributed to all stakeholders at least 24 hours before the meeting time.

How Do Stakeholders Prepare?

Each stakeholder is asked to review the WebApp description before the requirements gathering meeting and make a list of "content objects"[4] that are: (1) part of the environment that surrounds the system, (2) produced by the system, and (3) used by the system to perform its functions. In addition, each attendee is asked to make a list of functions that manipulate or interact with the content objects. Finally, lists of constraints (e.g., business rules that will impact the features provided) and performance criteria (e.g., speed, accuracy, privacy, security) are also developed. The attendees are informed that the lists are not expected to be exhaustive but are expected to reflect each person's perception of the system.

    Each person develops the lists described previously. Content objects described for the **SafeHomeAssured.com** WebApp might include:

---

4   A *content object* is a named collection of related information. Sometimes referred to as a "composite data item," a content object contains data items that take on a specific value when an instance of the object is defined.

- Company profile
- Product overview
- Product specifications
- Installation instructions
- Product database (includes pricing, items in inventory, shipping costs, etc.)
- Quotation templates
- Order forms
- Order entry database
- Layout image of user space
- User database (includes user identification, specialized security system configuration, other user-related info)
- Monitoring request form
- Monitoring "dashboard" for a contract user (includes account information, video window for monitoring, audio port for monitoring)
- Monitoring database
- Customer service dashboard (to be defined later)
- Tech support dashboard (to be defined later)

Each of these content objects represents a preliminary content requirement and also implies a set of functions that will be required to acquire, manipulate, or produce the content object.

The list of functions for the **SafeHomeAssured.com** WebApp might include:

- Provide product quotation
- Process security system order
- Process user data
- Create user profile
- Draw user space layout
- Recommend security system for layout
- Process monitoring order
- Get and display account info
- Get and display monitoring info
- Customer service functions (to be defined later)
- Tech support functions (to be defined later)

In a similar fashion, each stakeholder develops lists of constraints and performance criteria.

What Tasks Are Performed During an Elicitation Session?

As the requirements gathering meeting begins, the first topic of discussion is the need and justification for the new product—everyone should agree that the product is justified. Once agreement has been established, the facilitator indicates that the group must accomplish four tasks:

1. Define user categories, and develop descriptions for each category.

2. Refine content and functionality using the lists each person prepared.

3. Consider specific constraints and performance issues.

4. Write user scenarios for each user class.

Not all of these tasks are conducted within the time span of a single requirements gathering meeting, but all should be accomplished before the WebE process can proceed.

What Are the User Categories for the WebApp?

It can be argued that WebApp complexity is directly proportional to the number of user categories for the system. A set of fundamental questions must be addressed to define a user category:

- **What is the user's overall objective when using the WebApp?** For example, one user of **SafeHomeAssured.com** might be interested in gathering information about home management products. Another user might want to do a price comparison. A third user might want to purchase the *SafeHome* product. A fourth user already owns *SafeHome* and requires monitoring services or account information. Each represents a different user class or category, and each will have different needs and will navigate through the WebApp differently.

- **What is the user's background and sophistication level relative to the content and functionality of the WebApp?** If a user has a technical background and significant sophistication, elementary content or functionality will provide little benefit. Alternatively, a neophyte demands elementary content and functionality and would be confused if it were missing.

- **How will the user arrive at the WebApp?** Will arrival occur through a link from another website or search engine (this is likely to influence the design of the content and functionality within the WebApp) or will arrival occur in a more controlled manner through the home page?

- **What generic WebApp characteristics does the user like and dislike?** Different types of users may have distinct and predictable likes and dislikes. It's worth attempting to determine whether they do or do not. In many situations, the answer to this question can be ascertained by asking for their favorite and least favorite WebApps.

Using the answers to these questions, the smallest reasonable set of user classes should be defined. As requirements gathering proceeds, each defined user class must be considered when usage scenarios are developed.

How Are Content and Functional Requirements Identified?

The core activity of an elicitation meeting is the identification of content and functional requirements. Each stakeholder has begun this work by preparing lists of content objects and WebApp functions. Once the meeting begins, these lists can be displayed on large sheets of paper pinned to the walls of the room, displayed on adhesive-backed sheets stuck to the walls, or written on a whiteboard. Alternatively, the lists can be posted on an electronic bulletin board, at an internal website, or posted in a chat room environment for review prior to the meeting. Ideally, each listed entry should be capable of being manipulated separately so that lists can be combined, entries can be deleted, and additions can be made. At this stage, critique and debate are strictly prohibited.

Entries from individual lists are combined into a collective list that eliminates redundant entries, adds any new ideas that come up during the discussion, but does not delete anything. After collective lists for all topic areas (objects, functions, constraints, and performance) have been created, discussion—coordinated by the

---

SAFEHOME

A Requirements Gathering Meeting

The scene: A meeting room. The first requirements gathering meeting is in progress after basic top-level requirements have been established.

The players: The facilitator (you) and stakeholders from (1) business management, (2) marketing, (3) Web engineering, (4) security product support

The conversation:

Facilitator (pointing at whiteboard): So that's the current list of objects and functions for **SafeHome-Assured.com.**

Marketing: That about covers it from our point of view.

Product support (nodding toward the list): Does the "Get and display monitoring info" mean you want to allow customers to access remote video and audio over the net?

Marketing: Yeah . . . that will really set us apart from the competition.

Facilitator: Doesn't that also add some constraints?

Business manager: It sure does, both technical and legal.

Marketing: Meaning?

Team member: We better make sure an outsider can't hack into the system, disarm it, and then rob the customer's place or worse.

Business manager: Heavy liability on our part.

Team member: Very true.

Marketing: But we still need that . . . just be sure to stop a hacker from getting in.

Team member: That's easier said than done and . . .

Facilitator (interrupting): I don't want to debate this issue now. Let's note it as a constraint and proceed.

[One of the attendees serves as the recorder for the meeting and makes an appropriate note.]

Facilitator: I have a feeling there's still more to consider here.

[The group spends the next 30 minutes discussing other list entries.]

facilitator—ensues. The combined list is shortened, lengthened, or edited to properly reflect the WebApp to be developed. The objective is to develop a consensus list in each topic area. The lists are then set aside for later action.

How Are Constraints and Performance Issues Isolated?

You cannot build a successful WebApp without worrying about both internal and external constraints. *Internal constraints* are best understood by thinking about the technical environment in which the WebApp will reside and the project environment in which the WebApp will be built. A consideration of the *technical environment* might uncover specialized database protocols, the vagaries of different Web browsers, operating system characteristics, and client-server issues. All have some bearing on the design approach for the WebApp. The *project environment* encompasses available WebE tools, development hardware, software standards, and staff skill levels with various WebE technologies.

External constraints can be enumerated by considering the business and usage environment for the WebApp. Business rules, end-user idiosyncrasies, security demands, privacy issues, run-time performance, interoperability requirements, legal restrictions, and government regulations are but a few of the possible external constraints on the Web engineering work that is to be performed.

As an example of how a constraint might be identified, consider the preceding dialogue from the **SafeHomeAssured.com** requirements gathering meeting. In the dialogue, the following exchange occurred:

Team member: We better make sure an outsider can't hack into the system, disarm it, and rob the customer's place or worse.
Business manager: Heavy liability on our part.

These brief comments should raise a "constraint flag" for the team. It's obvious that very bad things could happen if the monitoring function or the content objects related to it were hacked. Therefore, security becomes a constraint, not because security isn't important for every WebApp, but because special measures over and above those that must be implemented for all WebApps may have to be implemented. The implication is that a *design emphasis on security and extensive security testing both will be required.* The impact of this on WebApp increment definition, resources, and scheduling will be determined during planning.

What Are Usage Scenarios?

Once the consensus lists identifying content objects, functions, and constraints have been completed, stakeholders are asked to play the role of a user (from a specific user category) and develop usage scenarios for one or more entries on each

SafeHome

Developing a Preliminary User Scenario

The scene: A meeting room, continuing the first requirements gathering meeting

The players: Members of the WebE team, members of the marketing organization (playing the role of end users), a product engineering representative, and a facilitator

The conversation:

Facilitator: We've been talking about security for access to **SafeHomeAssured.com.** I'd like to try something. Let's develop a user scenario for initial access to the home security function.

Marketing person: How?

Facilitator: We can do it a couple of different ways, but for now, I'd like to keep things really informal. Tell us [he points at a marketing person] how you envision accessing the system.

Marketing person: Um . . . well, this is the kind of thing I'd do if I was away from home and I had to let someone into the house, say a housekeeper or repair guy, who didn't have the security code.

Facilitator (smiling): That's the reason you'd do it . . . tell me *how* you'd actually do this.

Marketing person: The first thing I'd need is a PC. I'd log on to the website. I'd provide my user ID and . . .

Team member (interrupting): The Web page would have to be secure, encrypted, to guarantee that we're safe and . . .

Facilitator (interrupting): That's good information, but it's technical. Let's just focus on how the end user will use this capability. OK?

Team member: No problem.

Marketing person: So as I was saying, I'd log on to a website and provide my user ID and at least two passwords.

Team member: What if I forget my password?

Facilitator (interrupting): Good point, but let's not address that now. We'll make a note of that and call it an *exception.* I'm sure there'll be others.

Marketing person: After I enter the passwords, a screen representing all *SafeHome* functions will appear. I'd select the home security function. The system might request that I verify who I am, say by asking for my address or phone number or something. It would then display a picture of the security system control panel along with a list of functions that I can perform—arm the system, disarm the system, disarm one or more sensors. I suppose it might also allow me to reconfigure security zones and other things like that, but I'm not sure.

[As the marketing person continues talking, the facilitator takes copious notes. These form the basis for the first informal usage scenario. Alternatively, the marketing person could have been asked to write the scenario, but this would be done outside the meeting.]

of the lists.[5] Each usage scenario is typically one or two narrative paragraphs that describe how an end user would apply or create a content object or interact with a WebApp function. It should be noted, however, that more formal templates have been proposed and are called *use cases* [Bit03] [Coc01].

---

5 This can be done within the context of the meeting, or the meeting can terminate for a period of time while user scenarios are created off-line. Another approach is to ask an actual user to do this.

What Are Use Cases?

Use cases are a widely used approach for the creation of user scenarios. Use cases describe how a specific user category (called an *actor*) will interact with the WebApp to accomplish a specific action. The action may be as simple as acquiring defined content or as complex as conducting detailed user-guided control of remote monitoring equipment. The use case describes the interaction from the user's point of view.

In general, use cases are developed iteratively. Only those use cases necessary for the increment to be built are developed during the communication activity for the increment. In many situations only use cases for major WebApp functions (those considered during requirements gathering) are considered. These use cases may be refined during the analysis modeling activity (Chapter 7) for the increment.

Although developing and analyzing use cases takes time, it provides significant benefits:

- Use cases provide the detail necessary for effective planning and modeling activities.
- Use cases help the developer to understand how users perceive their interaction with the WebApp.
- Use cases help to compartmentalize Web engineering work because they can be organized into WebApp increments.
- Use cases provide important guidance for those who must test the WebApp.

Use cases have been characterized as a "contract for behavior" [Coc01]. The contract defines the way in which an actor[6] uses a WebApp to accomplish some goal. In essence, a use case captures the interactions that occur between producers and consumers of information and the system itself.

The concept of a use case is relatively easy to understand. It describes a specific usage scenario in straightforward language from the point of view of a defined actor. But how do we know: (1) what to write about, (2) how much to write about it, (3) how detailed to make our description, and (4) how to organize the description?

How Is a Use Case Created?

Requirements gathering provides us with the information needed to begin writing use cases. To begin developing a set of use cases, the functions or activities performed by a specific actor are listed. These may be obtained from a list developed by stakeholders or through conversations with customers or end users.

---

6   An *actor* is not a specific person, but rather a role that a person (or a device) plays within a specific context. An actor "calls on the system to deliver one of its services" [Coc01].

SAFEHOME

Developing Another Preliminary User Scenario

The scene: A meeting room, during the second requirements gathering meeting

The players: WebE team members, members of marketing, a product engineering representative, and a facilitator

The conversation:

Facilitator: It's time to continue talking about the **SafeHomeAssured.com** surveillance function. Let's develop a use case for access to it.

Team member: Who plays the role of the actor on this?

Facilitator: I think Meredith (a marketing person) has been working on that functionality. Why don't you play the role?

Meredith (marketing person): You want to do it the same way we did it last time, right?

Facilitator: Right . . . same way.

Meredith: Well, obviously the reason for surveillance is to allow the homeowner to check out the house while he or she is away, to record and play back video that is captured . . . that sort of thing.

Team member: The video will be digital. Is it stored on disk?

Facilitator: Good question, but let's postpone implementation issues for now. Meredith?

Meredith: Okay, so basically there are two parts to the surveillance function . . . the first configures the system including laying out a floor plan—we have to have tools to help the homeowner do this—and the second part is the actual surveillance function itself. Since the layout is part of the configuration function, I'll focus on the surveillance function only.

Facilitator (smiling): Took the words right out of my mouth.

Meredith: Okay . . . I want to gain access to the surveillance function via the Internet. I want to be able to display camera views on my PC and control pan and zoom for a specific camera. I specify the camera by selecting it from the house floor plan. I want to selectively record camera output and replay camera output. I also want to be able to block access to one or more cameras with a specific password. I also want the option of seeing small windows that show views from all cameras and then be able to pick the one I want enlarged.

Team member: Those are called thumbnail views.

Meredith: Okay, then I want thumbnail views of all the cameras. I also want the interface to the surveillance function to have the same look and feel as all other **SafeHomeAssured.com** interfaces. I want it to be intuitive, meaning I don't want to have to read a manual to use it.

Facilitator: Good job. Now, let's go into this function in a bit more detail . . .

The sidebar discussion suggests a function that we'll call *Access camera surveillance via the Internet* performed by a **HomeOwner** (end-user category). In addition, the following subfunctions (an abbreviated list) are implied but are as yet undefined:

- Select camera to view.
- Request thumbnails from all cameras.
- Display camera views in a PC window.
- Control pan and zoom for a specific camera.

- Selectively record camera output.

- Replay camera output.

As further conversations with the stakeholder (who plays the role of a homeowner) progress, the requirements gathering team can develop use cases for each of the subfunctions noted. Alternatively, the generation of use cases for the subfunctions can be delayed until the WebE modeling activity (Chapter 7).

In general, use cases are written first in an informal narrative fashion of a user scenario. If more formality is required, the same use case is rewritten using a structured format discussed later in this chapter.

To illustrate, consider a **SafeHomeAssured.com** function called *Access camera surveillance via the Internet.* The stakeholder who takes on the role of the **Home Owner** actor might write the following narrative:

Use case: *Access camera surveillance via the Internet*
Actor: HomeOwner
Narrative: If I'm at a remote location, I can use any PC with appropriate browser software to log on to the **SafeHomeAssured.com** website. I enter my user ID and two passwords, and once I'm validated, I have access to all functionality for my installed *SafeHome* system. To access a specific camera view, I select "Surveillance" from the major function buttons displayed. I then select "Pick a camera," and the floor plan of the house is displayed. I then select the camera that I'm interested in. Alternatively, I can look at thumbnail snapshots from all cameras simultaneously by selecting "All cameras" as my viewing choice. Once I choose a camera, I select "View" and a camera view appears in a viewing window that is identified by the camera ID. If I want to switch cameras, I select "Pick a camera" and the original viewing window disappears and the floor plan of the house is displayed again. I then select the camera that I'm interested in. A new viewing window appears.

Another way of writing the use case is to present the interaction as an ordered sequence of user actions. Each action is represented as a declarative sentence.

Use case: *Access camera surveillance via the Internet*
Actor: HomeOwner
Actions:

1. The homeowner logs on to the **SafeHomeAssured.com** website.
2. The homeowner enters his or her user ID.
3. The homeowner enters two passwords.
4. The system displays all major function buttons.
5. The homeowner selects "Surveillance" from the major function buttons.
6. The homeowner selects "Pick a camera."
7. The system displays the floor plan of the house.
8. The homeowner selects a camera icon from the floor plan.
9. The homeowner selects the "View" button.
10. The system displays a viewing window that is identified by the camera ID.
11. The system displays video output within the viewing window at one frame per second.

It is important to note that this sequential presentation does not consider any alternative interactions (the narrative is more free-flowing and did represent a few alternatives).

Of course, a description of alternative interactions is essential to a complete understanding of the function that is being described. Therefore, each step in the primary scenario is evaluated by asking the following questions [Sch98]:

- Can the actor take some other action at this point?
- Is it possible that the actor will encounter some error condition at this point? If so, what might it be?
- Is it possible that the actor will encounter some other behavior at this point (e.g., behavior that is invoked by some event outside the actor's control)? If so, what might it be?

Answers to these questions result in the creation of a set of secondary scenarios that are part of the original use case but represent alternative behavior.

For example, consider steps 6 and 7 in the primary scenario presented earlier:

6. **The homeowner selects "Pick a camera."**
7. **The system displays the floor plan of the house.**

Can the actor take some other action at this point? The answer is "yes." Referring to the free-flowing narrative, the actor may choose to view thumbnail snapshots of all cameras simultaneously. Hence, one secondary scenario might be "View thumbnail snapshots for all cameras."

Is it possible that the actor will encounter some error condition at this point? Any number of error conditions can occur as a computer-based system operates. In this context, we consider only error conditions that are likely as a direct result of the action described in step 6 or step 7. Again the answer to the question is "yes." A floor plan with camera icons may have never been configured. Hence, selecting "Pick a camera" results in an error condition: "No floor plan configured for this house."[7] This error condition becomes a secondary scenario.

Is it possible that the actor will encounter some other behavior at this point? Again the answer to the question is "yes." As steps 6 and 7 occur, the system may encounter an alarm condition. This would result in the system displaying a special alarm notification (type, location, system action) and providing the actor with a number of options relevant to the nature of the alarm. Because this secondary scenario can occur for virtually all interactions, it will not become part of the *Access camera surveillance via the Internet* use case. Rather, a separate use case—*Alarm condition encountered*—would be developed and referenced from other use cases as required.

---

7   In this case, another actor, the **SystemAdministrator,** would have to configure the floor plan, install and initialize (e.g., assign an equipment ID) all cameras, and test to be certain that each is accessible via the system and through the floor plan.

SafeHome

Use-Case Template for Surveillance Function

Use case: *Access camera surveillance via the Internet*

Primary actor: HomeOwner

Goal in context: To view output of camera placed throughout the house from any remote location via the Internet

Preconditions: System must be fully configured; appropriate user ID and passwords must be obtained.

Trigger: The homeowner decides to take a look inside the house while away.

Scenario:

1. The homeowner logs onto the **SafeHomeAssured.com** website.
2. The homeowner enters his or her user ID.
3. The homeowner enters two passwords (each at least eight characters in length).
4. The system displays all major function buttons.
5. The homeowner selects "Surveillance" from the major function buttons.
6. The homeowner selects "Pick a camera."
7. The system displays the floor plan of the house.
8. The homeowner selects a camera icon from the floor plan.
9. The homeowner selects the "View" button.
10. The system displays a viewing window that is identified by the camera ID.
11. The system displays video output within the viewing window at one frame per second

Extensions:

1. ID or passwords are incorrect or not recognized. See use case *Validate ID and passwords*
2. Surveillance function not configured for this system—system displays appropriate error message. See use case *Configure surveillance function.*
3. Homeowner selects "View thumbnail snapshots for all cameras." See use case *View thumbnail snapshots for all cameras.*
4. A floor plan is not available or has not been configured—display appropriate error message. See use case *Configure floor plan.*
5. An alarm condition is encountered. See use case *Alarm condition encountered.*

Priority: Moderate priority, to be implemented after basic WebApp functions

When available: Sixth increment

Frequency of use: Moderate

Channel to actor: Via PC-based or mobile device browser and Internet connection

Secondary actors: System administrator, cameras

Channels to secondary actors:

1. System administrator: PC-based system
2. Cameras: Wireless connectivity

Open issues:

1. What mechanisms protect unauthorized use of this capability by employees of CPI Corporation?
2. Is security sufficient? Hacking into this feature would represent a major invasion of privacy.
3. Will the system response via the Internet be acceptable given the bandwidth required for camera views?
4. Will we develop a capability to provide video at a higher frames-per-second rate when high-bandwidth connections are available?

Referring to the formal use-case template shown in the sidebar, the secondary scenarios are represented as extensions to the basic sequence described for *Access camera surveillance via the Internet.*

It's reasonable to ask whether all this is really necessary for every function that is identified. In general, it isn't. You should develop a narrative usage scenario for every major function that is to be delivered for a WebApp increment. However, if a function is particularly complex or important, a more detailed description (using the use-case template) may be required.

Identifying WebApp Increments

Recalling the iterative nature of the WebE process framework, the formulation and elicitation actions described earlier in this chapter are applied each time a new WebApp increment is to be developed. But how are the increments defined?

We derived overall WebApp requirements during the first iteration through the communication activity. These include the derivation of major content objects, WebApp functions, and usage scenarios (or use cases). Before planning for the first increment can commence, it is necessary to develop an ordered list of all potential increments to be deployed.[8]

One approach [Fuc98] is to create a stack of "cards" that contains one usage scenario or use case per card. Each card contains the name of the use case, a brief description, and an *effort indicator*—usually a number between 1 and 4. The effort indicator is assigned to each use case by the WebE team and provides an estimate of the relative degree of effort required to build the WebApp functionality required to implement the use case. A relatively simple scenario might be assigned an effort indicator of 1. A scenario requiring significant effort would be assigned an effort indicator of 4.

The cards are shuffled into random order and then distributed to selected stakeholders who are asked to arrange the cards into groupings that reflect how they would like content and functionality (implied by the usage scenarios) to be delivered. The manner in which cards are grouped is constrained by an *effort maximum, M.* No grouping of cards can have a cumulative effort indicator value that is greater than M, where M is defined by the WebE team and is a function of available resources and the desired delivery time for each increment.

As an example, we assume that the first communication activity for the **Safe-HomeAssured.com** WebApp has been completed, and stakeholders have defined a set of usage scenarios that are reflected in a stack of cards:

Card No.	Card Name	Effort Indicator
1	Learn about the company and its products	1
2	Download product specs	2
3	Get info that is customized to my user category	2

---

8   It is important to note that the ordered list of increments is likely to be revised a number of times before WebE work proceeds.

4	Look up a specific sensor	1
5	Get a product quote	2
6	Develop a layout from the space to be monitored	4
7	Get recommendations for sensor layout for my space	3
8	Place a product order	2
9	Request information on monitoring services	1
10	Place an order for monitoring services	2
11	Control sensors	3
12	Control cameras	3
13	Access camera surveillance via the Internet	4
14	Get account information	2

and so on . . .

The WebE team has established an effort maximum, $M = 4$, meaning that an increment can be defined only if it groups cards that have a combined effort indicator value of 4 or less. In addition, cards must also be grouped in a way that addresses functionality in a cohesive way.

In the case of the cards defined in the stack, the preliminary set of **SafeHome-Assured.com** increments might be:

Increment 1:   Use cases reflected in card 1.

Increment 2:   Use cases reflected in cards 2, 3, and 4

Increment 3:   Use cases reflected in cards 5 and 8

Increment 4:   Use cases reflected in cards 6 and 7[9]

Increment 5:   Use cases reflected in cards 9 and 10

Increment 6:   Use cases reflected in cards 11, 12, and 13

Increment 7:   Use cases reflected in card 14

When can the stakeholders expect deployment of these increments? We really won't know until we conduct planning—the next framework activity discussed in Chapter 5.[10]

It's also important to recognize that the first set of increments defined may be incomplete. As work proceeds, an important feature may be added to the WebApp, dictating the creation of one or more new use cases. As a consequence, new increments may be added, an existing increment may be modified, or a planned increment may be removed. The plan must reflect these changes going forward. But for now, we go with what we have.

---

9   In this case $M = 5$, but the increment still makes sense. The effort maximum is a useful guideline, but sometimes it must be violated.

10 And even then, we'll only have good schedule visibility on the first few increments, at best.

INFO

The Art of Negotiation

Learning how to negotiate effectively can serve you well throughout your personal and technical life. The following guidelines are well worth considering:

1. *Recognize that it's not a competition.* To be successful, both parties have to feel they've won or achieved something. Both will have to compromise.
2. *Map out a strategy.* Decide what you'd like to achieve, what the other party wants to achieve, and how you'll go about making both happen.
3. *Listen actively.* Don't work on formulating your response while the other party is talking. Listen. It's likely you'll gain knowledge that will help you to better negotiate your position.
4. *Focus on the other party's interests.* Don't take hard positions if you want to avoid conflict.
5. *Don't let it get personal.* Focus on the problem that needs to be solved.
6. *Be creative.* Don't be afraid to think outside of the box if you're at an impasse.
7. *Be ready to commit.* Once an agreement has been reached, don't waffle; commit to it and move on.

Negotiation

Ideally, communication determines stakeholder requirements in sufficient detail to proceed to subsequent framework activities for an increment. In reality, Web engineers and other stakeholders often enter into a process of negotiation, where a stakeholder may be asked to balance functionality, performance, and other product or system characteristics against cost and delivery time. The intent of this negotiation is to establish increment requirements that meet the needs of the customer while at the same time reflecting the real-world constraints (e.g., time, people, budget) that have been placed on the WebE team.

The best negotiators strive for a win-win result.[11] That is, the customer wins by getting a WebApp that satisfies the majority of his or her needs, and the WebE team wins by working toward realistic and achievable deadlines.

Before any negotiation begins, it's a good idea to determine each of the stakeholders' "win conditions" and to develop a strategy that will reconcile them into a set of win-win conditions for all concerned (including the WebE team).

SAFEHOME

Negotiating Requirements During Communication

The scene: A meeting room, during the second requirements gathering meeting

The players: WebE team members, members of marketing, a product engineering representative, and a facilitator

(continued)

---

11 Dozens of books have been written on negotiating skills (e.g., [Lew00], [Far97], and [Don96]). It is one of the more important things that a young (or old) Web engineer or manager can learn. Read one of these books.

SafeHome (continued)

The conversation:

Facilitator (addressing marketing members): I'd like to spend some time discussing card numbers 6 and 7. You know, *Space layout* and *Recommendations for monitoring layout.* Based on our preliminary use cases, it looks like you want as much automation as possible.

Marketing member: Ideally, it would be fully automatic. Just describe the house layout, and **Safe-HomeAssured.com** does the rest!

Team member (grimacing): We've got to talk about that.

Marketing member (looking mildly annoyed): This is really an important whiz-bang feature. We've got to have it.

Facilitator (recognizing that a negotiation has begun): Let's step back a moment and look at the issues. I agree with you [looking at marketing] that it's a feature that is very important. But we have to consider the complexity of a fully automated solution [looks at the WebE team members], its impact on delivery schedule, and the overall importance of full automation on revenue [looks at product engineering rep].

[Everyone shifts in their seats, but no one speaks.]

Facilitator: I'd like us to get to a place where your needs are satisfied [looking at marketing] but we keep delivery deadlines reasonable [looks at the WebE team members]. How do we get that done?

Team member: Look, we know it's a cool feature and we want to implement it. It's just that a fully automated solution is really complicated, and worse, it might result in recommendations that aren't really what the customer wants. We think a semiautomated solution, you know, where the customer is involved interactively, is a better way to go. Here's what I think we should do . . .

Facilitator: Hold up a sec. What do you think about that? [Looks at marketing.]

Marketing member: Well, if we can get the functionality we need, it might be okay, but I'll need to know more.

Facilitator (looking at a WebE team member): What do you propose?

[The negotiation continues until both parties come to an agreement. New use cases are created to reflect the new version of the features.]

Where We've Been . . . Where We're Going

The intent of the communication activity is to establish a set of requirements for the WebApp increment to be built. Communication, like all framework activities, occurs iteratively. During the first pass, overall WebApp requirements are delineated broadly, and from these requirements, a set of deployable increments is defined. Communication encompasses three WebE actions: formulation, elicitation, and negotiation.

Formulation identifies the scope of the increment to be built by examining business motivation, operational goals, and user characteristics. The intent is to provide a description of the scope of the WebE work to be performed. To derive the scope, stakeholders collaborate to establish priorities.

Elicitation gathers requirements by identifying the content objects that the WebApp increment will use and the functions that the increment will implement. Using a meeting format, requirements gathering tasks include definition of user categories, refinement of content and functionality, identification of constraints and performance issues, and the development of usage scenarios. The usage scenarios identified during elicitation are used to identify the WebApp increments that will be developed in subsequent iterations of the WebE process framework.

Negotiation attempts to reconcile conflicts between stakeholders. The intent is to establish a set of increment requirements that meets the needs of all the stakeholders while at the same time reflecting the real-world constraints (e.g., time, people, budget). The best negotiations strive for a win-win result.

Communication sets the stage for both planning and modeling—framework activities that can occur only after basic WebApp requirements have been identified. In Chapter 5, we'll explore how to establish a plan for deploying a WebApp increment.

References

[Bit03]   Bitner, K., and I. Spence, *Use Case Modeling,* Addison-Wesley, 2003.

[Coc01]   Cockburn, A., *Writing Effective Use Cases,* Addison-Wesley, 2001.

[Con02]   Constantine, L., and L. Lockwood, "User-Centered Engineering for Web Applications," *IEEE Software,* vol. 19, no. 2, March/April 2002, pp. 42–50.

[Don96]   Donaldson, M. C., and M. Donaldson, *Negotiating for Dummies,* IDG Books Worldwide, 1996.

[Far97]   Farber, D. C., *Common Sense Negotiation: The Art of Winning Gracefully,* Bay Press, 1997.

[Fuc98]   Fuccella, J., and J. Pizzolato, "Creating Web Site Designs Based on User Expectations and Feedback," *ITG Newsletter,* June 1998, www.internettg.org/newsletter/june98/web_design.html (accessed July 25, 2007).

[Gna99]   Gnado, C., and F. Larcher, "A User Centered Methodology for Complex and Customizable Web Applications Engineering," *Proc. First ICSE Workshop in Web Engineering,* ACM, Los Angeles, May 1999.

[Lew00]   Lewicki, R., Saunders, D., and J. Minton, *Essentials of Negotiation,* McGraw-Hill, 2000.

[Pow98]   Powell, T. A., *Web Site Engineering,* Prentice-Hall, 1998.

[Sch98]   Schneider, G., and J. Winters, *Applying Use Cases,* Addison-Wesley, 1998.

[Som97]   Somerville, I., and P. Sawyer, *Requirements Engineering,* Wiley, 1997.

5 PLANNING

Although many of us (in our darker moments) take Dilbert's view of project planning, it remains a very necessary activity when WebApps are built. Everyone plans to some extent, but the scope of planning activities varies among people involved in a WebE project. A Web engineer manages day-to-day work—planning, monitoring, and controlling technical tasks. A team leader plans, monitors, and coordinates the combined work of a WebE team. Other stakeholders generally have little interest in the details of the planning activity, but are *very* interested in the outcome. We plan so that their expectations can be met.

Because most WebApp increments are delivered over a time span that rarely exceeds 6 weeks, it's reasonable to ask: "Do we really need to spend time planning a WebApp effort? Shouldn't we just let a WebApp evolve naturally, with little or no explicit planning and only indirect management?" More than a few Web developers would opt for this approach, but that doesn't make them right!

Taking an agile approach to the planning activity, you adapt the effort and time spent on planning to the complexity of the WebApp increment to be deployed. If the WebApp increment is simple (e.g., the content is well defined and functions are straightforward), planning will take very little time. If, on the other hand, the increment is complex in terms of content, functionality, constraints, and performance, planning will require greater effort and will encompass each of the actions and tasks discussed in this chapter. Regardless of the characteristics of the increment, you must plan.

Understanding Scope

Much of the early effort expended during the communication activity (Chapter 4) focuses on a definition of WebApp scope. *Scope* is defined by answering the following questions:

Context. How does the WebApp fit into a business context, and what constraints are imposed as a result of the context?

Information objectives. What customer-visible content objects are used and produced by the WebApp increment?

Functionality. What functions are initiated by the end user or invoked internally by the WebApp to meet the requirements defined in usage scenarios?

Constraints and performance. What technical and environmental constraints will impact the framework activities that follow? What special performance issues (including security and privacy issues) will require design and construction effort?

Because it is difficult, if not impossible, to develop a meaningful plan without understanding the scope of the WebApp increment, the information derived during the communication activity must be examined with care. If scope is vague at this stage (and it may be), you have a bit of work to do before planning can commence.

What Communication Work Products Are Relevant?

All communication work products are relevant to the planning activity. In some cases, the only information available may be your written notes (*always* take notes!) and a set of usage scenarios that provide a description of the content and functions for the WebApp increment. If you take a more formal approach to communication, the following work products (Chapter 4) may be available for the planning activity:

- Statement describing business motivation for the overall WebApp
- Statement of overall objective for the WebApp
- List of user categories
- List of informational goals for the WebApp increment to be planned
- List of applicative (functional) goals for the WebApp increment to be planned
- Description of the increment (the statement of scope)
- List of content objects for the increment
- List of functions for the increment
- Set of usage scenarios that describe how each user category will interact with the increment

Although it's wonderful when all this information is available, it's not necessarily sufficient for the planning activity. The information developed during the communication activity may not be as complete as the WebE team would like. It's important to know what to do when this occurs.

What If Further Details Are Required to Understand the Increment?

Human beings tend to apply a divide-and-conquer strategy when they are confronted with a complex or vague problem. Stated simply, the problem is partitioned into smaller problems that are more understandable. Because the communication activity makes no attempt to fully define every aspect of the content and functions to be delivered by the WebApp,[1] an *elaboration* strategy can be used when further details are required to understand the scope of the WebApp increment in a more complete manner.

Elaboration begins with the information that has been developed as part of the communication activity. It is applied in two major areas: to the *content* that is to be delivered with the WebApp increment and to the *functions* that are invoked as part of all user scenarios for the increment.

Recalling the work performed in Chapter 4, the fourth increment of the **SafeHomeAssured.com** WebApp implemented two usage scenarios:

Develop a layout of the space to be monitored.
Get recommendations for sensor layout for my space.

The usage scenarios imply the existence of a number of major content objects and the functions that are related to them. However, these content objects and functions have *not* been explicitly identified during communication. You have three options: (1) proceed with planning and worry about the elaboration of content and functionality during the modeling activity, (2) do a bit of elaboration now, so that planning can be more reliable, or (3) do a complete elaboration to be sure you really understand this increment.

There is no "best" option here. The team may feel that technical work (in this case, analysis modeling) should begin (time is *always* of the essence) and may opt to develop the best plan they can with whatever information is now available. Alternatively, the team may choose to do a small amount of elaboration so that the plan can properly allocate technical work based on the content and functions that will be derived. Finally, the team may decide to do analysis modeling right now and completely elaborate before the plan is developed.

As an example, let's assume that the second option is chosen. The team will do a bit of elaboration now so that the plan can be completed but will delay the development of a more complete elaboration until the modeling activity commences.[2] Since the usage scenarios refer to a "space," the WebE team elaborates on the concept:

Space—a defined floor plan for a home or a small business
Content objects:
> **SpaceIdentifier**
> > **Name of space**
> > **Customer name**
> **Walls**
> > **Wall name (displayed as a number)**
> > **Start and end coordinates**

---

1   A more complete definition of content and function is developed as part of the analysis modeling action of the modeling activity.
2   It's important to note that the elaboration work performed now is not "wasted" in that it will save time and effort later in the process.

Doorways
   Wall ID
   Door size
   Door start coordinate
Windows
   Wall ID
   Window size
   Window start coordinate

. . . and so on for all content objects associated with this increment.

Functions (associated with "space"):
   Specify and draw walls
   Specify and draw doorways
   Specify and draw windows
   Compute size of each room
   Save/retrieve a named space
      Security protection is required
   Update/delete a named space
      Security protection is required
   Print a named space

. . . and so on for all functions associated with this increment.

The amount of effort associated with this elaboration is relatively small, but the payoff can be significant. For example, you now know that the team will have to develop at least seven functions associated with the creation of a user space. The work associated with this is allocated as part of the planning activity.

What If Gaps Still Exist in Your Understanding?

You cannot expect to achieve comprehensive understanding at the planning stage. You'll have to accept the fact that things remain a bit uncertain, even after you've elaborated the information derived during the communication activity—it's one of the risks inherent in all engineering work. More important, you'll have to complete the planning activity with imperfect information and move on.

As you move further into the WebE process, your understanding will improve as modeling is conducted. However, it's reasonable to assume that there will be a few surprises (some may be nasty) as construction proceeds. The team will have to adapt and move forward.

Refining Framework Activities

The WebE team must now choose the framework actions and tasks that are right for the remaining WebE work to be applied to the increment. Recalling our discussion from Chapter 3, the following framework activities must be refined for use on the increment to be built:

- **Modeling.** Actions and tasks that lead to the creation of analysis and design models that assist the WebE team and other stakeholders to better understand the WebApp and how it is to be constructed
- **Construction.** Actions and tasks required for code generation (either manual or automated) and testing
- **Deployment.** Actions and tasks that deliver the WebApp increment to the end users who evaluate it and provide feedback based on the evaluation

These framework activities are applicable to all WebApp increments. The problem is to refine the set of actions and tasks that are appropriate for this increment.

What Actions and Tasks Are Required?

WebE framework actions and tasks are refined by "melding" characteristics of the increment and the process. One way to accomplish this is to create a table similar to the one illustrated in Figure 5.1. The top row of the table lists the key content objects and functions to be delivered as part of the increment deployment. The first column lists the set of framework actions and tasks for modeling, construction, and deployment.

The WebE team selects the set of actions and tasks that are most appropriate for the WebApp increment to be engineered. Although some team members will argue in favor of a very sparse list, it is best to spend the time to develop a set of actions and tasks that will lead to a high-quality result. It's worth noting that just because a task is listed in the table it does not necessarily have to be used for every content object and function. The final decision is left to the Web engineer who will do the work. However, if the Web engineer decides to forego the WebE task, he or she must be able to justify the decision and is ultimately responsible for the quality of the work product produced.

Figure 5.1 illustrates only a portion of the table that would be created for the **SafeHomeAssured.com** WebApp.[3] In the portion shown, the content and functions for the usage scenarios are illustrated.

Develop a layout of the space to be monitored.
Get recommendations for sensor layout for my space.

Content objects—**Walls, Doorways,** and **Windows**—are listed in the first section of the top row. Functions (e.g., *Specify and draw walls*) are listed next.

---

3   This table is often created using a spreadsheet model, thereby facilitating modification and distribution among team members.

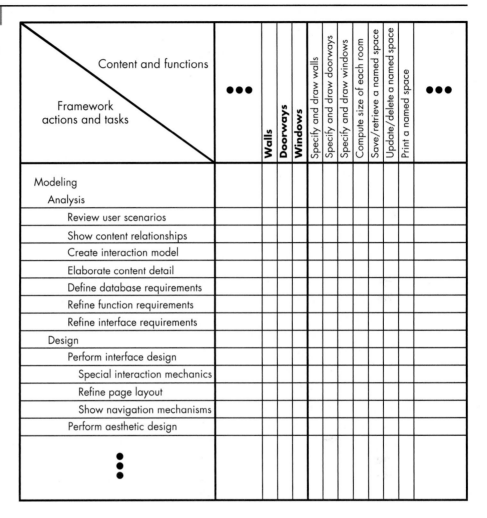

FIGURE 5.1

Melding the problem and the process.

After a brief discussion, the WebE team selects the set of tasks that will be used to model, construct, and deploy these content objects and functions. Referring to the figure, you'll note that the team has adapted the generic framework suggested in Chapter 3, rearranging some tasks, modifying others, and adding a few. In every instance, process agility and the quality of the end result will guide decision making. The internal matrix within the table is used to indicate which actions and tasks are applicable to which content and functionality. Not every action and task will be applied to every content object and function.

It is important to note that the set of actions and tasks defined for one increment is *not* necessarily the same set that is used for the next increment. The size and complexity of the work associated with each increment guides the WebE team in the selection of the framework tasks that will be applied.

What Work Products Will Be Produced?

The number of intermediate work products (e.g., modeling representations, interface sketches, navigation maps) should be kept to the minimum that is necessary to provide appropriate guidance for the next framework action or task. Three criteria should guide the team:

1. Is the work product absolutely necessary to better understand the WebApp increment and to achieve a high-quality result?

2. Will the work product serve as a useful foundation for work to be conducted in subsequent WebE tasks?

3. Does the work product provide information that can be used during the engineering of other WebApp increments?

If the answer to any of these questions is "yes," then you should consider creating the work product. Creating unnecessary work products not only wastes effort but can also calcify the WebApp and encourage developers to resist changes that might be very appropriate.

As an example, consider a situation in which the team is debating whether it is necessary to create an analysis modeling work product. The work product, in this case a collection of UML diagrams (Chapter 7), would certainly aid in understanding the increment and thereby improve quality. The diagrams would serve as a guide for subsequent design work and might be useful in the next two increments that are scheduled for deployment. Since all three criteria are met, the WebE team decides to develop the work product.

One team member argues against the decision.

"I have a very strong feeling that the stakeholders are going to change their minds about this capability," he states, "and we're going to have to update this collection of diagrams again and again. It'll waste time."

Everyone pauses for a moment. The Web engineer has made an excellent point. If changes to the content and functionality are likely, the work products in question will have to be updated with each change—a time-consuming and potentially error prone task. What to do?

The team leader ponders the situation for a moment.

"What if we create the work products assuming that no changes will occur. They'll be really useful to guide design," she says. "If you're right and the stakeholders do change their minds, we'll jettison these diagrams and make appropriate changes to the design itself."

The team spends a few moments discussing this and then revisits its decision.

What Is the Appropriate Way to Assess Quality?

You can do it right, or you can do it over again. If a WebE team stresses quality in all framework activities, the team reduces the amount of rework that it must do. That results in lower costs and, more importantly, improved time-to-market.

But it's not enough to talk the talk by saying that quality is important. You have to explicitly define what you mean when you say "WebApp quality" and define a set of tasks that will help ensure that every work product exhibits high quality.

When we discuss WebApp quality in this book, we refer to completeness and accuracy of the problem definition, the commodity of the solution design, the firmness of construction, and the overall degree to which the WebApp increment meets the needs of all stakeholders.[4]

In order to ensure the quality of work products as they are produced, the WebE team can conduct *pair walkthroughs*. This approach, adapted from the concept of *pair programming* in the *Extreme Programming* method [Bec99] [Jef01], suggests that all work products be reviewed by a pair of Web engineers. The producer of the work product presents it to another team member who looks for errors, inconsistencies, and omissions. Working together, the pair tries to improve the quality of the work product.

In cases where the work product is complex or its impact will be critical to the success of the project, the WebE team may schedule a *team walkthrough*—a review form that involves a number of team members and is guided by a distinct set of rules. A more detailed discussion of the mechanics of pair walkthroughs and further detail on team walkthroughs is presented later in this chapter.

SAFEHOME

Pair Walkthroughs

The scene: Meeting room in the Web engineering area before work on modeling begins

The players: Members of the **SafeHomeAssured.com** WebE team

The conversation:

Team leader: We're going to begin modeling tomorrow, and I'd like to go over the "pair programming" approach.

Team member 1: Pair programming? I thought we were going to just use pair walkthroughs. I'm confused.

Team member 2: It's really the same thing, at least as I understand it. You review as you're doing the work.

Team member 3: But we're going to each do our own work, right?

Team leader: You work as a *pair*.

Team member 3: Huh?

(continued)

---

4 In Chapter 3 we used the term *commodity* to refer to suitability of purpose. That is, does the design conform to stakeholder requirements? *Firmness* refers to the degree to which errors have been eliminated.

SAFEHOME (CONTINUED)

Team leader (looking for a paper in a folder and finding it): Listen to this quote from a paper [Wil99] I found on pair programming:

"In pair programming, *two* programmers are assigned to jointly produce *one* artifact (design, algorithm, code, etc.). The two programmers are like a coherent, intelligent organism working with one mind, responsible for every aspect of this artifact. One person is typing or writing, the other is continually reviewing the work. But, both are equal participants in the process. It is not acceptable to say or think things such as, 'You made an error in your design,' or 'That defect was from your part.' Instead, 'We screwed up the design,' or, better yet, 'We just got through test with no defects!' Both partners own everything." I think that just about sums it up.

Team member 2: So, two of us will work together to develop a model, looking for errors as we go.

Team member 1: Jeez. I don't know about this. Seems like a lot of redundancy to me. I think it'll slow us down.

Team leader: Exactly the opposite. In fact, there's a lot of anecdotal evidence that indicates we can deliver Web engineering work products faster and with higher quality—fewer bugs.

Team member 3: But I'm used to working alone. I don't know about this.

Team member 2: I say we give it a chance. If we crash and burn, we'll reevaluate, but I have a feeling that this will work.

Team member 3 (thinking for a moment): So there are no separate reviews when we use pair programming and walkthroughs?

Team leader: We might still have a team walkthrough at some point, but most of our quality control will occur as part of this approach.

[Team members nod without a lot of enthusiasm, but without any hostility.]

Here's the paper I just quoted from. Give it a read this morning, and we'll meet later in the day to discuss the pair programming approach in more detail.

How Should Change Be Managed?

If you don't manage change, it manages you. And that's never good. It's very easy for a stream of uncontrolled changes to turn a well-run WebE project into chaos. For that reason, planning for change is an essential part of the planning activity.

Changes arise from a number of different sources: (1) nontechnical stakeholders may have an afterthought[5] about the WebApp in general or the increment that is currently being developed, (2) end users may request different modes of interaction or demand different functions or content, or (3) Web engineers may learn that unexpected modifications are required to achieve WebApp requirements.

In every case, the change that is requested must be described unambiguously, evaluated to determine the impact on the increment and the overall WebApp, and assessed to estimate the level of effort required to make the change. The problem

---

5   The *afterthought* may be precipitated by new business requirements (e.g., the demographics of the projected market are different from those originally projected), new or modified content or functions (e.g., the content that was originally to be presented is not the content that is now desired), changes in management (e.g., a new executive manager "wants to go another way"), to name just a few.

is that all these change management activities take resources and time—things that are often in short supply as the WebE team is working on an increment. Yet, stakeholders want the changes to be made.

Later in this chapter we'll discuss change management—an umbrella activity that is designed to address the compelling need to make the changes that are requested, while at the same time lightening the immediate burden of change on a WebE team that is immersed in modeling, construction, and deployment.

Building a WebE Team

Web engineering emphasizes agility, and the agile philosophy (Chapter 2) stresses the importance of individual competency coupled with group collaboration. These are critical success factors for a WebE team. Cockburn and Highsmith [Coc01] note this when they write:

> Interestingly, people working together with good communication and interaction can operate at noticeably higher levels than when they use their individual talents. We see this time and again in brainstorming and joint problem-solving sessions. Therefore, agile project teams [WebE teams] focus on increasing both individual competencies and collaboration levels.

To make effective use of the competencies of each team member and to foster effective collaboration throughout a project, WebE teams should be *self-organizing*.

In the context of Web engineering, self-organization implies three things: (1) the WebE team organizes itself for the work to be done, (2) the team organizes the process framework to best accommodate its local environment, and (3) the team organizes the work schedule to best achieve delivery of the WebApp increment. Self-organization has a number of technical benefits, but more importantly, it serves to improve collaboration and boost team morale. In essence, the team serves as its own management. Ken Schwaber [Sch02] addresses these issues when he writes: "The team selects how much work it believes it can perform within the iteration [increment], and the team commits to the work. Nothing demotivates a team as much as someone else making commitments for it. Nothing motivates a team as much as accepting the responsibility for fulfilling commitments that it made itself."

How Do We Recognize a "Good" WebE Team?

The objective for every organization is to create a WebE team that exhibits cohesiveness. In their book, *Peopleware,* DeMarco and Lister [Dem98] discuss this issue:

> We tend to use the word team fairly loosely in the business world, calling any group of people assigned to work together a "team." But many of these groups just don't seem

like teams. They don't have a common definition of success or any identifiable team spirit. What is missing is a phenomenon that we call *jell.*

> A jelled team is a group of people so strongly knit that the whole is greater than the sum of the parts . . .
>
> Once a team begins to jell, the probability of success goes way up. The team can become unstoppable, a juggernaut for success . . . They don't need to be managed in the traditional way, and they certainly don't need to be motivated. They've got momentum.

DeMarco and Lister contend that members of jelled teams are significantly more productive and more motivated than average. They share a common goal, a common culture, and in many cases, a "sense of eliteness" that makes them unique.

Why Don't Teams Jell and What Can Be Done to Help?

Sadly, a WebE team can suffer from *team toxicity*—a malady defined by five factors that "foster a potentially toxic team environment" [Jac98]:

1. A frenzied work atmosphere in which team members waste energy and lose focus on the objectives of the work to be performed.
2. High frustration caused by personal, business, or technological factors that causes friction among team members.
3. "Fragmented or poorly coordinated procedures" or a poorly defined or improperly chosen process model that becomes a roadblock to accomplishment.
4. Unclear definition of roles resulting in a lack of accountability and resultant finger-pointing.
5. "Continuous and repeated exposure to failure" that leads to a loss of confidence and a lowering of morale.

In general, each of these toxins can be avoided if the WebE team is self-organizing. A self-organizing team has access to all information required to do the job, thereby avoiding a frenzied work environment in which people are scrambling to find vital information. A self-organizing team has control over the process that is employed, the work products that are produced, the work schedule that is defined, and the quality and change management activities that are implemented. Therefore, the team avoids the frustration that occurs when there is a lack of control. A self-organizing team establishes its own mechanisms for accountability (e.g., pair walkthroughs are a good way to accomplish this) and defines a series of corrective approaches when a member of the team fails to perform.

Every WebE team experiences small failures. The key to avoiding an atmosphere of failure is to establish team-based techniques for feedback and problem solving. In addition, failure by any member of the team must be viewed as a failure by the team itself. This leads to a team-oriented approach to corrective action, rather than the finger-pointing and mistrust that grows rapidly on toxic teams.

Can a WebE Team Manage Itself?

Some might argue that do-it-yourself team management is akin to do-it-yourself brain surgery, but we disagree (at least some of the time[6]). If a WebE team is experienced and competent, it is possible to develop WebApp increments without an official "project manager." A team leader should be appointed to coordinate communication and work tasks, but members of the team can assess progress and problems by conducting daily team meetings to coordinate and synchronize the work that must be accomplished for that day. These brief meetings (e.g., 15 to 20 minutes) address four key questions:

1. What have we accomplished since the last meeting?
2. What needs to be accomplished before the next meeting?
3. How will each team member contribute to accomplishing what needs to be done?
4. What roadblocks exist that have to be overcome?

SAFEHOME

Team Structure

The scene: Engineering manager's office

The players: Manager of the *SafeHome* product line and three members of the WebE team

Time: Prior to the initiation of the **SafeHomeAssured.com** project

The conversation:

Manager: Have you guys had a chance to look over the preliminary info on **SafeHomeAssured.com** that marketing's prepared?

Team leader: (nodding and looking at his team members): Yes. But we have a bunch of questions.

Manager: Let's hold on that for a moment. I'd like to talk about how we're going to structure the team, who's responsible for what . . . .

Team member 1: I'm really into the agile philosophy . . . I think we should be a self-organizing team.

Team leader: I agree. Given the tight time line and some of the uncertainty, and the fact that we're all really competent [laughs], that seems like the right way to go.

Manager: That's okay with me, but you guys know the drill.

(continued)

---

6 If a WebApp project is very complex, a large team or multiple teams may be required. In such cases (or in the case where the members of a team are inexperienced) a project manager can serve a vitally important role.

SafeHome (CONTINUED)

Team member 2: (smiling and talking as if she was reciting something): We make tactical decisions, about who does what and when, but it's our responsibility to get product out the door on time.

Team member 1: And with quality.

Manager: Exactly. But remember there are constraints. Marketing approves the increments to be produced—in consultation with us, of course.

Team member 2: And?

Manager: And, we're going to use the WebE process framework for the work.

Team member 2: But keep extraneous documentation to an absolute minimum.

Manager: Who is the liaison with me?

Team leader: We decided that I'll be the tech lead 'cause I have the most experience, so it's me, but feel free to talk to any of us.

Manager (laughing): Don't worry, I will.

As answers to each of these questions emerge, the team adapts its approach in a way that accomplishes the work to be performed. As each day passes, continual self-organization and collaboration move the team toward a completed WebApp increment.

How Do We Build a Successful Team?

In his best-selling book on a computer industry long past, Tracy Kidder [Kid00] tells the story of a computer company's heroic attempt to build a computer to meet the challenge of a new product built by a larger competitor.[7] The story is a metaphor for teamwork, leadership, and the grinding stress that all technologists encounter when critical projects don't go as smoothly as planned.

A summary of Kidder's book hardly does it justice, but these key points [Pic01] have particular relevance as you work to build an effective WebE team:

A set of team guidelines should be established. These encompass what is expected of each person, how problems are to be dealt with, and what mechanisms exist for improving the effectiveness of the team as the project proceeds.

Strong leadership is a must. The team leader must lead by example and by contact and must exhibit a level of enthusiasm that gets other team members to "sign up" psychologically for the work that confronts them.

Respect for individual talents is critical. Not everyone is good at everything. The best teams make use of individual strengths. The best team leaders allow individuals the freedom to run with a good idea.

---

7   Kidder's *The Soul of a New Machine,* originally published in 1981, is highly recommended reading for anyone who intends to make computing a career and everyone who already has!

Every member of the team should commit. The main protagonist in Kidder's book calls this "signing up."

It's easy to get started, but it's very hard to sustain momentum. The best teams never let an "insurmountable" problem stop them. Team members develop a "good enough" solution and proceed, hoping that the momentum of forward progress may lead to an even better solution later in the project.

Scott Rosenberg [Ros07] discusses the challenges that face software developers (and Web engineers) in a book with the intriguing title *Dreaming in Code*. He writes about an open source team working to develop a product called *Chandler* (**chandler.osafoundation.org**), innovative software for workgroup support. In discussing challenges that face technical teams, he writes:

> It's rare for a group of software developers to work together on a series of projects over time; in this they are less like sports teams or military units or musical ensembles and more like the forces of pros who assemble to make a movie and then disperse and recombine for the next film. So, while individual programmers and managers may carry with them a wealth of experience and knowledge of techniques that have served them well in the past, each time they begin a new project with a new team, they are likely to end up pressing the reset button and having to devise a working process from first principles.

We think Rosenberg has it half right. It is true that Web engineers and software developers in general are very much like a movie production company—each creative and knowledgeable in his area of specialty. But we don't think it's either necessary or desirable to "devise a working process from first principles" every time a new project is initiated. Successful teams can make use of a well-defined process framework without any reinvention. This saves them time, and, more importantly, it establishes a foundation from which a high-quality product can emerge.

What Are the Characteristics of a Good Team Leader?

In an excellent book on technical leadership, Jerry Weinberg [Wei86] suggests an MOI model of leadership:

Motivation. The ability to encourage technical people to produce to their best ability. This can be accomplished by providing incentives for high performance and imposing consequences for poor performance.

Organization. The ability to mold existing processes (or invent new ones) that will enable the initial concept to be translated into a final product.

Ideas or innovation. The ability to encourage people to create and feel creative even when they must work within bounds established for a particular WebApp.

Weinberg suggests that successful project leaders apply a problem-solving management style. That is, a leader of a WebE team should concentrate on understanding the problem to be solved, managing the flow of ideas, and at the same time, letting everyone on the team know (by words and, far more important, by actions) that quality counts and that it will not be compromised.

Managing Risk

Risk management encompasses a series of tasks that help a WebE team to understand and manage the many problems that can plague a WebApp project. A risk is a potential problem—it might happen, it might not. But, regardless of the outcome, it's a really good idea to identify it, assess its probability of occurrence, estimate its impact, and establish a contingency plan should the problem actually occur.

A WebE team considers risk at two different levels of granularity: (1) the impact of risk on the entire WebApp project, and (2) the impact of risk on the successful deployment of the WebApp increment currently being engineered.

At the project level, many risk-related questions must be asked and answered: Can planned WebApp increments be delivered within the time frame defined? Will these increments provide ongoing value for end users while additional increments are being engineered? How will requests for change impact delivery schedules? Does the team understand the required Web engineering methods, technologies, and tools? Is the available technology appropriate for the job? Will likely changes require the introduction of new technology?

At the increment level, concerns are more basic. Has the communication activity developed sufficient information for modeling, construction, and deployment? Is the refined process framework appropriate for the increment to be developed? Does the team have the right mix of skills to build this increment? Are content and function adequately defined? Does the increment pose a technology challenge?

Risk management is initiated during the planning activity but is actually an umbrella activity that is revisited throughout the process flow. The challenge for a WebE team is to do enough of it to be proactive about risk, but not so much that it slows other development work to a crawl. Let's examine the basics.

How Do We Identify Risks?

At some point during the planning activity, the WebE team collectively addresses the fundamental question: "What can go wrong?" Each team member is asked to make a list of risks that can be organized into one of the following categories: (1) people risks, (2) product risks, and (3) process risks.

People risks are potential problems that can be directly traced to some human action or failing. For example, it's likely that the WebApp increment will require components developed using XML, but the team currently has no one with XML experience. A technology-related people risk has been identified. Or maybe a specific stakeholder has been uncooperative in the past when information requests have been made, and yet, the required information is crucial to a successful outcome. A communication-related people risk has been identified.

Product risk can normally be traced to potential problems associated with WebApp content, functions, constraints, or performance. For example, a risk that could impact the tight delivery time for the first **SafeHomeAssured.com** increment (an informational WebApp) is discovered only after construction has commenced. A major content object (a comprehensive description of *SafeHome* products) is outdated and may require substantial modification before it can be deployed. A performance risk associated with a later **SafeHomeAssured.com** increment (in-home video monitoring) might be questionable control and monitoring interfaces for video and audio equipment.

Process risks are problems that are tied to the framework actions and tasks that have been chosen by the team. In some cases, too much process can be a potential risk. For example, the team has decided to do a thorough analysis model (Chapter 7) and has specified actions and tasks (and related work products) to accomplish this. For the fourth increment of the **SafeHomeAssured.com** WebApp (implement a layout for the space to be secured and recommend sensors for that space), a process risk might be that the work associated with developing a complete analysis model may be too time consuming and will cause a delay in design and construction activities.

The lists of possible risks are collected from team members and consolidated by category. The WebE team then meets to evaluate them.

How Do We Evaluate Risks?

Once a consolidated list of risks has been developed, the WebE team performs a quick evaluation. Each risk is briefly discussed and evaluated in two ways: (1) the likelihood or probability that the risk will become a reality, and (2) the consequences of the problems associated with the risk, should it occur. The intent is to consider risks in a manner that leads to prioritization. No WebE team has the time or the resources to address every possible risk with the same degree of rigor. By prioritizing risks, the team can allocate resources where they will have the most impact.

Once probability and impact have been estimated, the team can build a risk table.[8] A sample risk table is illustrated in Figure 5.2. The three columns of the

---

8   The risk table can be implemented as a spreadsheet model. This enables easy manipulation and sorting of the entries.

Sample risk
table prior to
sorting.

Risks	Probability	Impact
People		
Little XML experience on team	80%	3
Stakeholders uncooperative	60%	2
Senior manager may change midstream	40%	1
Product		
Informational content may be outdated	50%	2
Algorithms may not be adequately defined	80%	3
Security for WebApp more difficult than expected	80%	3
Database integration more difficult than expected	40%	3
Space def. capability more difficult than expected	70%	3
Process		
Not enough emphasis on communication	60%	2
Too many analysis tasks (too much time spent)	30%	1
Not enough emphasis on navigation design	40%	2
⋮	⋮	⋮

table reflect the risks, their probability (normally represented as a percentage), their impact on schedule and/or cost (often represented using an ordinal scale of 1 [low] to 4 [high]).

Once the columns of the risk table have been completed, the table is sorted by probability and then by impact. Alternatively, a composite score derived from *probability × impact* can be calculated and the table sorted on this basis. High-probability, high-impact risks percolate to the top of the table, and low-probability risks drop to the bottom. This accomplishes first-order risk prioritization. The team studies the resultant sorted risk table and defines a cutoff line. The *cutoff line* (drawn horizontally at some point in the table) implies that only risks that lie above the line will be given further consideration.

How Do We Develop Contingency Plans?

Since the overall development time span for each WebApp increment is short, written contingency plans are *not* developed as part of the WebE process framework. But that doesn't mean that the WebE team simply ignores high-priority risks.

The members of the team consider each risk that falls above the cutoff line in the risk table and answers three questions:

1. How can we avoid the risk altogether?

2. What factors can we monitor to determine whether the risk is becoming more or less likely?

3. Should the risk become a reality, what are we going to do about it?

The answers to these questions can be recorded (as informal notes) by the team leader.

SafeHome

Analyzing Risk

The scene: Meeting room in the Web engineering area during planning for the **SafeHomeAssured.com** WebApp

The players: All members of the WebE Team

The conversation:

Team leader (looking at the risk table shown in Figure 5.2): Okay, we've done a sort on the risk table, and three risks jump out at me: we have little XML experience on the team, security for the WebApp could be more complex than we think, and space definition capability—the layout design we're planning to deliver in increment 4—is definitely more complex than we think. The way I . . .

Team member 1 (interrupting): I think all three could kill us. In fact, I've really got to question the schedule for this stuff. It's nuts!

Team member 2: I have to agree. I'm just an XML rookie, and I may need help and . . .

Team member 3 (interrupting): And who on this team is really expert in the kind of security functionality we've got to implement for later increments? Not me, for sure . . .

Team leader (putting up his hands to stop the discussion): Guys, let's not get unhinged! I agree that all these issues represent risks, and that given the probability, it's likely that they will become reality. Our job is to determine what to do about 'em. Any ideas?

Team member 2: Well, Tyson McNeil [another software developer] knows XML really well. I suppose if I get into trouble . . .

Team leader: Let's be a bit more formal about it. I'll find out what Tyson's commitments are for the next 3 months. Maybe he could work part time for us when we need XML expertise. If not, we have to develop a reliable backup strategy.

Team member 1 (changing the subject): I have to believe that we've underestimated the effort required for the layout design function. I think we should go to the marketing guys right now and tell 'em.

Team leader: I have to agree. I'll speak with marketing and see if we can get some more time. If not, I want you to see if there's a stripped-down version of the capability we can deliver in the allotted time. I want that as an option if they're not willing to extend delivery.

Team member 1: I'm on it as soon as the meeting is over.

Team member 3: And what about security functionality?

Team leader (thinking a moment): I think we may need a bit of outside help. There are a few dollars in the project budget for consulting help. I'm going to try to line up a security expert right now.

Team member 1: What about the other risks?

Team leader: Except for potential problems with algorithm definition, they're lower probability, so for now, we'll let 'em slide. But we should talk about the algorithms . . .

Developing a Schedule

Fred Brooks, the well-known author of *The Mythical Man-Month* [Bro95], was once asked how software projects fall behind schedule. His response was as simple as it was profound: "One day at a time."

The reality of any technical project (whether it involves building a hydroelectric plant or developing a WebApp) is that hundreds of small tasks must occur to accomplish a larger goal. Some of these tasks lie outside the mainstream and may be completed without worry about impact on the completion date. Other tasks lie on the "critical path." If these critical tasks fall behind schedule, the completion date for the WebApp increment is put into jeopardy.

The WebE team's objective is to list all WebE actions and tasks for an increment, build a network that depicts their interdependencies, identify the tasks that are critical within the network, and then track their progress to ensure that any delay will be recognized "one day at a time." To accomplish this, the team leader must have a schedule that has been defined at a degree of resolution that allows progress to be monitored and the project to be controlled.

WebApp project scheduling is an activity that allocates the estimated effort for specific WebE tasks across the planned time line (duration) for building an increment. It is important to note, however, that the overall WebApp schedule evolves over time. During the first iteration of the WebE process framework, a macroscopic schedule is developed. This type of schedule identifies all WebApp increments and projects the dates on which each will be deployed. As the development of the increments gets under way, the entry for the increment on the macroscopic schedule is refined into a detailed schedule. Here, specific WebE tasks (required to accomplish an activity) are identified and scheduled.

Scheduling for WebE projects can be viewed from two rather different perspectives. In the first, an end date for the release of a WebApp has already (and irrevocably) been established. The WebE organization is constrained to distribute effort within the prescribed time frame. The second view of WebApp scheduling assumes that rough chronological boundaries have been discussed but that the end date is set by the WebE organization. Effort is distributed to make best use of resources, and an end date is defined after careful analysis of the WebApp. Unfortunately, the first situation is encountered far more frequently than the second.

What Is Macroscopic Scheduling?

As an example of macroscopic scheduling, consider the **SafeHomeAssured.com** WebApp. Recalling our discussion in Chapter 4, seven increments were identified for the project:

FIGURE 5.3

Time line for
macroscopic
project schedule.

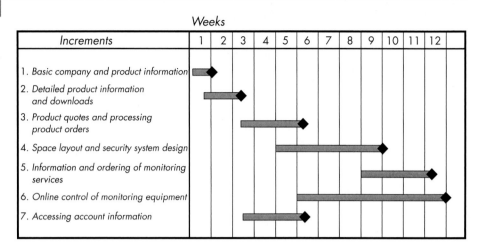

Increment 1:   Basic company and product information

Increment 2:   Detailed product information and downloads

Increment 3:   Product quotes and processing product orders

Increment 4:   Space layout and security system design

Increment 5:   Information and ordering of monitoring services

Increment 6:   Online control of monitoring equipment

Increment 7:   Accessing account information

The WebE team consults and negotiates with stakeholders and develops a *preliminary* deployment schedule for all seven increments. A time line for this schedule is illustrated in Figure 5.3.

It is important to note that the deployment dates (represented by diamonds on the time line) are preliminary and may change as more detailed scheduling of the increments occurs. However, this macroscopic schedule provides management with an indication of when content and functionality will be available and when the entire project will be completed. As a preliminary estimate, the team will work to deploy all increments with a 12-week time line. It's also worth noting that some of the increments will be developed in parallel (e.g., increments 3, 4, and 7). This assumes that the team will have sufficient people to do this parallel work.

What Is Increment Scheduling?

Once the macroscopic schedule has been developed, the team is ready to schedule work tasks for a specific increment. To accomplish this, you can use a generic process framework (Chapter 3) that is applicable for all WebApp increments. A *task list* is created by using the generic tasks derived as part of the framework as a starting point and then adapting these by considering the content and functions to be derived for a specific WebApp increment.

Each framework action (and its related tasks) can be adapted in one of four ways: (1) a task is applied as is, (2) a task is eliminated because it is not necessary for the increment, (3) a new (custom) task is added, and (4) a task is refined (elaborated) into a number of named subtasks that each becomes part of the schedule.

Recalling the discussion of the modeling activity in Chapter 3, we noted that the generic *design modeling* action could be accomplished by applying some or all of the following tasks:

- Design the interface.
- Design the aesthetic for the WebApp.
- Design the navigation scheme.
- Design the WebApp architecture.
- Design the content and the structure that supports it.
- Design functional components.
- Select appropriate design patterns.
- Design appropriate security and privacy mechanisms.
- Review the design.

As an example, consider the generic task *Design the interface* as it is applied to the fourth increment of **SafeHomeAssured.com.** Recall that the fourth increment implements the content and function for describing the living or business space to be secured by the *SafeHome* security system. Referring to Figure 5.3, the fourth increment commences at the beginning of the fifth week and terminates at the end of the ninth week.

There is little question that the *Design the interface* task must be conducted. The team recognizes that the interface design is pivotal to the success of the increment and decides to refine (elaborate) the task. The following subtasks are derived for the *Design the interface* task for the fourth increment:

- Develop a sketch of the page layout for the space design page.
- Review the layout with stakeholders.
- Design the space layout navigation mechanisms.
- Design the "drawing board" layout.[9]

---

9   At this stage, the team envisions creating the space by literally drawing the walls, windows, and doors using graphical functions. Wall lines will "snap" onto grip points. Dimensions of the wall will be displayed automatically. Windows and doors will be positioned graphically. The end user can also select specific sensors, cameras, etc., and position them once the space has been defined.

- Develop procedural details for the graphical wall layout function.
- Develop procedural details for the wall length computation and display function.
- Develop procedural details for the graphical window layout function.
- Develop procedural details for the graphical door layout function.
- Design mechanisms for selecting security system components (sensors, cameras, microphones, etc.).
- Develop procedural details for the graphical layout of security system components.
- Conduct pair walkthroughs as required.

These tasks become part of the increment schedule for the fourth WebApp increment and are allocated over the increment development schedule. They can be input to scheduling software (e.g., Microsoft Project) and used for tracking and control.

How Do We Estimate Effort and Time?

The focus of estimation for most WebE projects is on macroscopic, rather than microscopic, issues. The WebE team assesses whether a planned WebApp increment can be developed with available resources according to defined schedule constraints. This is accomplished by considering each increment's content and function as a whole. In essence, members of the WebE team ask, "Can we deploy the fourth **SafeHomeAssured.com** increment with three people working for 5 weeks, given our current understanding of the increment, the risks that we've identified, and the task list that we've defined for the work?"

If the team answers "yes," unanimously and without hesitation, no further estimation activities are required. On the other hand, if the team has trepidation about a delivery date that was forced on them by one or more stakeholders, two options are available: (1) voice your concerns but proceed anyway, or (2) do a small amount of detailed estimation in an effort to help yourselves and your stakeholders better understand the resources and time required.[10]

There are two viable (and quick) approaches to detailed estimation for WebApps. The first, *usage scenario–based estimation,* examines the usage scenarios (e.g., use cases) defined for the increment to be built. Examining the team's past history, you establish a value E_{avg}, which is the average effort (in person-days) required to deploy a usage scenario. To estimate the increment, count the number of usage scenarios and multiply by E_{avg}. The number can be adjusted based on the

---

10 What you're hoping to get, of course, is an extension to the delivery date.

FIGURE 5.4

Usage scenario–based estimation.

Usage Scenario	E_{avg}	Complexity	Effort
Develop a layout for the space to be monitored	14	2.5	35
Get recommendations for sensor layout for my space	14	2.0	28
Totals			63

perceived complexity of the usage scenarios. Once the effort is determined, it can be distributed across WebE actions and tasks along the project time line. Finally, the estimates can be used to assess the validity of the deployment dates for the increment. Figure 5.4 illustrates this approach for the fourth **SafeHomeAssured.com** increment, where the past history for the team indicates that $E_{avg} = 14$ person-days. Both usage scenarios to be implemented are considerably more complex than average with complexity multipliers of 2.5 and 2.0, respectively. Hence, the overall effort required to implement the fourth increment is estimated to be 63 person-days to be distributed over a delivery period of 5 weeks.

It's time for a word of caution. Inexperienced teams (and team leaders) assume a linear relationship exists between people, effort, and time. That is, if 63 person-days are required to model, construct, and deploy an increment, the work could be accomplished by one person working for 63 days, two people working for 32 days, three people working for 21 days, and so forth. Sadly, a linear relationship does not exist.

In reality, as more people become involved in a project, more effort is spent on communicating and coordinating (meetings, e-mail, etc.). Additional time is spent on things that have nothing to do with the project (e.g., telephone calls, coordinating the softball league), administrative issues (e.g., applying for a new health insurance plan), and other "nonproductive" work. As a consequence, it may take three people 25 or more calendar days to achieve 63 person-days of effort.

A second estimation approach uses a *product-process table*. In this approach, all major WebE actions are listed in the first column of the table. All major content objects and functions for an increment are listed in the first row. Team members estimate the amount of effort (in person-days) required to perform the WebE action for each content object and function. Figure 5.5 illustrates this estimation approach for the fourth **SafeHomeAssured.com** increment. This effort appears to be a bit more optimistic than scenario-based estimates. Both must be reconciled to provide a single estimate. The relatively complex content and functionality of increment 4 demands considerably more WebE effort than earlier increments.

Content and functions	Analysis	Design	Coding	Testing	Delivery	Feed-back	Total
Walls, doorways, windows	1	2	2	2	0.5	0.25	7.75
Sensors	0.5	1.5	1	1	0.25	0.25	4.5
Specify and draw walls,doorways, windows	1.25	3	3	3	1	0.25	11.5
Compute room size	0.5	1	2	1	0.5	0.25	5.25
Save/retrieve named space	0	1	1	0.5	0.5	0.25	3.25
Update/delete named space	0	1	1	0.5	0.5	0.25	3.25
Print named space	0	1	1	0.5	0.5	0.25	3.25
Recommend security hardware	0.5	3	2	2	0.5	0.25	8.25
Specify security hardware	0.5	2	2	3	0.5	0.25	8.25
Totals	4.25	15.5	15	13.5	4.75	2.25	55.25

How Do We Represent Task Interdependencies?

Some WebE tasks or actions cannot commence until the work product produced by another is available. Other tasks or actions can occur independently. Therefore, it should come as no surprise that individual WebE tasks have interdependencies based on their sequence.

When more than one person is involved in a WebE project, it is likely that development actions and tasks will be performed in parallel. When this occurs, concurrent tasks must be coordinated so that they will be complete when later tasks that require their work product(s) need to be performed.

A *task network,* also called an *activity network,* is a graphic representation of the task flow for a project. It is sometimes used as the mechanism through which task sequence and dependencies are input to an automated project scheduling tool. In its simplest form (used when creating a macroscopic schedule), the task network depicts the overall flow of Web engineering tasks. Figure 5.6 shows a schematic task network for the fourth **SafeHomeAssured.com** increment.

The concurrent nature of WebE actions and tasks leads to a number of important scheduling requirements. Because parallel tasks occur asynchronously, the team leader must determine intertask dependencies to ensure continuous progress toward completion of the increment. In addition, the team leader should be aware

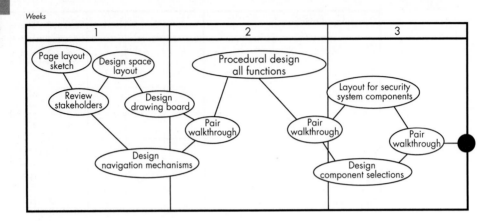

FIGURE 5.6

A task network for the fourth increment.

of those tasks that lie on the *critical path,* that is, tasks that must be completed on schedule if the increment as a whole is to be completed on schedule.

Managing Quality

A WebApp increment is modeled, constructed, and deployed over a relatively short time span. Once it is released to end users, the WebApp increment is exercised and feedback is provided to the WebE team. The feedback provides a reasonably good indication of what works and what doesn't.

It is tempting, therefore, to postpone any consideration of WebApp quality until after an increment is deployed, fixing problems when they're pointed out during the first days of usage. There are, of course, a number of flaws in this approach:

1. Quality problems found by end users are almost always much more expensive to correct than they would have been had they been uncovered earlier in the WebE process flow. Fixing a design error before the WebApp is constructed can be many times less expensive (in expended effort) than trying to correct a deployed WebApp.

2. Every problem uncovered by end users demands rework, and rework absorbs resources (people and effort) that would have been applied to the next increment. The overall project falls behind schedule.

3. Early users may not fully exercise the increment, leaving content and function untouched. Quality problems may exist in these untouched areas. They will be discovered later (and if you believe Murphy's law) at the worst possible time.

It is therefore advisable for every WebE team to focus on WebApp quality as increments are being engineered. But where do you focus?

What Quality Assurance Mechanisms Can the Team Use?

Although quality problems can arise from a variety of sources, their origins can often be traced to a failure to understand or achieve the needs of end users. Therefore, the first quality assurance mechanism for Web engineering is a thoughtful, thorough communication activity. In Chapter 4, we noted that communication elicits requirements from WebApp stakeholders. If care is taken as requirements gathering is conducted, then there will be less likelihood that errors. Inconsistencies or omissions will not be passed into subsequent framework activities. The *pair walkthrough* (discussed next) can be used to assess the quality of all work products developed as part of communication. In this case, the walkthrough participants include a Web engineer and one or more stakeholders.

Once requirements for content, function, constraints, and performance are passed forward to the modeling activity, analysis and design tasks commence. In every case, analysis and design models should be assessed for quality. At a minimum, the WebE team can create a generic checklist that you can use to assess the model. For more complex or critical models, a pair walkthrough can be conducted for each model that is created.

Once the WebApp increment code has been generated, a systematic sequence of tests (Chapter 15) can be initiated to assess the quality of the increment. It is important to note that tests must exercise all user requirements and at the same time examine technical aspects of the increment (e.g., architectural integrity, the correctness of a functional component or content object, and the validity of all links and navigation mechanisms).

The results of all quality assurance mechanisms should be recorded. This will assist the team when changes must be made and will also help the team to correct process weaknesses that led to a class of errors.

What Are the Mechanics of a Pair Walkthrough?

Earlier in this chapter, we noted that a pair walkthrough was an effective and agile mechanism for ensuring the quality of work products (e.g., analysis and design models, HTML or XML code, various scripts, and content and functions) that are produced as a consequence of WebE activities.

As an example of the mechanics of a pair walkthrough, we'll consider a portion of the analysis model of the fourth increment of the **SafeHomeAssured.com** WebApp. This increment implements a layout for the space to be monitored and recommends sensors for that space.

A member of the WebE team, working in conjunction with a specific stakeholder from the marketing department,[11] produces a portion of the analysis model (in this case, a graphical description of the user interface for implementing a space layout). As the interface model is developed, the Web engineer works together with a knowledgeable stakeholder (a marketing person who can play the role of an end user) and conducts an ongoing pair walkthrough. Both the Web engineer and the stakeholder review the interface model as it evolves, addressing questions such as:

- Is there anything about the page layout that is problematic?
- Are menu items meaningful, complete, and intuitive?
- Is the space layout scheme easy to use? Intuitive?
- Can you envision how you'd navigate to this page and from it to other functionality and content?
- Have we missed any key functionality or content on this page?
- What are you assuming about this model?

These and other questions are addressed repeatedly as the model evolves. The result is ongoing corrections and/or modifications to the model.

What Are the Mechanics of a Team Walkthrough?

There are situations in which the entire WebE team will review a work product. This situation occurs when the work product (e.g., a navigation design) may have broad impact for the entire WebApp, and hence it is important that everyone understands the issues and has input into the review.

Two team members use the "pair programming" approach to develop some aspect of the WebApp. Once they are convinced that the work product is complete in draft form, the pair (called the *producers* of the work product) asks other members of the team to participate in a *team walkthrough.* The producers give the other reviewers any information that has been produced (either in hard copy form, if feasible, or in electronic form). The reviewers promise to spend at least 30 to 45 minutes reviewing the work product and listing any issues, problems, or impressions based on the review.

Within 24 hours (preferably sooner), a team walkthrough begins. The producers of the work product begin by "walking through" the work product, explain-

---

11 Remember that nontechnical stakeholders are also considered to be active members of an agile WebE team.

ing what it represents and how the reader might interpret what is shown. As this occurs, the reviewers ask questions (often based on notes developed before the review) and point out potential problem areas. The producers note each of these without trying to solve them immediately. As the walkthrough proceeds, the participants follow these guidelines:

1. **Review the product, not the producer.** Conducted properly, the team walkthrough should leave all participants with a warm feeling of accomplishment. Conducted improperly, the walkthrough can take on the aura of an inquisition. Errors should be pointed out gently; the tone of the walkthrough should be loose and constructive; the intent should not be to embarrass or belittle, but rather to assist.

2. **Set an agenda and maintain it.** One of the key maladies of meetings of all types is drift. A walkthrough should be kept on track and on schedule.

3. **Limit debate and rebuttal.** When an issue is raised by a reviewer, there may not be agreement on its impact. Rather than spending time debating the question, the issue should be recorded for resolution later.

4. **Enunciate problem areas, but don't attempt to solve every problem noted.** A walkthrough is not a problem-solving session.

5. **Take written notes**. Notes may be entered directly into a notebook computer.

6. **Spend enough time to uncover quality problems, but not one minute more**. In general, a team walkthrough should be completed within 60 to 90 minutes at the most.

As an example of a situation in which a team walkthrough is required, the entire WebE team might decide to review aspects of the design model to help ensure that errors, inconsistencies, and omissions are uncovered before code generation commences prior to beginning the construction activity for the fourth **SafeHomeAssured. com** increment.

Do Criteria for Quality Exist for WebApps?

Even the best walkthroughs won't work if the people looking at the WebE work product don't know what to look for. The sidebar contains a comprehensive set of online resources [Qui01] that provide quality criteria and guidelines for WebApps.

INFO

Quality Criteria and Guidelines for WebApps

W3C: Style Guide for Online Hypertext	**www.w3.org/Provider/Style**
The Sevloid Guide to Web Design	**www.sev.com.au/webzone/design/guide.asp**
Web Pages That Suck	**www.webpagesthatsuck.com/index.html**
Resources on Web Style	**www.westegg.com/unmaintained/badpages**
Gartner's Web Evaluation Tool	**www.gartner.com/ebusiness/website-ings**
IBM Corp: Web Guidelines	**www-3.ibm.com/ibm/easy/eou_ext.nsf/ Publish/572**
World Wide Web Usability	**http://ijhcs.open.ac.uk**
Interface Hall of Shame	**www.iarchitect.com/mshame.htm**
Art and the Zen of Web Sites	**www.tlc-systems.com/webtips.shtml**
Designing for the Web: Empirical Studies	**www.microsoft.com/usability/webconf.htm**
Nielsen's useit.com	**www.useit.com**
Quality of Experience	**www.qualityofexperience.org**
SAP Design Guide	**www.sapdesignguild.org**
Creating Killer Web Sites	**www.killersites.com/core.html**
All Things at Web	**www.pantos.org/atw**
SUN's New Web Design	**www.sun.com/980113/sunonnet**
Tognazzini, Bruce: Homepage	**www.asktog.com**
Webmonkey	**http://hotwired.lycos.com/webmonkey/ design/?tw=design**
World's Best Websites	**www.worldbestwebsites.com**
Yale University: Yale Web Style Guide	**http://info.med.yale.edu/caim/manual**

Managing Change

Because an incremental process flow is used for Web engineering, it's relatively easy to manage change *if* you and other stakeholders have discipline and patience. Because the development time for an increment is short, it is often possible to delay the introduction of requested changes until the next increment, thereby reducing the disruptive effects associated with changes that must be implemented on the fly.

However, this strategy implies a subtle change in our approach to each increment. Not only does the *n* + 1st WebApp increment implement content and functionality associated with the increment, but it may also incorporate changes to content and functionality requested for the *n*th increment (changes that have been delayed until after the *n*th increment is initially deployed). Of course, this is only reasonable if none of those extra changes are "showstoppers"; that is, if the delivered increment (without the changes to be included in the next increment) is still an acceptable solution.

How Should Criticality and Impact of a Change Be Assessed?

In order to assess the criticality and impact of any requested change, each change should be categorized into one of four classes:

> **Class 1.** Content or function change that corrects a minor error or enhances local content or functionality
>
> **Class 2**. Content or function change that has an impact on other content objects or functional components within the increment
>
> **Class 3.** Content of function change that has a broad impact across a WebApp (e.g., major extension of functionality, significant enhancement or reduction in content, major required changes in navigation)
>
> **Class 4.** Major design change (e.g., a change in interface design or navigation approach) that will be immediately noticeable to one or more categories of end users

Once the requested change has been categorized, it can be assessed according to the algorithm shown in Figure 5.7.

Referring to the figure, class 1 and 2 changes are treated informally and are handled in an agile manner. For a class 1 change, a Web engineer evaluates the impact of the change, but no external review or documentation is required. As the change is made, standard check-in and check-out procedures are enforced by configuration repository tools (see Chapter 16 for details). For class 2 changes, it is incumbent on the Web engineer to review the impact of the change on related objects (or to ask other developers responsible for those objects to do so). If the change can be made without requiring significant changes to other objects, modification occurs without additional review or documentation. If substantive changes are required, further evaluation and planning are necessary.

Class 3 and 4 changes are also treated in an agile manner, but some descriptive documentation and more formal review procedures are required. A *change description*—describing the change and providing a brief assessment of the impact of the change—is developed for class 3 changes. The description is distributed to all members of the Web engineering team (including other stakeholders who have interest) who review it to better assess its impact. A change description is also developed for class 4 changes, but in this case, the review is conducted by all stakeholders.

When Do We Delay Making the Change?

As we noted in the introduction to this section, changes tend to disrupt work and delay the deployment of a WebApp increment. The reason for this is obvious—people who are working on content or functionality associated with an increment must stop what they're doing and address the change. This takes time.

FIGURE 5.7

Managing
changes for
WebApps.

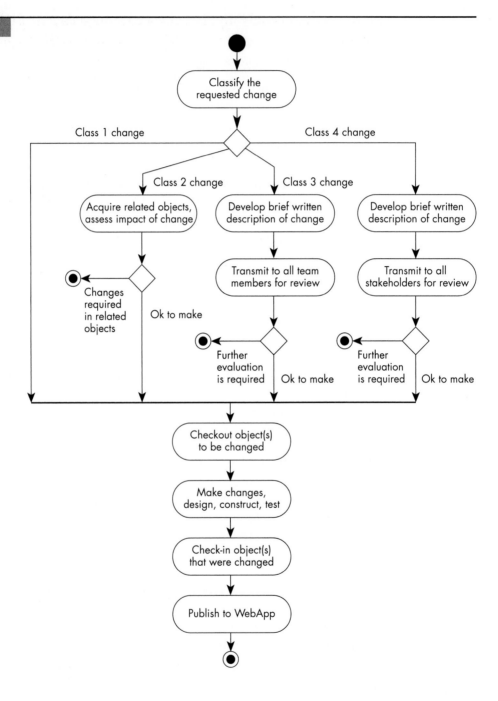

In order to avoid a disruption to the increment work schedule, a change associated with increment *n* should generally be addressed only after increment *n* is initially deployed. That is, changes are "locked out" of the increment while it is undergoing development. The requested changes must, of course, be evaluated and incorporated into the increment, but only after the increment has been delivered for the first time.

At this point you may be thinking: "My stakeholders won't put up with that approach. They request a change and want it implemented immediately."

We've encountered the same situation, but that doesn't mean that the "make the change now!" culture can't be changed. In order to change this culture, stakeholders must understand that changes are *not* free—they absorb resources and they take time. Therefore, the stakeholder is always left with a trade-off—work can be interrupted and changes can be made, but delivery dates will slip and costs will invariably escalate. In most situations, it is better to delay the implementation of a change until it can be accomplished in the least disruptive (and therefore, least costly and time consuming) manner.

There are situations, however, where a change should be made immediately. The change should be made immediately, if:

1. Delaying the change will result in more work than making it on the spot.

2. The usability of the increment by end users will be severely degraded without the change.

3. Significant monetary damages will occur if the change is not made immediately.

4. Regulatory or legal requirements demand that the deployment include the change.

If one or more of these criteria are met, you must make the change as part of the current increment.

SafeHome

A Request for a Change

The scene: Web engineering area as work progresses on increment 2, *Detailed product information and downloads*

The players: Two WebE team members and the team leader

The conversation:

Team leader: I just got a call from marketing. They want us to make a change, but I don't think it's too big a deal.

(continued)

SafeHome (continued)

Team member 1: But I thought the rule was no changes once we begin an increment.

Team leader: It is, but we still have to do a quick evaluation and determine how we're going to treat it.

Team member 2 (grimacing): Now? We're right in the middle of . . .

Team leader: I know, I know, but this shouldn't take more than 15 minutes.

[Both team members shrug, but they don't look happy.]

Team leader: They want us to add a new class of content objects for our product information content. They have a library of videos that describe how to install various monitoring devices, and they want to make that available to users.

Team member 1: So in addition to descriptive text, photos, product technical specs, and so on, they want a video?

Team leader: Uh huh.

Team member 2: Is there a video for every monitoring device?

Team leader: I'm not sure, but I'll call 'em and find out.

Team member 2: We need to know that, the size of the files, the format of the video, probably a bunch more that'll occur to me if I give it a bit more thought.

Team member 1: I assume they want it now.

Team leader: They do.

Team member 2: It looks like a class 1 or 2 change request to me. We'll have to modify our navigation design slightly to get at the video files, create the appropriate video display capability, and modify any internal links in our other product information objects. It'll be some work, but not a lot.

Team leader: How much is "not a lot"?

Team member 1: Give us the rest of the "15 minutes" and we'll tell you. And then?

Team leader: Well, we can delay until the next increment, but I'm inclined to make this mod right now. I suspect it might actually be more work if we delay it. We're not very far into increment 2, so . . .

Team member 1: Let's see how much effort is involved; then we'll decide.

Team leader: That's fair; stop by my cubical when you have a clearer estimate of the effort.

Should Changes Be Made to All Related Work Products?

Work products produced during the WebE process serve one of two purposes: (1) they can be an informal record of information gathered during a WebE activity (e.g., a list of content and functional requirements gathered during the communication activity), or (2) they can be a representation (model) of the WebApp that is used to guide subsequent WebE activities (e.g., an interface design model that will guide the coding of the interface during construction).

As a general rule of thumb, work products that fall into the first category need not be updated as changes are requested and made. However, work products in the second category should be modified to reflect any changes so that they remain useful in subsequent WebE activities.

It's important to note, however, that keeping *all* work products in the second category (e.g., design models) up to date can be burdensome for a WebE team. How then does the WebE team choose the work products that should be updated as changes are made?

A pragmatic approach is to answer this question: "What aspects of the design can be better represented as an executable implemention?" In some instances, the only permanent description of some aspect of the WebApp is the WebApp itself. For example, once the interface design model has been implemented in HTML, there is little reason to maintain the actual design model of the interface. Changes to the interface will be guided by the implementation, not the model. Hence, the model can be archived (for historical purposes), but need not be kept up to date. On the other hand, a design model of a complex function might be useful even after the function has been implemented and deployed. The reason for this is that the model is represented at a higher level of abstraction and will facilitate understanding by people who have not been involved in the original implementation. In this case, the functional model should be updated as changes are made to the function.

Tracking the Project

For a WebE project, on-time deployment of a WebApp increment is often the primary measure of overall progress. But before the increment is available, a Web engineer will inevitably encounter the question, "Where are we?"

To provide an answer to this question, you'll need to track progress as a WebApp increment is being developed. But how? For small and moderately sized Web engineering projects, an increment may be developed over a period of only 2 or 3 weeks. At best, intermediate milestones are informally defined, and the project schedule may not have been developed at a granularity that will aid in tracking.

Are There Any Macroscopic Indicators of Progress Problems?

At a macroscopic level, there are signs indicating that an increment (or the entire project) is in trouble. John Reel [Ree99] suggests 10 signs that indicate that an information systems project is in jeopardy. We have adapted these for WebApps:

1. The WebE team doesn't understand its customer's needs.
2. The WebApp scope is poorly defined.
3. Changes are managed poorly.
4. The chosen technology changes.
5. Business needs appear to be changing (or are ill defined).
6. Deadlines are unrealistic.
7. Users are not really interested in the WebApp.
8. Sponsorship is lost (or was never properly obtained).
9. The WebE team lacks people with appropriate skills.
10. Practitioners avoid best practices and lessons learned.

Throughout this and earlier chapters, we've discussed a WebE process that can help eliminate these problems. Take the process seriously and you'll avoid what some jaded industry professionals call the "90-90 rule." The first 90 percent of a system absorbs 90 percent of the allotted effort and time. The last 10 percent takes the other 90 percent of the allotted effort and time [Zah94]. The seeds that lead to the 90-90 rule are contained in the macroscopic indicators noted in the preceding list.

What Criteria Are Used to Track Progress?

One way to track progress as a WebApp increment is being developed is to poll the WebE team to determine which framework activities have been completed. However, this approach can be unreliable because completion of a framework activity is an indication of progress only if appropriate[12] work products have been developed.

Another approach is to determine how many user scenarios have been implemented and how many user scenarios (for a given increment) remain to be implemented. This provides a rough indication of the relative degree of "completeness" of the project increment.

If the WebE team has taken the time to construct a detailed work schedule for the increment, progress can be tracked by determining how many work tasks have been completed, how many work products have been produced and reviewed, and how much confidence individual team members have in the increment completion date.

Outsourcing WebE Work

A substantial percentage of WebApp development is outsourced[13] to vendors who (purportedly) specialize in the development of Web-based systems and applications. In such cases, a business (the customer) asks for a fixed price quote for WebApp development from two or more vendors, evaluates competing quotes, and then selects a vendor to do the work. But what does the contracting organization look for? How is the competence of a WebApp vendor determined? How does one know whether a price quote is reasonable? What degree of planning, scheduling, and risk assessment can be expected as an organization (and its outsourcing vendor) embarks on a major Web engineering effort?

---

12 In this context, an appropriate work product is one that is correct and establishes a solid foundation for the WebE work that follows.

13 Although reliable industry data are difficult to find, it is safe to say that this percentage is considerably higher than the one encountered in conventional software work. This may, of course, reduce somewhat as Web development skills become mainstreamed, but it is likely to always be high.

To answer these questions, we present a set of guidelines in the sections that follow. These are not intended to be a foolproof cookbook for the production of low-cost, on-time WebApps. However, they will help both the contracting organization and the vendor initiate work smoothly with a minimum of misunderstandings.

How Do We Initiate an Outsourced Project?

If outsourcing is the strategy to be chosen for WebApp development, an organization should perform a number of tasks before searching for a vendor to do the work.

1. **Communication should be performed internally.** The audience for the WebApp is identified, internal stakeholders who may have an interest in the WebApp are listed, the overall goals for the WebApp are defined and reviewed, the information and services to be delivered by the WebApp are specified, competing websites are noted, and qualitative and quantitative measures of a successful WebApp are defined. This information should be documented in a product specification that is provided to the outsourcing vendor.

2. **A rough design for the WebApp should be developed internally.** Obviously, an expert Web developer will create a complete design, but time and cost can be saved if the general look and feel of the WebApp is identified for the outsourcing vendor (this can always be modified during the preliminary stages of the project). The design should include an indication of the type and volume of content to be presented by the WebApp and the types of interactive processing (e.g., forms, order entry) to be performed. This information should be added to the product specification.

3. **A rough project schedule, including not only final delivery dates but also milestone dates, should be developed.** Milestones should be attached to deliverable increments of the WebApp as it evolves.

4. **A list of responsibilities for the internal organization and the outsourcing vendor should be created.** In essence, this task addresses what (information, contacts, and other resources) the outsourcing vendor will require of the internal organization.

5. **The degree of oversight and interaction by the contracting organization with the vendor should be identified.** This should include the naming of a vendor liaison and the identification of the liaison's responsibilities and authority, the definition of quality review points as development proceeds, and the vendor's responsibilities with respect to interorganizational communication.

All the information developed during these steps should be organized into a request for quote that is transmitted to candidate vendors.[14]

How Do We Select Candidate Outsourcing Vendors?

In recent years, thousands of Web design companies have emerged to help businesses establish a Web presence and/or engage in e-commerce. Many have become adept at the WebE process, but many others are little more than neophytes. In order to select candidate Web developers, you must perform due diligence. You should: (1) interview past clients to determine the Web vendor's professionalism, ability to meet schedule and cost commitments, and ability to communicate effectively, (2) determine the name of the vendor's chief Web engineer(s) for successful past projects (and later, be certain that this person is contractually obligated to be involved in your project), and (3) carefully examine samples of the vendor's work that are similar in look and feel (and business area) to the WebApp that is to be contracted. Even before a request for quote is offered, a face-to-face meeting may provide substantial insight into the "fit" between the contractor and vendor.

How Can We Assess the Validity of Price Quotes and the Reliability of Estimates?

Because relatively little historical data exist and the scope of WebApps is notoriously fluid, estimation is inherently risky. For this reason, some vendors will embed substantial safety margins into the cost quoted for a project. This is both understandable and appropriate. The question is *not* "Have we gotten the best bang for our buck?" Rather, the questions should be:

- Does the quoted cost of the WebApp provide a direct or indirect return on investment that justifies the project?
- Does the vendor that has provided the quote exhibit the professionalism and experience we require?

If the answers to these questions are "yes," the price quote is worth considering.

What Level of Project Management Will Be Needed?

The formality associated with project management tasks (performed by both the vendor and the contracting organization) is directly proportional to the size, cost, and complexity of the WebApp. For large, complex projects, a detailed project schedule that defines work tasks, software quality assurance checkpoints,

---

14 If WebApp development work is to be conducted by an internal group, nothing changes! The project is initiated in basically the same manner.

engineering work products, customer review points, and major milestones should be developed. The vendor and contractor should assess risk jointly and develop plans for mitigating, monitoring, and managing those risks that are deemed important. Mechanisms for quality and change management should be explicitly defined. Methods for effective communication between the contractor and the vendor should be established.

How Do We Assess the Schedule and Manage Scope?

WebApp development schedules span a relatively short period of time. Therefore, the development schedule should have a fine granularity. That is, work tasks and minor milestones should be scheduled on a daily time line. This fine granularity allows both the contracting organization and the vendor to recognize schedule slippage before it threatens the final completion date.

Because it is highly likely that the scope will change as a WebApp project moves forward, the WebE process model is adaptable and incremental. This allows the vendor's development team to "freeze" the scope for one increment so that an operational WebApp release can be created. The next increment may address scope changes suggested by a review of the preceding increment, but once the second increment commences, the scope is again frozen temporarily. This approach enables the WebApp team to work without having to accommodate a continual stream of changes, but still recognizes the continuous evolution characteristic of most WebApps.

Where We've Been . . . Where We're Going

The planning activity for Web engineering begins with a consideration of the project scope and leads to an understanding of business context, informational objectives, WebApp functionality, system constraints, and performance issues. This information is derived from work products produced during the communication activity.

An overall project plan provides a road map for the delivery of all WebApp increments, but the planning activity itself focuses on the tasks and work products to be produced for a specific increment. It also addresses the risk, quality, and change management mechanisms that will be applied as an increment is produced.

Planning is performed by all members of the WebE team and is coordinated by the team leader. Good WebE teams tend to jell and avoid the toxic characteristics that can create problems whenever a group of people work together.

Once planning is completed, technical work begins with the modeling activity. In the chapters that follow, we examine many different aspects of modeling as it is applied to WebApps.

References

[Bec99]   Beck, K., *Extreme Programming Explained: Embrace Change,* Addison-Wesley, 1999.

[Bro95]   Brooks, M., *The Mythical Man-Month,* Anniversary Edition, Addison-Wesley, 1995.

[Coc01]   Cockburn, A., and J. Highsmith, "Agile Software Development: The People Factor," *IEEE Computer,* vol. 34, no. 11, November 2001, pp. 131–133.

[Dem98]   DeMarco, T., and T. Lister, *Peopleware,* 2nd ed., Dorset House, 1998.

[Jac98]   Jackman, M., "Homeopathic Remedies for Team Toxicity," *IEEE Software,* July 1998, pp. 43–45.

[Jef01]   Jeffries, R., et al., *Extreme Programming Installed,* Addison-Wesley, 2001.

[Kid00]   Kidder, T., *The Soul of a New Machine,* Back Bay Books (reprint edition), 2000.

[Pic01]   Pickering, C., "Building an Effective E-Project Team," *E-Project Management Advisory Service,* Cutter Consortium, vol. 2, no. 1, 2001, **www.cutter.com/content/project/fulltext/summaries/2001/01/index.html** (accessed July 24, 2007).

[Qui01]   Quibeldey-Cirkel, K., "Checklist for Web Site Quality Assurance," *Quality Week Europe,* 2001.

[Ree99]   Reel, J. S., "Critical Success Factors in Software Projects, *IEEE Software,* May, 1999, pp. 18–23.

[Ros07]   Rosenberg, S., *Dreaming in Code,* Crown Publishers, 2007.

[Sch02]   Schwaber, K., "Agile Processes and Self-Organization," Agile Alliance, 2002, **www.agilealliance.org/system/article/file/784/file.pdf** (accessed July 24, 2007).

[Wei86]   Weinberg, G., *On Becoming a Technical Leader,* Dorset House, 1986.

[Wil99]   Williams, L., and R. Kessler, "All I Really Need to Know about Pair Programming I Learned in Kindergarten," University of Utah, 1999, **http://collaboration.csc.ncsu.edu/laurie/Papers/Kindergarten.PDF** (accessed July 24, 2007).

[Zah94]   Zahniser, R., "Timeboxing for Top Team Performance," *Software Development,* March 1994, pp. 35–38.

THE MODELING ACTIVITY

The written or spoken word is a wonderful and expressive vehicle for communication, but it is not necessarily a precise way to represent the content or functions to be delivered by a WebApp. Natural language can be ambiguous, contradictory, or unclear. Consider the following requirement: "Full product information should only be available to registered users." Apart from the lack of clarity about what is meant by "full product information," it is unclear when and how users might be recognized by the system as "registered," and even what is meant by "available." Should unregistered users be able to know that the extra information exists but not be able to see it? Or should they not even be allowed to know that it exists?

Modeling helps address this problem by using a combination of text, graphical, and diagrammatic forms to depict content and function, architecture and component detail, interfaces, navigation, and aesthetics in ways that are relatively easy to understand and, more important, straightforward to review for correctness, completeness, and consistency.

In Chapter 3 we discussed modeling briefly and stated that it is an activity that creates one or more conceptual representations of some aspect of the WebApp to be built. As shown in Figure 6.1, modeling in the WebE process flow involves two main actions: analysis and design. Before we focus on these actions and consider what "conceptual representations" might be relevant to them, we'll look at the concept of modeling a little more closely.

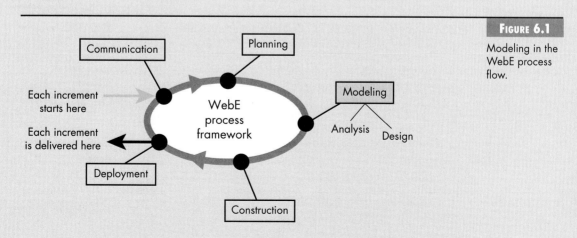

FIGURE 6.1

Modeling in the WebE process flow.

109

Modeling as a Concept

We model our perception of reality so that we can understand and change it, but our models of reality are not perfect. George Box, a famous industrial statistician, once noted that "all models are wrong, but some models are useful." What this means is that no model can ever capture all the near-infinite detail of that part of reality being modeled. (Otherwise it would be that reality!) However, when you create a model, you are aiming to capture the parts of reality that are useful and interesting to you. Therefore, a good model is only "wrong" (or really lacking in detail of reality) in ways that are irrelevant to you. The wrongness of the model is irrelevant to your purpose.[1] Indeed, by leaving some of the reality out of your models, you simplify them and focus on those things that are important to you and the WebE work you're about to perform.

How Do We Judge the Usefulness of a Model?

The only way we can judge the usefulness of a model is to understand the model's purpose. What is the model trying to help you understand? It is important to note, however, that the things that are important to understand vary at different times and for different people.

Let's consider a few of the **SafeHomeAssured.com** stakeholders. For the marketing manager of CPI, it is important to understand the way that users might respond to a particular product. The senior manager for product development might be more interested in understanding the connection between desired functionality and the capabilities and potential of different security or sensor technologies. CPI's engineering manager wants to understand the projected complexity of the WebApp content and functionality.

In each case, the parts of reality that are of interest are different. Taking heed of George Box's observation, the models used will need to be different. If modeling could be performed in a linear manner (as opposed to iteratively), we could move cleanly from one view of reality—one model—to the next, in a nice orderly fashion.

The problem is, as we have discussed earlier, Web engineering doesn't lend itself well to linear approaches. You need the agility to cope with changing requirements, changing technologies, changing people—changing reality. In this environment, the *relationships* between the models become much more important. As we

---

1   It is important to note, however, that a WebApp model can be just plain wrong. If we omit important details, exhibit inconsistent representations, don't listen to stakeholders, or commit many other sins, we've built a model that is, at best, of little use to anyone and, at worst, dangerous.

SafeHome

A Debate about Modeling

The scene: Meeting room in the Web engineering area before work on modeling begins

The players: Members of the **SafeHomeAssured.com** WebE team

The conversation:

Team leader: I'm hearing some grumbling about modeling. At least one of us wants to get right into coding and creating Web pages.

Team member 2: That would be me.

Team member 1 (mildly annoyed): Why am I not surprised? You've been down on the WebE process from the beginning.

Team leader (looking at WebE team member 2): The thing I don't understand about your position is that the process seems to be working for this WebApp. We did a pretty good job gathering requirements, and our plan seems rational. So far the process works.

Team member 2: But modeling is guaranteed to slow us down. We're not here to create unnecessary models; we're here to build **SafeHomeAssured.com.**

Team member 3: Who said anything about building *unnecessary* models?

Team member 1: We don't build models for models' sake, we'll build 'em when something is unclear or very complex.

Team member 2: But then how can we be sure they're right?

Team leader: That's why we use pair programming and pair walkthroughs for every model we create.

Team member 2: There's still no guarantee they're right.

Team member 1: You're missing the point. The intent isn't to build a perfect model. It's to provide us with a better understanding of some aspect of the WebApp. That will allow us to construct the WebApp in less time, with fewer errors.

Team member 2: In theory.

Team member 3 (laughing): It doesn't look like we're going to convince you, but since the rest of us are signed up, you're coming along for the ride. If you're right, I'll be the first to say so.

Team leader: Look, let's model only when we really need to, but when it's necessary, we model. Agreed?

[Heads nod with varying degrees of enthusiasm.]

share information contained within the models, stakeholders are better able to appreciate other stakeholders' perspectives.

Can Models Be Used to Understand Business Constraints?

Business activities and the technology that supports them have become intimately intertwined. This facilitates powerful support for business activities, but it also means that organizations have become increasingly constrained by the inherent limitations of the technology.

As we have already discussed, a model that is constructed appropriately has the potential to allow Web engineers to understand business and user requirements and the design that is intended to fulfill them. But equally important in a rapidly evolving business environment, an effective model allows developers and business analysts to see how a WebApp, its architecture, or its supporting technology might impose constraints on a business organization.

As an example of this "reverse modeling" effect, consider the **SafeHomeAssured. com** WebApp. The interface design model for the fourth increment (introduced in Chapters 4 and 5) results in a design that enables the end user to develop a layout of *SafeHome* security hardware in order to represent the physical space to be secured or monitored. This technological approach makes demands of the end user (who must be willing to spend time describing the space) and therefore constrains CPI to sell Web-based monitoring only to people who are willing to do a spatial layout. This will probably eliminate a nontrivial percentage of the potential market. The CPI marketing department, upon examining the interface design model, immediately recognizes the implied constraint and begins discussing how people who don't want to do the layout graphically can still achieve their goals. This leads to consideration of two new business rules:

1. Potential customers can choose to send a set of house or business floor plans to CPI's customer service. The plans will then be translated by CPI staff into a layout.

2. Potential customers can call CPI, and a sales representative will be sent out to meet with them.

The first proposed business rule allows CPI to accommodate a larger universe of customers. The second proposed rule, although interesting, is ultimately rejected because the company does not want to build a sales force. This illustrates how the **SafeHomeAssured.com** interface design model (as well as other models) can be used in reverse to drive the creation of a new business rule.

The Models We Create

By now we hope you'll agree that models can help you to understand aspects of a project more clearly. But what models should you build? Obviously, this will depend on what it is you want to understand.[2] The best way to identify areas where better understanding (through modeling) is required is to think about the combination of two things: (1) the process being followed (and, hence, the *viewpoints* that are relevant to the activities, actions, and tasks being carried out), and (2) the product being developed (and, hence, the *things* that need to be understood and modeled). We'll begin by looking at each of these in turn and then see how they combine to provide us with a clear view of what to model.

---

2   It will also depend upon the amount of time you have to do the modeling work.

What Does the Process Tell Us About Modeling?

Let's go back and look again at the WebE process that was originally outlined in Chapter 3—particularly Figure 3.2. One of the key WebE activities is *modeling,* and this includes two main actions: *analysis* and *design.* Both of these are aimed at producing models, though in quite different ways. Analysis examines stakeholder requirements in an effort to understand what the WebApp should be doing.

Basically, analysis modeling helps you to understand the nature of the problem being addressed and the "shape" of the WebApp that will allow you to address that problem. There are a number of different elements to this that relate to different points of view. CPI's executive vice president for business development will be interested in the business environment and the business opportunities that might be created by leveraging WebApps. CPI's marketing manager will be interested in how users will interact with, and respond to, a WebApp. CPI's senior manager for product development will be interested in the specific requirements for the WebApp. Each set of interests is related to the others, but represents a different point of view that may dictate a different model.

Conversely, design modeling is about understanding the internal structure of the WebApp being developed and how this creates the shape of the WebApp that was identified by the analysis model. And again, there will be different points of view. CPI's system architect will focus on the overall structure of the WebApp, the broad technologies that are being used, and how the WebApp interfaces to other systems. The information architect will emphasize the nature, structure, and management of the content within the WebApp. A programmer on the WebE team will be most interested in the lower-level functional detail that enables the actual implementation.

What Does the WebApp Tell Us About Modeling?

In Chapter 1 we considered different categories of WebApps (e.g., informational, download, customizable, interaction). Each of these categories blends its focus on information, functionality, and behavior in a different way. Similarly, a Web engineer will focus on different facets of the WebApp—interface, content, navigation, functionality—at different stages of the WebE process. A functionally complex application (e.g., an auction site that integrates detailed support for workflows) is more likely to need thorough functional modeling. An application that involves rich, diverse information (such as a news site) will likely demand a focus on content modeling and interaction models that depict how users interact with that content.

Apart from the type of application, areas of uncertainty in the application can also affect the types of models constructed. For example, consider a functionally rich application in which the functionality is well defined and understood, but the nature of the content is unclear. It makes more sense for the WebE team to focus (at least initially) on models that help clarify the uncertainties in the content.

Modeling Frameworks

A number of researchers have suggested frameworks that provide clarification of the set of models that might be used in Web engineering. In addition to suggesting specific model types, the frameworks often aim to establish terms and concepts that are relevant. The majority of these have a focus on application architecture and so are often referred to as *architecture frameworks*.

One of the earliest, most comprehensive, and widely used of these is the Zachman framework [Zac87] [Sow92], shown in Figure 6.2. Referring to the figure, the

---

FIGURE 6.2

The Zachman framework.
Source: Reprinted from **www.zifa.com/framework.html** with permission of John Zachman.

Zachman framework contains two dimensions. The first dimension describes the perspectives of stakeholders of the application and includes the following viewpoints: planner, owner, designer, builder, and subcontractor. The second dimension presents six questions: *what* (data), *how* (function), *where* (network), *who* (people), *when* (time), and *why* (motivation). The two dimensions establish a 5 × 6 matrix of cells. Each cell describes a unique model, an architecture or a description that is relevant to a particular question asked by a particular stakeholder. A number of other popular frameworks—including the 4+1 View Model of architecture [Kru95] and the Model Driven Architecture (MDA) [OMG01]—provide similar insights.[3] A good discussion of these frameworks and their relevance in Web engineering is given in [Kon05].

Is There a Modeling Framework for the Web?

Older modeling frameworks (such as the Zachman framework) were developed for conventional information technology (IT) applications. Their direct applicability to the development of WebApps is questionable. A workable modeling framework for WebApps should be able to accommodate the development of open and modularized architectures for the Web. Similarly, reusable information and components and an increased emphasis on the quality of the user interface—all characteristics of Web architectures—must be accommodated.

A modeling framework that is more suitable to the Web was jointly developed by one of the authors of this book (David) along with several colleagues—Xiaoying Kong and Li Liu [Kon05]. This revised framework, called the *Web Application Architecture Framework* (WAAF), classifies concerns related to the development of WebApps along two dimensions. As shown in Table 6.1, each row (the horizontal dimension) presents the perspective of the different participants in the WebE process: business owners, WebApp users, information architects, application architects, developers, and testers. The vertical dimension (columns) classifies the architectures into four categories that capture the main modeling domains: structure (*what*), behavior (*how*), location (*where*), and pattern. The first three categories (*what, how, where*) mirror those in the Zachman framework. The fourth category (pattern) has been added based on the growing recognition of the importance of patterns[4] in software applications generally and in WebApps in particular [Pla02]

---

3   There are a range of other frameworks beyond those already mentioned. Many of these have been developed for particular application domains, such as the Federal Enterprise Architecture Framework (FEAF—promotes shared development for U.S. federal processes); Command, Control, Computers, Intelligence, Surveillance, and Reconnaissance (C4ISR) architectural framework (gives architectural guidance for U.S. Department of Defense–related domains); and the Treasury Enterprise Architecture Framework (TEAF—supports the U.S. Treasury's business processes in terms of work products).

4   Patterns are general solutions to commonly encountered problems. They are typically represented as a description or template describing how to solve the problem and can be used in different contexts. Design patterns for WebApps are discussed in Chapter 13.

TABLE 6.1   WEB APPLICATION ARCHITECTURE FRAMEWORK (WAAF) MATRIX

	Structure (What)	Behavior (How)	Location (Where)	Pattern
Planning Architecture (Planner's Perspective)	List of things important to the business	List of processes the business performs	List of locations in which the business operates	Possible business models and patterns
Business Architecture (Business Owner's Perspective)	e.g., business entity relationship model	e.g., business process model	e.g., business entity location model	e.g., business model patterns
User Interface Architecture (User's Perspective)	e.g., user interface structure model	e.g., user interface flow model	e.g., user site map model	e.g., interface templates, navigation patterns
Information Architecture (Information Architect's Perspective)	e.g., information dictionary	e.g., information flow model	e.g., information node location model	e.g., information scheme patterns
System Architecture (System Architect's Perspective)	e.g., system functioning module/submodule/server page structure	e.g., workflow model of module/submodule/server page	e.g., site mapping model of modules/submodules/server pages	e.g., design patterns, presentation styles
Web Object Architecture (Developers' Perspective)	e.g., physical object relationship	e.g., algorithms in source code	e.g., network deployment model	e.g., cots, components, code library
Test Architecture (Tester's Perspective)	e.g., test configuration	e.g., test procedure	e.g., test deployment	e.g., templates, standards of test document

[Mon03]. Each cell in the framework is a model, a description, or an architecture, as appropriate.[5]

How Does Modeling Relate to the WebE Process?

The WAAF framework provides an indication of which models (*work products* in the terminology of the WebE process) are appropriate for which purpose and audience. However, we need to go one step further and consider how these might relate to the specific actions and tasks of the modeling activity within the WebE framework. The modeling activity contains two main actions—analysis and design. Each of these actions requires a set of WebE tasks and related work products that will be discussed in detail in Chapters 7 to 13. At this point, however, it might be useful to examine how they fit together into the WAAF framework. Analysis and design actions are composed of the following WebE tasks:

---

5   Some of these will be discussed in Chapters 7 to 11.

Analysis Modeling (Chapter 7)

A-1. Decide whether a requirements model is needed.

A-2. Represent WebApp content.

A-3. Identify content relationships.

A-4. Refine and extend user scenarios.

A-5. Review user scenarios.

A-6. Create an interaction model for complex scenarios.

A-7. Refine interface requirements.

A-8. Identify functions.

A-9. Define constraints and performance requirements.

A-10. Identify database requirements.

Design Modeling (Chapters 8 to 13)

D-1. Design the aesthetic for the WebApp.

D-2. Design the interface.

D-3. Design the navigation scheme.

D-4. Design the WebApp architecture.

D-5. Design the content and the structure that supports it.

D-6. Design functional components.

D-7. Design appropriate security and privacy mechanisms.

D-8. Review the design.

Each task uses existing information acquired during earlier framework activities or from earlier models (or other work products) and adds new information that results in the modification of existing models or the construction of new ones. We'll leave the specifics of how this is accomplished until later chapters, but a few examples might help illustrate what we mean.

Consider task A-6, *Create an interaction model for complex scenarios*. As shown in Figure 6.3, the execution of this task involves understanding the relationship between user tasks and the content that is required for each task, as well as relevant application states.[6] It might also require information on business processes and information structures. Input to task A-6 typically includes broad business-level information (i.e., the business owner's perspective) on both structure and

---

6 An *application state* is an externally observable characterization of the condition of the application. For example, the state of an airline reservation application might have a user logged in, with a completely selected flight, but no confirmation or payment.

WAAF models
associated with
the analysis task,
*Create an inter-
action model
for complex
scenarios.*

	Structure (What)	Behavior (How)	Location (Where)	Pattern
Planning Architecture (Planner's Perspective)				
Business Architecture (Business Owner's Perspective)				
User Interface Architecture (User's Perspective)				
Information Architecture (Information Architect's Perspective)				
System Architecture (System Architect's Perspective)				
Web Object Architecture (Developers' Perspective)				
Test Architecture (Tester's Perspective)				

behavior. In this context, *structure* is defined by examining business entities and the relationships between them—such as the information being exchanged with customers. *Behavior* is defined by examining business workflows. The outcome is a model that depicts how the users interact with the application (i.e., the application behavior) from the user's point of view.

As a simple example of task A-6, consider increment 5, *Information and ordering of monitoring services,* for **SafeHomeAssured.com.** Business-level structure addresses the specific information that must be acquired to set up a new user for monitoring services. This might include specific data items as well as the structure of the database that is used as a foundation for customers who use *SafeHome* monitoring services. Business-level behavior addresses the workflow that has been established to have a user register for monitoring services, including the collection of appropriate user information, validation and vetting (for security purposes) of the user, specification of payment options and choices, and a myriad of other details that are required to "sign up" a user. In addition, user requirements for sign-up would also have to be modeled in some manner. It should be noted that the actual design of the interface for increment 5 does not occur until task D-2.

Figure 6.4 shows the information required and the model created by design task D-3, *Design the navigation scheme.* In this case, the task involves input from the user's perspective—on both structure (i.e., the content and relationships be-

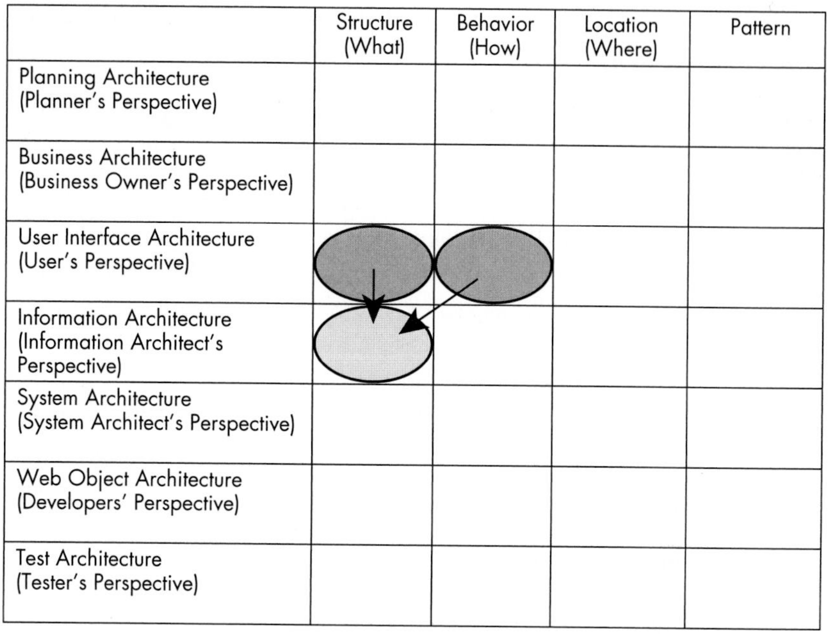

FIGURE 6.4

WAAF models associated with design task, *Design the navigation scheme.*

	Structure (What)	Behavior (How)	Location (Where)	Pattern
Planning Architecture (Planner's Perspective)				
Business Architecture (Business Owner's Perspective)				
User Interface Architecture (User's Perspective)				
Information Architecture (Information Architect's Perspective)				
System Architecture (System Architect's Perspective)				
Web Object Architecture (Developers' Perspective)				
Test Architecture (Tester's Perspective)				

tween the content that the user interacts with) and behavior (i.e., the user's interaction model). The output is a model of the application information architecture.

As a simple example of task D-3, consider increment 4, *Space layout and security system design,* for **SafeHomeAssured.com.** User-level structure addresses the specific information that must be specified by the user to create a space layout and how one data item relates to others within the context of increment 4. It specifies the flow of user actions that are required to create the space layout, coupled with system responses that flesh out the layout and recommend security monitoring devices. This information is passed to the "information architect" (in WAAF jargon) who establishes the overall interface structure.

The WAAF provides an overall framework that can help a WebE team to choose the types of models that might suit different WebE actions and tasks. The actual models that are available for analysis and design will be discussed in chapters 7–13.

Modeling Languages

In the context of Web engineering, a *modeling language* incorporates a set of notations, terms, and/or symbols, as well as the rules for establishing associations between them. A modeling language often has a formally structured representation as well as a set of graphical elements. Since there are many different facets of a WebApp that can be modeled, your WebE team may encounter two different types of languages:

- A very rich language capable of a diversity of modeling
- A range of different languages each specialized for a particular purpose

UML (Unified Modeling Language)[7] [Rum98] falls into the former category and contains a rich modeling notation that incorporates a wide diversity of different models. WebML [Cer00], on the other hand, is much more specialized, focusing on a particular aspect of design that is relevant to WebApps. We'll discuss both of these in more detail later in this chapter.

Gu, Henderson-Sellers, and Lowe considered Web modeling languages in some detail, including the extent to which modeling languages don't meet WebApp modeling requirements [Gu02]. Many of these requirements relate to the way that we might want to model the architecture of WebApps. Modeling requirements are decomposed into functional, informational and general requirements. The sections that follow provide a summary of the key elements of this earlier work.

What Capabilities Should Exist to Model Functionality?

In order to model the *functionality* delivered by a WebApp, a modeling language should provide the following capabilities:

- **Ability to model integration and connectivity.** Modeling languages must be able to represent the integration of (sub)systems and resources. In many organizations, the newly developed WebApp needs to work closely together with existing core-business applications. This challenge requires that the modeling language provide support for integrating the WebApp with these legacy applications in a seamless manner. Similarly, since the integration of components is largely dependent on the interface specifications, modeling languages need to provide the ability to model and document component interfaces accurately and unambiguously and be able to represent the connectivity mechanisms.

- **Ability to support pattern modeling.** Both research and practical experience suggest that it is desirable to use patterns whenever possible. This includes support for the modeling of those aspects that are common between different problems and solutions. A modeling language should be able to identify the *variation points* in models and/or patterns (i.e., those aspects that will typically vary from one application to the next, even when the pat-

---

7   See **www.omg.org/uml/** for a detailed discussion of UML.

tern is generally applicable) and the rules regarding when and how these variation points are applied in certain scenarios [Fon00].

- **Ability to represent concepts in a technology-neutral fashion.** The technologies supporting WebApps are changing rapidly. It is therefore unwise to create a WebApp specification or design an architecture that is dependent upon specific technologies. Indeed, technology-neutral design is very much needed in WebApp development.

- **Ability to model sophisticated system functionality.** Many, if not most, WebApps will support critical business processes and workflows that are an important part of the organization's business model.[8] These processes will often involve complex functionality, which should be able to be represented. It should also be possible to define business rules and constraints that are used to ensure the integrity of the entire application.

What Capabilities Should Exist to Model Information Content?

The ability to model content is pivotal to the successful implementation of many complex WebApps. Web information specifications, architectures, and designs address content and how it is managed, information structuring and access, user contextualization, design of and support for navigation, and information viewpoints and presentation issues. A modeling language should provide the following *information modeling* capabilities:

- **Ability to model presentation-level concepts.** Compared with conventional software applications, the presentational design of WebApps has its own unique characteristics, including more sophisticated functionality at the presentation level, various media types at the presentation level, and use of modeling languages by non-IT focused designers (e.g., graphical designers, multimedia producers, authors, and market analysts).

- **Ability to model navigational structure and behavior.** The ability to represent complex navigational behaviors and structures is a key feature of WebApps. It is important to be able to represent not only the navigation, but also the context of the navigation.

- **Ability to model user interactions with the information.** WebApps typically support very sophisticated user interactions that are influenced by a range of factors. Two key factors are a rich diversity of information sources

---

8 A business model defines both strategic and tactical mechanisms (e.g., the modeling of business workflows, information and order tracking, and transaction processing) that enable a business (or a part of a business) to attract customers, produce and sell products, and generate revenue.

and complex modes of access (e.g., reactive, proactive, guided, free-form, exploratory).

- **Ability to model user roles and user groups.** The success of WebApps is largely dependent on user satisfaction. This implies that you need to understand users' roles and objectives. But it also means that it is critical to model aspects such as personalization.

- **Ability to model content.** The effective management of content is a critical success factor of WebApp development. Content management (Chapter 16) usually involves, but is not restricted to, the design of the content structure, mostly expressed in the format of database schemata.

What Generic Capabilities Should Exist in a Modeling Language?

Apart from support for WebApp functional and information architecture modeling, it is also critical for modeling languages to provide a set of generic capabilities, such as linking the functional and informational aspects of WebApp models in a consistent and cohesive fashion. A modeling language should provide the following *generic* capabilities:

- **Ability to model business domain concepts.** Experience suggests that a key characteristic of most WebApps is a very strong linkage between the business model and the technical architecture.[9] As a consequence, the quality of the modeling will largely depend on the developers' understanding of the business models and the required changes to them, in the context of the impact from Web technologies. To facilitate and document this understanding, modeling languages need to provide the ability to model business domain concepts (e.g., business processes, business entities, workflows, business rules), together with the roles and responsibilities of users. Business-related development and modeling artifacts are usually created and used by developers from both IT and business backgrounds. As a result, the modeling of business domain concepts needs to be designed with the consideration of target user types so that these model artifacts can be easily understood, communicated, and modified within and across development teams and business units.

- **Ability to link business models with the technical architecture.** Early in this chapter, we noted the importance of "reverse modeling." Modeling lan-

---

9   In other words, the nature of the WebApp typically has a more direct and greater impact on the business and how it operates than might be the case with other applications. This is taken to the extreme with organizations like eBay, whose business model simply couldn't exist in the absence of the WebApps that support it. But even with more conventional organizations, the same thing applies. For example, think about how online banking applications have become a mainstay for modern financial institutions.

guages need to provide the ability to represent the linkage between the business model and the technical architecture and between the model elements in the business model and the model elements in the technical architecture. This interconnection needs to be represented at various abstraction levels.

- **Ability to link information with functionality.** The integrity and cohesion of a WebApp is largely dependent on a close and yet flexible interconnection between its information architecture and its functional architecture (this will be discussed in more detail in Chapter 8). It is critical to link information and functional architectures so that the WebApp can successfully address business needs in a coherent way [Low01].

- **Ability to maintain system integrity.** The integrity of WebApps can be challenged by aspects such as the complexity of the WebApp, so changes to requirements caused by stakeholder uncertainty, rapid changes in technologies, continuous evolution of application functionality and structure, and the

---

SAFEHOME

Preparing for Modeling

The scene: Web engineering area the day after a 2-day short course in UML (a modeling language that will be discussed in later chapters) has been completed

The players: Members of the **SafeHomeAssured.com** WebE team

The conversation:

Team member 1: I think I understand the mechanics of UML and how it applies to normal software, but it's still not all that clear to me how much of it we should use during our WebApp analysis and design.

Team member 2: I say we use it sparingly. There're so many possible diagrams and we're time pressed as it is.

Team leader: Two comments that the instructor made stick with me. We'll need to "link business models with the technical architecture" and "link information with functionality."

Team member 3: What does that mean, exactly?

Team member 1: The way I see it, we use UML to model specific business requirements for **SafeHomeAssured.com** that marketing wants. We also use it to show how WebApp content relates to the built-in functions that manipulate the content.

Team member 2: And what if requirements are straightforward?

Team leader: We probably don't need a UML model.

Team member 3: The instructor also said something about thinking about the entire "life cycle" of the WebApp.

Team member 1: Yeah, I remember that. If we do a good job, then the models we create can support changes that we make after the fact.

Team member 2 (smiling): But I thought we'd do such a good job modeling there wouldn't be any changes.

Team member 1: Get real, there'll always be changes! But the UML models could make them easier to deal with, particularly in a year or two when someone else might have to make them.

Team leader: But that's only true if they're accurate and up to date.

Team member 2: And that's why we don't want to create too many of them. We'd never be able to keep them accurate and up to date.

Team leader: No argument there.

combination of multiple disciplines and technological areas. Modeling languages can help ensure application integrity by being based on a representation that supports automatic integrity and referential checking of the models.

- **Ability to support understanding and communication.** To facilitate communication during WebApp development, modeling languages should provide the ability to represent various aspects of the WebApps at different abstraction levels[10] and from different viewpoints. It is also important to provide coordinated interconnections between these abstraction levels. That is, when one aspect of the WebApp model is changed, the potential impact of the change can be identified and highlighted in the relevant aspects of related models.

- **Ability to support Web system life cycle management.** Because WebApps exhibit fine-grained evolution during their life cycle, maintenance (e.g., correcting, adapting, and enhancing the WebApp) plays an increasingly important role. Modeling languages, therefore, need to support models that can be easily evolved, as well as facilitate identification and understanding of those aspects of models that are likely to be difficult to change.

Existing Modeling Approaches

There is a rich diversity of different modeling languages and an almost equally rich set of information that discusses the various strengths and weaknesses of these languages. One attempt to consider the strengths and weaknesses of existing modeling languages is reported in [Gu02]. In this work a set of Web-specific modeling languages—OOHDM [Sch98], WebML [Cer00], Koch [Koc00], WAE [Con02], W2000 [Bar01] and HDM-Lite/Autoweb [Fra00]—were considered in terms of the extent to which they address the requirements outlined in the preceding sections. The results of this evaluation are shown in Table 6.2.

Referring to the table, basic modeling requirements are well considered by most modeling approaches. There are, however, other aspects that are not covered at all. For example, the following aspects are not typically well supported by any of these modeling languages:

- Ability to model integration and connectivity
- Ability to model sophisticated system functionality
- Ability to model business domain concepts
- Ability to link information architecture with functional architecture

---

10 An abstraction level refers to the level of product or technical detail that is represented for a WebApp.

TABLE 6.2   MODELING LANGUAGE GAP ANALYSIS

Requirements for Modeling Languages	OOHDM	WebML	Koch	WAE (Conallen)	W2000	HDM-lite/ Autoweb
Ability to model integration and connectivity	N	N	N	P	P	P
Ability to support pattern modeling	Y	N	N	P	P	N
Ability to represent concepts in a technology-neutral fashion	P	Y	Y	P	Y	Y
Ability to model sophisticated system functionality	N	N	N	P	N	N
Ability to model presentation-level concepts	Y	Y	Y	N	N	Y
Ability to model navigational structure and behavior	Y	Y	Y	P	P	Y
Ability to model user interactions with information	P	Y	Y	P	Y	Y
Ability to model user roles and groups	N	Y	N	P	Y	Y
Ability to model content	Y	Y	Y	P	Y	Y
Ability to model business domain concepts	P	P	P	P	P	P
Ability to link business model with technical architecture	P	P	P	P	P	P
Ability to link information architecture with functional architecture	N	N	N	N	P	N
Ability to maintain system integrity	N	P	N	N	P	P
Ability to support understanding and communication	Y	Y	P	P	Y	Y
Ability to be process independent	N	Y	Y	Y	N	N
Ability to support Web system life cycle management	P	P	P	P	P	P

Source: From [Gu00].

Legend: Y = yes, N = no, P = partial.

FIGURE 6.5

Existing model-
ing approach
gap analysis.
Source: Adapted from
[Gu02].

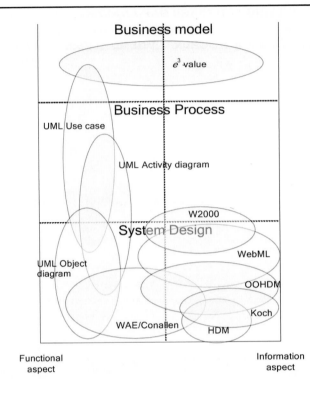

Functional
aspect

Information
aspect

In the following chapters we will say a lot more about how we might handle the modeling of these aspects.

The relative focus of various modeling languages is shown in Figure 6.5. Referring to the figure, use cases and UML-based modeling notations tend to provide good coverage of the functional elements of software applications in general and WebApps in particular. But UML does not provide good representational tools to capture the informational elements of WebApps. The specialized Web modeling notations that have been developed address informational elements (at least in part) but don't provide good connections to the functional modeling. Most don't provide good modeling connections from or to the business models and processes that are so important in most WebApps.

Where We've Been . . . Where We're Going

In this chapter we've examined modeling as a concept. The modeling activity for Web engineering creates different representations of reality. The usefulness of these representations is defined by the audience that uses them and by a set of criteria that create a Web Application Architecture Framework (WAAF) for modeling.

A variety of modeling languages is available for the description of WebApps. Ideally, these languages exhibit a set of functional, informational, and general requirements that lead to effective models for analysis and design. In this chapter we've described these fundamental requirements and presented a very brief overview of some of these languages. In the following chapters we'll show you how to develop effective models for WebApps. In Chapter 7 we'll look at analysis modeling, and in Chapter 8 we'll focus on the models used in the design of WebApps. Throughout, we'll consider how to select the right models for different tasks and how to apply and interpret these models.

References

[Bar01] Baresi, L., G. Garzotto, and P. Paolini, "Extending UML for Modelling Web Applications," *Proc. 34th Hawaii International Conference on System Sciences,* 2001, Hawaii, p. 3055.

[Cer00] Ceri, S., P. Fraternai, and A. Bongio, "Web Modelling Language (WebML): A Modelling Language for Designing Web Sites," *Proc. WWW9/Computer Networks,* vol. 33, 2000, pp. 137–157. See also **www.webml.org/** (accessed July 25, 2007).

[Con02] Conallen, J., *Building Web Applications with UML*, 2nd ed., Addison Wesley Professional, 2002.

[Fon00] Fontoura, M., W. Pree, and B. Rumpe, "UML-F: A Modelling Language for Object-Oriented Frameworks," *Proc. ECOOP 2000—Object-Oriented Programming: 14th European Conference,* Sophia Antipolis and Cannes, France, June 2000, Springer, pp. 63–82.

[Fra00] Fraternali, P., and P. Paolini, "Model-Driven Development of Web Applications: the AutoWeb System," *ACM Transactions on Office Information Systems,* vol. 18, no. 4, 2000, pp. 323–382.

[Gu02] Gu, A., B. Henderson-Sellers, and D. Lowe, "Web Modelling Languages: the Gap Between Requirements and Current Exemplars," *Paper presented at the AusWeb '02: The Eighth Australian World Wide Web ConferenceAusWeb,* Sunshine Coast, Australia, July 2002, pp. 5–10. See also **http://ausweb.scu.edu.au/** (accessed July 25, 2007).

[Koc00] Koch, N., H. Baumeister, R. Hennicker, and L. Mandel, "Extending UML to Model Navigation and Presentation in Web Applications," *Modelling Web Applications in the UML Workshop, UML2000,* York, England, October 2000.

[Kon05] Kong, X., L. Liu, and D. Lowe, "Separation of Concerns: A Web Application Architecture Framework," *Journal of Digital Information,* vol. 6, no. 2, 2005, **http://jodi.tamu.edu/Articles/v06/i02/Kong/** (accessed July 25, 2007).

[Kru95] Kruchten, P., "The 4+1 View Model of Architecture," *IEEE Software,* vol. 12, no. 6, 1995, pp. 42–50.

[Low01] Lowe, D., and B. Henderson-Sellers, "Web Development: Addressing Process Differences," *Cutter IT Journal*, vol. 14, no. 7, 2001, pp. 11–17.

[Mon03] Montero, S., P. Díaz, and I. Aedo, "Formalization of Web Design Patterns Using Ontologies," *Atlantic Web Intelligence Conference 2003*, Madrid, Spain, May 5–6, pp. 179–188.

[OMG01] Object Management Group, "Model Driven Architecture," 2001, **www.omg.org/mda/** (accessed July 25, 2007).

[Pla02]   Platt, M., "Microsoft Architecture Overview," 2002, **http://msdn2.microsoft.com/en-us/library/ms978007.aspx** (accessed July 25, 2007).

[Rum98] Rumbaugh, J., I. Jacobson, and G. Booch, *The Unified Modeling Language Reference Manual*, Addison-Wesley, 1998.

[Sch98]   Schwabe, D., and G. Rossi, "Developing Hypermedia Applications Using OOHDM," *Workshop on Hypermedia Development Processes, Methods and Models (Hypertext '98)*, Pittsburgh, 1998.

[Sow92] Sowa, J. F., and J. A. Zachman, "Extending and Formalizing the Framework for Information Systems Architecture," *IBM Systems Journal* vol. 31, no. 3, 1992, pp. 590–616.

[Zac87]   Zachman, J. A., "A Framework for Information Systems Architecture," *IBM Systems Journal* vol. 26, no. 3, 1987, pp. 454–471.

ANALYSIS MODELING FOR WEBAPPS

It is impossible to begin the design and construction of a WebApp increment if you have no understanding of what is required. That's why the Web engineering process suggests a communication activity (Chapter 4) as an organized way of eliciting requirements from stakeholders. The result is a set of requirements[1] for each WebApp increment to be built.

But how do we know if these requirements are sufficient? Or complete? Or even unambiguous and noncontradictory? This is the purpose of *analysis modeling* for WebApps. It helps to ensure that you have clarity in your understanding of what you're building.

Understanding Analysis in the Context of WebE

Web developers are often skeptical when the idea of requirements analysis for WebApps is suggested. "After all," they might argue, "the WebE process must be agile, and analysis is time consuming. It'll slow us down just when we need to be designing and building the WebApp."

Problem analysis does take time, but solving the wrong problem takes even more time. The question for every WebApp developer is simple: Are you *sure* you understand the requirements of the problem? If the answer is an unequivocal "yes," then it may be possible to skip analysis modeling, but if the answer is "no," then requirements analysis should be performed. Steve Franklin [Fra03] comments on this issue when he writes:[2]

> Frequently, developers go straight to the coding phase without really understanding what they are trying to build or how they want to build it. Server-side coding is often done ad hoc, database tables are added as needed, and the architecture evolves in a sometimes unintentional manner. *But some modeling and disciplined software engineering* can make the software development process much smoother and ensure that the Web system is more maintainable in the future.

Can disciplined analysis modeling and an agile approach to WebApp development peacefully coexist? We think the answer is "yes," but only if

---

1   These requirements will almost certainly be incomplete, but they provide a starting point for the modeling actions that follow.
2   Emphasis added.

the WebE team recognizes that analysis modeling must be tuned to the size of the problem and the nature of the design tasks that follow.

How Much Analysis Is Enough?

Web engineers should understand the role of analysis well enough to be able to know just how much of it needs to be carried out. The degree to which analysis modeling is emphasized depends on the following size-related factors:

- Size and complexity of the WebApp increment
- Number of stakeholders (analysis can help to identify conflicting requirements coming from different sources)
- Size of the WebE team
- Degree to which members of the WebE team have worked together before (analysis can help develop a common understanding of the project)
- Degree to which the organization's success is directly dependent on the success of the WebApp

The converse of these points is that as the project becomes smaller, the number of stakeholders fewer, the development team more cohesive, and the application less critical, it is reasonable to apply a more lightweight analysis approach.

Although we suggest that it is a good idea to analyze the problem *before* beginning design, it is not true that *all* analysis must precede *all* design. In fact, the design of a specific part of the WebApp only demands an analysis of those requirements that affect that part of the WebApp. As an example from **SafeHomeAssured. com,** we could validly design the overall site aesthetics (layouts, color schemes, etc.) without having analyzed the functional requirements for the e-commerce capabilities associated with product purchasing. The WebE team only needs to analyze that part of the problem that is relevant to the design work for the increment to be delivered.

Can We Analyze Using a Prototype?

For many WebApps, the best analysis approach is *not* modeling. Rather, when the WebE team must understand page layout or aesthetic requirements, the best option is often to build a quick prototype.[3] In this context, a *prototype* is a stripped-down version of one or more aspects of the WebApp increment (often implemented in plain HTML). The prototype provides a feel for page layout and aesthetics, naviga-

---

3   In many cases, it can take longer to build an effective analysis model than it does to build a quick design prototype.

tional mechanisms, and in more limited cases, functionality and information content, without implementing all of these in a complete manner.

The WebApp prototype can be used to evaluate the requirements on which it is based and is often useful as a contribution to the final construction of the WebApp. Stakeholders can test-drive the prototype and immediately note things they like and things that simply don't work. They can point out omissions and tune their perception of what is really required. All of this is an excellent vehicle for understanding.

Although the prototyping approach can work very well, it can also lead to problems. All too often stakeholders use the prototype and then ask whether it will be in production shortly (say, tomorrow?). The WebE team tells the stakeholders that the prototype is for demonstration purposes only and that it has many flaws that make it inappropriate for production usage. Yet, the stakeholders insist.

Too often, the WebE team succumbs to this request. "We can probably live with these flaws," someone on the team ventures. "After all, we'll have part of our

---

SAFEHOME

Prototyping in Lieu of Modeling

The scene: The Web engineering area at CPI Corporation

The players: Two members of the **SafeHome-Assured.com** team working as a pair, who are beginning the modeling activity for increment 3, *Product quotes and product order processing*

The conversation:

Team member 1: I spent some time with marketing, and they've given me their business workflow for quotes and order processing. Nothing too difficult, but lots of CPI-specific requirements. We'll have to access the order entry database from the WebApp, and . . .

Team member 2 (interrupting): So, we're going to model this using UML?

Team member 1: I don't think UML is right or necessary here, although I do think we'll need to refine the use cases, and UML might be appropriate there. What I'd like to do is to build an order entry prototype, show it to marketing, get their OK, and then use it to drive the full design and construction of this increment.

Team member 2: But what about other technical requirements, like integrating with the existing databases and . . .

Team member 1: The requirements are fairly straightforward for those parts, so all of that can wait for the design stage.

Team member 2: So instead of a UML model—except maybe to flesh out the use cases—we create a prototype using *WebCarpenter*? [*WebCarpenter* is a fictitious off-the-shelf tool that the team has chosen for the generation of Web pages.]

Team member 1: Uh huh. And that means we're going to be doing some design work as well, but why not? It puts us further down the road, gives the marketing guys a good look at what they'll get, and will be a lot quicker than UML.

Team member 2: Let's do it. Just gotta be sure that marketing understands that what we'll show them is a prototype, not an operational WebApp.

WebApp already built, and time really is tight. We'll implement a few patches and proceed with what we've got." The result can be a poorly designed WebApp that may be difficult to adapt and enhance.

Does prototyping work? Absolutely! But only if your team understands its dangers as well as its benefits.

Is Analysis Distinct from Design?

Many people assume that technology—and particularly software technology—is infinitely malleable and that any stakeholder requirement, no matter how bizarre, can be implemented within a WebApp simply by molding the technology to meet the need. Unfortunately, this can be a recipe for disaster.

The technologies that we use as part of Web engineering have a certain "grain" associated with them. As any carpenter knows, if you try to cut and shape with the grain of wood, then things go smoothly. But as soon as you work against the grain, things can become much more difficult.[4]

If you construct a WebApp in which there is a good fit between the stakeholder requirements and technological capability, it's likely that the project and the end result will succeed. But if you try to do things that cut across the technology, then the engineering work and the product it produces become much more complex, time consuming, and expensive.

For example, part of the "grain" of the Web is its distributed client-server architecture. A requirement for guaranteed rapid WebApp response time cuts across this grain (primarily because of the latency associated with communication between the client and server). If the WebE team must meet this requirement, complex engineering solutions (e.g., using Ajax) must be developed. Conversely, a requirement for simple access to the WebApp from any location runs with the grain, aligning with the distributed nature of Web technologies, and would therefore be simple to design and implement.

So what are we getting at here? Stated simply, some requirements will be inherently much more difficult and costly to implement than others. While analysis might help you understand the requirements themselves, only design can help you understand the *costs*[5] of construction. The cost of implementing a requirement must be considered by the WebE team and other stakeholders to determine

---

4   Or, if this analogy doesn't work for you, think about how much more difficult it is to walk across or against the flow of pedestrian traffic in a busy shopping mall, compared with walking with the flow.

5   In this context, the *costs* of construction include aspects such as the people and skills required to do the work, the time required to implement the requirement, the integration difficulty for the requirement, and the modifications to other content or functions that will be necessary to accommodate the requirement.

whether the need (requirement) is worth the cost and how the cost might affect the way the requirement is prioritized.

Of course, this doesn't mean that you should ignore analysis and jump straight into the design. Whether the WebE team chooses to analyze informally, build a prototype, or complete more formal analysis models (discussed throughout this chapter), understanding the problem (and the stakeholder requirements that define it) is as important as ever—but it does need to be interwoven with the design.

Analysis Modeling for WebApps

We hope you now agree that understanding the problem—gathering requirements and analyzing them—is an important part of developing a WebApp. But how do we actually *analyze* requirements? A useful way to answer this question is to consider the answers to four other key questions:

1. What are the inputs to analysis modeling?
2. What are the outputs from analysis?
3. What analysis tasks can and should we carry out?
4. What tools can we use to help us model?

What Are the Inputs to Analysis Modeling?

The WebE process incorporates a communication activity (Chapter 4) that identifies the information that becomes input to analysis modeling. This input includes stakeholders and user categories, the business context, defined informational and applicative goals, general WebApp requirements, and usage scenarios. This information is represented in the form of natural language descriptions, rough outlines, sketches, and other informal representations.

Analysis takes this information, structures it using a formally defined representation scheme (where appropriate), and then produces more rigorous models as an output. The analysis model provides a detailed indication of the true structure of the problem and provides insight into the shape of the solution.

This might make a little more sense if we consider an example. In Chapter 4, we discussed possible **SafeHomeAssured.com** functions—including one that was called *Access camera surveillance via the Internet*. At the time, this function seemed relatively clear and was described in some detail as part of a use case. We reproduce one version of the use case:

Use case: *Access camera surveillance via the Internet*
Actor: HomeOwner
Narrative: If I'm at a remote location, I can use any PC with appropriate browser software to log on to the **SafeHomeAssured.com** website. I enter my user ID and two levels of passwords,

and once I'm validated, I have access to all functionality for my installed **SafeHome** system. To access a specific camera view, I select "surveillance" from the major function buttons displayed. I then select "pick a camera," and the floor plan of the house is displayed. I then select the camera that I'm interested in. Alternatively, I can look at thumbnail snapshots from all cameras simultaneously by selecting "all cameras" as my viewing choice. Once I choose a camera, I select "view" and a camera view appears in a viewing window that is identified by the camera ID. If I want to switch cameras, I select "pick a camera" and the original viewing window disappears and the floor plan of the house is displayed again. I then select the camera that I'm interested in. A new viewing window appears.

Before we continue, you should examine this use case again to see if you can see anything that is missing, ambiguous, or unclear.

Okay—could you find anything? No doubt some of the issues you identified are aspects of the solution that would naturally emerge during the design. Examples might be the specific layout of the function buttons, their aesthetic look and feel, the size of snapshot views, the placement of camera views and the house floor plan, or even minutiae such as the maximum and minimum length of passwords. Some of these aspects really are just design decisions (such as the layout of the buttons), and others are requirements (such as the length of the passwords) that don't fundamentally influence the architectural design decisions.

But some issues you identified are things that might actually influence the overall design itself and relate more to a thorough understanding of the requirements. We'll examine some of these as we progress through this chapter, but to give you an initial sense of some of the missing information, consider the following questions:

- What video resolution is provided?

- What occurs if an alarm condition is encountered while the camera is being monitored?

- How does the system handle cameras that can be panned and zoomed?

- What information should be provided along with the camera view (e.g., location, time and date, last previous access)?

None of these questions were identified or considered in the initial development of the use case, and yet, the answers could have a substantial effect on different aspects of the design.

What we are really saying is that although the communication activity provides a good foundation for understanding, analysis refines this understanding by providing additional interpretation. As the problem structure is delineated as part of the analysis model, questions invariably arise. It is these questions that fill in the gaps—or in some cases, actually help us to find the gaps in the first place.

To summarize, the inputs to the analysis model will be the information collected during the communication activity—anything from an informal note in an e-mail to a detailed project brief complete with comprehensive usage scenarios and product specifications.

What Are the Outputs from Analysis?

Earlier in this chapter we noted that the goal of analysis is to understand stakeholders' needs. Stated another way, analysis provides a disciplined mechanism for representing and evaluating WebApp content and function, the modes of interaction that users will encounter, and the environment and infrastructure in which the WebApp resides.

Each of these characteristics can be represented as a set of models that allow the WebApp requirements to be analyzed in a structured manner. While the specific models depend largely upon the nature of the WebApp, we can identify four main classes of models and the associated analysis that is supported by these models:

1. **Content model.** Identifies the full spectrum of content to be provided by the WebApp. Content includes text, graphics and images, and video and audio data.

2. **Interaction model.** Describes the manner in which users interact with the WebApp.

3. **Functional model.** Defines the operations that will be applied to WebApp content and describes other processing functions that are independent of content but necessary to the end user.

4. **Configuration model.** Describes the environment and infrastructure in which the WebApp resides.

Each of these models can be developed using a representation scheme (often called a "language") that allows its intent and structure to be communicated and evaluated easily among members of the WebE team and other stakeholders. As a consequence, a list of key issues (e.g., errors, omissions, inconsistencies, suggestions for enhancement or modification, and points of clarification) are identified and acted upon.

What Analysis Tasks Can and Should We Carry Out?

Analysis tasks will obviously be focused on the construction and interpretation of the models discussed in the previous subsection "What Are the Outputs from Analysis?" Typical analysis tasks include:

- Determine whether a requirements model is needed
- Represent WebApp content
- Identify content relationships

- Refine and extend usage scenarios
- Review usage scenarios
- Create an interaction model for complex scenarios
- Refine interface requirements
- Identify system functions
- Define constraints and performance requirements
- Identify database requirements
- Represent functional requirements
- Represent navigational requirements

Later in this chapter we'll examine how these tasks are applied to create the models that are output from the analysis action.

What Tools Can We Use to Help Us Model?

Although many software tools exist for the construction of WebApps, relatively few have been developed specifically for analysis. However, that doesn't mean that a WebE team is left without tool support. Four categories of tools can be used as analysis is conducted:

UML tools. Used to create analysis models in the Unified Modeling Language, a modeling notation that is widely used in the software engineering community.

Prototyping tools. Virtually any WebApp construction tool (e.g., Adobe *GoLive*) can be used to create an operational prototype. These tools allow fast layout, integration of content, and the development of rough aesthetics, all appropriate for the creation of a quick prototype.

Issue tracking tools. Can be used to record and track the resolution of issues that arise out of interpretation of the emerging analysis models.

Content management tools. Can be used to model the nature and structure of content objects that are used as part of the WebApp.

For a listing of current tools that may help your team to conduct effective analysis, visit the website that supplements this book.

How Do We Decide Whether Modeling Is Necessary and Which Approach Is Best?

To analyze or not to analyze? It's a reasonable question that a WebE team should ask and answer before proceeding to design. In some cases, a WebApp is complex and business-critical. A combination of prototyping and other modeling forms may be required. In other cases, it may be possible that only a small subset of WebApp features needs rigorous analysis, while others are sufficiently understood based on information gathered as part of the communication activity. Finally, the WebApp may be quite simple (even if it is large). The WebE team may decide to proceed directly to design.

Earlier in this chapter, we identified some of the criteria that must be considered when determining the need for rigorous analysis. The following list of questions about your project provides a good starting point:

- Is the functionality or content of the WebApp increment complex enough to require a solution of more than just a few pages or some simple scripts?

- Do complex relationships exist among different content classes, and do these have an impact on how the WebApp is implemented?

- Does the WebApp increment produce information that will be critical to the user?

- Does the WebApp increment deliver functions that are not well understood at the moment? Are these functions algorithmically complex?

- Does the WebApp increment have a significant impact on already deployed increments? On increments that will be developed later?

- Is the WebApp business-critical?

SafeHome

Analysis Modeling

The scene: SafeHomeAssured. com WebE team meeting room prior to the commencement of increment 3, *Get a product quote and place an order*

The players: The WebE team leader and two other members of the WebE team

The conversation:

Team leader: Okay, we've finished increment 2, and everybody is happy with the result.

Team member 1: No more changes?

Team leader: Nope, just the ones we've already implemented.

Team member 2: Cool. What's next?

Team leader: We can begin work on the next increment—building the product quote and ordering sections of the WebApp. Marketing has modified the use cases, but nothing too dramatic. [Hands over card 5, *Get a product quote*, and card 8, *Place a product order*.] I assume you've both had a look at these. I've highlighted the changes.

Team member 1 (reading and nodding): I think both of these use cases are pretty simple. We should be able to just dive straight into the design and get this one over and done with pretty quickly.

Team member 2 (frowning): Yeah, maybe, but . . .

(continued)

SAFEHOME (CONTINUED)

Team leader (looking at team member 2): You don't sound all that convinced.

Team member 2: Well, it's probably nothing, but I'm just a little concerned that maybe there are a few things that we're overlooking.

Team member 1 (exasperated): Oh, come on. It's just a simple quote request and order system. Just about every other site on the Web has one of these, and they're all pretty simple. I agree that some of the later stuff on surveillance is a little more complex, but not this.

Team leader (to team member 1): Look, you're probably right, but it can't hurt to spend just a few minutes looking at this a little more carefully before we dive in.

Team member 2 (looking relieved): The thing that worries me is whether we've really understood the nature of the quotes that **SafeHome** provides. This use case we developed with them earlier shows a simple process of locating a product and then asking for a quote, but I'm sure I heard the client say something about differential pricing for different classes of customers. Surely that complicates things?

Team leader: Hmmm. Go on . . . [looking interested].

Team member 2: And once a customer puts in an order for a product, we don't even yet know what payment options the client is willing to accept and whether there is a limit on where the client is willing to deliver to, and . . .

Team leader (interrupting): Okay, okay, I get the point. I agree that we need to look at the requirements a little more carefully. It seems to me that the core functionality is pretty clear, but the content to support this is vague—things like pricing models, payment types, etc. How about we begin by working on a content model and then see where that leads us?

Team members 1 and 2: [Both nod agreement.]

- Will the WebApp increment have a possible impact on the other operations of the business or the relationship that the business organization has with its stakeholders?

- Is there any possibility that stakeholders are unsure of the requirements for the WebApp increment?

- Are there more than one or two user classes, and will they use the WebApp in substantially different ways?

- Is there a strong probability that errors, omissions, or inconsistencies were introduced during the communication activity?

If you answered "yes" to any of the preceding questions, then you should consider building an analysis model. A key factor worth remembering is that you should focus the modeling on those aspects where there is a lack of clarity or where there is a potential for confusion.

Understanding the Users

At the end of the day, the people who use the WebApp will judge its success. For this reason, it is important that the WebE team understands who its users will be, what background and skills the users have, how each user category perceives the

WebApp, and what features and performance will be required to provide a successful user experience.

Much of this information is acquired as part of the communication activity (Chapter 4). Each user category is defined as requirements are gathered, and a description of users within the category is developed by answering the following questions:

- What is the user's overall objective when using the WebApp?
- What is the user's background and sophistication level relative to the content and functionality of the WebApp?
- How will the user arrive at the WebApp?
- What generic WebApp characteristics does the user like and dislike?

At the beginning of the analysis, you should reexamine these categories and descriptions a little more carefully to ensure that you have understood them thoroughly. This might include defining a user hierarchy and then refining the usage scenarios that have already been developed.

Why Is It Necessary to Revisit the User Hierarchy?

User categories were identified as part of the communication activity (Chapter 4), and in many cases they are relatively straightforward and remain unchanged as analysis is conducted. However, as more is learned about the problem domain during analysis modeling, it may become necessary to refine a simple set of two or three user categories into a hierarchy. This can help a WebE team to better understand the relationships between the different categories of users and the WebApp itself. This hierarchy can also be important when defining coherent sets of functionality and content that might be visible to different users.

The users of **SafeHomeAssured.com** are sufficiently well defined and do not need further refinement into a more detailed hierarchy. However, just to illustrate the approach, we depict a user hierarchy in Figure 7.1.[6]

Those readers who are already conversant in UML may note that we have liberally adapted the UML *actor* symbol in this diagram. UML allows the "modeling" of actors, but in UML an actor strictly represents the idealization of a particular interaction with the system—rather than a user. The same user may participate in

---

6 **Important Note:** In numerous places throughout this book, including Figure 7.1, we make use of UML notation. If you are *not* familiar with UML, you might want to spend some time at the following Web resources which provide basic UML primers:
- Object Management Group—UML: **www.uml.org/**
- UML Tutorial, Ian Grahame: **http://uml.tutorials.trireme.com/**
- UML Primer: **http://vinci.org/uml/**

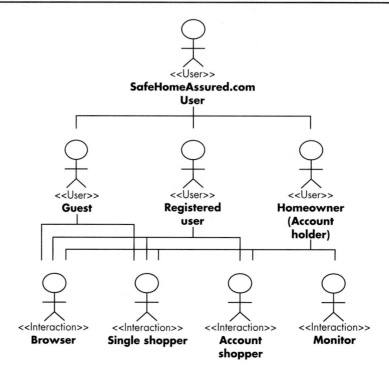

different interactions (and therefore be represented as different actors), but that user will carry his or her context across these roles. In our view, it is important to model the user context and not just the individual interactions. To achieve these we show both the different users (using the «user» actors) and the different types of interactions in which those users participate (using the «interaction» actors).

For **SafeHomeAssured.com** there are three main types of users, who can carry out four different types of interactions: (1) *guests* can browse the public information on products and download specs, as well as purchase products (but the system won't remember their preferences); (2) *registered users* have access to the same functionality as guests, but the system will remember their preferences as well as allow them to purchase on an account; (3) *registered homeowners* can browse information and buy products, but can also have their system monitored online.

For each «user» actor we need to understand the nature of the user category—its context, needs, and behaviors. In Chapter 4 we talked about user profiles and where we might find this information (often from the marketing department). At that preliminary stage, however, the profile will probably be relatively informal.

When we perform analysis, it might be necessary to examine user profiles in a little more detail and see if there is anything we have overlooked.

A typical user profile considers age, gender, background, expertise and knowledge, and applicative and informational goals. In some cases this information will be relatively straightforward. In others you might need to actively investigate the users—using techniques such as user interviews, surveys, or focus groups. For example, the **SafeHomeAssured.com** WebE team may need to clarify what skills the WebApp users have (in terms of knowing how to most effectively use the Web to monitor their premises). An excellent example of an approach to user profiling is available at the Australian Government website **www.agimo.gov.au/publications/2004/06/toolkit**.

Do We Apply Usage Scenarios as Is?

Just as the communication activity helps us to understand user characteristics, it also results in the definition of usage scenarios (use cases) that describe how different user categories will interact with the WebApp in different situations. For

---

SafeHome

Refining Use Cases

The scene: WebE team meeting room prior to the commencement of increment 3, *Get a product quote and place an order*

The players: The WebE team leader and two other members of the WebE team

The conversation:

[. . . carrying on from a previous conversation about the need for more detail in the use-case descriptions . . .]

Team leader: So, we're agreed then that these two use cases need more work. [He points at card 5, *Get a product quote*, and card 8, *Place a product order*.] The question is, How should we approach this?

Team member 2: Well, if we look at the use-case diagram, we can see that placing an order is really an extension of obtaining a quote. We talked about this last week, where it makes more sense for someone to obtain a quote, and once they have the quote they can place an order—rather than the more usual process of simply dumping things into a shopping basket and then checking out.

Team member 1 (looking a little puzzled): I still don't really understand why we are taking that approach.

Team member 2: Yeah, I was puzzled at first as well, but after marketing explained it, it made more sense. We want to couple placing an order as tightly as possible with getting a quote, as a way of maximizing the likelihood of getting the user to complete the order. If we make it simple to get a quote, but hard to place the order, customers might rethink the order before it gets committed.

Team member 1: Oh, OK—I get it. So once they have the quote, the ordering step should be really quick and simple! We haven't really got that cleanly captured in our use cases. I guess this means that we should modify the use cases—and the use-case diagram—to make this more explicit.

[They then proceed to work on some modifications to the use cases.]

many projects, the usage scenarios will be somewhat rudimentary, that is, sufficient for initial planning and estimation[7] but not detailed enough for analysis and design. It is likely that at least some use cases will require substantial elaboration. In addition, as analysis proceeds, the actions defined in one use case must be examined in the context of user actions defined in other use cases.

In Chapter 4 we identified a set of 14 usage scenarios for **SafeHomeAssured. com,** each of which could be represented using a use case. As an example of use case refinement, consider the sidebar discussion about the *Get a product quote* use case.

Another key aspect of refining use cases is to identify possible overlaps and hence changes that might be beneficial as the system is implemented. For example, increment 3 of the development involves the implementation of two use cases: *Get a product quote* and *Place an order*. Increment 5 also involves two use cases: *Request information on monitoring services* and *Place an order for monitoring services*. Note that both of these involve *placing an order,* though one is for products and one is for services. If you were to implement increment 3 without considering this commonality, you would probably end up building a product ordering system that was difficult to modify later for also ordering services—or at least difficult to reuse. In Figure 7.2 we show how this might be represented in a use-case diagram.

It's also worth noting that finding commonalities in use cases can also be important in terms of simplifying the application design and, as a consequence, reducing the effort required for implementation and improving the usability of the application. For example, consider an event promotion WebApp where one class of users (*venue patrons*) can view descriptions of events to be held at selected venues, such as sporting, cultural, or music events. A second class of users (*venue owners*) have access to edit the event descriptions for their venues. This might initially sound like two different use cases (*View event information* and *Edit event information*), but the design will be greatly simplified if we realize that in both cases the information is made available, but in one use case that information can also be changed; that is, *Edit event information* can be seen as an extended version of *View event information*. It may be quite feasible for the same design (and most of the same code) to be used for both, but in the *View* use case, the edit functionality is disabled (and/or hidden).

Even if the WebE team decides to apply usage scenarios as is, analysis can identify areas of commonality among use cases and establish interconnections that may be of use to designers as the WebApp is created. Creating a diagram similar to the one illustrated in Figure 7.2 takes relatively little time and may provide substantial insight.

---

7   Planning and estimation are used for establishing the preliminary set of WebApp increments.

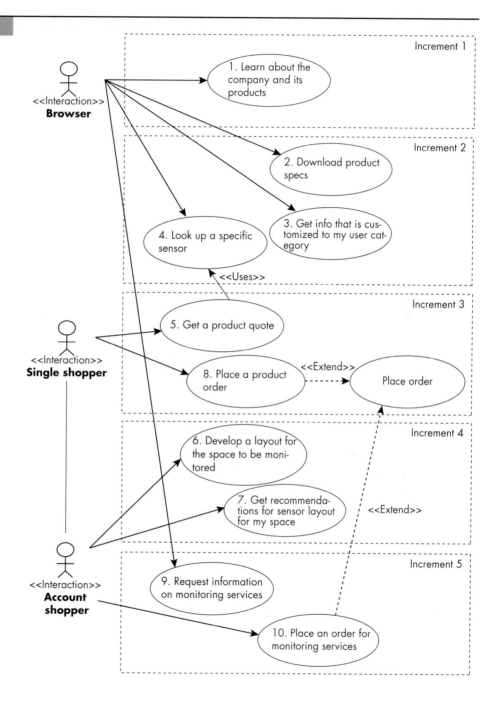

FIGURE 7.2

Use-case
diagram for
**SafeHome-
Assured.com.**

The Content Model

Using information gathered during the communication activity and refinements made during analysis, the WebE team should now have a clear understanding of the users and the use cases that describe the users' interactions with the WebApp. The next step is to develop a *content model*—a representation that provides a clear indication of the content that is required to support a usage scenario.

What Are the Structural Elements of the Content Model?

The content model contains structural elements that provide an important view of content requirements for a WebApp. These structural elements encompass content objects (e.g., text, graphical images, photographs, video images, audio) that are presented as part of the WebApp. In addition, the content model includes all *analysis classes*—user-visible entities that are created or manipulated as a user interacts with the WebApp. Analysis classes manifest themselves in one of the following ways:

- *External entities* (e.g., other systems, databases, people) that produce or consume information to be used by the WebApp
- *Things* (e.g., reports, displays, video images) that are part of the information domain for the problem
- *Occurrences or events* (e.g., a quote or an order) that occur within the context of a user's interaction with a WebApp
- *Roles* (e.g., retail purchasers, customer support, salesperson) played by people who interact with the WebApp
- *Organizational units* (e.g., division, group, team) that are relevant to an application
- *Places* (e.g., manufacturing floor or loading dock) that establish the context of the problem and the overall function of the WebApp
- *Structures* (e.g., sensors, monitoring devices) that define a class of objects or related classes of objects

An analysis class encompasses attributes that describe it, operations that effect behavior required of the class, and collaborations that allow the class to communicate with other classes.

Attributes define an analysis class. They clarify what the class means in the context of the problem space. To develop a meaningful set of attributes for an analysis class, you should study a use case and select those "things" that reasonably belong to the class. In addition, the following question should be answered for each class: *What data items (composite and/or elementary) fully define this class in the context of the problem at hand?*

Operations define the behavior of a class. Although many different types of operations exist, they can generally be divided into four broad categories: (1) operations that manipulate content in some way (e.g., adding, deleting, reformatting, selecting), (2) operations that perform a computation, (3) operations that inquire about the state of an object, and (4) operations that monitor an object for the occurrence of a controlling event. Operations are accomplished by manipulating attributes and must have "knowledge" of the nature of the class's attributes.

A class can use its own operations to manipulate its own attributes, thereby fulfilling a particular responsibility. Alternatively, a class can fulfill a responsibility by collaborating with other classes. *Collaborations* identify relationships between classes. When classes collaborate to achieve some requirement, they can be organized into an architectural element (e.g., a subsystem) of the WebApp during design.

Like other elements of the analysis model, the content model is derived from a careful examination of use cases developed for the WebApp. Use cases are examined to extract content objects and analysis classes. To accomplish this, a Web engineer can perform a "grammatical parse" [Pre05] on the use cases developed for the WebApp to be built. Classes are determined by underlining each noun or noun clause and entering it into a simple table. Synonyms should be noted. If the class is required to implement a solution, then it is part of the solution space; otherwise, if a class is necessary only to describe a solution, it is part of the problem space.

For simple WebApps, you may be able to jump straight from the use cases to content objects and then on to other aspects of the analysis model. But more complex WebApps require a more structured approach to the definition of analysis classes. One useful approach makes use of *Web information exchange diagrams* [Ton04].

What Is an Information Exchange and How Is It Represented?

Use cases (and other similar notations such as usage scenarios) describe the ways in which users will interact with a WebApp, and therefore they implicitly capture the *exchanges of value* between different users that the WebApp enables.[8] For example, with **SafeHomeAssured.com,** the first use case is *Learn about the company and its products.* This represents an interaction between the user and **SafeHomeAssured.com.** This interaction occurs because the user gains something of value—information

---

8 A key concept in many approaches to business modeling is *value exchange.* For any business interaction to occur, there must be (perceived) value to all the participants in that interaction. By understanding and modeling these exchanges of value, we can improve the business.

about the company that helps the user determine if **SafeHomeAssured.com** is trustworthy. **SafeHomeAssured.com** in return gets something of value—the potential for future business from that user.

One approach to understanding the content required in a WebApp is to look at these exchanges of value (as captured by the use cases) and determine the implied exchanges of information that are required to support the value exchange. This is the basis of *Web information exchange diagrams* (WIED). A subset of WIED notation is shown in Figure 7.3.

Applying the notation shown in Figure 7.3, a typical WIED for the information on sensor locations used in **SafeHomeAssured.com** is shown in Figure 7.4. In this figure you'll note that analysis of the use cases has resulted not only in the identification of the information that is exchanged in each interaction, but also the internal interdependencies between these information items. This can be crucial in helping to identify possible constraints on the application. For example, obtaining recommendations for a sensor layout requires information that can only have been obtained by a prior development of a layout. This shows the tight coupling that exists between these two particular use cases. Similarly, a discussion based on this diagram might identify that users could specify the sensors to be monitored, even if a floor plan has not yet been entered, but the first version only allows the list of registered sensors to be displayed as part of a floor plan layout. A subsequent amendment to this diagram, possibly added as a hand-drawn addition, suggests a mechanism for providing users with a list of their registered sensors, even if they have not provided a floor plan.

Once one or more WIEDs have been developed for a WebApp, you can then progress to a relatively straightforward identification of the content that is required for each information unit.

How Are Content Objects Defined?

Content can be developed prior to the implementation of the WebApp, while the WebApp is being built, or long after the WebApp is operational. In every case, it is incorporated via navigational reference into the overall WebApp structure. A *content object* might be a textual description of a product, an article describing a news event, an action photograph taken at a sporting event, a user's response on a discussion forum, an animated representation of a corporate logo, a short video of a speech, or an audio overlay for a collection of PowerPoint slides. The content objects might be stored as separate files, embedded directly into Web pages, or generated dynamically from database information. In other words, a content object is any item of cohesive information that is to be presented to an end user.

Content objects are identified either from the information units in a Web information exchange diagram, or (in simpler applications where a WIED model is not

WebML-
compliant

UML-
compliant

Actor Unit

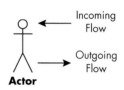

Supplied Information Unit

Derived Information Unit

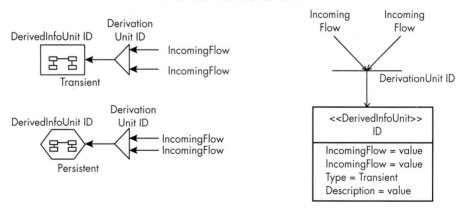

FIGURE 7.4

Partial information
exchange diagram for
SafeHomeAssured.com.

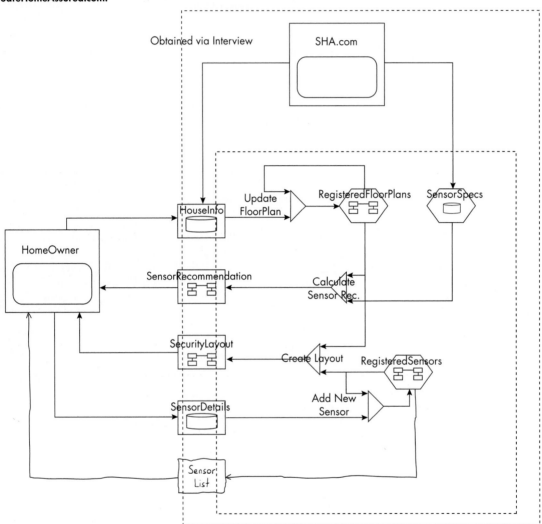

necessary) directly from use cases by examining the scenario description for direct and indirect references to content. For example, in the use case S*elect SafeHome components,* we encounter the sentence:

I will be able to get descriptive and pricing information for each product component.

This same information is also shown in the WIED model. Although there is no direct reference to content, it is implied. You could meet with the author of the use case and gain a more detailed understanding of what "descriptive and pricing information" means. In this case, the author of the use case might indicate that "descriptive information" includes (1) a one-paragraph general description of the component, (2) a photograph of the component, (3) a multiparagraph technical description of the component, (4) a schematic diagram of the component showing how it fits into a typical **SafeHome** system, and (5) a thumbnail video that shows how to install the component in a typical household setting.

It is important to note that each of these content objects must be developed (often by content developers who are *not* Web engineers) or acquired for integration into the WebApp architecture (discussed in Chapter 9).

SafeHome

Defining Content Objects

The scene: WebE team area prior to the commencement of analysis modeling for increment 2, *Detailed product information and downloads*

The players: Two members of the WebE team working as a pair

The conversation:

Team member 1: So the next step is to define the content, right?

Team member 2: Yep, we'll examine all of the use cases that relate to this increment, select the appropriate content objects, maybe build a model, if it's necessary, and . . .

Team member 1 (interrupting): Two questions. One, I'm not clear on how we select content objects, and two, I thought that we had agreed to keep modeling to a minimum.

Team member 2: Selecting the objects is a bit of an art, but one way that really does work is to do a grammatical parse. For example, look at this excerpt from one of the use cases for this increment: "I want to be able to get <u>product information</u> for any of the *SafeHome* components. The description of a *SafeHome* component will include all <u>product identification data</u> as well as <u>descriptive information</u>."

Team member 1: Why the underlining?

Team member 2: It provides an inkling of the content object, but it doesn't go far enough. We need to know what "product identification data" and "descriptive information" are—what the component elements are. So [drawing a diagram], I talked with marketing and here's what we came up with [a rough sketch similar to Figure 7.5].

Team member 1: I see, so info about a *SafeHome* component includes a description, and the other items you drew . . . sort of a hierarchy.

Team member 2: That'll get us started. Then we'll need to figure out what operations, if any, are needed to manipulate the content objects. For example, we'll need to *stream and display* any video objects, and . . .

Team member 1 (interrupting): I thought you said we'd have to model this stuff.

Team member 2 (smiling): We just did.

Team member 1: Huh?

Team member 2 (smiling): This drawing [referring to Figure 7.5] is called a data tree, and it's a reasonable way to model a hierarchy of content objects.

Team member 1: That was easy.

Team member 2: Modeling doesn't have to be a big deal, timewise.

FIGURE 7.5

Data tree for a
*SafeHome-
Assured.com
Component.*

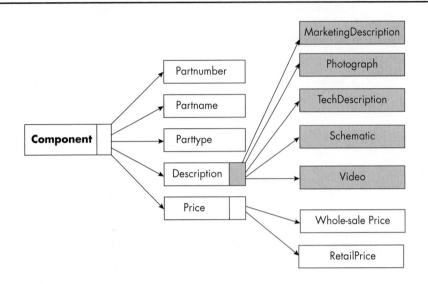

Is There a Simple Way to Depict Content Relationships and Content Hierarchy?

In many instances, a simple list of content objects, coupled with a brief description of each object, is sufficient to define the requirements for content that must be designed and implemented. However, in some cases, the content model may benefit from a richer analysis—such as *entity relationship diagrams* [Baq04] or *data trees* [Sri01]. These graphical representations depict the relationships among content objects and/or the hierarchy of content maintained by a WebApp.

Consider the data tree created for a **SafeHomeAssured.com** component shown in Figure 7.5. The tree represents a hierarchy of information that is used to describe a component (later we will see that the **SafeHomeAssured.com** component is actually an analysis class for this application). Simple or composite data items (one or more data values) are represented as unshaded rectangles. Content objects are represented as shaded rectangles. In the figure, **Description** is defined by five content objects (the shaded rectangles). In some cases, one or more of these objects would be further refined as the data tree expands.

You can create a data tree for any content that is composed of multiple content objects and data items. The data tree is developed in an effort to define hierarchical relationships among content objects and to provide a means for reviewing content so that omissions and inconsistencies are uncovered before design commences. In addition, the data tree serves as the basis for content design.

How Do We Select and Represent Analysis Classes for WebApps?

As we have already noted, analysis classes are user-visible entities that are created or manipulated as a user interacts with the WebApp, while content objects represent the raw information or media that is used within a WebApp. Analysis classes organize content objects so that they can be combined and manipulated.

We have also seen that an analysis class encompasses attributes that describe it, operations that affect behavior required of the class, and collaborations that allow the class to communicate with other classes. Analysis classes are derived by examining each use case. To illustrate, consider the use case *Access camera surveillance via the Internet* that was introduced in Chapter 4.

SafeHome

Use Case for Surveillance

Use case: *Access camera surveillance via the Internet*

Primary actor: Homeowner

Goal in context: To view output of cameras placed throughout the house from any remote location via the Internet

Preconditions: System must be fully configured; appropriate user ID and passwords must be obtained.

Trigger: The homeowner decides to take a look inside the house while away.

Scenario:

1. The homeowner logs on to the **SafeHome** products website.

2. The homeowner enters his or her user ID.
3. The homeowner enters two passwords (each at least eight characters in length).
4. The system displays all major function buttons.
5. The homeowner selects "surveillance" from the major function buttons.
6. The homeowner selects "pick a camera."
7. The system displays the floor plan of the house.
8. The homeowner selects a camera icon from the floor plan.
9. The homeowner selects the "view" button.
10. The system displays a viewing window that is identified by the camera ID.
11. The system displays video output within the viewing window at one frame per second.

A quick grammatical parse of the use case identifies three candidate classes (underlined): **HomeOwner, Camera,** and **House.** A first-cut description of each class is shown in Figure 7.6.

The **HomeOwner** class encompasses the information that is retained about a **HomeOwner** user of the system, including name, user ID, and passwords. One or more **HomeOwner** objects can also be linked to zero or more **House** objects, which can contain floor plans. A floor plan can in turn be associated with **Camera** objects. Some of these class attributes are single or composite data items, and others are content objects. Operations relevant to the class are also shown.

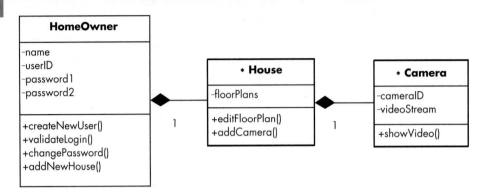

FIGURE 7.6

Example analysis classes for the use case, *Access camera surveillance via the Internet.*

Each use case identified for **SafeHomeAssured.com** is parsed for analysis classes. Class models similar to the one described in this section are developed for each use case.

The Interaction Model

The vast majority of WebApps enable a "conversation" between an end user and application functionality, content, and behavior. This conversation can be described using an *interaction* model that can be composed of one or more of the following elements: (1) use cases, (2) sequence diagrams, (3) state diagrams,[9] and/or (4) user interface prototypes. In addition to these representations, the interaction is also represented within the context of the navigation model (described later in this chapter in section "Relationship-Navigation Analysis").

Where Do Use Cases Come into Play?

Use cases are the dominant element of the interaction model for WebApps. It is not uncommon to describe 100 or more use cases when large, complex WebApps are analyzed, designed, and constructed. However, a relatively small percentage of these use cases describes the major interactions between end-user categories (actors) and the system. Other use cases refine the interactions, providing the analysis detail necessary to guide the design and construction.

In many instances, a set of use cases is sufficient to describe the interaction at an analysis level (further refinement and detail will be introduced during design). However, when the interaction sequence is complex and involves multiple analysis classes or many tasks, it is sometimes worthwhile to depict it using a more rigorous diagrammatic form.

---

9   Sequence diagrams and state diagrams are modeled using UML notation.

What Are Sequence Diagrams and When Should They Be Developed?

UML *sequence diagrams* provide a shorthand representation of the manner in which user actions (the dynamic elements of a system defined by use cases) collaborate with analysis classes (the structural elements of a system). Since analysis classes are extracted from use case descriptions, there is a need to ensure that traceability exists between the classes that have been defined and the use cases that describe system interaction. Conallen [Con00] writes: "The merging of dynamic and structural elements of the [analysis] model is the key link in the traceability of the model and should be taken very seriously."

A sequence diagram for the *Access camera surveillance via the Internet* use case is shown in Figure 7.7. The vertical axis of the diagram depicts actions that are defined within the use case. The horizontal axis identifies the analysis classes that are used as the use case proceeds. For example, a user logs in to the WebApp,

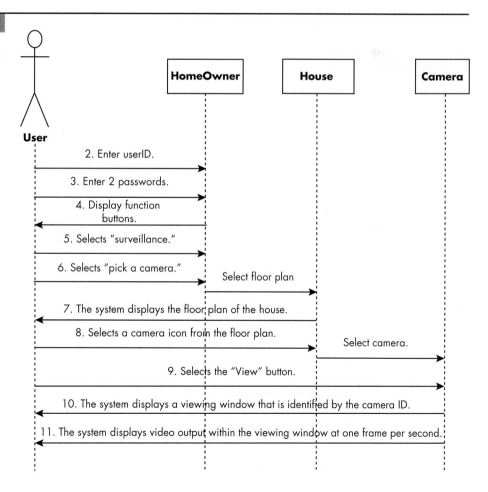

FIGURE 7.7

Sequence diagram for use case, *Access camera surveillance via the Internet.*

User

HomeOwner   House   Camera

2. Enter userID.

3. Enter 2 passwords.

4. Display function buttons.

5. Selects "surveillance."

6. Selects "pick a camera."

Select floor plan

7. The system displays the floor plan of the house.

8. Selects a camera icon from the floor plan.

Select camera.

9. Selects the "View" button.

10. The system displays a viewing window that is identified by the camera ID.

11. The system displays video output within the viewing window at one frame per second.

navigates the relevant options, and selects a camera. The video from that camera is then displayed. The movement across and down the sequence diagram ties each analysis class to use case actions. If a use case action is missing from the diagram, you should reevaluate the description of analysis classes to determine if one or more classes are missing. Sequence diagrams can be created for each use case and the analysis classes defined for the use case.

How Do State Diagrams Represent the Behavior of a WebApp?

The UML *state diagram* provides another representation of the dynamic behavior of the WebApp as an interaction occurs. Like most modeling representations used in Web engineering, the state diagram can be represented at different levels of abstraction. State diagrams are most useful when a user interaction triggers a change in the state of the WebApp—and hence changes the way in which it might react to a user.

A *change of state* occurs when the user observes a new mode of behavior for the WebApp. For example, when a user who is browsing product descriptions requests a product quote, the request triggers a change of state from a *product overview* state to a *product quotation* state. The WebApp look and feel observed by the user may also change as a consequence.

Often these changes of state will relate to interconnections between different use cases. For example, the *Access camera surveillance via the Internet* use case involves selecting a camera from a floor plan—but this is only possible if that user has previously configured (or had **SafeHomeAssured.com** configure) a floor plan. In other words, the **HomeOwner** class (see Figure 7.6) may or may not have a valid **House,** and when a **House** does exist, it may or may not have a valid **FloorPlan.**

Figure 7.8 depicts a partial, top-level (high level of abstraction) state diagram for the interaction between a customer and the **SafeHomeAssured.com** WebApp. This state diagram shows that the WebApp's response to various events within the *Access camera surveillance via the Internet* use case will depend upon the state of the application and, in particular, on whether a house is available for the customer and there is a valid house plan. The state diagram indicates the events that are required to move the new customer from one state to another, the information that is displayed as a state is entered, the processing that occurs within a state, and the exit condition that causes a transition from one state to another.

Do We Really Need Use Cases, Sequence Diagrams, and State Diagrams to Fully Describe the Interaction Model?

Because use cases, sequence diagrams, and state diagrams all present related information, it is reasonable to ask why all three are necessary. In some cases, they are not. Use cases may be sufficient in some situations, particularly if you have

FIGURE 7.8

Partial state
diagram for
construction of
house plans.

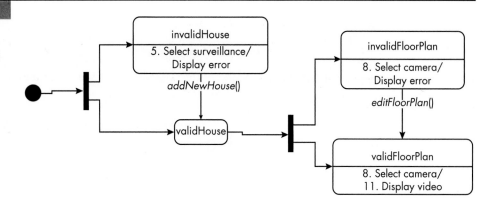

documented the exceptions thoroughly. However, use cases provide a rather one-
dimensional view of the interaction. Sequence diagrams present a second dimension that is more procedural (dynamic) in nature. State diagrams provide a third
dimension that is more behavioral and contains information about potential navigation pathways that is not provided by use cases or the sequence diagrams.

When all three dimensions are used, omissions or inconsistencies that might
escape discovery in one dimension become obvious when a second (or third) dimension is examined. It is for this reason that large complex WebApps can benefit
from an interaction model that encompasses all three representations.

Key factors affecting whether or not use cases, sequence diagrams, and state
diagrams are all necessary include the complexity of the overall increment, the
consequences of an error for users, (imagine the consequences if an unauthorized
user gained access to the video cameras inside your home!) and the likely difficulty
associated with rectifying an error later in the WebE process.

Why Is It a Good Idea to Build an Interface Prototype?

The layout of the user interface, the content it presents, the interaction mechanisms it implements, and the overall aesthetic of the user-WebApp connections
have much to do with user satisfaction and the overall acceptability of the WebApp.
Although it can be argued that the creation of a user interface prototype is a design
activity, it is a good idea to perform it during the creation of the analysis model.
The sooner that a physical representation of a user interface can be reviewed, the
higher the likelihood that end users will get what they want. The design of user
interfaces is discussed in detail in Chapter 9.

Because WebApp construction tools are plentiful, relatively inexpensive,
and functionally powerful, it is best to create the interface prototype using such
tools. The prototype should implement the major navigational links and represent
the overall screen layout in much the same way that it will be constructed. For

FIGURE 7.9

Example
screenshot of the
**SafeHome-
Assured.com**
home page.

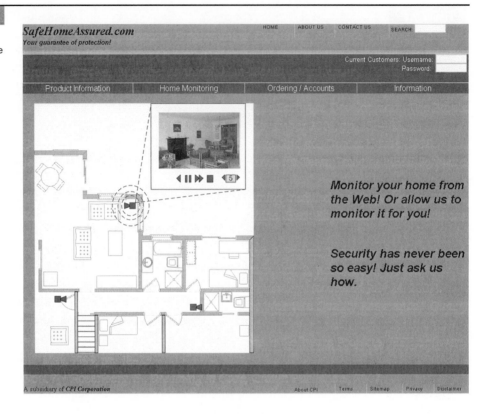

example, if five major system functions are to be provided to the end user, the prototype should represent them as the user will see them upon first entering the WebApp. Will graphical links be provided? Will a left-hand (or right-hand) menu be displayed? What other information will the user see? Questions like these should be answered by the prototype. Figure 7.9 illustrates a screenshot of an early prototype of the **SafeHomeAssured.com** home page. This prototype uses the layout and video monitoring capabilities of *SafeHome* as a selling tool and also provides the visitor with links to other important WebApp features. The prototype may not activate these links, but they are provided to give the reviewer a feel for the manner in which navigation will be initiated. It is important to note that this prototype can, and often does, change dramatically before the final interface design is developed.

The Functional Model

Many WebApps deliver a broad array of computational and manipulative functions that can be associated directly with content (either using it or producing it) and that are often a major goal of user-WebApp interaction. For this reason, the WebE team should analyze functionality in addition to content and interaction.

The *functional model* addresses two processing elements of the WebApp, each representing a different level of procedural abstraction: (1) user-observable functionality that is delivered by the WebApp to end users, and (2) the operations contained within analysis classes that implement behaviors associated with the class.

User-observable functionality encompasses any processing functions that are initiated directly by the user. For example, a financial WebApp might implement a variety of financial functions (e.g., a *college tuition calculator* or a *retirement savings calculator*). These functions may actually be implemented using operations within analysis classes, but from the point of view of the end user, the function (more correctly, the data provided by the function) is the visible outcome.

At a lower level of procedural abstraction, the analysis model describes the processing to be performed by analysis class operations. These operations manipulate class attributes and are involved as classes collaborate with one another to accomplish some required behavior.

Regardless of the level of procedural abstraction, the UML *activity diagram* can be used to represent processing details. At the analysis level, activity diagrams should only be used where the functionality is relatively complex. Much of the complexity of many WebApps occurs not in the functionality provided, but rather with the nature of the information that can be accessed and the ways in which this can be manipulated.

There are two good examples of complex functionality in **SafeHomeAssured.com** that would benefit from a careful analysis by the WebE team. The first is the use case *Get recommendations for sensor layout for my space*. The user has already developed a layout for the space to be monitored and, in this use case, selects that layout and requests recommended locations for sensors within the layout. **SafeHomeAssured.com** responds with a graphical representation of the layout with additional information on the recommended locations for sensors. The interaction is quite simple; the content is somewhat more complex, but the underlying functionality is very sophisticated. The system must undertake a relatively complex analysis of the floor layout in order to determine the optimal set of sensors. It must examine room dimensions, the location of doors and windows, and coordinate these with sensor capabilities and specifications. No small task!

The second example is the use case *Control cameras*. In this use case, the interaction is relatively simple, but there is the potential for complex functionality, given that this "simple" operation requires complex communication with devices located remotely and accessible across the Internet. A further possible complication relates to negotiation of control when multiple authorized people attempt to monitor and/or control a single sensor at the same time.

Figure 7.10 depicts an activity diagram for the *takeControlOfCamera()* operation that is part of the **Camera** analysis class used within the *Control cameras* use case. An activity diagram is similar to a flowchart, illustrating the processing flow and

FIGURE 7.10

Activity diagram
for the *take
ControlOf
Camera()*
operation.

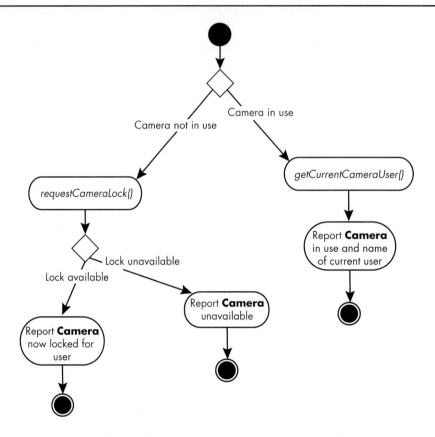

logical decisions within the flow. It should be noted that two additional operations
are invoked within the procedural flow: *requestCameraLock()*, which tries to lock
the camera for this user, and *getCurrentCameraUser()*, which retrieves the name of
the user who is currently controlling the camera. The construction details indicate
how these operations are invoked, and the interface details for each operation are
not considered until WebApp design commences.

The Configuration Model

WebApps must be designed and implemented in a manner that accommodates a
variety of environments on both the server side and the client side.[10] The Web-
App can reside on a server that provides access via the Internet, an Intranet, or an

---

10 The *server side* hosts the WebApp and all related system features that enable multiple users
    to gain access to the WebApp via a network. The *client side* provides a software environment
    (e.g., browsers) that enable end users to interact with the WebApp on the user's desktop.

Extranet. Server hardware and operating system environments must be specified. In addition, interoperability considerations on the server side must be considered. If the WebApp must access a large database or interoperate with corporate IT applications, then appropriate interfaces, communication protocols, and related collaborative information must be specified.

Client-side software provides the infrastructure that enables access to the WebApp from the user's location. In general, browser software is used to deliver WebApp content and functionality that is downloaded from the server. Although standards do exist, each browser has its own peculiarities. For this reason, the WebApp must be thoroughly tested within every browser configuration that is specified as part of the configuration model. For example, some Intranet WebApps might be able to assume that a specific client will be used, whereas most publicly accessible WebApps must accommodate a broad range of clients.

In some cases, the configuration model is nothing more than a list of server-side and client-side attributes. However, for more complex WebApps, a variety of configuration complexities (e.g., distributing load among multiple servers, caching architectures, remote databases, multiple servers serving various objects on the same Web page) may have an impact on analysis and design. The UML *deployment diagram* can be used in situations in which complex configuration architectures must be considered.

For **SafeHomeAssured.com** the public content and functionality should be specified to be accessible across all major Web clients (i.e., those with more than 0.1 percent market share or greater[11]). Conversely, it may be acceptable to restrict the more complex control and monitoring functionality (which is only accessible to *HomeOwner* users) to a smaller set of clients. The configuration model for **SafeHomeAssured.com** will also specify interoperability with existing product databases and monitoring applications.

Relationship-Navigation Analysis

In the context of Web applications, each architectural element has the potential to be linked to all other architectural elements. Indeed, linking mechanisms and the navigation they enable provide a key access tool within WebApps. But as the volume of content and the complexity of the user interaction increases, the number of links increases and, hence, the navigational complexity throughout the WebApp also

---

11 Determining market share for browsers is notoriously problematic and varies depending on which survey is used. Nevertheless, at the time of writing, Internet Explorer and Firefox were the only browsers that were reported in excess of 10 percent market share, and Netscape, Mozilla, Opera, and Safari the only other ones consistently above 0.1 percent.

increases. The question, then, is how to establish the appropriate links between content objects and among the functions that provide user-required capabilities.

Relationship-navigation analysis (RNA) provides a series of analysis steps that strive to identify relationships among the elements uncovered as part of the creation of the analysis model.[12] Yoo and Bieber [Yoo01] describe RNA in the following manner:

> RNA provides systems analysts with a systematic technique for determining the relationship structure of an application, helping them to discover all potentially useful relationships in application domains. These later may be implemented as links. RNA also helps determine appropriate navigational structures on top of these links. RNA enhances system developers' understanding of application domains by broadening and deepening their conceptual model of the domain. Developers can then enhance their implementations by including additional links, metainformation, and navigation.

The RNA approach is organized into five steps:

1. **Stakeholder analysis.** Identifies the various user categories, and establishes an appropriate stakeholder hierarchy

2. **Element analysis.** Identifies the content objects and functional elements that are of interest to end users

3. **Relationship analysis.** Describes the relationships that exist among the WebApp elements

4. **Navigation analysis.** Examines how users might access individual elements or groups of elements

5. **Evaluation analysis.** Considers pragmatic issues (e.g., cost-benefit) associated with implementing the relationships defined earlier

The first two steps in the RNA approach were discussed earlier in this chapter. In the sections that follow, we consider methods for establishing the relationships that exist among content objects and functions.

How Do We Establish Relationships Between Content Objects and Functionality?

Yoo and Bieber [Yoo01] suggest a list of questions that can help you to assess the relationships among *elements* (content objects or functions) that have been identified within the analysis model. The following list, adapted for WebApps, is representative [Yoo01]:

- Is the element a member of a broader category of elements?

- What attributes or parameters have been identified for the element?

---

12 It should be noted that RNA can be applied to any information system and was originally developed for hypermedia systems in general. It can, however, be adapted nicely for Web engineering.

- Does descriptive information about the element already exist? If so, where is it?
- Does the element appear in different locations within the WebApp? If so, where?
- Is the element composed of other smaller elements? If so, what are they?
- Is the element a member of a larger collection of elements? If so, what is it and what is its structure?
- Is the element described by an analysis class?
- Are other elements similar to the element being considered? If so, is it possible that they could be combined into one element?
- Is the element used in a specific ordering of other elements? Does its appearance depend on other elements?
- Does another element always follow the appearance of the element being considered?
- What pre- and postconditions must be met for the element to be used?
- Do specific user categories use the element? Do different user categories use the element differently? If so, how?
- Can the element be associated with a specific formulation goal or objective? With a specific WebApp requirement?
- Does this element always appear at the same time as other elements appear? If so, what are they?
- Does this element always appear in the same place (e.g., same location of the screen or page) as other elements? If so, what are they?

The answers to these and other questions can help you to position the element in question within the WebApp and to establish relationships among elements. It is possible to develop a relationship taxonomy and to categorize each relationship identified as a result of the questions noted. If you have further interest, refer to [Yoo01] for more detail.

How Do We Analyze Navigational Requirements?

Once relationships have been developed among elements defined within the analysis model, you should consider the requirements that dictate how each user category will navigate from one element (e.g., content object) to another. The mechanics of navigation are defined as part of design. At this stage, you must consider overall navigation requirements. The following questions should be addressed:

- Should certain elements be easier to reach (require fewer navigation steps) than others? What is the priority for presentation?

- Should certain elements be emphasized to force users to navigate in their direction?
- How should navigation errors be handled?
- Should navigation to related groups of elements be given priority over navigation to a specific element?
- Should navigation be accomplished via links, search-based access, or some other means?
- Should certain elements be presented to users based on the context of previous navigation actions?
- Should a navigation log be maintained for users?
- Should a full navigation map or menu (as opposed to a single "back" link or directed pointer) be available at every point in a user's interaction?
- Should navigation design be driven by the most commonly expected user behaviors or by the perceived importance of the defined WebApp elements?
- Can users "store" their previous navigation through the WebApp to expedite future usage?
- For which user category should optimal navigation be designed?
- How should links external to the WebApp be handled? Overlaying the existing browser window? As a new browser window? As a separate frame?

These and many other questions should be asked and answered as part of navigation analysis.

The Web engineering team and its stakeholders must also determine overall requirements for navigation. For example, will a "site map" be provided to give users an overview of the entire WebApp structure? Can a user take a "guided tour" that will highlight the most important elements (content objects and functions) that are available? Will a user be able to access content objects or functions based on defined attributes of those elements (e.g., a user might want to access all photographs of a specific building or all functions that allow computation of weight)?

Relationship-navigation analysis leads to a set of requirements for navigation. From these requirements, it is possible to develop an information architecture—the first step in high-level navigational design (Chapter 10).

To illustrate this, consider how the following question applies to **SafeHome-Assured.com:** *For which user category should optimal navigation be designed?* As shown in Figure 7.1, there are three main classes of user—guests, registered users, and homeowners. Considering the prototype home page (see Figure 7.9), we can see the navigational options that are implicitly available to each of these users. A quick discussion between the **SafeHomeAssured.com** system architect and the CPI marketing team indicates that navigational support should be optimized to attract new customers (i.e., navigation requirements for the user class *guests* should take precedence). Considering this navigation requirement, the current home page does not provide a clear path for *guests* to determine how to register with **SafeHomeAssured.com.**

Where We've Been . . . Where We're Going

The purpose of analysis modeling is to build upon information derived during the communication activity, refining and modeling WebApp requirements, and as a consequence, establishing a much deeper understanding of the nature of the WebApp to be built. In addition, analysis modeling transforms the requirements into a form that naturally leads to the design.

Analysis modeling refines a WebE team's understanding of the users and the tasks they perform. Usage scenarios (use cases) provide a key mechanism for capturing this and are the catalyst for all subsequent requirements analysis and modeling activities.

Four analysis tasks contribute to the creation of a complete analysis model: (1) content analysis identifies the full spectrum of content to be provided by the WebApp, (2) interaction analysis describes the manner in which the user interacts with the WebApp, (3) functional analysis defines the operations that will be applied to WebApp content and describes other processing functions that are independent of content but necessary to the end user, and (4) configuration analysis describes the environment and infrastructure in which the WebApp resides. Finally, relationship-navigation analysis identifies relationships among the content and functional elements defined in the analysis model and establishes requirements for defining appropriate navigation links throughout the system. A series of questions helps to establish relationships and identify characteristics that will have an influence on navigation design.

Analysis modeling is the first technical action in the Web engineering process. By refining, improving, and structuring the WebE team's understanding of requirements, it establishes a firm foundation for design.

In the chapters that follow, we delve into design—the technical kernel of Web engineering. We begin by exploring overall system and architectural design issues in Chapter 8.

References

[Baq04] Baqui, S., *Database Design Using Entity Relationship Diagrams,* Auerbach, 2004.

[Con00]   Conallen, J., *Building Web Applications with UML*, Addison-Wesley, 2000.

[Fra01]   Franklin, S., "Planning Your Web Site with UML," *webReview*, 2001, **www. ddj.com/documents/s=2659/nam1012432061/index.html** (accessed July 30, 2007).

[Fra03] Franklin, S., "Applying Rational tools to a simple J2EE-based project Part 9: Wrapping up development and testing," December 4, 2003, http://www.ibm. com/developerworks/rational/library/337.html (accessed October 11, 07).

[Pre05]   Pressman, R. S., *Software Engineering: A Practitioner's Approach,* 6th ed., McGraw-Hill, 2005.

[Sri01]   Sridhar, M., and N. Mandyam, "Effective Use of Data Models in Building Web Applications," 2001, **www.2002.org/CDROM/alternate/698/** (accessed July 30, 2007).

[Ton04] Tongrungrojana, R., and D. Lowe, "WIED: A Web Modelling Language for Modelling Architectural-Level Information Flows," *Journal of Digital Information*, vol. 5, no. 2, 2004, **http://jodi.tamu.edu/Articles/v05/i02/Tongrungrojana/** (accessed July 30, 2007).

[Yoo01] Yoo, J., and M. Bieber, "A Systematic Relationship Analysis for Modeling Information Domains," in M. Rossi and K. Siau (eds.), *Information Modeling in the New Millennium,* Idea Group, 2001, **http://web.njit.edu/~bieber/pub/ millenium-v3.pdf** (accessed July 30, 2007).

WEBAPP DESIGN

To this point in the Web engineering process, you've worked to en-sure that you have a clear understanding of the WebApp to be built. But you've spent relatively little time considering how to go about build-ing it. In this chapter and Chapters 9 through 11, we consider the design activities that set the stage for the construction of the WebApp itself and every increment that will be delivered to the end users.

As a consequence of analysis modeling (Chapter 7), you have estab-lished who will use the WebApp, what tasks users will perform, what functionality is required to support those tasks, what information must be exchanged, and the content that supports this information. Finally, you have identified the nature of the interaction that ties these elements together.

In this chapter and the ones that follow, we consider the concepts, principles, and methods that are required to transform an understanding of what the WebApp should do into a representation of what the WebApp should be. In other words, we are ready to move from *what* to *how*, from *WebApp analysis* to *WebApp design*.

Design for WebApps

In his authoritative book on Web design, Jakob Nielsen [Nie00] states: "There are essentially two basic approaches to design: the artistic ideal of expressing yourself and the engineering ideal of solving a problem for a customer." During the first decade of Web development, many develop-ers chose an approach based on the artistic ideal. Design occurred in an ad hoc manner and was usually conducted as HTML was generated. Design evolved out of an artistic vision that itself evolved as WebApp construction occurred.

Even today, some proponents of agile software development (Chap-ter 2) use WebApps as poster children for the development of applica-tions based on "limited design." They argue that WebApp immediacy and volatility mitigate against formal design, that design evolves as an ap-plication is built (coded), and that relatively little time should be spent on creating a detailed design model. This argument has merit, but only for relatively simple WebApps—when a single developer can design the architecture and build the WebApp while maintaining a detailed mental picture of the design. When content and function are complex; when the size of the WebApp encompasses hundreds of content objects, functions, and analysis classes; when multiple people become involved in the design; and when the success of the WebApp will have a direct impact on the success of the business, then design should not be taken lightly. We must be careful not to mistake *limited design* (which is inappropriate except for simplistic applications) for *lightweight design*. In the latter, the design is carried out meticulously, but possibly with aspects of the design being developed incrementally and with the results documented through prototypes that evolve into the actual WebApp.

This reality leads us to Nielsen's second approach—"the engineering ideal of solving a problem for a customer." Web engineering adopts this philosophy, and a more rigorous approach to WebApp design enables it to be achieved by developers. In every instance, a design model should be created before construction begins, but a good Web engineer recognizes that the design will evolve as more is learned about stakeholder requirements as the WebApp is built. Therefore, the level of detail needed in the design model will be highly dependent on how volatile the requirements are likely to be.

The creation of an effective design will typically require a diverse set of skills. Sometimes, for small projects, a single developer may need to be multiskilled. For larger projects, it may be advisable and/or feasible to draw on the expertise of specialists: Web engineers, graphic designers, content developers, programmers, database specialists, information architects, network engineers, security experts, and testers. Drawing on these diverse skills allows the creation of a model that can be assessed for quality and improved *before* content and code are generated, tests are conducted, and end users become involved in large numbers. If analysis is where *WebApp quality is established,* then design is where the *quality is truly embedded.*

What Does a WebApp Designer Need to Know?

A WebApp designer should have a good understanding of the characteristics that make a good design—both generically and for a specific WebApp. Generically, a good design should guide the WebApp construction and ensure that the solutions that are developed maximize simplicity, consistency, identity, robustness, and usability. For the design to be an effective guide to the construction, it should also be understandable and incorporate an appropriate level of detail. But what level of detail is appropriate? In the case of WebApp design, we need enough information to make the design useful, but not so much that the design process becomes burdensome.

In terms of specific WebApps, the design needs to cover those aspects that are relevant to that WebApp. For some applications, security will not be an issue at all and the design can effectively ignore this aspect (or at least deal with it informally during the construction). For other applications, security may be critical. This means that designers should have a good understanding of the security issues that the design must address.

What Is Logical Design?

Design for WebApps encompasses both logical design and physical design. *Logical design* involves the identification of those abstract things that have to occur inside the WebApp in order to meet stakeholder requirements and conform to the analysis model (Chapter 7). For example, for **SafeHomeAssured.com** to provide the required information and functionality, it would need to include a security monitoring subsystem, an order management subsystem, and a customer management subsystem (among others). At this level we are not considering the actual WebApp software components or the hardware on which these components might operate, but rather the logical building blocks that provide the desired functionality and content.

What Is Physical Design?

The *physical design* maps our understanding of the logical design into the actual physical elements to be implemented as part of the WebApp—items such as Web servers, database servers, content management systems, processing scripts, Web pages, and other WebApp components. At this level you consider the overall system physical architecture and then drill down into the detailed system components.

For example, increment 2 of **SafeHomeAssured.com** includes support for downloading the specs of available products. In the logical design, you develop a conceptual architecture that includes a product information repository where the product information is stored and a product management subsystem that supports access to this content.[1] In the physical design, you then determine how these components will actually be implemented. For example, you could choose to use off-the-shelf content management software[2] for these subsystems. Instead, since the application is relatively simple, is maintained by a single person; and the content is stable, not subject to constant evolution, and is already stored in a database, the **SafeHomeAssured.com** development team decides to use the existing stand-alone database for the product information repository, and hand-coded ASP (Active Server Pages) scripts to access this content for the product management.

---

1   These aspects are shown in more detail in the conceptual architecture illustrated in Figure 8.4.
2   See the CMS Matrix website (**www.cmsmatrix.org/**) for typical software that might be appropriate in implementing the product management subsystem.

What Information Is Created as a Consequence of Design?

The primary output of all design tasks is a *design model* that encompasses content, aesthetics, architecture, interface, navigation, and component-level design issues. The design model provides sufficient information for the WebE team to construct the final WebApp (or at least those WebApp increments currently being designed). During the design, alternative solutions are considered, and the degree to which the current design model will lead to an effective implementation is also assessed.

In this chapter we examine the overall design process and how to ensure consistency between logical and physical design and between functional and information design. We will look at the key issues that affect your approach to design and how you should address these issues.

In Chapters 9–13 we consider specific design tasks. Chapter 9 addresses interaction design and how it forms a basis for ensuring the connection between user requirements and WebApp design. Chapter 10 examines the design of the information aspects that support the interaction. Chapter 11 considers system functionality and the techniques required to represent the design of WebApp functions. In Chapter 12 we move from logical design into the physical design and construction and show how you can map the logical elements into components that can be implemented. Finally, in Chapter 13 we consider design patterns and how these can help improve the design.

Design Goals

In her regular column on Web design, Jean Kaiser [Kai02] suggested a set of design goals that are applicable to virtually every WebApp regardless of application domain, size, or complexity:

> **Simplicity.** Although it may seem old-fashioned, the aphorism "all things in moderation" applies to WebApps. There is a tendency among some designers to provide the end user with too much: exhaustive content, extreme visuals, intrusive animation, enormous Web pages—the list is long. Rather than *feature-bloat*, it is better to strive for moderation and simplicity. To get a sense of how true this can be, consider the simplicity of the interface for one of the most widely used sites on the Web—**www.google.com**—(while the interface is simple, the underlying functionality is incredibly complex).
>
> Content should be informative but succinct and should use a delivery mode (e.g., text, graphics, video, audio) that is appropriate to the information that is being delivered. Aesthetics should be pleasing, but not overwhelming (e.g., using too many colors tends to distract the user rather than enhance

the interaction), and the architecture should achi̇

in the simplest possible manner. Navigation sho

navigation mechanisms should be intuitively ṛ

tions should be easy to use and easier to understṣ.

Consistency. This design goal applies to virtually every e.

sign model. Content should be constructed consistently (e.g., text ṛ

and font styles should be the same across all text documents, and graphiṛ

art should have a consistent look, color scheme, and style). Graphic design

(aesthetics) should present a consistent look across all parts of the WebApp.[3]

Architectural design should establish templates that lead to a consistent

hypermedia navigation structure. Interface design should define consistent

modes of interaction, navigation, and content display. Navigation mecha-

nisms should be used consistently across all WebApp elements. As Kaiser

[Kai02] notes, "Remember that to a visitor, a Web site is a physical place. It is

confusing if pages within a site are not consistent in design."

Identity. The aesthetic, interface, and navigational design of a WebApp

must be consistent with the application domain for which it is to be built.

A Web site for hip-hop musicians will undoubtedly have a different look and

feel than a WebApp designed for a financial services company. The WebApp

architecture will be entirely different, interfaces will be constructed to ac-

commodate different categories of users, and navigation will be organized

to accomplish different objectives. A Web engineer (and other design con-

tributors) should work to establish an identity for the WebApp through the

design.

Robustness. Based on the identity that has been established, a WebApp

often makes an implicit promise to a user. The user expects robust content

and functions that are relevant to the user's needs. If these elements are

missing or insufficient, it is likely that the WebApp will fail.

Navigability. We have already noted that navigation should be simple

and consistent. It should also be designed in a manner that is intuitive and

predictable for users. That is, users should be able to understand how to

move about the WebApp without having to search for navigation links or

instructions. For example, if a page contains a field of graphic icons or im-

ages, some of which can be used as navigation mechanisms, these must be

identified in some obvious manner. Nothing is more frustrating than trying

to find the appropriate live link among many graphical images.

---

3 Web technologies such as cascading style sheets (CSSs) were designed, in part, to support this
   objective—by providing a style definition that could be used across an entire site, thereby facilitating consistency.

It is also important to position links to major WebApp content and functions in a predictable location on every Web page. If page scrolling is required (and this is often the case), links at the top and bottom of the page make the user's navigation tasks easier.

Visual appeal. Of all software categories, Web applications are unquestionably the most visual, the most dynamic, and the most unapologetically aesthetic. Beauty (visual appeal) is undoubtedly in the eye of the beholder, but many design characteristics (e.g., the look and feel of content, interface layout, color coordination, the balance of text, graphics and other media, and navigation mechanisms) do contribute to visual appeal.

Compatibility. Most WebApps will be used in a variety of environments (e.g., different hardware, Internet connection types, operating systems, and browsers) and must be designed to be compatible with each.

A design that achieves each of these goals will be pleasing to the end user and bring credit to the WebE team.

Establishing Design Guidelines

The scene: SafeHomeAssured. com WebE team meeting room just before design is to commence for the first increment

The players: The WebE team leader and all team members

The conversation:

Team member 1 (before everyone arrives): I don't see why we need standards for this increment. It's just a simple informational site.

Team member 2: That's true, but the other increments are more complex, and besides, we better all get on the same page before we begin design and construction. [Pauses and looks up to see the team leader enter.]

Team leader: I thought it would be a good idea to discuss overall design guidelines for the work we're going to do on **SafeHomeAssured.com.** [He hands out a six-page document to each team member.] What I've done is modified a set of WebApp design guidelines that a friend gave me—I'd like to walk through it, get your comments and suggestions, and use it as a straw man for our work.

Team member 3 (looking around the table): All of us have worked on WebApps before. Do we really need to constrain ourselves with "standards." Aren't we going to be a self-organizing team?

Team leader (smiling but firm): First, these are guidelines, not rigid standards. Second, even self-organizing teams have to be consistent. What these guidelines will give us is a consistent approach to design. Nobody is going to tell you how to design low-level stuff, but the overall design feel of **SafeHome-Assured.com** has to be solid . . . and consistent.

[The team leader walks through the document. There is substantial discussion, more than a few objections and counterproposals, but general agreement that the idea of design guidelines is a good one. The walkthrough continues with navigation design guidelines.]

Team leader: Okay, the next section covers navigation design.

[Everyone spends a few moments perusing that section.]

Team member 1: This suggests that all major functions be presented in a left-hand column with scroll-

SafeHome (CONTINUED)

down subfunctions when a major function is selected. That's pretty much the way we envisioned the interface during analysis.

Team member 4: Yeah, but it also says that we want to constrain the navigation mechanisms to text links within a page. I can see a number of places where we might like to use graphical icons, for example . . .

Team leader (interrupting and making a note): I agree, that's too restrictive. I've made a note to modify it.

Team member 2: This suggests that we "limit navigation depth to four levels maximum." I'm not sure what that means.

Team member 1: It means that any content or functionality should be accessible with no more than four mouse clicks on navigation links. It's a good idea . . . keeps things simple, but I'm not sure it's always doable.

Team member 3: We can always have exceptions, if they're really warranted.

Team leader: I agree.

Team member 4: It also says that . . .

[The conversation continues for each design guideline.]

Design and WebApp Quality

Design goals provide the WebE team with a set of global objectives, but how can the members of the team determine whether these goals have been achieved? What characteristics can be assessed to determine the quality of a WebApp design?

From a generic viewpoint, design results in a "model" that is used to guide the construction of the WebApp. The model, regardless of its form, should contain enough information to reflect how stakeholder requirements (defined during the communication activity and in the analysis model) are to be translated into content and executable code. But design must also be specific. It must address key quality attributes of a WebApp in a manner that enables you to build and test effectively.

This means that in order to undertake effective WebApp design, you need to have a good understanding of WebApp quality. A good starting point is to examine what users of the WebApp might expect.

How Do Users Perceive Quality?

Every person who has surfed the Web or used a corporate Intranet has an opinion about what makes a "good" WebApp. The Web abounds with websites that provide information about good and bad WebApp designs and give examples of each (at least examples that the authors of the information believe illustrates good or bad quality).[4]

---

4   For examples of sites that compare good and bad designs see the following:
Vincent Flinder's Web Pages That Suck, **www.webpagesthatsuck.com/**
Bad Human Factors Designs, **www.baddesigns.com/**
Kerlins.Net Web Design, **http://kerlins.net/bobbi/technology/webdesign/**
CoolHomePages Web Site Design Learning and Tutorials Academy, **www.coolhomepages.com/cda/10commandments/**
Poor Web Design Examples, **www.4webmarketing.biz/webdesign/poorwebdesign.htm**
Sunday Software's Good and Bad Church Websites, **www.sundaysoftware.com/good-badsites.htm**

Individual viewpoints vary widely. Some users enjoy flashy graphics; others want simple text. Some demand copious information; others desire an abbreviated presentation. Some like sophisticated analytical tools or database access; others like to keep it simple.

In fact, the user's perception of goodness (and the resultant acceptance or rejection of the WebApp as a consequence) might be more important than any technical discussion of WebApp quality. For example, consider Thomas Edison, the inventor of the phonograph. Despite the brilliance of his invention, the companies he established to market the phonograph all failed—primarily because he understood the technology but not his end users. As a result, his marketing focused on the technology, rather than the entertainment benefits that the device provided for consumers. His competitors marketed a phonograph that was possibly not as technologically advanced, but was much better adapted to users, and they succeeded (at least financially) while Edison failed.

But how is WebApp quality perceived? What attributes must be exhibited to achieve goodness in the eyes of end users and at the same time exhibit the technical characteristics of quality that will enable you to correct, adapt, enhance, and support the application over the long term?

In reality, all the general characteristics of software quality apply to WebApps. However, the most relevant of these characteristics—usability, functionality, reliability, efficiency, and maintainability—provide a useful basis for assessing the quality of Web-based systems.

Is There a User-Centric Model for Assessing Design Quality?

No matter how many quality criteria a WebApp meets, it will fail if end users do not like it or are unhappy with it. For this reason, it is important to establish a user-centric model for WebApp quality. One useful model that provides a worthwhile basis for evaluating (and hence, guiding) WebApp design is the *Technology Acceptance Model* (TAM) [Dav89]. TAM is widely used in information systems research and models how users accept and use a new technology (in this case a new WebApp is the technology under consideration). The model includes two key measures: *perceived usefulness* (PU), the extent to which the user believes that the technology will help achieve operational goals; and *perceived ease of use* (EOU), the extent to which the user believes that the system is easy to use (takes minimum effort).

TAM has subsequently evolved into TAM2 [Ven00] and UTAUT (Unified Theory of Acceptance and Use of Technology) [Ven03].[5] Although these models are primarily intended as research tools, they do provide some useful insights into the

---

5 A good overview of UTAUT can be found at York University's Unified theory of acceptance and use of technology website, **www.istheory.yorku.ca/UTAUT.htm**

factors that affect how users react to a WebApp.[6] For example, Table 8.1 lists the items used in UTAUT, modified to refer specifically to WebApps instead of general technology systems.

As each WebApp increment is introduced, a questionnaire containing the questions posed in Table 8.1 could be provided to a representative set of end users. Where appropriate, the questions could be customized to suit the particular Web App being developed. Once the answers are statistically analyzed, the results can provide the WebE team with an indication of user-centric perceptions of design (and construction) quality.

TABLE 8.1   ITEMS USED IN EVALUATING USERS RESPONSE TO A WEBAPP

Performance expectancy

U6[7]: I would find the WebApp useful in my job.

RA1: Using the WebApp enables me to accomplish tasks more quickly.

RA5: Using the WebApp increases my productivity.

OE7: If I use the WebApp, I will increase my chances of getting a raise.

Effort expectancy

EOU3: My interaction with the WebApp would be clear and understandable.

EOU5: It would be easy for me to become skillful at using the WebApp.

EOU6: I would find the WebApp easy to use.

EU4: Learning to operate the WebApp is easy for me.

Attitude toward using technology

A1: Using the WebApp is a bad/good idea.

AF1: The WebApp makes work more interesting.

AF2: Working with the WebApp is fun.

Affect1: I like working with the WebApp.

Social influence

SN1: People who influence my behavior think that I should use the WebApp.

SN2: People who are important to me think that I should use the WebApp.

SF2: The senior management of this business has been helpful in the use of the WebApp.

SF4: In general, the organization has supported the use of the WebApp.

Facilitating conditions

PBC2: I have the resources necessary to use the WebApp.

---

6   Reading about UTAUT will provide you with useful insight into design quality from a user's point of view.

7   The item labels used in Table 8.1 are those specified in UTAUT and are derived from the original sources that contributed to the development of UTAUT. For example, item OE7 refers to an item on Outcome Expectations (which occurs within Social Cognitive Theory). The PBC items refer to Perceived Behavioral Control (from the Theory of Planned Behavior). Full details are available in [Ven03].

TABLE 8.1   (CONTINUED)

PBC3: I have the knowledge necessary to use the WebApp.

PBC5: The WebApp is/is not compatible with other WebApps I use.

FC3: A specific person (or group) is available for assistance with WebApp difficulties.

Self-efficacy

I could complete a job or task using the WebApp . . .

SE1: If there was no one around to tell me what to do as I go.

SE4: If I could call someone for help if I got stuck.

SE6: If I had a lot of time to complete the job for which the WebApp was provided.

SE7: If I had just the built-in help facility for assistance.

Anxiety

ANX1: I feel apprehensive about using the WebApp.

ANX2: It scares me to think that I could lose a lot of information using the WebApp by hitting the wrong link.

ANX3: I hesitate to use the WebApp for fear of making mistakes I cannot correct.

ANX4: The WebApp is somewhat intimidating to me.

Behavioral intention to use the WebApp

BI1: I intend to use the WebApp in the next <n> months.

BI2: I predict I would use the WebApp in the next <n> months.

BI3: I plan to use the WebApp in the next <n> months.

Source: Adapted from [Ven03].

As an example of the use of UTAUT, consider the sidebar that describe a discussion among members of the **SafeHomeAssured.com** team.

SafeHome

Assessing Design Quality

The scene: SafeHomeAssured.com WebE team meeting room during a design review meeting for increment 5, *Monitoring services*

The players: The WebE team leader and the WebE interface designer

The conversation:

Interface designer: I've done an assessment of users' reactions to the initial interface design prototype for this increment. There's one aspect that is worrying me, and I'd like to go over it with you.

Team leader: What's the problem?

Interface designer: Well, I used the UTAUT approach you showed me and adapted it with a few additional questions related to specific issues with this increment. Most of the results look fine—except for the answers to the questions about user anxiety.

Team leader: Refresh my memory. What were the questions?

Interface designer: Sure. Here's a list of the questions. [The interface designer hands over a sheet with the following written on it (in part)]:

SAFEHOME (CONTINUED)

Anxiety

ANX1: I feel apprehensive about using the monitoring service.

ANX2a: It scares me to think that I could lose a lot of information using the **SafeHomeAssured.com** monitoring services.

ANX2b: I am worried about an unauthorized person being able to access my home security information or functionality.

ANX3: I hesitate to use the monitoring services for fear of making mistakes I cannot correct.

ANX4: The monitoring services are somewhat intimidating to me.

Interface designer: We gave this to a sample of 20 prospective users and asked them to rate the questions on a standard five-point Likert scale ranging from strongly disagree to strongly agree. In the questions on anxiety, the answers to ANX3 and ANX4 were OK, which probably means that the users generally were happy with the interface. The problem was

with the first three questions. The scores for all three of these were much more problematic than anything else in the interface. I then went back to the users and discussed this with them in more detail. It turns out that they are really worried about other people breaking into the system and accessing their security devices. Basically doing things like watching them using their own cameras or even disabling the security devices so that they can break in.

Team leader: But we already have excellent security around all these functions.

Interface designer: Yep, but that security isn't really visible to them. I think we need to change the interface a little to make the security aspects more visible to the user.

Team leader: OK. How about coming back to me tomorrow with some suggestions about how we might do this?

A formal approach such as UTAUT would be overkill for many Web engineering projects. However, when a WebApp is business-critical, when user acceptance is pivotal to business success, and when users' perceptions of usefulness and ease of use are difficult to discern using less formal approaches, a question-based format such as UTAUT, followed by statistical analysis, can provide the WebE team with important guidance.

What Is a Quality Framework?

If a cross section of end users answers each of the questions contained in Table 8.1, the WebE team would gain insight into the efficacy of the WebApp it has created. But an assessment of the goodness of a WebApp from the user's point of view (although very important) is not the only arbiter of quality. For example, an e-commerce site might be extremely well designed from the user's perspective given that it provides easy access to useful information, but fails to actually sell any products. In addition to the user-centric model, there are a number of different quality frameworks that identify a broad set of quality characteristics that should be considered during design.

Olsina and his colleagues [Ols99] have prepared a "quality requirement tree" that identifies a set of technical attributes—usability, functionality, reliability,

FIGURE 8.1

Quality require-
ments tree.
Source: From [Ols99].

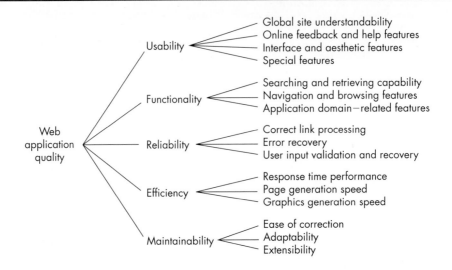

efficiency, and maintainability—that lead to high-quality WebApps.[8] Figure 8.1 summarizes their work. The criteria noted in the figure are of particular interest to Web
engineers who must design, build, and maintain WebApps over the long term.

Offutt [Off02] extends the five major quality attributes noted in Figure 8.1 by
adding the following attributes:

Security. WebApps have become heavily integrated with critical corporate
and government databases. E-commerce applications extract and then store
sensitive customer information. For these and many other reasons, WebApp
security is paramount in many situations. For example, with **SafeHome-
Assured.com** it is crucial that unauthorized users can't gain access to other
users' home security information. The key measure of security is the ability
of the WebApp and its server environment to rebuff unauthorized access
and/or thwart an outright malevolent attack. A detailed discussion of
WebApp security is beyond the scope of this book. If you have further interest, see [Cro07], [Das07], or [Kal03].

Availability. Even the best WebApp will not meet users' needs if it is
unavailable. In a technical sense, availability is the measure of the percentage of time that a WebApp is available for use. The typical end user expects
WebApps to be available 24/7/365. Anything less is deemed unacceptable.[9]

---

8   These quality attributes are quite similar to those often quoted for software applications. The
     implication is that quality characteristics are universal for all software.
9   This expectation is, of course, unrealistic in all but the most extreme cases. Most major
     WebApps must schedule downtime for fixes and upgrades. We can, however, ensure (through
     use of server farms, careful design of the maintenance and deployment servers, etc.) that the

But uptime is not the only indicator of availability. Offutt [Off02] suggests that "using features available on only one browser or one platform" makes the WebApp unavailable to those with a different browser or platform configuration. The user will invariably go elsewhere.

Scalability. Can the WebApp and its server environment be scaled to handle 100, 1000, 10,000, or 1,000,000 users? Will the WebApp and the systems with which it is interfaced handle significant variation in volume and load, or will responsiveness drop dramatically (or cease altogether)? It is not enough to build a WebApp that is *usually* successful. It is equally important to build a WebApp that can *continuously* accommodate the burden of success (significantly more end users) and become even more successful.

Time-to-market. Although time-to-market is not a true quality attribute in the technical sense, it is a measure of quality from a business point of view. The first WebApp in the market often captures a disproportionate number of end users.

In a more general sense, Miller [Mil00] suggests the following "dimensions of quality." These should be considered by Web engineers, but they represent a view of quality that is more visible to end users.

Time. How rapidly does the WebApp change? How much has a WebApp changed since the last upgrade? How do you highlight the parts that have changed?

Structural. How well do all the parts of the WebApp hold together? Are all links inside and outside the WebApp working? Do all the images work? Are there parts of the WebApp that are not connected?

Content. Does the content of critical pages match what is supposed to be there? Do key phrases exist continually in highly changeable pages? Do critical pages maintain quality content from version to version? What about dynamically generated HTML pages?

Accuracy and consistency. Are today's copies of the pages downloaded the same as yesterday's? Close enough? Are the data presented accurately enough? How do you know?

Response time and latency. Does the Web server respond to a browser request within certain parameters? In an e-commerce or workflow context, how is the end-to-end response time after information is submitted? Are there parts of a site that are so slow the user becomes frustrated?

---

transition to new versions of WebApps occurs in such a small time window that it is transparent to users.

Performance. Is the browser-server connection quick enough? How does the performance vary by time of day, load, and usage? Is performance adequate for e-commerce applications?

As a WebApp designer, you can use each of these questions as a crib sheet when designing the WebApp interface, navigation approach, layout, and aesthetics.

Is There a Way to Assess Content Quality?

Billions of Web pages are available for those in search of information on the World Wide Web. Even well-targeted Web searches result in an avalanche of content. With so many sources of information to choose from, how does the user assess the quality (e.g., veracity, accuracy, completeness, timeliness) of the content that is presented within a WebApp? Tillman [Til00] suggests a useful set of criteria for assessing the quality of content:

- Can the scope and depth of content be easily determined to ensure that it meets the user's needs?
- Can the background and authority of the content's authors be easily identified?
- Is it possible to determine the currency of the content, the last update, and what was updated?
- Is the content and its location stable (i.e., will it remain at the referenced URL)?

In addition to these content-related questions, the following might be added:

- Is content credible?
- Is content unique? That is, does the WebApp provide some unique benefit to those who use it?
- Is content valuable to the targeted user community?
- Is content well organized? Indexed? Easily accessible?

Is There a Single Quality Checklist I Can Use?

It certainly would be nice if we could develop a single, definitive quality checklist for WebApps. The problem is that different WebApp stakeholders see different quality characteristics as important. Each stakeholder plays a different role and has a different point of view. In addition, different WebApps have different requirements and quality needs.

To help you, we've synthesized a checklist from the various sources discussed earlier. It provides an overall summary of important issues that can be used as a basis for informing the design and undertaking design reviews.

EVALUATING DESIGN

WebApp Design IQ Checklist

The following WebApp Design IQ (Importance/Quality) Checklist (derived from the sources discussed in this book) provides a set of key WebApp characteristics that need to be considered during design. By considering these items, both Web engineers and end users can quickly assess overall WebApp quality and then focus their attention on quality items that need further consideration.

For each quality item listed, give a score to both I and Q and compute the product of the two values. Those items that have an overall rating (product) of 5 or higher potentially need further consideration. Those that have a rating of 10 or higher are areas of major concern.

I(mportance) rating: Rate the importance of the characteristic for the WebApp.

> 0 = minimal significance for this WebApp
>
> 5 = high significance for this WebApp

Q(uality) rating: Rate the current quality level of the WebApp design or implementation.

> 0 = minimal quality concerns for this WebApp
>
> 5 = substantial quality concerns for this WebApp

I Q Rating   Design Characteristic

I   Q   **Usability**

☐ × ☐ = _____   Global understandability (appropriate metaphors, etc.)

☐ × ☐ = _____   Appropriate feedback and help features

☐ × ☐ = _____   Interface intuitiveness (learnability)

☐ × ☐ = _____   Structural navigability

☐ × ☐ = _____   Navigation integrity (link correctness, completeness, etc.)

☐ × ☐ = _____   Site overviews (maps, trails, bread crumbs, etc.)

I   Q

☐ × ☐ = _____   User adaptation and customization

☐ × ☐ = _____   Other: _____

Content

☐ × ☐ = _____   Content completeness (scope and depth)

☐ × ☐ = _____   Content correctness

☐ × ☐ = _____   Content currency

☐ × ☐ = _____   Content relevance

☐ × ☐ = _____   Content accuracy and authoritativeness

☐ × ☐ = _____   User perceptions of content

☐ × ☐ = _____   Other: _____

Functional

☐ × ☐ = _____   Functional accessibility

☐ × ☐ = _____   Functional consistency

☐ × ☐ = _____   Functional correctness

☐ × ☐ = _____   Searching and indexing capabilities

☐ × ☐ = _____   Exception handling and error recovery

☐ × ☐ = _____   Other: _____

Nonfunctional

☐ × ☐ = _____   Data security

☐ × ☐ = _____   User perception of security

☐ × ☐ = _____   WebApp availability

☐ × ☐ = _____   WebApp extensibility

☐ × ☐ = _____   WebApp responsiveness and performance

☐ × ☐ = _____   Other: _____

Developmental

☐ × ☐ = _____   Ease of correction

☐ × ☐ = _____   Extensibility and adaptability

☐ × ☐ = _____   Other: _____

WebApp design should attempt to address each of these quality needs, but in reality they sometimes conflict with one another. For example, the marketing department of a financial services company (a highly competitive environment) wants an end user to enter the company's website as quickly and effortlessly as possible. Conversely, the stakeholders with responsibility for privacy and security want to ensure that the website cannot be breached by those with malevolent intent, even if this retards the user's ability to enter the site. The WebApp design must respond to these conflicting (but still valid) requirements.

The checklist on the preceding page represents only a small sampling of the issues that should be addressed as the design of a WebApp evolves, but it has been developed to address the key issues and then focus the designer's attention on those issues that need further attention. An important goal of Web engineering is to develop systems in which affirmative answers are provided to all quality-related questions.

The Design Process

It's time to begin discussing WebApp design more explicitly. In order to conduct design in a way that achieves high quality, you should understand and apply key design tasks—the "how" of WebApp design.

What Are the Elements of WebApp Design?

In his early book on Web design, Powell [Pow00] attempts to define design in the context of Web engineering:

> Defining Web design is very difficult. To some, design focuses on the visual look and feel of a Web site. For others, Web design is about the structuring of information and the navigation through a document space. Others might consider design to be mostly about the technology used to build interactive Web applications. In reality, Web design includes all of these things and maybe more.

Web design focuses on many different aspects of the Web-based system. Because the appropriate mix of aesthetics, content, and technology will vary depending upon the nature of the WebApp, the design activities that are emphasized will vary for each project. A key Web engineering skill is the effective integration of these various elements.

Design begins by focusing on issues that are important to the one stakeholder who will use the WebApp day in and day out—the end user. Virtually all WebApps have a strong interactive component. It follows that the design of the interaction is pivotal to user acceptance and critical to the success of the WebApp itself. Therefore, interaction design is the place where WebApp design begins.

FIGURE 8.2

The WebApp
design pyramid.

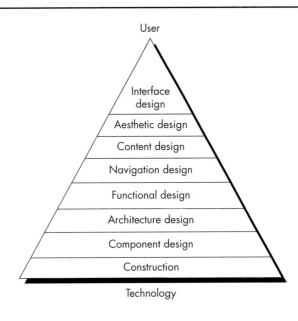

And where does design stop? The answer to this question seems easy—design stops when construction (e.g., HTML coding) begins. But there are two problems with this simplistic answer. The first is that often the distinction between design and construction is blurred. Many aspects of the design are identified through prototypes that become the basis for the construction. Secondly, even the best designer cannot foresee every contingency that is encountered during the construction activity. Some construction problems require redesign, and as a consequence, design continues well into the construction activity.

So design begins with the interface and ends after construction is completed. But what happens in between?

Figure 8.2 depicts a *design pyramid* that contains the design actions (levels) that occur as a complete design model is created. The top two levels of the pyramid—*interface design* and *aesthetic design*—form the basis of user's interaction with the system, and therefore can be grouped together as *interaction design*.[10] We consider each of these aspects individually:

- *Interface design* describes the structure and organization of the user interface. It includes a representation of screen layout, a definition of the modes of interaction, and a description of navigation mechanisms. For sites with more than simplistic functionality, it may also include descriptions of the workflow sequences and related issues.

---

10 Interaction design is considered in detail in Chapter 9.

- *Aesthetic design,* also called *graphic design,* describes the look and feel of the WebApp. It includes color schemes, geometric layout, text size, font and placement, the use of graphics, and related aesthetic decisions.

The next two levels of the pyramid focus on information: the content that underpins the WebApp, the way in which that content is organized, and the manner in which the user travels through the WebApp to access content or functionality. We consider each of these design tasks individually:

- *Content design* defines the layout, structure, and outline for all content that is presented as part of the WebApp. It establishes the relationships among content objects.

- *Navigation design* represents the navigational flow between content objects and for all WebApp functions. It describes the ways in which the user locates and interacts with the content.

The design of both content and navigation is discussed in detail in Chapter 10.

WebApps have evolved to provide significant functionality in addition to a wide variety of content, all tied to the application domain under consideration. For example, the **SafeHomeAssured.com** WebApp provides a wide array of functional capabilities (e.g., allows users to define space layouts, place product orders, monitor a house via the Internet) in addition to a broad collection of content (e.g., product descriptions, specifications, photos). In some cases the functionality will follow well-established patterns. For example, business-to-consumer (B2C) WebApps use catalogs, shopping carts, and checkouts. In other cases the functionality may be highly specialized. When design focuses explicitly on functionality, we describe it in the following way:

- *Functional design* identifies the overall behavior and functionality that is supported by the WebApp—including aspects such as workflow support, content and interface adaptation and/or customization, order entry, database processes, computational functions, and others.

Functional design is considered in Chapter 11.

The bottom levels of the design pyramid—classified as *technical design*—consider how the interface, navigation, content, and functions will be integrated together and implemented. Technical design provides a basis for the construction activity that follows. It considers both the WebApp architecture and the design of WebApp components.

- *Architecture design* identifies the overall structure for the WebApp. *Conceptual architecture design* identifies the conceptual components for the WebApp and the way in which these are interconnected. It ensures that the various aspects of the application are appropriately integrated.[11] *Technical architecture design* identifies the technical components and the interactions between the components that are required to construct the WebApp.

- *Component design* develops the detailed processing logic required to implement functional components that support a complete set of WebApp functions.

It is worth clarifying the distinction between the conceptual and the technical architecture. The conceptual architecture outlines the major functional and information components that are required for the system. For example, a simple e-commerce application might require a product catalog (with content and searching-browsing functionality), a purchasing system (with shopping basket management and payment functionality), a customer management system (for tracking user purchases and performing site adaptation and recommendations), and possibly an administration subsystem (for management of registrations, purchase requests, etc.).

This compares with the technical architecture that shows how the specific design components of the conceptual architecture map into the specific technologies used to implement the WebApp. For example, an e-commerce application may include a Web server, a payment gateway, a content management system, and a number of HTML pages and ASP scripts.

What Are the Characteristics of the Design Process?

The WebE design pyramid clarifies the design tasks that should be performed to create a high-quality WebApp. But what about the process for actually carrying out the design? When should each of these design tasks be considered and to what depth?

To answer these questions, let's begin by looking at the overall Web engineering process and then see what this tells us about the design. In earlier chapters, we have noted that Web engineering produces a WebApp incrementally. The implication is that you can deliver increasingly more robust and complex levels of content and functionality to end users through a series of increments. The very nature of the Web facilitates this strategy in two ways.

First, the transition from one WebApp increment to a more robust increment is generally transparent to the user. Although work must occur on the part of the WebE team, no action is required at the end-user level.[12] It is therefore much more reasonable to adopt an incremental design and release strategy.

---

11 For example, we can have a particular navigation design that controls the way in which users interact with the WebApp, but this navigation is modified by functionality that adapts the WebApp for different users. It is important that in integrating the navigation and functional elements, overall integrity is maintained.

12 Contrast this to conventional software, where a new version requires reinstallation (and the complexities associated with it) that is often performed by the end user.

The second characteristic that facilitates an incremental process is more subtle. WebApp interfaces are partitioned into sequences of pages that are accessed through navigational pathways. This means that additional content and/or functionality can be added to an application with minimal disturbance to the existing content and functionality. The new increment may require a change to the existing WebApp that is as simple as a new link on a single page.

What Does an Incremental WebE Process Imply for the Design Activity?

During the communication and planning activities (Chapters 4 and 5) WebApp increments are described. During analysis modeling they are specified in more detail. The design tasks discussed in the earlier section "What Are the Elements of WebApp Design" must be applied to each increment. There is, however, an important preliminary or initial design step related to overall architectural integrity.

The sidebar discussion, conducted by members of the **SafeHomeAssured.com** WebE team, raises an important issue. Throughout this book, we emphasize the

---

SafeHome

Initial Design

The scene: SafeHomeAssured. com WebE team meeting room where the initial design meeting for increment 1, *Basic company and product information,* is being conducted

The players: The WebE team leader and two other members of the WebE team

The conversation:

Team member 1: Well, finally we can start to get our teeth into some actual design. It'll be good to see the first pieces of the WebApp start to take shape and to produce something that can be used.

Team member 2: Yeah, definitely. I was looking at the description for this first increment. It's pretty simple—just some basic information. A sort of "Hi, we're here" set of pages. I figure we can throw these together pretty quickly over the next week. A couple of pages sitting on a standard Apache Web server on a Linux box—simple really—and that also means that we can start using some nice version control software I found for Linux recently. I say we just dive into the design of the information.

Team leader: Hold on a minute. Sure, this first

increment is really simple—particularly since it doesn't really need any sophisticated hardware or server software, but if we make an arbitrary decision at this point on a particular platform just because it doesn't really matter, then we might get ourselves into trouble with a later increment when it does matter. Have you thought through what might be some of the higher-level architectural constraints imposed by other increments?

Team member 2 (frowning): No, not really. I didn't think it mattered.

Team leader: Well, consider the increment that does the space layout. The software that we use inhouse all runs on PCs and uses a bunch of proprietary libraries that I think are only available on a PC! If we lock ourselves into a Linux platform now, it could create all sorts of problems when we come to that particular increment.

Team member 1: Good point. I guess we need to start off thinking about the broader architecture. Once we get that right, we can dive into the specifics of any of the increments.

need for agility and suggest that it become a pivotal philosophy as WebApps are built. Further, some proponents of agile process models argue that developers should avoid building into the system anything that might be relevant to a future increment. The intent is to stay sharply focused on the increment to be delivered and not become sidetracked with "extraneous" detail.

There are, however, many situations in which a broader consideration of WebApp architectural issues is not only justified, but mandatory. Some agile approaches do try to address this to a limited extent, but others fail to emphasize the importance of architectural design and, as a result, major architectural problems can occur. For example, a key step in Extreme Programming (XP) [Bec99] [Bec05] is to develop a *system metaphor,* but this is intended to support developer communication and understanding during the design process, rather than ensuring application integrity.

This problem can be addressed by beginning the overall design with a consideration of the full set of increments (or at least as representative a sample as possible) and the consequent development of overall conceptual and technical architectures. Once the basic elements of these architectures are in place, the design and construction of each increment can begin.

This then results in the design process outlined in Figure 8.3. As can be seen from this figure the overall structure of the conceptual and technical architectures is initially developed, but the design of the relevant aspects of these architectures is deferred until it is needed for particular WebApp increments. As each WebApp increment is then designed, the interaction layers are designed, and these then inform the detailed design of the core architectural components and the informational and functional layers. Once these are in place, the relevant conceptual components of these design models can then be mapped into the technical design.

Initial Design of the Conceptual Architecture

The conceptual architecture provides an overall structure for the WebApp design. It represents the major functional and information components for the WebApp and describes how these will fit together. The specific architecture will be dependent on the nature of the WebApp, but in every case, it should ensure a sound integration between the WebApp information and the WebApp functionality.

High-level design activities for conventional software development often focus on the functional aspects of an application.[13] Essentially, a system architect tries to determine[14] the functional building blocks or subsystems that the system might

---

13 Object-oriented approaches are an exception—problem classes flow out of an analysis model and are coupled with methods that manipulate them.

14 *Intuit* might be a better word to describe the actual process, given that most authors view architectural design as a creative process.

FIGURE 8.3

The WebE design process.

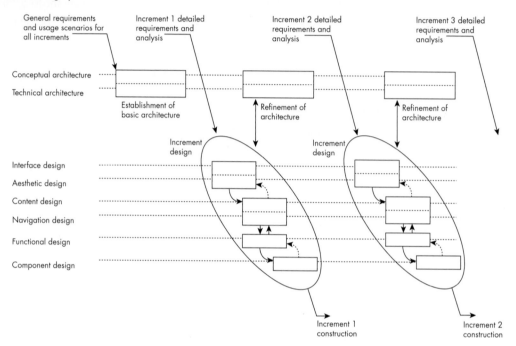

require. The result is often documented as a block diagram showing these subsystems and the interfaces between them.

When this process is applied to WebApps, it can be problematic. It properly identifies functional subsystems, but it often overlooks informational building blocks or only considers them quite peripherally. So how do you achieve an effective balance between information and functionality in the conceptual architecture?

A good place to start is with workflows or functional scenarios (which are an expression of the system functionality) and information flows (described in Chapter 7). If you look for commonalities across the workflows or key functionalities, you can identify the major functional components. If you look for commonalities across the information flows, then you can identify the major information components.

As a simple example, consider the following set of key functionalities for **SafeHomeAssured.com** (identified in Chapter 4):

- **Provide product quotation**
- **Process security system order**
- **Process user data**
- **Create user profile**
- **Draw user space layout**

- Recommend security system for layout
- Process monitoring order
- Get and display account info
- Get and display monitoring info
- Customer service functions (to be defined later)
- Tech support functions (to be defined later)

From these key functionalities we can identify the following partial list of *functional subsystems:*

- **UserManagement.** Manages all user functions, including user registration, authentication and profiling, user-specific content, and interface adaptation and customization.

- **ProductManagement.** Handles all product information, including pricing models and content management.

- **OrderHandling.** Supports the management of customer's orders.

- **AccountAdministration.** Manages customer's accounts, including invoicing and payment.

- **SecuritySystemSupport.** Manages user's space layout models and recommends security layouts.

- **SecuritySystemMonitoring.** Monitors customer's security systems and handles security events.

And, of course, there are overall management subsystems:

- **ClientInterface.** Provides the interface between users and the other subsystems, as required to satisfy user's needs.

- **SystemMaintenance.** Provides maintenance functionality, such as database cleaning.

Now, consider the content objects that were also introduced in Chapter 4:

- Company profile
- Product overview
- Product specifications
- Installation instructions
- Product database (includes pricing, items in inventory, shipping costs, etc.)
- Quotation templates
- Order forms
- Order entry database
- Layout image of user space
- User database (includes user identification, specialized security system configuration, other user-related info)
- Monitoring request form

- Monitoring "dashboard" for a contract user (includes account information, video window for monitoring, audio port for monitoring)
- Monitoring database
- Customer service dashboard (to be defined later)
- Tech support dashboard (to be defined later)

From this list we can identify a set of key *information components:*

- Users
- Company information
- Product information
- Quotations and orders
- Security system configurations (space models and system layouts)
- Security system data (dynamic monitoring information)

The challenge of architectural design is to link the functional subsystems and information components in an effective manner. To accomplish this, the WebApp designer develops a hybrid model that links functional components to the information that each component manipulates. The hybrid model also links users to the information and functions with which they interact.

Figure 8.4 shows an initial conceptual architecture for **SafeHomeAssured.com.** In this figure, the linkage between various functional subsystems and information components is shown. Several aspects of this architecture are worth noting. The first is that the only static pages that are included in the design are the company information pages. All remaining content is dynamically generated from underlying data sources to suit different users. This dynamic generation is carried out by the various functional subsystems. The second interesting aspect of the architecture is that the main client interface (which would incorporate the actual Web server at the technical architecture level) uses the various other subsystems to generate the required pages to deliver to the user. And finally, the **SafeHomeAssured.com** Web-App also incorporates global configuration files and style templates that govern the overall look and feel of the site.

The design of a conceptual architecture can be used to initiate the design process and to establish a starting point for the detailed design of each increment. The architecture would be refined and amended based on knowledge gained during later design tasks, but in essence it forms a baseline that should ensure reasonable integrity as each increment is developed.

Initial Design of the Technical Architecture

The conceptual architecture provides an overall structure for the WebApp design, and the *technical architecture* shows how this can be mapped into specific technical components. We'll discuss much more on the technical components in Chapters 12

FIGURE 8.4

Example (partial) **SafeHomeAssured.com** conceptual architecture.

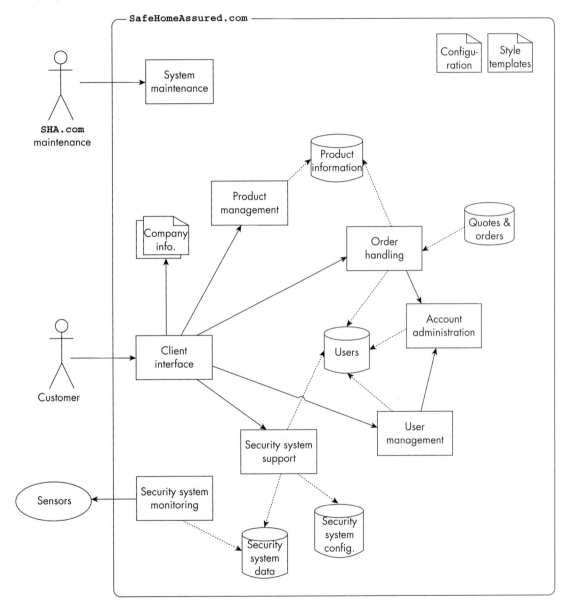

and 14. For now, it's worth noting various key issues that impact on the decisions made about the technical components.

Any decision made about how one component might map into the technical architecture will affect the decisions about other components. This can occur for a number of reasons, but it is often because a technical component provides broad-based support or puts constraints on other components. For example, the WebE team may choose to design **SafeHomeAssured.com** in a way that stores product information as XML files. Later, the team discovers that the content management system doesn't easily support access to XML content, but rather assumes that the content will be stored in a conventional relational database. One component of the technical architecture conflicts with constraints imposed by another component.

Many (possibly most) technical components are developed without a single narrow focus in mind. Rather, they are designed to be as broadly applicable as possible. Hence these components will often provide considerable flexibility, but also significant complexity. A fully blown commercial-strength content management system would obviously provide the functionality required for a simple static website, but would also provide much additional functionality that is not needed. This unnecessary functionality can then complicate the development—distracting the developers and requiring additional effort to manage. In some cases, a much simpler technical solution will be more appropriate.

Finally, the specific choices of technical components that make up the technical architecture depend not just on the specific needs imposed by the conceptual architecture, but also on the environment in which it will be operating (e.g., the WebApp hosting environment might be based on a Linux platform) and the skills of the development team.

Where We've Been . . . Where We're Going

WebApp design is a combination of art and engineering. To be effective, a good design must accommodate each of the requirements established by stakeholders during the communication activity. But it must also accommodate the inevitable changes to requirements that will occur throughout the design and into construction and delivery. Design begins by focusing on the way in which a user will interact with an application and then moves to consider the functions and information content that will be required to meet stakeholders' needs. It then proceeds to physical design, in which the logical elements are mapped into a representation that can be implemented as part of the WebApp. The primary output of the design activity is a design model that encompasses interface descriptions, aesthetics, content, navigation, architecture, and component-level design issues.

Every WebApp designer must be cognizant of a set of generic design goals: simplicity, consistency, identity, robustness, navigability, visual appeal, and compatibility. In addition, a variety of quality frameworks can be applied to WebApp design. These quality criteria provide a set of objectives for achieving WebApp design quality. In addition, a user-centric quality model provides a solid indication of the degree to which end users like the technology that the WebApp delivers. WebApp designers can apply a Design IQ Checklist that serves to assess the importance of various quality criteria and the degree to which the WebE team has met each of the criteria.

The design process is an agile, iterative collection of design actions that are applied to each WebApp increment as it is created. A design pyramid can be used to describe a set of design actions that are performed (with varying degrees of emphasis) for each WebApp increment. The design actions include interface design, aesthetic design, content design, navigation design, functional design, architecture design, and component design.

Each of the design actions represents a challenge for the WebE team. In the chapters that follow, we'll consider the mechanics of each design action in some detail.

References

[Bec99] Beck, K., *Extreme Programming Explained: Embrace Change,* Addison-Wesley, 1999.

[Bec05] Beck, K., and C. Andres, *Extreme Programming Explained: Embrace Change,* 2nd ed., Addison-Wesley, 2005.

[Cro07] Cross, M., *Developer's Guide to Web Application Security,* Syngress, 2007.

[Dav89] Davis, F. D., "Perceived Usefulness, Perceived Ease of Use, and User Acceptance of Information Technology," *MIS Quarterly,* vol. 13, no. 3, 1989, pp. 319–342.

[Das07] Daswani, N., et al., *Foundations of Security,* Apress, 2007.

[Kai02] Kaiser, J., "Elements of Effective Web Design," About, Inc., 2002, **http://webdesign.about.com/library/weekly/aa091998.htm** (accessed September 15, 2004).

[Kal03] Kalman, S., *Web Security Field Guide,* Cisco Press, 2003.

[Mil00] Miller, E., "The Website Quality Challenge," *Software Research, Inc.,* 2000, **www.soft.com/eValid/Technology/White.Papers/website.quality.challenge.html** (accessed July 31, 2007).

[Nie00] Nielsen, J., *Designing Web Usability,* New Riders Publishing, 2000.

[Off02] Offutt, J., "Quality Attributes of Web Software Applications," *IEEE Software,* March/April, 2002, pp. 25–32.

[Ols99]   Olsina, L. et al., "Specifying Quality Characteristics and Attributes for Web Sites," *Proc. 1st ICSE Workshop on Web Engineering*, ACM, Los Angeles, May 1999.

[Pow00] Powell, T., *Web Design*, McGraw-Hill/Osborne, 2000.

[Til00]   Tillman, H. N., "Evaluating Quality on the Net," *Babson College*, May 30, 2000, **www.hopetillman.com/findqual.html#2.**

[Ven00] Venkatesh, V., and F. D. Davis, "Theoretical Extension of the Technology Acceptance Model: Four Longitudinal Field Studies," *Management Science* vol. 46, no. 2, February 2000, pp. 186–204.

[Ven03] Venkatesh, V., M. G. Morris, G. B. Davis, and F. D. Davis, "User Acceptance of Information Technology: Toward a Unified View," *MIS Quarterly*, vol. 27, no. 3, 2003, pp. 425–478.

INTERACTION DESIGN

Every user interface—whether it is designed for a WebApp, a traditional software application, a consumer product, or an industrial device—should exhibit the following characteristics: easy to use, easy to learn, easy to navigate, intuitive, consistent, efficient, error-free, and functional. It should provide the end user with a satisfying and rewarding experience. Interface design concepts, principles, and methods provide a Web engineer with the tools required to achieve this list of attributes.

Interaction design for WebApps begins not with a consideration of technology or tools, but with a careful examination of the end user. During analysis modeling (Chapter 7), a user hierarchy was developed. Each user category may have subtly different needs, may want to interact with the WebApp in different ways, and may require unique functionality and content. This information is derived during the communication activity (Chapter 4), may be refined during analysis modeling, and is revisited as the first step in interaction design.

Dix [Dix99] argues that you should design an interface so that it answers three primary questions for the end user:

Where am I? The interface should (1) provide an indication of the WebApp that has been accessed[1], and (2) inform users of their location in the content hierarchy.

What can I do now? The interface should always help users understand their current options—what functions are available, what links are live, what content is relevant?

Where have I been, where am I going? The interface must facilitate navigation. Hence, it must provide a "map" (implemented in a way that is easy to understand) of where users have been and what paths they may take to move elsewhere within the WebApp.

An effective WebApp interface must provide answers for each of these questions as end users navigate through content and functionality.

---

1   Each of us has bookmarked a website page, only to revisit it later and have no indication of the website or the context for the page (as well as no way to move to another location within the site).

Interface Design Principles and Guidelines

The user interface of a WebApp is its "first impression." Regardless of the value of its content, the sophistication of its processing capabilities and services, and the overall benefit of the WebApp itself, a poorly designed interface will disappoint the potential user and may, in fact, cause the user to go elsewhere. Because of the sheer volume of competing WebApps in virtually every subject area, the interface must grab a potential user immediately.

Bruce Tognozzi [Tog01] defines a set of fundamental characteristics that all interfaces should exhibit and, in doing so, establishes a philosophy that should be followed by every WebApp interface designer:

> Effective interfaces are visually apparent and forgiving, instilling in their users a sense of control. Users quickly see the breadth of their options, grasp how to achieve their goals, and do their work.
>
> Effective interfaces do not concern the user with the inner workings of the system. Work is carefully and continuously saved, with full option for the user to undo any activity at any time.
>
> Effective applications and services perform a maximum of work, while requiring a minimum of information from users.

You might argue that everybody recognizes these things and every interface designer wants to achieve them. And yet, each of us has seen more than a few really bad interfaces and, surely, will continue to see many more.

What Principles Do We Apply to Design Effective Interfaces?

In order to design an effective interface, Tognozzi [Tog01] identifies a set of over-riding design principles:[2]

> **Anticipation.** *A WebApp should be designed so that it anticipates the user's next move.* For example, consider a customer support WebApp developed by a manufacturer of computer printers. A user has requested a content object that presents information about a printer driver for a newly released operating system. The designer of the WebApp should anticipate that the user might request a download of the driver and should provide navigation facilities that allow this to happen without requiring the user to search for this capability.
>
> **Communication.** *The interface should communicate the status of any activity initiated by the user.* Communication can be obvious (e.g., a text message)

---

2   Tognozzi's original principles have been adapted and extended for use in this book. See [Tog01] for further discussion of these principles.

or subtle (e.g., a sheet of paper moving through a printer to indicate that printing is under way). The interface should also communicate the user's status (e.g., the user's identification) and location within the WebApp content hierarchy.

Consistency. *The use of navigation controls, menus, icons, and aesthetics (e.g., color, shape, layout) should be consistent throughout the WebApp.* For example, if underlined blue text implies a navigation link, content should never incorporate blue underlined text that does *not* imply a link. In addition, an object, say a yellow triangle, used to indicate a caution message before the user invokes a particular function or action, should not be used for other purposes elsewhere in the WebApp. Finally, every feature of the interface should respond in a manner that is consistent with user expectations.[3]

Controlled autonomy. *The interface should facilitate user movement throughout the WebApp, but it should do so in a manner that enforces navigation conventions that have been established for the application.* For example, navigation to secure portions of the WebApp should be controlled by a user ID and a password, and there should be no navigation mechanism that enables a user to circumvent these controls.

Efficiency. *The design of the WebApp and its interface should optimize the user's work efficiency, not the efficiency of the Web engineer who designs and builds it or the client-server environment that executes it.* Tognozzi [Tog01] discusses this when he writes:

> This simple truth is why it is so important for everyone involved in a software project to appreciate the importance of making user productivity goal one and to understand the vital difference between building an efficient system and empowering an efficient user. This truth is also key to the need for close and constant cooperation, communication, and conspiracy between engineers and human interface designers if this goal is to be achieved.

Flexibility. *The interface should be flexible enough to enable some users to accomplish tasks directly and others to explore the WebApp in a somewhat random fashion.* In every case, it should enable users to understand where they are and provide users with the functionality to undo mistakes and retrace poorly chosen navigation paths.

Focus. *The WebApp interface (and the content it presents) should stay focused on the user task(s) at hand.* In all hypermedia there is a tendency to route the user to loosely related content. Why? Because it's very easy to do! The

---

3   Tognozzi [Tog01] notes that the only way to be sure that user expectations are properly understood is through comprehensive user testing (Chapter 16).

problem is that users can rapidly become lost in many layers of supporting information and lose sight of the original content that they wanted in the first place. The WebApp interface and its content should stay focused on whatever objective users must accomplish.

Fitt's law. *"The time to acquire a target is a function of the distance to and size of the target"* [Tog01]. Based on a study conducted in the 1950s [Fit54], Fitt's law "is an effective method of modeling rapid, aimed movements, where one appendage (like a hand) starts at rest at a specific start position, and moves to rest within a target area." If a sequence of selections or standardized inputs (with many different options within the sequence) is defined by a user task, the first selection (e.g., mouse pick) should be physically close to the next selection. For example, a WebApp home page interface for an e-commerce site that sells consumer electronics provides the following menu options:

> Get a gift suggestion
>
> Buy a product
>
> Comparison shop
>
> Ask a question
>
> Get technical support

Each of these options implies a set of follow-on user choices or actions. For example, the "Buy a product" option requires that the user enter a product category followed by the product name. The product category (e.g., audio equipment, televisions, DVD players) appears as a pull-down menu as soon as "Buy a product" is selected. The next choice is then immediately obvious (it is nearby), and the time to acquire it is negligible. If, on the other hand, the choice appeared on a menu that was located on the other side of the screen, the time for the user to acquire it (and then make the choice) would be far too long.

User interface objects. *A vast library of reusable human interface objects (and patterns) has been developed for WebApps. Use them.* Any interface object that can be "seen, heard, touched or otherwise perceived" [Tog01] by an end user can be acquired from any one of a number of object libraries.

Latency reduction. *Rather than making the user wait for some internal operation to complete (e.g., downloading a complex graphical image), the WebApp should use multitasking in a way that lets the user proceed with work as if the operation has been completed.* In addition to reducing latency, delays must be acknowledged so that the user understands what is happening. This includes (1) providing audio feedback (e.g., a click or bell tone) when a selection does not result in an immediate action by the WebApp, (2) displaying an animated clock or progress bar to indicate that processing is under way, and (3) providing some entertainment (e.g., an animation or text presentation) while lengthy processing occurs.

Learnability. *A WebApp interface should be designed to minimize learning time and, once learned, to minimize relearning required when the WebApp is revisited.* In general the interface should emphasize a simple, intuitive design that organizes content and functionality into categories that are obvious to the user.

Metaphors. *An interface that uses an interaction metaphor is easier to learn and easier to use, as long as the metaphor is appropriate for the application and the user.* A metaphor should call on images and concepts from the user's experience, but it does not need to be an exact reproduction of a real-world experience. For example, an e-commerce site that implements automated bill paying for a financial institution uses a checkbook metaphor (not surprisingly) to assist the user in specifying and scheduling bill payments. However, when "writing" a check, the user need not enter the complete payee name but can pick from a list of payees or have the system select a payee based on the first few typed letters. The metaphor remains intact, but the user gets an assist from the WebApp.

Maintain work product integrity. *A work product (e.g., a form completed by the user, a user-specified list) must be automatically saved so that it will not be lost if an error occurs.* Each of us has experienced the frustration associated with completing a lengthy WebApp form only to have the content lost because of an error (made by us, by the WebApp, or in transmission from client to server). To avoid this, a WebApp should be designed to auto-save all user-specified data. The interface should support this function and provide the user with an easy mechanism for recovering "lost" information.

Readability. *All information presented through the interface should be readable by young and old.* The interface designer should emphasize readable type styles, font sizes, and color background choices that enhance contrast.

Track state. *When appropriate, the state of user interactions should be tracked and stored so that users can log off and return later to pick up where they left off.* In general, cookies can be designed to store state information. However, cookies are a controversial technology, and other design solutions may be more palatable for some users.

Visible navigation. *A well-designed WebApp interface provides "the illusion that users are in the same place, with the work brought to them"* [Tog01]. When this approach is used, navigation is not a user concern. Rather, the user retrieves content objects and selects functions that are displayed and executed through the interface.

Each of these design principles is applied as the preliminary interface design is created and when the design is reviewed (see sidebar).

SafeHome

Interface Team Walkthrough

The scene: SafeHomeAssured.com team leader's office

The players: Team leader and two members of the WebE team

The conversation:

Team member 1 (to team leader): Have you had a chance to take a look at our preliminary interface design [Figure 7.9] for **SafeHome-Assured.com?**

Team leader: Yeah . . . I went through it from a technical point of view, and I have a bunch of notes. I e-mailed 'em to you this morning.

Team member 1: Haven't looked at my e-mail yet . . . give me a summary of the important issues.

Team leader: Overall, you've done a good job, nothing groundbreaking, but it's a typical interface, decent aesthetics, reasonable layout. You hit all the important functions . . .

Team member 2 (smiling ruefully): But?

Team leader: Well, there are a few things . . . .

Team member 1: Such as . . .

Team leader: You guys remember the very first iteration on the home page where the major functions displayed in the menu were

About the company
Describe your home
Get *SafeHome* component recommendations
Purchase a product
Get technical support

The problem was that we left out some things, and those functions weren't at the same level of abstraction. So we retooled the whole thing, and you came up with this [points at the preliminary prototype from Figure 7.9].

Team member 2 (smiling): I like it.

Team leader: So do I, but marketing wants greater emphasis on the company and wants distinct photos of the product and services. So . . . I think our main menu should be:

About the company
Home security
Monitoring services
Our technology
Contact us

There'll be lots of subfunctions under each of these major options. Might think about having them pop us as a submenu when the top-level option is chosen. Each of the submenu options will lead the user to a separate Web page with its own layout, content objects, and functions.

Team member 1: But don't we want to register users who want to go directly to pages that meet their needs? We have no direct mechanism to do that here.

Team leader: You're right. It might not be a bad idea to provide a log-in like we had on the previous interface prototype iteration. I'll run it past marketing, but I think we can proceed as is for now.

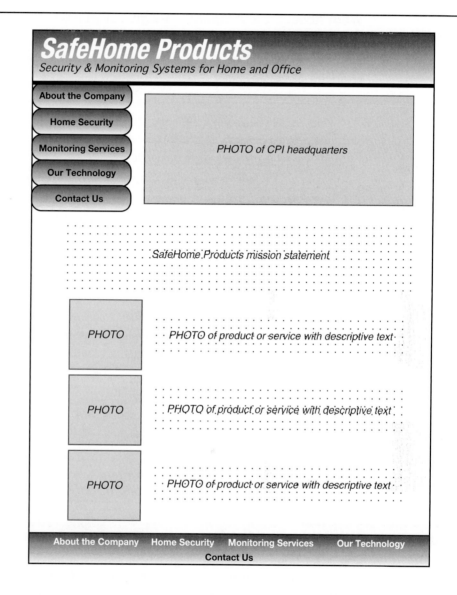

FIGURE 9.1

Home page preliminary design layout.

As a result of modifications suggested during the preliminary interface design review, the WebE team produces a new home page interface design,[4] as illustrated in Figure 9.1.

---

4 Recall that we noted that the preliminary interface design (Figure 7.9) would likely change as the WebE team moved further into design.

What About Some Pragmatic Design Guidelines?

Nielsen and Wagner [Nie96] suggest a few pragmatic interface design guidelines (based on their redesign of a major WebApp) that provide a nice complement to the principles suggested earlier:

- Reading speed on a computer monitor is approximately 25 percent slower than reading speed for hard copy. Therefore, *do not force the user to read voluminous amounts of text,* particularly when the text explains the operation of the WebApp or assists in navigation.

- *Avoid "under construction" signs*—they raise expectations and cause an unnecessary link that is sure to disappoint or frustrate users.

- *Users prefer not to scroll.* Important information should be placed within the dimensions of a typical browser window.

- *Navigation menus and head bars should be designed consistently and should be available on all pages that are available to the user.* The design should not rely on browser functions (e.g., the back arrow) to assist in navigation.

- *Aesthetics should never supersede functionality.* For example, a simple button might be a better navigation option than an aesthetically pleasing, but vague image or icon whose intent is unclear.

- *Navigation options should be obvious, even to the casual user.* The user shouldn't have to search the screen to determine how to link to other content or services.

A well-designed interface the improves the user's perception of the content or services provided by the site. It need not necessarily be flashy, but it should always be well structured and ergonomically sound.

Interface Design Workflow

Interface design for WebApps begins with the identification of user, task, and environmental requirements. These activities are performed as part of requirements gathering and modeling discussed earlier in this book. Once user tasks have been identified, user scenarios (use cases) are created and analyzed to define a set of interface objects and actions.

Information contained within the analysis model (Chapter 7) forms the basis for the creation of a screen layout that depicts graphical design and placement of icons, definition of descriptive screen text, specification and titling for windows, and specification of major and minor menu items. Tools are then used to prototype and ultimately implement the interface design model.

The following tasks represent a rudimentary workflow for WebApp interface design:

1. **Review user characteristics and categories, user tasks, use cases, and related information contained in the analysis model and refine as required.**

2. **Develop a rough design prototype of the WebApp interface layout.** An interface prototype (including the layout) may have been developed as part of the analysis modeling activity. If the layout already exists, it should be reviewed and refined as required. If the interface layout has not been developed, the WebE team should work with stakeholders to develop it at this time. A preliminary interface design for **SafeHomeAssured.com** (a modified version of the prototype created as part of analysis modeling) is shown in Figure 9.1.

3. **Map user objectives into specific interface actions.** For the vast majority of WebApps, the user will have a relatively small set of primary objectives (typically, between four and seven primary objectives). These should be mapped into specific interface actions as shown in Figure 9.2. In essence, the design must answer the following question: "How does the interface enable the user to accomplish each objective or provide the launching point for relevant tasks?"

4. **Define a set of user tasks that are associated with each action.** Each interface action (e.g., "Buy a product") is associated with a set of user tasks. These tasks have been identified during analysis. During design, they must

FIGURE 9.2

Mapping user objectives into interface actions.

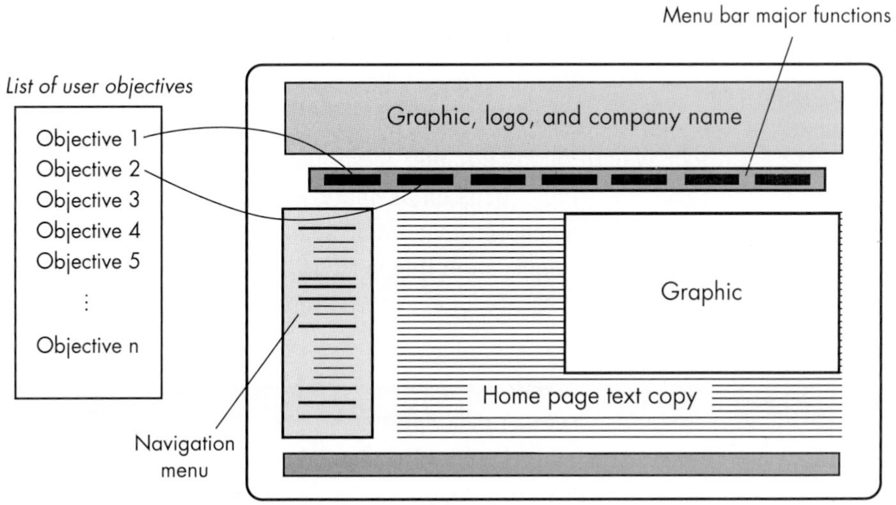

be mapped into specific interactions that encompass navigation issues, content objects, and WebApp functions.

5. **Develop screen images for each interface action.** As each action is considered, a sequence of screen images should be created to depict how the interface responds to user interaction. Content objects should be identified (even if they have not yet been designed and developed), WebApp functionality should be shown, and navigation links should be indicated.

6. **Refine interface layout and screen images using input from aesthetic design.** Web engineers complete a rough layout, but the aesthetic look and feel for a major commercial site is often developed by artistic, rather than technical, professionals—such as graphic designers. Aesthetic design (discussed later in this chapter) is integrated with the work performed by the interface designer.

7. **Identify user interface objects that are required to implement the interface.** This task may require a search through an existing class library to find those reusable objects (classes) that are appropriate for the WebApp interface. In addition, any custom classes are specified at this time.

8. **Develop a procedural representation of the user's interaction with the interface.** This optional task uses UML sequence diagrams and/or activity diagrams to depict the flow of activities (and decisions) that occurs as the user interacts with the WebApp.

9. **Develop a behavioral representation of the interface.** This optional task makes use of UML state diagrams to represent state transitions and the events that cause them. Control mechanisms (i.e., the objects and actions available to the user to alter a WebApp state) are defined.

10. **Describe the interface layout for each state.** Using design information developed in tasks 2 and 5, associate a specific layout or screen image with each WebApp state described in task 9.

Pair walkthroughs (Chapter 5) should be conducted throughout all these design tasks and should focus on usability. In addition, it's important to note that the design workflow chosen by a WebE team should be adapted to the special requirements of the application that is to be built. Therefore, all 10 design tasks may not always be necessary for every WebApp interface.

Interface Design Preliminaries

A key tenet of the WebE process model is this: *You'd better understand the problem before you attempt to design a solution.* In the case of interface design, understanding the problem means understanding (1) the people (end users) who will interact with the system through the interface, (2) the tasks that end users must perform to do their work, (3) the content that is presented as part of the interface, and (4) the environment in which these tasks will be conducted. In the sections that follow, we examine each of these elements of interface analysis[5] with the intent of establishing a solid foundation for the design tasks that follow.

How Do We Understand the Characteristics of WebApp Users?

The phrase *user interface* is probably all the justification needed to spend some time understanding the user before worrying about technical matters. Each user has a mental image of the WebApp that may be different from the mental image developed by other users. In addition, the user's mental image may be vastly different from your design model. The only way that you can get the mental image and the design model to converge is to work to understand the users themselves as well as how these people will use the system.[6] Information from a broad array of sources can be used to accomplish this:

User interviews. The most direct approach is for members of the WebE team to meet with end users to better understand their needs, motivations, work culture, and a myriad of other issues. This can be accomplished in one-on-one meeting or through focus groups.

Sales input. Salespeople can meet with the customer and users on a regular basis and can gather information that will help the WebE team to categorize users and better understand their requirements.

Marketing input. Market analysis can be invaluable in the definition of market segments and an understanding of how each segment might use the software in subtly different ways.

Support input. Support staff can have discussions with users on a daily basis. They are the most likely source of information on what works and what doesn't, what users like and what they dislike, what features generate questions, and what features are easy to use.

The following set of questions (adapted from [Hac98]) will help you to better understand the users of a WebApp in a business setting:

- Are users trained professionals, technicians, clerical or manufacturing workers?

---

5   Some or all of these activities may have already been conducted as part of the communication activity (Chapter 4) or analysis modeling (Chapter 7).

6   Much, if not all, of the information about users and their needs should really be collected during requirements gathering and analysis. If these Web engineering actions have been performed properly, you will have enough information to understand the user. However, there are times when you must derive this information.

- What level of formal education does the average user have?
- Are the users capable of learning from written materials, or have they expressed a desire for classroom or mentor-based training?
- Are users expert typists or keyboard-phobic?
- What is the age range of the user community?
- Will the users be represented predominately by one gender?
- How are users compensated for the work they perform?
- Do users work normal office hours, or do they work until the job is done?
- Is the WebApp to be an integral part of the work users do, or will it be used only occasionally?
- What is the primary spoken language among users? What domain-specific language is used?
- What are the consequences if a user makes a mistake using the system?
- Are users experts in the subject matter that is addressed by the system?
- Do users want to know about the technology that sits behind the interface?

The answers to these and similar questions will allow you to understand who the end users are, what is likely to motivate and please them, how they can be grouped into different user classes or profiles, what their mental models of the system are, and how the user interface must be characterized to meet their needs.

How Do We Elaborate the Content Objects That Are Identified?

An interface designer also examines usage scenarios and other information obtained from the user and extracts the content objects that are manipulated by the tasks that the user performs. These objects can be categorized into classes. Attributes of each class are defined, and an evaluation of the actions applied to each object provide you with a list of operations.

In Chapter 7, we defined a data tree (Figure 7.5) for a **SafeHomeAssured.com** content object called **Component.** If you have responsibility for interface design you would examine the content object and use the description of **Component** to help in the layout of the interface. You should recognize that all users will have an interest in the object **Component** and will view it as a product specification for some component of *SafeHome.* Key content that must be presented via the interface include the product name, serial number, part category, description, price, photo, technical description, and other related information.

You then create the layout shown in Figure 9.3. This Web page is the template for each product specification. Note that the form of the page remains identical to

FIGURE 9.3

Security
products page
layout.

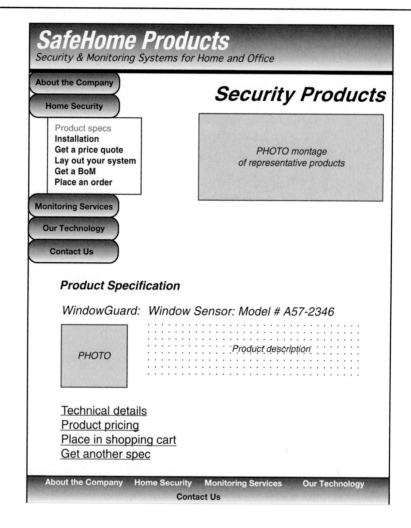

Figure 9.1, though navigation menus[7] are expanded to reflect the tasks that will be applied to the **Component** (product specification) content object. The product name, category, part number, description, and photo are represented as shown in the figure.

Applying the design principles discussed earlier in this chapter, the interface design encourages ease of understanding and use. For example, rather than

---

7 You have chosen to use pull-down navigation menus for subfunctions (e.g., "Product specs," "Installation," "Get a price quote"), while always allowing the user to have access to major functions that were presented on the home page.

providing technical details directly, the user can navigate to them (not every user has an interest and their inclusion would make the page very busy) via the "Technical details" navigation link. Other product specification-related navigation links— "Product pricing," "Place in shopping cart," and "Get another spec"— are shown in the lower left-hand corner of the page.

What Tasks Do the Users Perform?

In Chapters 4 and 7, we emphasized the need to obtain answers to the following questions:

- What work will the user perform in specific circumstances?
- What tasks and subtasks will be performed as the user does the work?
- What specific problem domain objects will the user manipulate as work is performed?
- What is the sequence of work tasks—the workflow?
- What is the hierarchy of tasks?

Hopefully, these questions have been answered before design commences.

In earlier chapters we noted that the use case describes the manner in which an actor (in the context of user interface design, an actor is always a person) interacts with a system. When used as part of task analysis, the use case is developed to show how an end user performs some specific work-related task. In most instances, the use case is written in an informal style (a simple paragraph) in the first person.

As a result of requirements gathering (Chapter 4), the **SafeHomeAssured.com** WebE team defined an increment named *Develop a layout from the space to be monitored.* The interface designer reviews the use case for this increment:

Use case: *Develop a layout for the space to be monitored*
Actor: Any user
Description: I want to configure a security system by first representing the layout of a "space" (i.e., house, office/retail space) in which the security sensors and monitoring devices are to be installed. To accomplish this, I must be able to use a "drafting tool box" that will allow me to draw walls, windows, and doors for the floor plan. I must be able to specify dimensions for walls, doors, and windows; orient them properly; and represent security sensors and monitoring devices as required. Each of these drawing elements (walls, windows, doors, sensors, monitoring devices) must be capable of being moved and rotated. I want to be able to have SafeHomeAssured.com analyze the floor plan layout I develop and recommend sensor and monitoring device placement. I want to save a floor plan by name, retrieve it at a later time, edit it, and delete it. Once the floor plan and sensor placement are complete, I want to be able to order the configuration of sensors and monitoring devices. All of these actions must be secure.

This use case provides a basic description of the interface for the floor plan layout. From it, you can extract tasks, objects, and the overall flow of the interaction. In addition, extended WebApp features that might please the user can also be conceived. For example, multifloor spaces were not explicitly mentioned in the use case but are essential for a complete floor plan layout capability. You recognize this and provide additional functionality. The resultant interface design for the floor plan layout is shown in Figure 9.4.

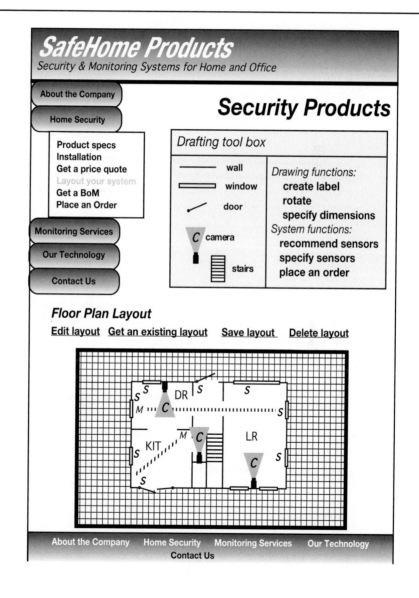

How Do We Elaborate the Tasks That Are Identified?

Task analysis can be applied in two ways. As we have already noted, a WebApp is often used to replace stand-alone software or a manual or semiautomated activity. To understand the tasks that must be performed to accomplish the goal of the activity, you must understand the tasks that humans currently perform (when using the existing approach) and then map these into a similar (but not necessarily identical) set of tasks that are implemented in the context of the WebApp user interface. Alternatively, you can study the known requirements (including use cases) for the WebApp and derive a set of user tasks.

Regardless of the overall approach to task analysis, as a designer you must define and classify tasks. One approach is stepwise elaboration. For example, let's reconsider the use case *Develop a layout for the space to be monitored.* This use case explicitly cites a number of major tasks and implies a larger number of subtasks. Each major task can be elaborated into subtasks that are implemented as part of the interface. For example, consider the following use case excerpt:

I must be able to use a "drafting tool box" that will allow me to draw walls, windows, and doors for the floor plan. I must be able to specify dimensions for walls, doors, and windows; orient them properly; and represent security sensors and monitoring devices as required. Each of these drawing elements (walls, windows, doors, sensors, monitoring devices) must be capable of being moved and rotated.

Referring to Figure 9.4, a **DraftingToolBox** (a content object) is implemented in the interface design. Within **DraftingToolBox,** drawing subfunctions—*Create a label, Rotate,* and *Specify dimensions* are noted explicitly. Functions that enable the user "to draw walls, windows, and doors for the floor plan" must be implemented but are not explicitly named in the interface. To accomplish the drawing function, **Wall, Window,** and **Door** objects are dragged and dropped to form the floor plan grid toward the bottom of the interface layout.

Other system functions—*Recommend sensors* and *Specify sensors*—imply a collection of complex functional components that implement specialized algorithms to perform those functions. These functional components are initiated when the user selects the appropriate link within **DraftingToolBox.**

The "Place an order" link allows the user to navigate to the e-commerce section of the **SafeHomeAssured.com** WebApp. However, internal data structures must be created to store the list of all sensors and monitoring devices that have been manually specified or automatically recommended. This data structure will then be used to develop a bill of materials and a price quote that are necessary to complete an order.

The interface design should be reviewed against the use case to ensure that each explicit and implicit user task is adequately addressed. As design work proceeds, the model of the interface should accommodate each of the tasks in a way that is consistent with the *user model* (the profile of a typical WebApp user) and *system perception* (what the user expects from the WebApp).

How Do We Design for Different Users with Different Roles?

When a number of different users, each playing different roles, makes use of a user interface, it is sometimes necessary to go beyond task analysis and object elaboration and apply *workflow analysis.* This technique allows you to understand how a work process is completed when several people (and roles) are involved. Consider a drug company that intends to implement a system that fully automates the process of prescribing and delivering prescription drugs. The entire process[8] will revolve around a Web-based application that is accessible by physicians (or their assistants), pharmacists, and patients. Workflows can be represented effectively with a UML swimlane diagram (a variation on the activity diagram)—particularly where there are multiple users or other entities participating in the interaction.

We consider only a small part of the work process—the situation that occurs when a patient asks for a refill. Figure 9.5 presents a swimlane diagram that indicates the tasks and decisions for each of the three roles noted in the preceding paragraph. This information may have been elicited via interview or from use cases written by each actor. Regardless, the flow of events (shown in the figure) enables the interface designer to recognize a number of key interface characteristics:

1. Each user implements different tasks via the interface; therefore, the look and feel of the interface designed for the patient will be different from the one designed for pharmacists or physicians.

2. The interface design for pharmacists and physicians must accommodate access to and display of information from secondary information sources (e.g., access to inventory for the pharmacist and access to information about alternative medications for the physician).

3. Many of the activities noted in the swimlane diagram can be further elaborated using task analysis and/or object elaboration (e.g., *Fills prescription* could imply a mail-order delivery, a visit to a pharmacy, or a visit to a special drug distribution center).

As the interface is analyzed, the process of elaboration continues. Once the workflow has been established, a task hierarchy can be defined for each user type. The hierarchy is derived by a stepwise elaboration of each task identified for the user. For example, consider the user task *Requests that a prescription be refilled.* The following task hierarchy is developed:

---

8 This example has been adapted from [Hac98].

FIGURE 9.5

Swimlane
diagram for
prescription refill
function.

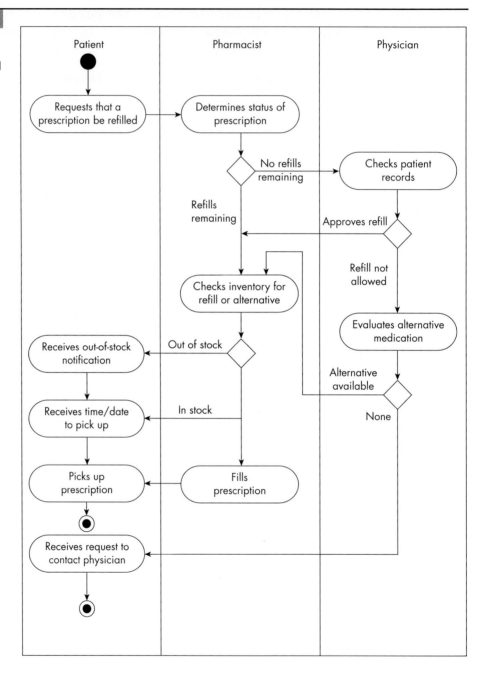

Requests that a prescription be refilled

- *Provide identifying information*
  - ○ *Specify name*
  - ○ *Specify userID*
  - ○ *Specify PIN and password*
- *Specify prescription number*
- *Specify date and time refill is required*

To complete the *Requests that a prescription be refilled* tasks, three subtasks are defined. One of these subtasks, Provide identifying information, is further elaborated in three additional sub-subtasks.

How Is Content Integrated into the Interface Description?

The user tasks we identified in the preceding section ("How Do We Design for Different Users with Different Roles?") lead to the presentation of a variety of different types of content. For modern applications, display content can range from character-based reports (e.g., a spreadsheet), graphical displays (e.g., a histogram, a 3D model, a picture of a person), or specialized information (e.g., audio or video files). Content objects may be (1) generated by components (unrelated to the interface) in other parts of the WebApp, (2) acquired from data stored in a database that is accessible from the application, or (3) transmitted from systems external to the WebApp.

The format and aesthetics of the content (as it is displayed by the interface) must be considered as part of interface design. Some of the questions you should consider are as follows:

- Are different types of data assigned to consistent geographic locations on the screen (e.g., do photos always appear in the upper right-hand corner)?
- Can the user customize the screen location for content?
- Is proper on-screen identification assigned to all content?
- If a large report is to be presented, how should it be partitioned for ease of understanding?
- Will mechanisms be available for moving directly to summary information for large collections of data?
- Will graphical output be scaled to fit within the bounds of the display device that is used?
- How will color be used to enhance understanding?
- How will error messages and warnings be presented to the user?

As each question is answered, the design requirements for content presentation are established.

Interface Design Steps

Once design preliminaries have been completed, all tasks (or objects and actions) required by the end user have been identified in detail and the interface design activity commences. Interface design, like all WebE design, is an iterative process. Each user interface design step occurs a number of times, each elaborating and refining information developed in the preceding step.

Although many different user interface design models have been proposed, all suggest some combination of the following steps:

1. Using information developed during design preliminaries, define interface objects and actions (operations).

2. Define events (user actions) that will cause the state of the user interface to change. Model this behavior.

3. Depict each interface state as it will actually look to the end user. Create an aesthetic, and lay out all navigation mechanisms, content objects, and related information.

4. Indicate how the user interprets the state of the system from information provided through the interface.

In some cases, you may begin with sketches of each interface state (i.e., what the user interface looks like under various circumstances) and then work backward to define objects, actions, and other important design information. Regardless of the sequence of design tasks, you should: (1) always follow the design principles and guidelines discussed earlier in this chapter, (2) model how the interface will be implemented, and (3) consider the environment (e.g., display technology, operating system, development tools) that will be used.

How Are Interface Objects and Actions Translated into a Layout?

Once interface objects and actions have been defined and elaborated iteratively, they are categorized by type. Target, source, and application objects are identified. A *source object* (e.g., a report icon) is dragged and dropped onto a *target object* (e.g., a printer icon). The implication of this action is to create a hard-copy report. An *application object* represents application-specific data that are not directly manipulated as part of screen interaction. For example, a mailing list is used to store names for a mailing. The list itself might be sorted, merged, or purged (menu-based actions), but it is not dragged and dropped via user interaction.

SafeHome

Designing a Layout

The scene: The Web engineering area at *CPI Corporation*

The players: Two members of the **SafeHome-Assured.com** team working as a pair, who are designing the page layout for the use case, *Access camera surveillance via the Internet*

The conversation:

Team member 1: This use case we have from analysis doesn't provide us with a lot of detail.

Team member 2: Agreed, but it's probably enough to get started. We'll have to elaborate as required.

Team member 1: Will marketing be around if we have questions?

Team member 2: They better be. They're part of the team.

[Team member 1 draws a sketch for the camera surveillance page (Figure 9.6).]

Team member 1: Whaddaya think?

Team member 2: Well . . . I think we need to make some mods. First, look at this use case. They

explicitly want to select the camera, sensors, etc., from the floor plan. I don't see a floor plan.

Team member 1: I thought it would complicate the page, and besides, it'll be more work to implement. I used a list of camera and other sensors . . . we could add their location . . . same thing.

Team member 2: Nah, it isn't, and besides, we have to work with the use cases we have.

Team member 1 (sighs): Alright, you have a point. Then we've got to parse the use case and pick out key content objects and the operations that we'll need to manipulate them and then, what?

Team member 2: We need to be sure that all the content objects appear within the interface design and that all the operations are implemented in some manner.

Team member 1: You know, I just noticed that we're not providing any way to control camera functions, you know, on/off, pan/zoom.

Team member 2: That's one of the ops we have to implement.

[Both team members work on a revised sketch that is a precursor to Figure 9.7.]

When you are satisfied that all important objects and actions have been defined (for one design iteration), perform the screen layout. Like other interface design activities, screen layout is an iterative process in which graphical design and placement of icons, definition of descriptive screen text, design and placement of navigation mechanisms, specification and titling for windows, and definition of major and minor menu items are conducted. If a real-world metaphor is appropriate for the application, it is specified at this time and the layout is organized in a manner that complements the metaphor.

To provide a brief illustration of the design steps noted previously, we revisit a **SafeHomeAssured.com** function called *Access camera surveillance via the Internet*. The stakeholder who takes on the role of the **HomeOwner** actor might write the following use case:

Use case: *Access camera surveillance via the Internet*
Actor: HomeOwner

FIGURE 9.6

Preliminary
sketch for the
*Camera Surveil-
lance* interface.

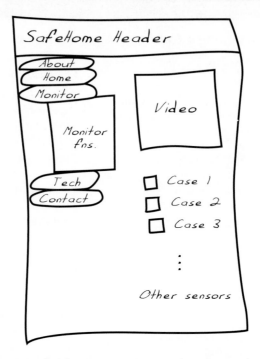

Narrative: If I'm at a remote location, I can use any PC with appropriate browser software to log on to the ***SafeHomeAssured.com*** website. I enter my user ID and two levels of passwords, and once I'm validated, I have access to all functionality for my installed *SafeHome* system. To access a specific camera view, I select "Surveillance" from the menu options displayed. I then select "Pick a camera," and the floor plan is displayed. I then select the camera that I'm interested in. Alternatively, I can look at thumbnail snapshots from all cameras simultaneously by selecting "All cameras" as my viewing choice. Once I choose a camera, I select "View" and a camera view appears in a viewing window that is identified by the camera ID. I can pan and zoom the camera I have selected. If I want to switch cameras, I again select "Pick a camera" and the original viewing window disappears. I then select the camera that I'm interested in. A new viewing window appears.

Based on this use case, the following homeowner tasks, objects, and data items are identified:

- *Accesses* the **SafeHome** system
- *Enters* an **ID** and **Password** to allow remote access
- *Displays* **FloorPlan** and **SensorLocations**
- *Displays* **VideoCameraLocations** on floor plan
- *Selects* **VideoCamera** for viewing
- *Views* **VideoImages** (four frames per second)
- *Pans* or *zooms* the **VideoCamera**

Objects (boldface) and actions (italics) are extracted from this list of user tasks.

A preliminary design layout of the screen layout for video monitoring is created (Figure 9.7).[9] To invoke the video image, a video camera location icon, *C*, located in the floor plan displayed in the monitoring window is selected. In this case, a camera location in the living room (LR) is selected. The video image window appears, displaying a video from the camera located in the living room. The zoom and pan control slides are used to control the magnification and direction of the video image. To select a view from another camera, the user selects "Pick a camera" from the menu and a new video window replaces the original.

The preliminary design layout for the interface shown in Figure 9.7 would have to be supplemented with additional figures (sketches) representing the expansion of each menu item within the menu bar, indicating what actions are available for each monitoring services mode (state). After review of the preliminary design, two issues arise:

- The zoom and pan sliders should be placed immediately below the video window.

- Stakeholders would like to have the capability to record the streaming video, and replay it.[10]

Given these issues, the preliminary design is revised as shown in Figure 9.8.

What About the Design of Navigation Mechanisms for the Interface?

As we noted earlier in this chapter, the objectives of a WebApp interface are to: (1) establish a consistent window into WebApp content and functionality, (2) guide the user through a series of interactions with the WebApp, and (3) organize the navigation options and content available to the user. To achieve a consistent interface, you should first use aesthetic design (considered in the section "Aesthetic Design" that follows) to establish a coherent look for the interface. This encompasses many characteristics, but must emphasize the layout and form of navigation mechanisms. To guide user interaction, you may draw on an appropriate metaphor[11] that enables the user to gain an intuitive understanding of the interface. To implement navigation options, you can select from one of a number of interaction mechanisms:

---

9   Note that this differs somewhat from the implementation of these features in earlier chapters. This might be considered a first-draft design and represents one alternative that might be considered.

10 This represents a new feature for the WebApp and would have to be negotiated to ensure that increment delivery dates can be maintained or adjusted.

11 In this context, a *metaphor* is a representation (drawn from the user's real-world experience) that can be modeled within the context of the interface. A simple example might be a slider switch that is used to control the auditory volume of an .mpg file.

- **Navigation menus.** Key word menus (organized vertically or horizontally) list key content and/or functionality. These menus may be implemented so that the user can choose from a hierarchy of subtopics that is displayed when the primary menu option is selected. Referring to Figure 9.8, the key word menus are organized vertically on the left of the Web page. Selecting a major function (e.g., monitoring services) causes a submenu to appear as

FIGURE 9.7

Preliminary design layout for the monitoring services interface.

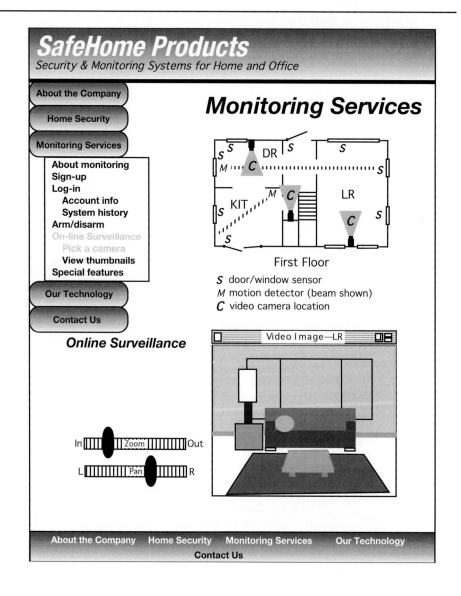

shown. The subfunctions contained within the menu can then be selected to meet the user's needs.

- **Graphic icons.** Buttons, switches, and similar graphical images enable the user to select some property or specify a decision. Referring again to Figure 9.8, the slide switches and recorder controls for the video image are graphic icons that are consistent with a video metaphor.

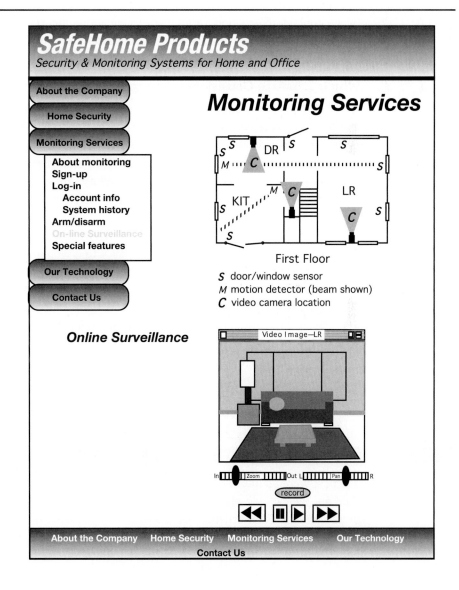

- **Graphic images.** Graphical representations are selectable by the user and implement a links to content objects or WebApp functionality. In Figures 9.7 and 9.8, the floor plan layout contains a variety of graphical images (e.g., the camera icon) that can be selected by the user.

One or more of these control mechanisms should be provided at every level of the content hierarchy.

It is important to distinguish between the layout of navigation mechanisms (an interface design issue) and the design of navigation for the WebApp. Navigation design, discussed in Chapter 10, focuses on the semantics of the navigational flow between content objects and for all WebApp functions. Interface design implements the semantics using a syntax of navigation mechanisms (menus, icons, images).

Why Is Interface Consistency So Important?

A well-designed WebApp interface should be both internally and externally consistent. As we have already noted, *internal consistency* demands that the aesthetics of each Web page have the same look and feel, that navigation mechanisms are used in a uniform manner, that content objects have the same fundamental design characteristics, and that input and output from WebApp functions exhibit a regularity that is predictable and pleasing. Internal consistency allows the user to develop an interactive rhythm that leads to high ratings for usability.

But internal consistency is not enough. The WebApp must also exhibit *external consistency.* Like it or not, the typical visitor to a WebApp will not spend much time there. It's likely that the visitor will arrive after visiting other websites and will leave to travel to still other WebApps. As Nielsen [Nie00] notes: ". . . users feel that they are using the Web as a whole rather than any specific site." It is for this reason that your WebE team must abide by current interface design conventions, making your WebApp's interface conventions consistent with those used across the Web. If you don't (after all, each of us likes to be creative and think outside the box), you risk alienating visitors who may not have the time or the inclination to learn a new interaction paradigm.

Aesthetic Design

The best WebApp interfaces are efficient in their presentation of content and function, but they should also be aesthetically pleasing. Aesthetic design, also called *graphic design,* is an artistic endeavor that complements the technical aspects of both interface design and content design. Without it, a WebApp may be useful, but

unappealing. With it, a WebApp draws its users into a world
a visceral, as well as an intellectual level.

But what is aesthetic? There is an old saying, "beauty exi
holder." This is particularly appropriate when aesthetic desig
sidered. To perform effective aesthetic design, we again retur ......erarchy
developed as part of the analysis model (Chapter 7) and ask, "Who are the WebApp's
users, and what WebApp look do they desire?"

How Do We Create an Aesthetically Pleasing Layout?

Every Web page has a limited amount of "real estate" that can be used to support
nonfunctional aesthetics, navigation features, informational content, and user-
directed functionality. The development of this real estate is planned during aesthetic design.

Like all aesthetic issues, there are no absolute rules when screen layout is
designed. However, a number of general layout guidelines are worth considering:

- **Don't be afraid of white space.** It is inadvisable to pack every square
  inch of a Web page with information. The resulting clutter makes it difficult for the user to identify needed information or features and creates
  visual chaos that is not pleasing to the eye. Referring back to Figure 9.3,
  the designer has chosen to provide a navigation link to content describing
  technical details rather than incorporating this content on the existing page.
  The reason is to keep the page from becoming too busy and preserve white
  space.

- **Emphasize content.** After all, that's the reason the user is there. Nielsen
  [Nie00] suggests that the typical Web page should be 80 percent content
  with the remaining real estate dedicated to navigation and other features.
  Referring back to Figure 9.1, the **SafeHomeAssured.com** home page is almost
  all content, providing the user with a picture of what *SafeHome* products
  are about.

- **Organize layout elements from top-left to bottom-right.** The vast
  majority of users will scan a Web page in much the same way as they scan
  the page of a book—top-left to bottom-right. If layout elements have specific
  priorities, high-priority elements should be placed in the upper-left portion
  of the page real estate.

- **Group navigation, content, and functionality geographically within
  the page.** Humans look for patterns in virtually all things. If there are no
  discernable patterns within a Web page, user frustration is likely to increase

(due to unnecessary searching for needed information). The interface design (e.g., Figure 9.3) for **SafeHomeAssured.com** places all major functions in the upper left-hand corner and has all content presented left to right and top to bottom.

- **Don't extend your real estate with the scrolling bar.** Although scrolling is often necessary (especially once you drill down to the detailed content pages), most studies indicate that users would prefer not to scroll. It is better to reduce page content or to present necessary content on multiple pages. The interface designer for the **SafeHomeAssured.com** WebApp violates this rule (it may be necessary to scroll to certain functionality or content), arguing that necessary content overrides a desire to limit scrolling.

- **Consider resolution and browser window size when designing the layout.** Rather than defining fixed sizes within a layout, the design should specify all layout items as a percentage of available space [Nie00].

- **Design the layout for freedom of navigation.** The generic layout of all WebApp pages should assume that the user will navigate to the page in ways that are not expected (e.g., via a direct link from a search engine). The layout should be designed to accommodate unpredictable arrival without confusion (on the part of the user). It is also important to ensure that a user is not allowed to navigate to a secure page without first passing through security validation. For example, if a visitor tried to navigate directly to the **SafeHomeAssured.com** monitoring services page shown in Figure 9.8, the visitor would be redirected automatically to the *log-in* page.

- **Don't assume that the layout will be consistent across different display devices and browsers.** Design the layout so that it is effective on both large and small displays, using features that are properly translated on the majority of popular browsers.

- **If you use photos, make them small format with the option to enlarge.** Large JPEG files can take time to download. Most users will be satisfied with a thumbnail photo as long as they have the option to look at a larger version.

- **If you want a cohesive layout, look, and feel across all WebApp pages, use a cascading style sheet (CSS).** A CSS allows you to specify one look and feel (e.g., font type, size, and style) across all Web pages. Just as important, the CSS lets you modify the look and feel across all pages by making changes to only one file.

Nielson [Nie00] suggests an interesting design exercise when he states: ". . . go through your design elements and remove them one at a time. If your design works without a certain element, kill it. Simplicity always wins over complexity . . ."

SAFEHOME

Reviewing the Aesthetic Design

The scene: The Web engineering area at CPI Corporation

The players: Two members of the **SafeHome-Assured.com** team working as a pair, who are conducting a pair walkthrough on the aesthetic design of the product specification page (Figure 9.3)

The conversation:

Team member 1 (looking at Figure 9.3): I'm generally pleased with this. It seems to work.

Team member 2: I've been thinking about it, and we have some aesthetic problems.

Team member 1: What problems? Functions are delineated nicely top-left. We use plenty of white space. The product info is easy to find on the page.

Team member 2 (gently interrupting): I'm not so sure that the product info is easy to find. Users working on a small screen will have to scroll to see it. Worse, they'll have to scroll to see the links to technical details, product pricing, and so on.

Team member 1 (thinking for a moment): Yeah, you're right about the scrolling. What if we get rid of the photo montage and move the product specification content upward on the page?

Team member 2: That'd work, but we have to be sure we don't crowd stuff. Remember, white

space. [She pauses for a moment.] There's something else.

Team member 1 (interrupting): Before you get to it, I just noticed something. We never provided a mechanism for increasing the size of the component photo. I'll note it so we can make the change. What were you going to say?

Team member 2: Aesthetically, I think we can do a better job with the links to technical details, product pricing, etc. Right now, they're very basic and visually unappealing, don't you think?

Team member 1: Actually, you're right, and the fact that they're low on the page and removed from the other functions is not the best. Maybe what we need to do is create a third level of functionality that pops up once "Product Specs" is chosen.

Team member 2: I like that. All functions appear upper-left. But we have to be sure that the functional hierarchy doesn't become too busy.

Team member 1: It's doable, but the functional hierarchy has to appear on all pages where it's needed—consistency and all that.

Team member 2: We've got a few changes to make.

Team member 1: Piece of cake.

What Leads to an Effective Graphic Design?

Graphic design considers every aspect of the look and feel of a WebApp. The graphic design process begins with layout and proceeds into a consideration of global color schemes, text types, sizes, and styles; the use of supplementary media (e.g., audio, video, animation); and all other aesthetic elements of an application.

A comprehensive discussion of graphic design issues for WebApps is beyond the scope of this book. You can obtain design tips and guidelines from many websites that are dedicated to the subject. For example,

Design & Publishing eZine	**www.graphic-design.com**
Grantastic Designs	**www.grantasticdesigns.com**
Web Page Design for Designers	**www.wpdfd.com**

or from one or more print resources (e.g., [Bag01], [Clo01], or [Hei02]).

Usability

In an insightful paper on usability, Larry Constantine [Con95] asks a question that has significant bearing on the subject: "What do users want, anyway?" He answers this way:

> What users really want are good tools. All software systems, from operating systems and languages to data entry and decision support applications, are just tools. End users want from the tools we engineer for them much the same as we expect from the tools we use. They want systems that are easy to learn and that help them do their work. They want software that doesn't slow them down, that doesn't trick or confuse them, that doesn't make it easier to make mistakes or harder to finish the job.

Constantine argues that usability is not derived from aesthetics, state-of-the-art interaction mechanisms, or built-in interface intelligence. Rather, it occurs when the architecture of the interface fits the needs of the people who will be using it.

A formal definition of usability is somewhat illusive. Donahue and his colleagues [Don99] define it in the following manner: "Usability is a measure of how well a computer system . . . facilitates learning; helps learners remember what they've learned; reduces the likelihood of errors; enables them to be efficient, and makes them satisfied with the system."

The only way to determine whether "usability" exists within a WebApp you are building is to conduct a usability review once the interface design has been established. Watch users interact with the WebApp design prototype, and answer the following questions [Con95]:

- Is the WebApp usable without continual help or instruction?
- Do the rules of interaction and navigation help a knowledgeable user work efficiently?

- Do interaction and navigation mechanisms become n
  become more knowledgeable?
- Has the WebApp been tuned to the physical and social
  it will be used?
- Are users aware of the state of the WebApp? Do users know where they are
  at all times?
- Is the interface structured in a logical and consistent manner?
- Are interaction and navigation mechanisms, icons, and procedures consis-
  tent across the interface?
- Does the interaction anticipate errors and help users correct them?
- Is the interface tolerant of errors that are made?
- Is the interaction simple?

If each of these questions is answered "yes," it is likely that usability has been achieved.

Among the many measurable benefits derived from a usable system are increased sales and customer satisfaction, competitive advantage, better reviews in the media, better word of mouth, reduced support costs, improved end-user productivity, reduced training costs, reduced documentation costs, and reduced likelihood of litigation from unhappy customers [Don99].

Design Issues

As the design of a WebApp interface evolves, five common design issues almost always surface: system response time, user help facilities, error information handling, accessibility, and internationalization. Unfortunately, many designers do not address these issues until relatively late in the design process (sometimes the first inkling of a problem doesn't occur until an operational increment has been deployed). Unnecessary iteration, project delays, and customer frustration often result. It is far better to establish each as a design issue to be considered at the beginning of interface design, when changes are easy (at least when compared with the difficulty in addressing them later in the development) and costs are low.

What Factors Affect Response Time and
What Can We Do to Improve It?

System response time for WebApps is complicated by many factors: instantaneous load on the server, the bandwidth of the client-server connection, the processing speed of the client, the complexity of content and the functions that create it, and the capabilities of the browser. It should come as no surprise that response time is the primary complaint for many WebApps. In general, system response time is measured from the point at which the user performs some control action (e.g., hits the return key or clicks a mouse) until the WebApp responds with desired output or action.

System response time has two important characteristics: duration and variability. If the duration of system response is too long, user frustration and stress is the inevitable result. *Variability* refers to the deviation from average response time, and in many ways, it is the most important response time characteristic. Low variability enables the user to establish an interaction rhythm, even if response time is relatively long. For example, a 1-second response to a command will often be preferable to a response that varies from 0.1 to 2.5 seconds. When variability is significant, the user is always off balance, always wondering whether something different has occurred behind the scenes.

Because so many factors affect response time, it is difficult for a designer to create a design (at any level) that guarantees a short, predictable (low variability) response. At the interface design level,[12] it is important to weigh specific requirements for the WebApp against its overall hardware, software, and communication characteristics. For example, if the WebApp is likely to service a very high number of users, the server configuration must be designed to accommodate the load; if the communication bandwidth for the average user is predicted to be relatively low, the use of large content objects (such as large photographs, graphics files, or video content) should be avoided when possible; if a processing function is extremely complex and compute intensive, it might be best to segment it into client-side and server-side functionality to maximize processing speed or, alternatively, to warn the user if a selection (of a processing function or content object) will require a significantly longer response or download time than normal. It is also worthwhile to provide a graduated time scale that provides the user with an indication of the percent completion of the operation. In extreme cases, the use of technologies such as AJAX can overcome some of the limitations of the Web and improve response times.

How Should We Design "Help" Facilities?

You should strive to create a WebApp interface that is intuitive and, therefore, completely self-explanatory. But almost every user of an interactive, computer-based system requires help now and then. Therefore, you should provide a set of obvious mechanisms for those in need of help. Once the user navigates to a "help" facility, a graduated solution context should be provided:

1. Most common problems can be answered with a *Frequently asked questions* (FAQ) facility. But many WebApps design this facility as an afterthought, making it extremely sparse and therefore useless. The FAQ should be cate-

---

12 It is important to note that system response time is also a function of content design, component-level design, and even architectural design.

gorized by topic, have a wide variety of common and not-so-common questions (that are updated regularly), and be detailed in its level of response.

2. An online *Help* facility should be provided for particularly complex websites. The user guide should have a detailed table of contents, a search facility, and an extremely detailed index.

3. A technical support link should be provided as a last resort.

A number of design issues [Rub88] must be addressed when an online help facility is developed:

- *Will help be available for all WebApp functions and at all times during system interaction?* Options include help for only a subset of all functions and actions or help for all functions.

- *How will the user request help?* Options include a "Help" menu item or a navigation icon (e.g., a stylized question mark).

- *How will help be represented?* Options include a separate window, a reference to a PDF document (less than ideal), or a one- or two-line suggestion produced in a fixed screen location.

- *How will the user navigate back to normal interaction?* Options include a return button displayed on the screen or the browser back button (less than ideal).

- *How will help information be structured?* Options include a "flat" structure in which all information is accessed through a key word or a layered hierarchy of information that provides increasing detail as the user proceeds into the structure via hyperlinks.

Purists will argue that none of this should be necessary if the interface designer does a proper job. But pragmatists (our position) recognize that even solid designs cannot anticipate every question and eliminate every problem.

How Should the Interface Handle Errors?

A well-designed WebApp interface should anticipate errors and help the user to avoid them. However, when errors do occur, the interface should provide an immediate, recognizable, and understandable notification of the error.

As an example of a commonly encountered scenario in which error avoidance and error notification are weak, consider the following:

Prior to a download or order on a commercial WebApp, the user must check a box that indicates that he agrees to abide by licensing or other rules. The box is often small and is placed in a visually obscure location. Therefore, it is often missed and not checked. The user submits his "order," and nothing appears to happen. Puzzled, the user scans the Web page and after some searching finds the following message (often in red small text): *Your request cannot be processed because an error has occurred or information is missing.*

There is no indication of what error occurred or what information is missing. The user must recheck his actions until he determines that the box has not been checked. This is a frustrating and time-consuming sequence of events.

In this scenario we encounter two problems. First, the interface designer failed to help the user avoid an error in the first place. By placing the checkbox in a visually obscure location, the designer makes the likelihood of an error (not checking the box) much higher. Second, the error message itself is weak. It should state: *You have forgotten to check the licensing box. Please do so now and resubmit.* No ambiguity and no wasted time.

In general, every error message or warning produced by a WebApp should have the following characteristics:

- The message should describe the problem in jargon that users can understand.
- The message should make it clear what options users have to rectify the problem and/or recover from the error.
- The message should indicate any negative consequences of the error (e.g., potentially corrupted data files) so that users can check to ensure that they have not occurred (or correct them if they have).
- The message should be accompanied by an audible or visual cue. That is, a beep might be generated to accompany the display of the message, or the message might flash momentarily or be displayed in a color that is easily recognizable as the error color.
- The message should be nonjudgmental. That is, the wording should never place blame on the user.

Because no one really likes bad news, few users will like an error message no matter how well designed. But an effective error message philosophy can do much to improve the quality of a WebApp and will significantly reduce user frustration when problems do occur.

What Is "Accessibility" and How Does It Apply to Interface Design?

As WebApps become ubiquitous, Web engineers must ensure that interface design encompasses mechanisms that enable easy access for those with special needs. *Accessibility* for users (and developers) who may be physically challenged is an imperative for moral, legal, and business reasons. A variety of accessibility guidelines (e.g., [W3C03]) provide detailed suggestions for designing interfaces that achieve

SAFEHOME

Design Issues as the Interface Evolves

The scene: The Web engineering area at CPI Corporation

The players: Two members of the **SafeHome-Assured.com** team working as a pair, who have completed the interface design for the *Camera Surveillance* increment

The conversation:

Team member 1 (looking at Figure 9.8 and examining related work products): You know, something occurred to me as I was finishing up the documentation of this.

Team member 2: What?

Team member 1: We forgot to specify the design of any increment-specific help facility or any error-handling features.

Team member 2 (grimacing): Jeez. You're right, but we have to move into deployment or we'll never deliver this increment on time.

Team member 1 (thinking a moment): I agree. Why don't we spend an hour making a list of error conditions that are specific to camera surveillance,

and then we'll design and implement the error processing during construction.

Team member 2: Good strategy. We can do the same thing for camera surveillance "help." Then implement the help facility during construction.

Team member 1: Maybe we should check with marketing to determine how sophisticated they want the help facility to be. No one said much about this, and there's no mention of it in the use cases.

Team member 2: But we need a help facility, whether they mentioned it or not.

Team member 1: Agreed. But we can do a sophisticated one or something simple.

Team member 2: Since no one mentioned it, why don't we go with a simple FAQ for this increment. If we get feedback asking for more, we'll address it in another WebApp increment.

Team member 1: Given the time line, that's a reasonable approach. Let's go that way.

Team member 2: Good. Let's start making a list of possible error conditions.

varying levels of accessibility. Others [e.g., [App07] and [Mic07]) provide specific guidelines for "assistive technology" that addresses the needs of those with visual, hearing, mobility, speech, and learning impairments. Guidelines for developing accessible software can also be found at the IBM Human Ability and Accessibility Center, **www-03.ibm.com/able/access_ibm/disability.html.**

What Is "Internationalization" and How Does It Apply to WebApps?

Web engineers and their managers invariably underestimate the effort and skills required to create user interfaces that accommodate the needs of different locales and languages. Too often, interfaces are designed for one locale and language and then jury-rigged to work in other countries. The challenge for interface designers is to create "globalized" WebApps. That is, user interfaces should be designed to accommodate a generic core of functionality that can be delivered to all who use the WebApp. *Localization* features enable the interface to be customized for a specific cultural market.

A variety of internationalization guidelines (e.g., [IBM07]) are available to Web engineers. These guidelines address broad design issues (e.g., screen layouts may differ in various markets) and discrete implementation issues (e.g., different alphabets may create specialized labeling and spacing requirements). The *Unicode* standard [Uni07] has been developed to address the daunting challenge of managing dozens of natural languages with hundreds of characters and symbols.

Where We've Been . . . Where We're Going

The user interface is the window into WebApp content and function. In many cases, the interface molds a user's perception of the quality of the system. If the "window" is smudged, wavy, or broken, the user may reject powerful functions and content. In fact, a weak interface may cause an otherwise well-designed and solidly implemented application to fail.

A wide array of principles and guidelines help the designer to create an effective user interface. These can be summarized with the following rules: (1) place the user in control, (2) make interaction easy for the user, and (3) make the interface aesthetic and consistent. An organized design process should be conducted to achieve an interface that abides by these rules.

Interface design begins with a series of analysis tasks that define the profiles of various end users and delineate user tasks and actions with use cases, task and object elaboration, workflow analysis, and hierarchical task representations.

Once tasks have been identified, a set of interface objects and actions is extracted from the user scenarios that describe each task. This provides a basis for creation of a screen layout that depicts graphical design and placement of icons, definition of descriptive screen text, specification and titling for windows, and specification of major and minor menu items. Design issues such as response time, command and action structure, error handling, and help facilities are considered as the design model is refined.

In the design chapters that follow, we'll examine aspects of WebApp design that move slowly away from the user's world and toward the technical domain of the WebApp as a computer-based system. In Chapter 10, we'll start this journey by considering information design—the representation of content objects and the mechanisms that allow a user to navigate among them.

References

[App07] Apple Inc., *Accessibility,* 2007, **www.apple.com/accessibility/** (accessed August 6, 2007).

[Bag01] Baggerman, L., and S. Bowman, *Web Design That Works,* Rockport Publishers, 2001.

[Clo01]   Cloninger, C., *Fresh Styles for Web Designers,* New
          2001.

[Con95]   Constantine, L, "What DO Users Want? Engineerin
          ware," *Windows Tech Journal,* December 1995, **www.forUse.com** (access
          gust 6, 2007).

[Dix99]   Dix, A., "Design of User Interfaces for the Web," *Proc. of User Interfaces to
          Data Systems Conference,* September 1999, **www.comp.lancs.ac.uk/computing/users/
          dixa/topics/webarch/** (accessed August 6, 2007).

[Don99]   Donahue, G., S. Weinschenck, and J. Nowicki, "Usability Is Good Busi-
          ness," Compuware Corp., July 1999, **http://www.half-tide.com/ResourcesFiles/
          UsabilityCost-BenefitPaper.pdf** (accessed August 6, 2007).

[Fit54]   Fitts, P., "The Information Capacity of the Human Motor System in Con-
          trolling the Amplitude of Movement," *Journal of Experimental Psychology,*
          vol. 47, 1954, pp. 381–391.

[Hac98]   Hackos, J., and J. Redish, *User and Task Analysis for Interface Design,* Wiley,
          1998.

[Hei02]   Heinicke, E., *Layout: Fast Solutions for Hands-on Design,* Rockport Pub-
          lishers, 2002.

[IBM07]   IBM, "Overview of Software Globalization," 2007, **www-128.ibm.com/
          developerworks/xml/library/x-i18n1.html** (accessed August 6, 2007).

[Mic07]   Microsoft, *Accessibility,* 2007, **www.microsoft.com/enable/** (accessed August 6,
          2007).

[Nie00]   Nielsen, J., *Designing Web Usability,* New Riders Publishing, 2000.

[Nie96]   Nielsen, J., and A. Wagner, "User Interface Design for the WWW," *Proc.
          CHI '96 Conf. on Human Factors in Computing Systems,* ACM Press, 1996,
          pp. 330–331.

[Rub88]   Rubin, T., *User Interface Design for Computer Systems,* Halstead Press
          (Wiley), 1988.

[Tog01]   Tognozzi, B., "First Principles," *askTOG,* 2001, **www.asktog.com/basics/
          firstPrinciples.html** (accessed August 6, 2007).

[Too02]   Toor, M., "The Top Twenty Web Design Tips," 2002, **www.graphic-design.
          com/Web/feature/tips.html** (accessed August 6, 2007).

[Uni07]   Unicode, Inc., *The Unicode Home Page,* 2007, **www.unicode.org/** (accessed
          August 6, 2007).

[W3C03]   World Wide Web Consortium, *Web Content Accessibility Guidelines,* 2003,
          www.w3.org/TR/2003/WD-WCAG20-20030624/ (accessed August 6, 2007).

10

INFORMATION DESIGN

Content is at the heart of almost every WebApp. Indeed, for the vast majority of Web-based systems and applications, "Content is King."[1] Effective user interfaces, straightforward navigation, and rich functionality are all important, but many WebApps that have exhibited these characteristics have failed because they lacked meaningful content or because the content could not be located.

In Chapter 9 we examined user interface design. If you think about it for a moment, the user interface for most WebApps is a gateway to content, and content (along with the functions that manipulate it) is what enables the user to achieve the objectives identified during the communication activity (Chapter 4). In this chapter we consider how to provide the substance underneath the user interface—we will focus on *information design*.

There are really only three key issues[2] that should be considered when a WebE team performs information design:

- **Content.** What content is available?
- **Composition.** What views on that content do you wish to provide users?
- **Navigation.** How do the users gain access to those views?

There are different levels of abstraction at which you might consider these information design issues. For example, are you considering the high-level information architecture of a WebApp or the low-level detailed design of the specific content on each page? Are you designing the access strategy across major information categories or the specific navigation options within a narrow collection of content options?

The specific content requirements of a WebApp are first considered during the communication activity (Chapter 4) and are then elaborated and structured during analysis modeling (Chapter 7). During early elicitation sessions of the communication activity, Web engineers and other stakeholders identify the initial content objects (a named collection of related information). Elicitation also considers the user's overall goals in

---

1 See Bill Gates, "Content Is Where the Money Is on the Internet," 1996, **www.microsoft. com/billgates/columns/1996essay/essay960103.asp** (accessed January 23, 2006) and David Callan, "Content is King," undated, **www.akamarketing.com/content-is-king.html** (accessed August 7, 2007)

2 A fourth issue—how is the content managed?—will be considered in Chapter 12.

accessing the content and their background as it relates to interpreting the content. Finally, the communication activity results in the development of user scenarios or use cases that illustrate the use of the content.

During analysis modeling, members of the WebE team often construct a content model. The content model makes use of Web information exchange diagrams (Chapter 7) that can be used to help in the refinement of content objects. The result is a clear set of content specifications for the WebApp, but not necessarily the ways in which this information will be arranged within the WebApp.

In this chapter we consider how this content can be organized, accessed, and managed—the information design for the WebApp. We begin by examining the high-level information architecture—what its role is, what it contains, and how it can be developed. We'll then consider detailed information design and the specific navigation structures that are required to access content. Finally, we'll draw both the high-level information architectural design and the low-level navigation design approaches together into an information design workflow that can be applied to your WebApp projects.

Information Architecture

The overall goal of information design is to translate content requirements, usually in the form of a detailed set of content objects, into a specific information design for the WebApp. The overall strategy for information design usually combines both a bottom-up approach and a top-down approach.

Bottom-up information design is commonly used for small WebApps and simply involves designing and building actual Web pages and progressively linking these together so that the information views and the structure of the WebApp emerge organically. However, for larger WebApps a bottom-up approach can result in a solution that frustrates a user's attempts to locate information, presents that information (when it is found) out of context, and restricts easy accommodation of changes.

A *top-down information design* approach considers the overall organization, interrelationships, and structure of major content categories within a WebApp. This high-level design approach addresses aspects of the WebApp such as the overall structure of the application, the way in which the information is organized, and the ways in which users might access that information. This is the realm of the *information architecture.*

What Is an Information Architecture?

The term *information architecture* (IA) is widely used in the Web engineering community, and yet, although each person seems to know exactly what it means, definitions vary dramatically from person to person. In an effort to remove this lack of consistency, a number of organizations (e.g., the *Information Architecture Institute*[3]), websites (e.g., IAWiki **www.iawiki.net/**), publications (e.g., *Boxes and Arrows*[4]), and conferences (e.g., the annual IA Summit[5]) are dedicated to information architecture. The role of an *information architect* is commonly encountered within a WebE team that is working on a large project.

An information architecture might be as simple as a site map that represents the basic WebApp navigational structure. Alternatively, an IA may be a detailed model that provides a comprehensive overview of the approach for structuring, managing, and accessing information within a WebApp. One definition[6] of an IA that captures the need to focus on the user's tasks is: *"The structural design of an information space to facilitate task completion and intuitive access to content"* [Ros02].

The IA provides a skeleton around which all information aspects of the WebApp are built. To elaborate on this a little further, let's change our focus for a moment and consider an example from the world of residential architecture.

Think about what a set of architectural plans for a house might actually show you. The plans will certainly indicate major structural elements of the house along with the materials from which the structure will be constructed. From the location of the major structural elements—room layout, stairs, walls, doors, windows—the internal space, and hence the effectiveness of the architectural solution, can be evaluated. The plans will also show how the house relates to its environment—the compass orientation of the house, its relationship to major environmental elements on the property (e.g., a pond or brook, rock outcroppings) and the slope of the land on which the house sits. Finally, the plans will show the location of the main access (e.g., driveway, walks) to the house and what other things border the property on which the house sits.

In other words, the architectural plans for a house show the basic structure and its context—those things that define the overall *shape* and usability of the residence. More detailed architectural information (e.g., plumbing and electrical layouts) can be incorporated as additional layers of information.

Because architectural plans show the relationship between the house and its surrounding environment, it is possible to evaluate whether the design is appropriate for its surroundings. The *utility* of the resultant house will be dependent not only on its structure but on how that structure relates to its environment.

An IA for a WebApp is (or should be) analogous to a set of architectural plans for a house. It should describe the basic information "structure" of the solution,

---

3   **iainstitute.org**

4   **www.boxesandarrows.com/**

5   ASIS&T Information Architecture Summit 2007, **www.iasummit.org/**

6   A good discussion on the various definitions for IA can be found at IAWiki, **www.iawiki.net/
    DefiningTheDamnThing** (accessed August 8, 2007).

but also position this within the overall information "landscape" in which the WebApp exists.

What Are the Elements of an Information Architecture?

In their seminal text on information architecture, Rosenfeld and Morville [Ros02] describe IA in terms of a Venn diagram containing three intersecting circles representing context, content, and users. In their introductory chapter they state:

> Some web sites provide logical structures that help us find answers and complete tasks. Others lack any intelligible organization and frustrate our attempts to navigate through them. We can't find the product we need; we can't locate the report we found last week; we're lost inside an online shopping cart. These web sites may remind us of buildings that fail: houses with flat roofs that leak, kitchens with no counter space, office towers with windows you can't open, and maze-like airports with misleading signs . . .
>
> However, as designers of web sites, we should not become trapped by the metaphor of building architecture . . . we'll also talk about information ecologies, knowledge economies, digital libraries, and virtual communities. We learn what we can from each analogy, and we leave the baggage behind.

They then go on to define IA:

In.for.ma.tion ar.chi.tec.ture *n*
1. The combination of organization, labeling, and navigation schemes within an information system.
2. The structural design of an information space to facilitate task completion and intuitive access to content.
3. The art and science of structuring and classifying web sites and intranets to help people find and manage information.
4. An emerging discipline and community of practice focused on bringing principles of design and architecture to the digital landscape.

In other words, an IA is the high-level design that creates the structure of the information space to be used within the WebApp.

What Are the Characteristics of a Good Information Architecture?

Hardman, Bulterman, and van Rossum [Har93] give a list of ideal requirements for a hypermedia information model—most of which apply equally well to WebApp IAs. They list:

- **Composition with multiple, dynamic data.** The model must support the ability to group different information items into a presentation and the expression of constraints among these items.

  Example: **SafeHomeAssured.com** could include multimedia presentations on the use of the various sensors. Should these presentations occur in a new window? Should they auto-repeat on completion?

- **Higher-level presentation specification.** The model should be able to specify constraints across multiple information items. For instance, we might want to indicate that a certain class of image (such as items of artwork) should never be presented without including the artist's name.

    Example: In **SafeHomeAssured.com** whenever private information is presented to a user (such as account information or home security details), the user's name and log-in status should be displayed as part of the strategy of building user confidence.

- **Temporal relations.** Certain information items may have time-based relationships, which can be important to their presentation (e.g., a link to information about an event might only be relevant up until that event is held).

    Example: With **SafeHomeAssured.com,** consideration would need to be given to the inclusion or exclusion of information on recent sensor monitoring events. How many should be presented to the user? At what point are they no longer considered relevant? How are they built into the architecture?

- **Context for links and link semantics.** An important characteristic of many WebApps, particularly those that support adaptation and personalization, is the ability to control the presentation depending upon which links are followed. This might be described in a use case as, "If I follow link A, then show the result in a new window. If I follow link B, then replace the current information with the result."

    Example: When users choose to view their current sensor layout in **SafeHomeAssured.com,** the house plans should be presented in a new window.

In addition to these requirements, it is reasonable to add others:

- **Separation of content and information.** Content is the collection of data sources that are available for use. Information is what is useful to the users of the WebApp. A good IA will differentiate between these.

    Example: With **SafeHomeAssured.com** the product catalog contains a rich set of data on different pricing structures, and most of this information may never be shown to most users. For a particular user, the product information that is displayed is likely to be some modified subset of this data, combined with user information.

- **Separation of information and application.** A WebApp IA should differentiate between the information that a user would find meaningful, and the structural ways in which this information might be arranged and accessed.

Example: In **SafeHomeAssured.com** we wouldn't embed the classification of the products directly into the product information, but rather as a separate classification schema.

- **Separation of application and presentation.** If we separate the presentation mechanisms from the application, then the portability and genericity of applications (the ability to be applied to other applications or problems with minimal change) will be substantially enhanced.

    Example: In **SafeHomeAssured.com** the formatting of the products would not be embedded into the product catalog. Rather, it would be represented as presentation template(s).

We use each of the requirements discussed in this section to assess the quality and usefulness of the IA.

SafeHome

The Information Architect

The scene: SafeHomeAssured.com team leader's office as the communication activity commences

The players: Team leader and two members of the **SafeHomeAssured.com** WebE team

The conversation:

Team leader: How are your preliminary communication meetings going?

Team member 1: We've got the stakeholders developing use cases, and it's going okay.

Team leader: What do we know so far?

Team member 2: One thing for sure—this Web-App is going to have a reasonably sophisticated information architecture.

Team member 1: What do you mean, "information architecture"?

Team member 2: You know, the structure of content, the way we organize content objects, the way we navigate to it, that sort of thing.

Team leader: What we don't want is for the architecture to just happen in some ad hoc way. It's the

first thing we should really design, and I think one guy should develop a straw man for the team.

Team member 2: The information architect.

Team leader (nodding in agreement): I'd like you to take on that role. Are you comfortable with the responsibility?

Team member 2: Sure. I did some IA in my last job, read some books on IA. I think I can do it.

Team member 1: What criteria do you use? To do the design, I mean.

Team member 2: Well, first we have to wait until we get all the use cases. Then we analyze them, derive the content objects that we'll need, understand the functions that are applied to the objects, and understand which user groups need which content and how they'll need to get to it—navigation.

Team member 1: That's all part of analysis, isn't it?

[Team member 2 nods.]

Team leader: But you really didn't answer the question. What makes a good information architecture?

[Team member 2 discusses the characteristics covered in the preceding section.]

How Do We Develop an Information Architecture?

As we noted in an earlier subsection, an IA should describe the basic information "structure" of the WebApp and how users might interact with that structure. The structure will usually revolve around a broad *blueprint* for the site combined with taxonomies, ontologies,[7] and/or controlled vocabularies that assist in giving some formalism to the model. The way in which users interact with the WebApp will often be captured through *wireframes*[8] and supported by consideration of the role of other access mechanisms such as search tools.

The degree of complexity that is used to represent a WebApp IA varies greatly. In some cases, a WebE team will develop a site map and argue that it represents an information architecture for the WebApp. Even when the site map is very rich in structure (such as the one shown in Figure 10.1), it remains only a site map and often won't provide sufficient detail about the overall WebApp design, nor will it allow the overall structure to be fully evaluated against user goals.

In some cases, a site map might be supplemented with a discussion of user interactions with the WebApp and the way in which these interactions influence the information organization. Although this approach provides greater insight, it does not explicitly model the nature of the information exchange that does occur and the internal interrelationships between information domains within the WebApp structure. Nor does a discussion of user interactions provide an effective consideration of the information environment in which the system exists.

Rosenfeld and Morville [Ros02] discuss a comprehensive approach to the development of an IA, involving five key phases: research, strategy, design, implementation, and administration. The first two phases are the most critical to the successful development of an IA.

The first phase, *research,* focuses on understanding the context of the IA—background material, goals, business context, users, and likely content. Each of these aspects of a WebApp has been discussed previously during the communication activity (Chapter 4) and analysis modeling (Chapter 7).

The second phase, *design,* is the core of the IA development process. Rosenfeld and Morville [Ros02] discuss this in the following way:

> Design is where you shape a high-level strategy into an information architecture, creating detailed blueprints, wireframes, and metadata schema that will be used by graphic designers, programmers, content authors, and the production team. This phase is typically where information architects do the most work, yet quantity cannot drive out

---

7   An *ontology* is a formal domain model that represents the objects in the domain, the attributes of those objects, and the relationships between the objects. The model supports reasoning about the domain.

8   A *wireframe* shows the basic size, location, and layout of the components that make up a WebApp page.

FIGURE 10.1

An example site map.
Source: Copyright Dynamic Diagrams, **www.dynamicdiagrams.com/case_studies/sec_web.html.** Reproduced with permission.

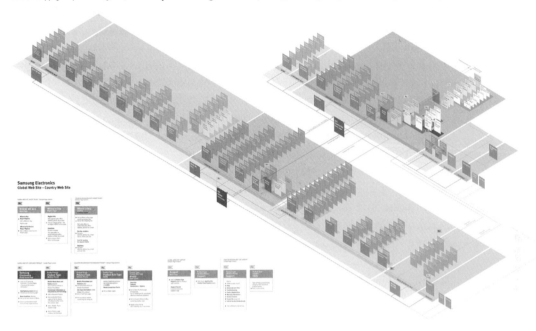

quality. Poor design execution can ruin the best strategy. For an information architect, the meat is in the middle and the devil is in the details.

In other words, the IA progressively emerges through the development of suitable design models of the information structure. In the sections that follow, we'll consider some of the issues in developing an IA and then present models that address those issues. First, we look at information organization and then examine other models that depict how information is accessed.

Organizing Content

Imagine going back 20 years to a time before the availability of networked access to huge repositories of information. If you were asked to determine the specific view of a particular politician on a given item of legislation, how would you have proceeded? You could have gone to your local library, found copies of the legislative records, and looked up the debates on that legislation. Now, imagine how difficult that would have been if you arrived at the library only to find that someone had pulled all the books off the shelves and thrown them into a huge pile on the floor. Or worse still—if they had removed all the pages from each book and shuffled them. Your search would be almost impossible!

The organization of the information space within a WebApp serves much the same purpose as the organization of books within a library and pages within each book—it allows users to find what they need. But information organization can also serve other purposes. For example, an e-commerce application might have an information structure designed to ensure that users see information that encourages them to make additional purchases. Consider the role of specialized user adaptation functions within **Amazon.com.** These ensure that specific books will be presented to each Amazon customer based on that customer's prior navigation and purchases.

In **SafeHomeAssured.com** we might adapt the content so that when users log in, they are provided with a "home page" that includes suggestions for new sensors that are suited to work well with those already installed, or newer, more secure versions to replace those already installed.

Brick-and-mortar libraries use information categorizations (structures) that have evolved over hundreds of years.[9] Information architects design customized structures that may be unique for a particular WebApp. These structures need to be intuitive and take into account the ways in which the users are most likely to expect information to be arranged. In some cases this arrangement will be inherent in the information itself—consider the natural ordering of information in an online telephone directory. In other cases a metaphor can be adopted that provides a natural structuring. Once the user is aware of the metaphor (e.g., a shopping cart), the information structure is easily understood. The need for these structures is well articulated by Rosenfeld and Morville [Ros02] when they state, "The way we organize, label, and relate information influences the way people comprehend that information. As information architects, we organize information so that people can find the right answers to their questions."

Regardless of the sophistication of a WebApp interface and aesthetics, the bottom line is almost always information acquisition. If the internal structure of content is disorganized, it will be extremely difficult, if not impossible, for a WebE team to design and implement navigation and searching mechanisms that will provide end users with the information they need.

Structuring the Information Space

Before we look at a particular information model, let's consider what general types of information structures are possible and how these structures might be used in different applications. When you structure information during the information design, you are trying to define explicitly the ways in which users might mentally

---

9   The original Dewey decimal classification was developed by Melvil Dewey in 1876.

manage the information—the structures that they have built or learned or assumed about the information.

For example, consider a WebApp that contains a repository of biographical information about famous people, including Bill Clinton, George W. Bush, Meg Ryan, and Billy Bob Thornton. How would this information be grouped? Would Clinton and Bush (U.S. Presidents) be grouped separately from Ryan and Thornton (actors)? Or would Clinton and Thornton (both born in Arkansas) establish one group while Bush and Ryan (both born in Connecticut) establish another? Obviously, it would depend on the likely knowledge of the users and why they were using the WebApp.

What Information Structures Are Possible?

The information structures that are created during information design can be classified in various ways as illustrated in Figure 10.2. It is important to note that WebApps can utilize more than one information structure. For example, an educational WebApp might organize high-level training materials using a linear structure. The user has to first complete topic 1 before progressing to topic 2. But within a given topic, information can be organized into a hierarchical structure allowing a user to go through different subtopics in any order. Alternatively you can overlay different structures onto the same underlying information so that it can be accessed and utilized differently depending upon the context. Often the structure used will reflect the types of information that you are trying to represent.

Linear structures. This information structure can be used in a number of ways within a WebApp. For example, it can be used to retain the sequential structure of an original paper document or to control access when the user should be guided through a sequence of steps dictated by a prescribed sequence of events. Linear structures are encountered when a predictable sequence of interactions (with some variation or diversion) is common. A classic example might be a tutorial presentation in which pages of information along with related graphics, short videos, or audio are presented only after prerequisite information has been presented. The

---

FIGURE 10.2

Example information structures.
Source: From [Low99]. Reprinted with permission.

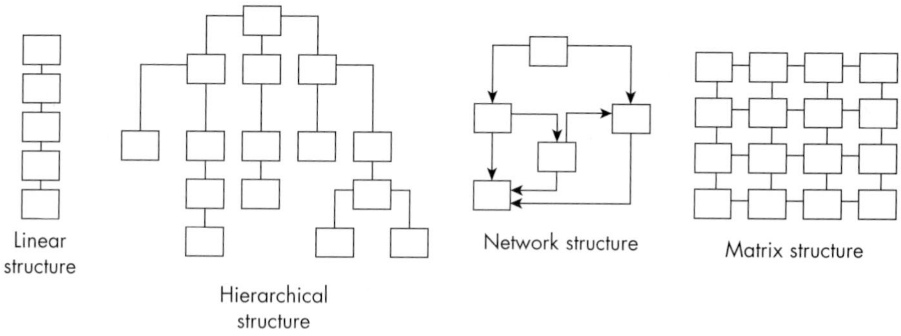

Linear structure

Hierarchical structure

Network structure

Matrix structure

sequence of content presentation is predefined and generally linear. Another example might be a product order entry workflow in which information must be specified in a particular order. As content and processing become more complex, a purely linear flow (as shown in Figure 10.2) gives way to more sophisticated branched structures (though still directed along particular pathways) in which alternative content may be invoked or a diversion to acquire complementary content occurs.

Matrix (or grid) structures.   This architectural option can be applied when WebApp content is organized categorically in two (or more) dimensions. For example, consider the case in which a WebApp provides details on procedures for car repair. A matrix structure is chosen. Horizontal access to the matrix is divided into information on different problems (steering faults, ignition problems, etc.), and vertical access to the matrix is divided into information describing symptoms, causes, solutions, tools, and procedures. Hence, users might navigate the grid horizontally if they are trying to solve a particular problem and then vertically to understand the nature of that problem. This WebApp architecture is useful only when highly regular content is encountered [Pow00].

Hierarchical structures.   This structure is undoubtedly the most common WebApp architecture and is used to reflect natural information taxonomies. Selecting the right taxonomy is a substantial challenge, particularly when the information is not homogeneous. In many cases multiple different hierarchies might be appropriate. Earlier we gave an example of a site focused on famous people. We might have one hierarchy in which a person can be located by profession (Famous people → Profession → Entertainer → Actor → Cinema → Comedy → Adam Sandler) and the same people arranged in a second hierarchy based on their origins (Famous people → Origins → Birth location → New York → Adam Sandler).

Network or graph structures.   These architectural elements are composed of associative links that bind common or related concepts together within the information space. A network structure can be very effective in cross-connecting related aspects within a WebApp and allowing users substantial navigational flexibility. They are most commonly used as an overlay on top of a hierarchical structure. If used judiciously, a network structure can help users browse productively. If overused, users can be confused by the choices or lose a sense of where they are and what information is available. An excellent example of a network structure is **www.wikipedia.com.** The Wikipedia content has some categorizations but is based on an incredibly rich set of cross references among the content rather than a natural hierarchy.

The architectural structures discussed in the preceding paragraphs can be combined to form composite structures. The overall architecture of a WebApp may be hierarchical, but part of the structure may exhibit linear characteristics, while

ing upon the context. In the example shown, the list of orders can be included in the ordering page, which might also include information on placing new orders, and the user information pages, which might also include basic user account information.

If you would like to learn more about blueprints, two good sources of additional information have been developed by Christina Wodtke [Wod06] and at IAWiki.[12]

Accessing Information

Apart from the actual information structure of the WebApp, there are a number of other factors that affect the ability of users to achieve their goals. These generally relate to navigational mechanisms and characteristics:

- WebApp mechanisms that allow users to understand what navigation options are available at any given time
- Interface mechanisms that provide users with an indication of where they are and what they are currently seeing
- Navigation mechanisms that allow users to travel within the information structure.

We consider each of these mechanisms in the sections that follow.

How Do We Ensure That the User Understands the Context and Doesn't Get Lost?

Have you ever navigated into a complex WebApp and felt "lost in hyperspace"? When this happens, you lose track of where you are within (or beyond) the WebApp. It's a common problem that can leave the user disoriented and unable to acquire needed information or invoke appropriate functionality. It also makes it difficult to interpret the information that has already been acquired. An excellent example of this was conveyed to David Lowe by a student in a Web design class:

> Several years ago I was arranging a fancy dinner for some friends who were visiting, and realized that the ideal start to the meal would be a seafood bisque. Not being able to find a good recipe in any of my books, I did a search on the Web. After looking at several options, I picked one out that looked unusual and proceeded to make the soup. My guests were highly complimentary about both the soup and the meal, and we all had a wonderful time. Unfortunately, the next day everyone who had been to the dinner fell violently ill, including myself.
>
> After recovering, I got to wondering—what part of the dinner might have been at fault? I couldn't remember all the ingredients I had put into the bisque so I redid the search and found the original website. It turned out that the page I had jumped to directly from the search engine only described the bisque—but when I backtracked to

---

12 Visit **http://iawiki.net/SiteMaps.**

the homepage for the site (by cutting back the URL) I discovered that it was a site that contained home remedies for various medical problems, disguised as nice meals to make them more palatable. Oh no! I had served to my guests a home remedy for severe constipation!

While this is a somewhat "severe" example (and just possibly apocryphal—though the student asserted that it did actually occur to him), this does illustrate the importance of ensuring that information is always presented within a clear context. It also highlights that a significant cause of this problem is jumping into the middle of a WebApp as a result of a search query.

The following guidelines can help users to know where they are and define the context of the information they are seeing:

Clear labeling. The WebE team should develop a set of local standards that lead to a clear set of labels for all link anchors. The labels should accurately describe the destination of the link and can be crucial for ensuring that

---

SafeHome

Creating a Data Dictionary

The scene: SafeHomeAssured. com workspace

The players: The information architect and other WebE team members

The conversation:

Information architect: I've noticed that not everybody is using terminology consistently as we develop various aspects of the preliminary design.

Team member 1: For example, some of us are using the term *sensor* to refer to any device that we sell; others are using it just for some detection devices and not others.

Team member 2: We'll get it sorted out . . . eventually.

Information architect: Not good enough. I guarantee that if we're inconsistent in naming things we'll make mistakes, some of them subtle. They'll come back to bite us.

Team member 1: What do you propose?

Information architect: Part of my job is to develop a data dictionary—so that we all have consistent definition of content objects and the like. Here, look at this . . . it's a start.

[The team reviews a two-page document that begins:

The following terms are the standard accepted terms to be used within the **SafeHomeAssured. com** WebApp:

Product. A security device that is available for purchase and installation in a home security setup

Sensor. A product that is able to monitor some aspect of home security

Networked sensor. A product that, when configured, is able to be monitored online

Connected sensor. A product that has been installed and configured for online monitoring

Floor plan. Details of the arrangement of a physical space, and the location and ID of any sensors within that space

Account. Details of all orders (past and pending) associated with a given account holder, as well as current payment details, etc.

Order. A request (provisional, confirmed, or completed) for services and/or products

Team members make suggestions for modifications and additions.]

users understand where they have landed when following a link. Indeed, it can be useful to ensure that the labels are not only clear but consistent across the site. Many information architects establish a WebApp "dictionary" of terms to be used across the entire WebApp design.

Breadcrumbs. It's always a good idea to know where you've come from as you navigate deep into an information structure.[13] *Breadcrumbs* provide a navigation pathway description that is included on each Web page. The pathway describes where the current page fits within the information structure. As an example, consider a breadcrumb pathway for a **SafeHomeAssured.com** user who has accessed the surveillance feature remotely and is in the process of selecting a camera from a house floor plan (from which surveillance video will be displayed). Compare this to the blueprint in Figure 10.5b:

Monitoring $\longrightarrow$ **Floor Plan (ID:34)** $\longrightarrow$ **Sensor (ID:653)**

This breadcrumb pathway indicates the navigation choices that the user has made (or could have made—if she jumped straight to a location through a search) to get to the floor plan.

Identity. Each Web page should clearly identify the nature of the site or subsite to which presented information belongs.[14] It should also (when possible) provide an indication of the context, the purpose of the WebApp, and also provide links to the "home" page.

How Do We Help the User Move Through the Information Structure?

A user's ability to acquire information easily can be impaired as the complexity and size of a WebApp information structure grows. To avoid this problem, an information architect should tune navigational support to the specific characteristics of the IA and design search mechanisms that lead the user to desired information while filtering out extraneous content. The goal is to help experienced users achieve their navigational goals more quickly[15] and to provide inexperienced users with additional navigational support.

If an information architect has done a good job, the resultant design of a WebApp information structure will be very clear, allowing users to navigate to the required information without any doubt or confusion. But as a user becomes more experienced, the designer might consider providing a mechanism that allows the

---

13 Recall that it's a good idea to limit the depth to which a user must navigate to acquire needed information.

14 If this guideline had been followed, the unpleasant circumstances described in the introduction to this section could have been avoided.

15 This is analogous to the numerous shortcut keys that are available within most software applications—key combinations that allow users to perform tasks more rapidly as they become more experienced.

user to "jump" directly to desired information without having to traverse a long (and tedious[16]) navigational path. While browser techniques such as *bookmarking* support this on the user side, there are other things that the information architect can do to help. Some simple examples include:

Global links. These links are provided on every Web page and point to commonly visited WebApp locations or functions. They allow a user to jump to those locations without having to return to the home page or follow other prescribed navigational pathways. Typical examples include: Home, Help, Contact, Site map, Index, Search, News, About, Register, and Log-in.

Shortcuts. These are ways of bypassing the normal navigational route and jumping over intermediate steps straight to a particular location within the information space. The most common example of this is the use of submenus that allow users to bypass intermediate pages.

Breadcrumbs and trails. We have already noted that breadcrumbs are useful for helping users to locate themselves. But breadcrumbs (represented as active links) can also allow users to return quickly to any intermediate point along the navigation pathway between the home page and their current location.

The draft structure for **SafeHomeAssured.com** shown in Figure 10.3 gives several examples of these types of links.

In a way, each of the preceding mechanisms allows the user to "subvert" the prescribed manner in which information is accessed. The benefits of controlled access to information must always be weighed against ease of use and facility of access.

What Guidelines Are Available for Implementing Searching Mechanisms?

Most large WebApps incorporate searching mechanisms. In fact, searching allows a user to bypass the imposed navigational structure and jump directly to specific locations within the WebApp, and as a result, it is often the first choice for users who need information "now!"

In many cases, a search engine is attached to a WebApp after it has been designed and implemented. Although this can provide useful support for users, it can also cause problems. An add-on search engine does not take into account which WebApp components should be indexed. This means that the user may be pointed to inappropriate information (e.g., a component designed for one user category may become available to another user category) and will be able to wander the

---

16 At least from the point of view of the "experienced" user.

FIGURE 10.6

Example of the constrained use of a search engine.
Source: From [Low99, figure 5.5]. Reprinted with permission.

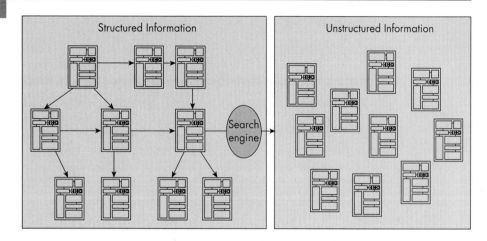

information space in an unconstrained manner. It also means that the search functionality is not truly an integrated component of the overall application.

Figure 10.6 illustrates one approach to a controlled integration of a search engine into an application. A search engine can often be used more profitably by constraining its scope. That is, the search can be used as an access mechanism into a region of the information space that either does not contain well-structured information or has a complex information structure. Referring to the figure, structured information on the left is accessed using conventional navigation mechanisms. These pages are excluded from the search domain. However, pages on the right of the figure (representing unstructured information) are less amenable to prescribed navigation and therefore become the focus of the search function.

As an example in **SafeHomeAssured.com,** consider access to information on products. Much of the content and function provided by the WebApp is best accessed via prescribed navigational mechanisms. However, a search function might be beneficial for the user who is looking for specific security or monitoring products. A search function constrained to that part of the **SafeHomeAssured.com** information domain could be implemented.

Of course, search engines can be used effectively across an entire WebApp. The problem, however, is that a global approach often results in too many search "hits," rather than too few. Users are inundated with possible locations of the information they desire and often waste time navigating to unproductive locations.

The appropriate use of a search engine can be understood by considering the types of usage patterns that are likely and the information structure(s) that will exist. Given these two factors, the suitability of a search engine and the scope of its operation can be determined. Searching can become particularly useful when the underlying information is structured (e.g., in a database or as XML files) and/or contains accessible metadata. In this case the search can be constrained to particular fields within the data.

A number of other factors should be considered in search engine design. These include the mechanism and/or frequency of updating the underlying indexes, and information gathering processes and their efficiency (especially for large indexes). These will typically not affect the search functionality (except where performance constraints place restrictions) and can often be relegated to the technical design stage of WebApp development.

Can Searching Mechanisms Lead to Problems?

A search engine will bypass the information structures and identify possible destinations anywhere within a given region of the information space. This introduces two possible problems.

The first problem is related to the possibility that the navigation structure was imposed so that the user would follow a certain logical sequence through the information. Breaking this sequence (by using the search engine to jump outside the link structure) could possibly destroy the logical flow of concepts and ideas and hence damage the effectiveness of the WebApp. The severity of this problem will depend on the particular class of application (for example, this is likely to be a much greater problem for educational applications than reference applications). The solution is to exercise care in generating the indexes and allowable destinations for the results of searches. In **SafeHomeAssured.com,** we obviously wouldn't want to include in the search results the intermediate pages in the order-processing workflow.

The second problem occurs when the user becomes disoriented ("lost in hyperspace") as a consequence of the unconstrained jumping that searching facilitates. This is partly a result of the content discontinuity (long "conceptual" distances are traversed instantly) and partly a result of the sudden change in context. Again, the only reasonable solution is to design carefully both the search engine (so that only reasonable jumps are allowed) and the context of each page or node that is likely to be the destination of a search-based jump (so that the context facilitates user reorientation). It is also important to ensure that all potential destinations include clear information on their location within the information space. Breadcrumbs can be an effective mechanism for achieving this.

Wireframe Models

Earlier, we discussed the role of blueprints as one element of a design model for information structures. *Wireframes* serve a parallel purpose in describing how an individual page (or pages) within a WebApp might look conceptually. While a wireframe does not depict the graphic design of a page, it does capture the core information and navigation elements that should be present on the page and the approximate arrangement of these elements. In essence, a wireframe is an artificial screen dump without the graphic design or actual instantiated content.

Figure 10.7 illustrates the wireframe for one of a number of design alternatives for the home page for **SafeHomeAssured.com.** Referring to the figure, the wireframe model helps prioritize the various information and navigation elements and position them for maximum understanding. In general, wireframes are created for key pages within a WebApp—those pages that are exemplars of the design or that contain particularly crucial elements.

A common question is whether a wireframe is an information design tool or an interaction design tool. The answer is that it can be either but should be both. We can develop a wireframe that highlights the key interactions triggered from

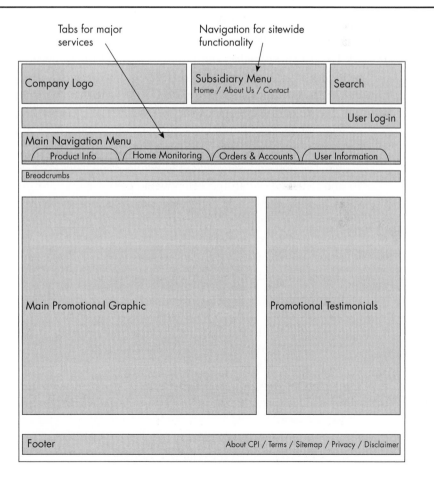

FIGURE 10.7

Example wire-frame for the **SafeHome-Assured.com** home page.

that location within the WebApp. But the same wireframe can also be used to explore the integration of the content and what the information structure would look like from that point within the WebApp.

Navigation Design: Creating the Detailed Structure

The information architecture describes the structure and organization of the WebApp. In addition, it implicitly describes the mechanisms required to find and access content and how all these fit together. However, you must still create the specific navigation design at a local level. In this section we examine some possible approaches for accomplishing this. In the next section, "Summarizing the Design Process," we put everything together and recommend an overall information design process.

How Have Information Design and Navigation Design Models Evolved?

Approaches to the detailed design of information space navigation have evolved over the past two decades. During the 1980s and 1990s, hypertext researchers considered issues of navigational structure in complex information spaces. When the Web appeared, it was natural for them to extend this work and apply it to WebApps.[17]

The *Dexter Hypertext Reference Model* [Hal94] (a model that predates the Web) is an attempt to capture the main abstractions that exist in a range of hypermedia applications. The Dexter model represents a hypermedia application as three layers. The bottom layer, called the *within-component layer,* represents the contents and structure within the components of the application. The middle layer, called the *storage layer,* is the core of the Dexter model and depicts the basic structure of a hypermedia application composed of *nodes* (which can be either atomic or contain other nodes) and the *links* between nodes. Nodes are anchored to the contents in the bottom layer. The top layer, called the *run-time layer,* captures the functionality to access and manipulate the data structures. This is shown schematically in Figure 10.8.

The Dexter model was not intended as a design model but rather as a reference model for comparing hypermedia systems and models. It does, however, emphasize that it is important to model the underlying content and to consider how this content will be arranged for the purpose of access. It also implies that presentation is a separate issue from structure.

---

17 This is despite early concerns within the hypertext community that the Web was not a worthwhile hypertext system. Indeed, a submission to the 1991 Hypertext Conference by Tim Berners-Lee—the inventor of the Web—was rejected!

FIGURE 10.8

The Dexter
Hypertext Refer-
ence Model.
Source: Adapted from
[Hal94].

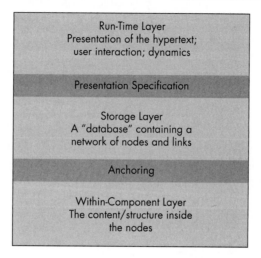

These concepts have been adopted by other hypermedia design models and subsequently were adapted to the Web. Many of these models were based on *entity-relationship modeling* or *object-oriented modeling*.[18]

In general, these techniques were either developed explicitly for modeling information in the context of the Web or have been adapted to this domain. The specific structure, notations, and emphasis vary for each modeling approach. But in every case, the design involves understanding and modeling the underlying information, modeling the way in which the information will be seen by the user, and using the inherent relationships between the underlying information sources to suggest appropriate navigational links.

One of the key limitations of many of the early methods—particularly those that most closely drew on concepts and techniques from hypermedia—was that they focused almost entirely on the detailed information structures and ignored both the higher-level architecture (as we discussed earlier in this chapter) and the integration of complex functionality. Although this is not a major limitation for small-scale informational WebApps (Chapter 1), it is a problem for WebApps that incorporate rich functionality (e.g., e-commerce applications, online banking, auction sites).

---

18 Examples of these early methods included the *Relationship Management Methodology* (RMM) [Isa95], the *Object-Oriented Hypermedia Design Model* (OOHDM) [Sch98], EORM [Lan94], work by Lee [Lee97], WSDM [Det97], and *Web Modeling Language* (WebML) [Cer00]. Other work focuses on how a system is likely to be used [Gue00] and how that impacts the information domain and resultant navigation, and the use of formal methods (HadeZ [Ger99]) using the Z notation to specify conceptual, structural, and perspective schemas.

Web Application Extensions (WAE) [19] [Con99] is one approach that attempts to avoid this problem by adapting UML to accommodate Web functionality. In addition, it attempts to link a user's view of the system (as seen through the interaction with Web pages) to the back-end processes that support this interaction. In the subsections that follow, we'll examine two illustrative navigation design methods—RMM and WebML— and see how they can be applied.

How Is the RMM Model Used for Navigation Design?

The *Relationship Management Methodology* (RMM) [Isa95] is an early navigation design approach that encompasses the following set of activities: feasibility analysis, entity-relationship (E-R) modeling, slice design, navigation design, and construction. Each activity consists of a series of steps and a set of work products (e.g., a "feasibility document" is produced at the end of feasibility analysis). Three RMM activities have relevance in our discussion of information design: ER modeling, slice design, and navigation design.

The *E-R modeling* [20] activity defines the information domain of the application by identifying content (data) objects, attributes, relationships, and various type indicators that comprise the WebApp information space. Content objects are represented by a labeled rectangle. Relationships are indicated with a labeled line connecting objects. The nature of the *connection* between data objects and relationships is established using a variety of special symbols—though there are a number of different ER notations that are in common use. In **SafeHomeAssured.com** we would model users, accounts, products, sensors, and other objects. A partial ER model for **SafeHomeAssured.com** is given in Figure 10.9a. It is worth noting that modeling, even at this level, can lead to the identification of important unresolved issues. In creating the **SafeHomeAssured.com** ER model, the cardinality of the relationship between *sensors* and *floor plans* is considered—which leads to the question of whether or not a sensor can exist on more than one floor plan. The resolution of this (after discussions with the client) is that the floor plans need not be orthogonal (i.e., they can overlap—and hence two floor plans can contain the same sensor). This is because the user might wish to create different but overlapping floor plans that support monitoring of different parts of a home at different times.

The *slice design* activity follows ER modeling and determines detailed information structure and access mechanisms. Basically, this step is about grouping con-

---

19 WAE is discussed later in this chapter in the section, "Is It Possible to Create Models That Link Content and Functionality?"

20 A comprehensive discussion of E-R modeling is beyond the scope of this book. For further guidance see the tutorial "How to Draw Entity Relationship Diagrams" at SmartDraw.com, **http:// www.smartdraw.com/tutorials/software-erd/erd.htm** (accessed August 8, 2007) or the discussion on entity-relationship diagrams at Webopedia, **http://itmanagement.webopedia.com/TERM/E/ entity_relationship_diagram.html** (accessed August 8, 2007).

tent from the domain (captured in the ER model) into collections that can or should be presented together in order to be useful and meaningful. A slice of information might be a small section of an entity (e.g., the name of a user entity or a photo of a product entity), or pieces of information from several entities that are grouped together (e.g., a floor plan combined with the name and type of sensors included within that floor plan). Slices represent a collection of information that is useful for a user when grouped together. They are often constructed hierarchically, gradually combining small items of information and other information collections into progressively richer collections.

A good example of a rich slice in **SafeHomeAssured.com** is shown in Figure 10.9b. In this figure, the rectangles with rounded corners are the underlying information entities, the ovals are attributes within those entities, and the segments are the slices used to combine the entity attributes. This figure shows an information slice that captures the information to be shown to a user (as a single page) after logging in. The slice contains details of the user (e.g., name and last access—included by embedding a previously defined slice), any recent purchase orders, and the current status of these orders (again, using another slice), as well as the name of any floor plans associated with that user and the last five monitoring events associated with each floor plan. Notice that this slice is made up of other slices of information, which are ultimately drawn from the underlying domain model. In practice, these domain entities would likely be implemented as entries in a database (or some other form of information repository, such as XML pages) and the slices would be a suitable query onto this content.

Even without understanding the specific notation of this slice design, it should be clear that this approach allows the designer to collect sections of information together into meaningful units. The slice design guidelines emphasize that each slice represents a whole information unit for the user and is predicated on domain analysis.

The third design step in RMM is *navigation design*—where the links between the various slices are identified. Slice design creates the information units that have interest for various user categories. Ultimately, these information units are aggregated and are transformed into Web pages. The navigation design links these pages by selecting all slices that are the target of a link derived from an ER diagram. Figure 10.9c shows a fragment of a navigation design for **SafeHomeAssured.com.**

The RMM design activities can be bottom-up, top-down, or a combination of the two. For example, in a bottom-up approach the designer can focus initially on each information entity and then on the more general access mechanisms. In a top-down approach the designer focuses first on the general structures during the slice design, and then converts these into lower-level presentation units. In practice the process is likely to be an iterative approach combining both top-down and

FIGURE 10.9

RMM modeling of **SafeHome-Assured.com:**
(a) partial ER model,
(b) m-slice diagram for the main user information, and
(c) partial navigation design.

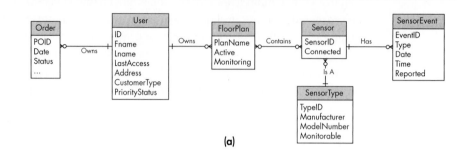

(a)

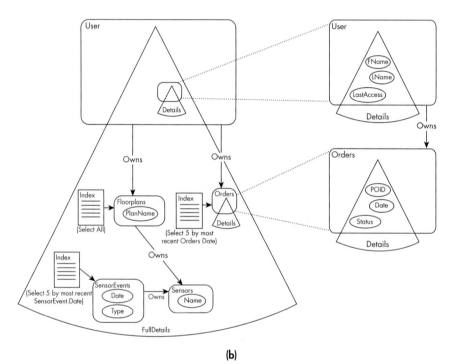

(b)

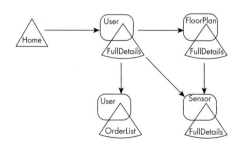

(c)

bottom-up. It is also worth pointing out that during this step the designers have to identify the components and the way in which they are most likely to be accessed. This means that an understanding of the users and their context is quite important.

RMM focuses on modeling the underlying content, the user viewpoints into this content, and the navigational structures that interlink the content. The RMM design process is somewhat subjective and provides relatively little guidance about how to ensure that the slices—and hence, the navigational structures—are grouped most appropriately. It assumes the designer will know (intuitively) which slices are most appropriate and helpful to the user.

How Can WebML Be Used to Create a Navigation Design?

A more recently developed, and richer, notation than RMM is the *Web Modeling Language* (WebML) [Cer00]. This modeling language incorporates robust support for aspects such as workflow modeling, presentation and content adaptation, personalization, and design patterns. It is supported by a CASE (computer-aided software engineering) tool (albeit one that is still rather crude), modeling templates, and a rich set of technical resources.[21]

Figure 10.10 shows the WebML model for the same **SafeHomeAssured.com** RMM example shown in Figure 10.9. Referring to the figure, the basic models in WebML are similar to those in RMM and other design approaches. WebML begins with a data model (broadly equivalent to the RMM ER model). This is then used in the construction of the hypertext model that describes both the content composition and the site navigation. The *composition* specifies which pages compose the WebApp and which content units make up a page (analogous to the slice diagrams in RMM). The *navigation model* expresses how pages and content units are linked to form the WebApp. WebML also includes a *presentation model* that expresses the layout and graphic appearance of pages (independently of the output device and of the rendition language), and a *personalization model* that expresses how the other models change for different user categories.

Is It Possible to Create Models That Link Content and Functionality?

RMM and WebML focus almost entirely on information structures and largely ignore the integration of complex functionality into these structures. WebML does include a number of *operation units* that can be used in the navigation model, but these are best suited to the representation of how the functionality is woven into the user interaction and content presentation, rather than the detailed functional

---

21 Full details on WebML can be found at WebML.org, **www.webml.org** (accessed August 8, 2007).

FIGURE 10.10

WebML modeling of **SafeHomeAssured.com:** (a) partial data model and (b) partial hypertext model.

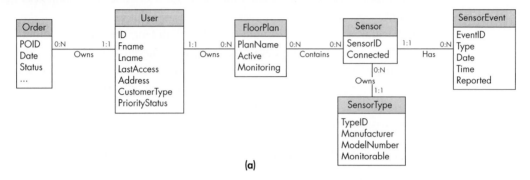

(a)

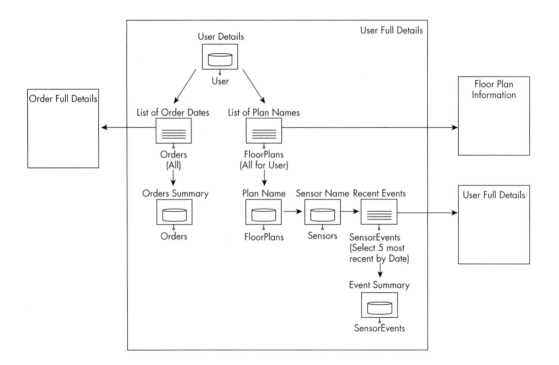

(b)

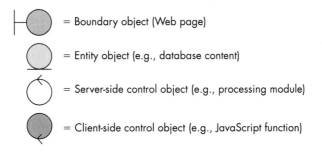

FIGURE 10.11

Example WAE model fragment for **SafeHome-Assured.com.**

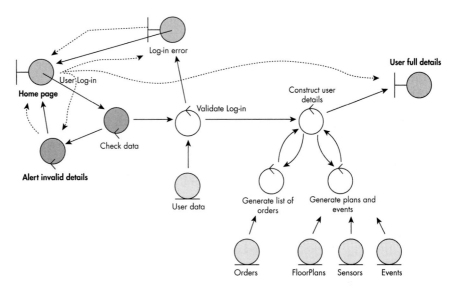

design. Although this is not a major limitation for informational WebApps, it is a problem for WebApps that incorporate sophisticated functionality.[22]

Web Application Extension for UML (WAE) [Con99] is a design approach that links the informational perspective with functional WebApp components. It indicates how functional components generate and/or provide information and how the information (through aspects such as link activation or form submission) triggers functional components. Specifically, WAE models the connection between client-side content and behavior, and server-side functionality.

Figure 10.11 provides a small fragment of a WAE model for **SafeHomeAssured. com.** In this example, both informational and functional elements are included. The functional elements will be discussed in detail in Chapter 11. The informational ele-

---

22 Today, almost all major WebApps (e.g., e-commerce applications, online banking, auction sites) incorporate reasonably sophisticated functionality.

ments include boundary objects (i.e., the Web pages or other components—such as alert boxes—with which the user interacts) and entity objects (i.e., the data sources that provide the content for inclusion in the pages). The other components provide details of how and entity objects are connected.

Does the Structure of the Web Itself Have an Impact?

The World Wide Web was originally conceptualized as a set of protocols that provided a common interface to different applications, rather than as an information application itself. A distributed client-server model continues to be used for access to information and other resources, but the Web does not provide a formal model for information management and access.

Information design can result in the creation of reasonably complex information structures, but the Web itself utilizes a simple node-link model of information structure. Information is presented in nodes, and the nodes are interconnected with simple point-to-point, unidirectional, noncontextual, untyped links. Nodes remain the basic information units, and it is really the links that provide rich navigation functionality.

As the Web has evolved, a complex array of modifications and add-ons have been developed to circumvent the constraints that result from a simple model of hypermedia. Much of the complexity in the construction phase of WebApps occurs when a WebE team attempts to map information designs into the functionality support provided by the Web. For example, the mechanisms used to present information have evolved substantially from the original text-only nodes to a set of very complex media compositions supported by various browsers. Early examples included the use of frames to improve contextualization of information and Java applets to improve the integration of media. More recent examples include the use of technologies such as Ajax. Today, a variety of modifications extend the constrained hypermedia functionality supported by the Web. Examples include the use of plug-ins to provide multiple destination links and applications that provide a map of the interrelationships between information at a website. Most of the modifications have, however, focused on nonhypermedia aspects such as interface improvement and better media handling.

Summarizing the Design Process

Throughout this chapter we have discussed information architectures, blueprints, wireframes, and detailed navigation models. But how do we bring all of these together into an actual design process?

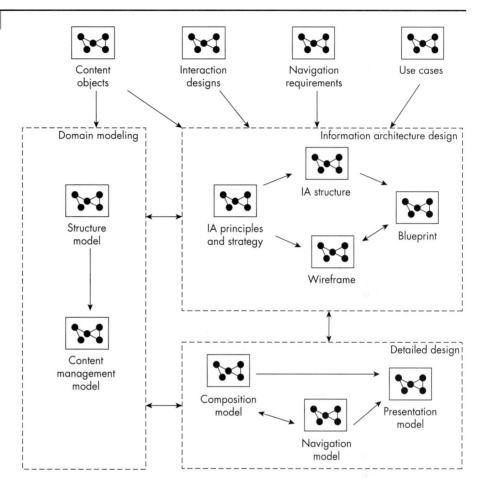

Key design tasks—domain modeling, information architecture design, and detailed design—and their resultant work products are shown in Figure 10.12.

Domain modeling focuses on transforming content objects into a clear model that can be used as the foundation for the information design. The domain model includes a structure model such as those used in WebML or WAE, and a content management model (Chapter 16) that maps the content into manageable forms.

Guided by the principles, characteristics, and techniques discussed earlier in this chapter, the designer creates a model of the information architecture. The information architect uses information produced as part of interaction design and the overall navigation requirements that are driven by the relationships between content objects. The structure of the information space is specified, and a strategy for organizing and managing content is defined. The strategy identifies (1) the approach that will be used for managing content, (2) whether metadata is an issue, (3) how the architecture will be maintained, and (4) what tools will be considered for use. Site blueprints and wireframes are developed and iteratively refined.

The information architecture design is then used as a basis for the detailed design (when necessary). Detailed design encompasses a composition (or slice) model that groups content from the structure model into the specific user-level components. This composition model is jointly developed with the low-level navigation model that defines link structures in detail. Finally, the presentation model maps specific information components into the interface represented in a wireframe model.

It's important to note that the formality of the design process should be tuned to the characteristics of the WebApp to be built. Before you dive into information design and create a comprehensive set of complex models, recognize that the degree of formality with which information design is conducted depends on a variety of issues:

- **Application scale.** As size and complexity (of the WebApp, content objects, and their interrelationships) grows, it becomes more and more important to represent things in a way that enables the WebE team to assess the quality of the design *before* construction begins.

- **Information volatility.** If content is highly dynamic (e.g., the content for an online auction site), it becomes increasingly important to establish a clear structural model as well as a sound set of IA principles and strategies. Conversely, detailed design models become less useful because they would have to be updated too frequently to be of use, and detailed models could inappropriately constrain the WebApp evolution. In addition, the access mechanisms captured in the blueprint must consider the dynamic nature of the content. The blueprint and access mechanisms become central in the information design process.

- **Application volatility.** If overall requirements for a WebApp are likely to change frequently (e.g., the business environment is evolving and unpredictable), the WebApp designer should focus on those aspects of the WebApp and the information space that are known to be stable.[23] Detailed designs are less useful because it would be difficult to maintain them effectively.

- **User heterogeneity.** A WebApp that supports a single homogeneous set of users will be much simpler to design, insofar as the user context will remain relatively consistent. In this case the IA structure and blueprint become

---

23 If nothing is stable, it's reasonable to ask why the project has been initiated.

somewhat less important and the wireframe more important. Conversely, as end-user diversity increases (hence, user goals and tasks become more diverse), it becomes more difficult to ensure that there is overall consistency in the information structures and information access paths. Consequently, the blueprint increases in importance.

- **Application criticality.** Although WebApp quality is always important, it becomes the central focus of the WebE team when a WebApp is mission-critical. In order to ensure quality, the team should conduct a series of reviews that focus on design work products. The models that are created as a consequence of information design can be assessed to ensure that quality will be constructed when the WebApp is built.

The decision about the appropriate depth of modeling for a specific WebApp project should be made early during the design process and not left to an ad hoc decision driven by time pressures.

Where We've Been . . . Where We're Going

For almost all WebApps, content is crucial. Indeed it sits at the core of the application and can be seen as the skeleton upon which the WebApp is built. Even if a WebApp has a well-designed interface and effective functionality, it can be difficult to use and will be open to misinterpretation (recall the seafood bisque example earlier in this chapter if the information design is weak).

The heart of a WebApp information design is the information architecture (IA). The IA describes how information will be organized, accessed, and managed. Indeed, the IA is often the only part of the design that needs to be explicitly documented—given that the detailed information design is much more fluid and often continuously evolving. In fact, this fluidity at a low level makes a solid, carefully constructed IA all the more important. If the IA is flawed, it will allow the inevitable low-level evolution to corrupt the application.

Although a range of models can be used, blueprints and wireframes (or variants of these) typically are the most important models to construct. The blueprint establishes a stable baseline for information access and management. The wireframe forms the bridge to the interaction design. Other models complement these and clarify specific details or approaches.

If the information design forms the "skeleton" of a WebApp, then the muscles, tendons, and joints—those things that make the skeleton move and achieve something—are the functional components of the WebApp. In Chapter 11 we consider how the functional elements are designed and then look at how these are bound to the information designs to create an effective whole.

References

[Cer00]   Ceri, S., P. Fraternali, and A. Bongio, "Web Modeling Language (WebML): A Modeling Language for Designing Web Sites," in *Proc. WWW9 Conference,* Amsterdam, 2000, pp. 137–157.

[Che96]   Chen, M. S., J. S. Park, and P. S. Yu, "Data Mining for Path Traversal Patterns in a Web Environment," in *Proc. International Conference on Distributed Computing Systems,* Chicago, October 1–4, 1996, pp. 385–393.

[Con99]   Conallen, J., *Building Web Applications with UML,* Object Technology Series, Addison-Wesley, 1999, p. 336.

[Coo99]   Cooley, R., B. Mobasher, and J. Srivastava, "Data Preparation for Mining World Wide Web Browsing Pattern," *Knowledge and Information Systems* vol. 1, no. 1, 1999, pp. 5–32.

[Det97]   De Troyer, O., and C. Leune, "WSDM: A User-Centered Design Method for Web Sites," In *Proc. 7th International World Wide Web Conference,* Elsevier, Brisbane, Australia, 1997, pp. 85–94.

[Ger99]   German, D. M., and D. D. Cowan, "Formalizing the Specification of Web Applications," *Lecture Notes in Computer Science,* Issue 1727, Springer Verlag, 1999, pp. 281–292.

[Gue00]   Guell, N., D. Schwabe, and P. Vilain, "Modeling Interactions and Navigation in Web Applications," In *Proc. World Wide Web and Conceptual Modeling'00 Workshop—ER'00 Conference,* Salt Lake City, 2000, pp. 115–127.

[Hal94]   Halasz, F., and M. Schwartz, "The Dexter Hypertext Reference Model," *Communications of the ACM* vol. 37, no. 2, 1994, pp. 30–39.

[Har93]   Hardman, L., D. Bulterman, and G. van Rossum, "The Amsterdam Hypermedia Model: Extending Hypertext to Support Real Multimedia," *Hypermedia Journal* vol. 5, no. 1, 1993, pp. 47–69.

[Isa95]   Isakowitz, T., E. Stohr, and P. Balasubramanian, "RMM: A Methodology for Structured Hypermedia Design," *Communications of the ACM* vol. 38, no. 8, 1995, pp. 34–44.

[Lan94]   Lange, D., "An Object-Oriented Design Method for Hypermedia Information Systems," *HICSS-27: Proc. 27th Hawaii International Conference on System Sciences,* Maui, Hawaii, 1994, pp. 366–375.

[Lee97]   Lee, S. C., "A Structured Navigation Design Method for Intranets," In *Proc. Third Americas Conference on Information Systems,* Association for Information Systems (AIS), Indianapolis, 1997.

[Low99]   Lowe, D., and W. Hall, *Hypermedia and the Web: An Engineering Approach,* Wiley, 1999.

[Pow00]   Powell, T., *Web Design,* McGraw-Hill/Osborne, 2000.

[Ros02]   Rosenfeld, L., and P. Morville, *Information Architecture for the World Wide Web,* 2nd ed., O'Reilly, 2002.

[Sch98]   Schwabe, D., and G. Rossi, "Developing Hypermedia Applications Using OOHDM," presented at *Workshop on Hypermedia Development Processes, Methods and Models (Hypertext'98),* Pittsburgh, 1998.

[Spi98]   Spiliopoulou, M., and L. C. Faulstich, "WUM: A Tool for Web Utilization Analysis," *EDBT, Workshop WebDB'98, LNCS 1590,* Springer Verlag, March 1998, pp. 184–203.

[Tak97]   Takahashi, K., and E. Liang, "Analysis and Design of Web-based Information Systems," presented at *7th International World Wide Web Conference,* Brisbane, Australia, 1997.

[Ton03]   Tongrungrojana, R., and D. Lowe, "WebML+: Connecting Business Models to Information Designs," *SEKE: 15th International Conference on Software Engineering and Knowledge Engineering,* eds., K. Zhang and J. Debenham, Knowledge Systems Institute, 2003, pp. 17–24.

[Wod06] Christina Wodtke, "Information Architecture: Blueprints for the Web," 2006, **www.eleganthack.com/blueprint/author.php** (accessed August 8, 2007).

11

Functional Design

Content might be the core of a WebApp, but functionality makes it sing and dance. The users of modern WebApps expect that robust content will be coupled with sophisticated functionality and that this functionality will allow them to magnify their understanding of content, characterize content in different ways, personalize their interaction, and provide added value to their website visit. It is for this reason that WebApp designers spend increasingly greater amounts of project effort on the design of functionality that will be incorporated into each WebApp increment.

WebApp Functionality

Modern WebApps are radically different from those that existed during the early days of the Web, and possibly the greatest change has been in the incorporation of progressively more sophisticated and complex functionality. As we noted in Chapter 1, the earliest Web-based applications focused on providing access to content. This was accomplished using the core Web architecture and the earliest forms of HTML and the Hypertext Transfer Protocol (HTTP). As time passed, HTML was extended to allow more sophisticated formatting and the subsequent introduction of style sheets.

Simple functionality began to emerge through the use of server-side scripting[1] and client-side plug-ins. The inexorable push for more sophisticated and seamless levels of user interaction then led to the introduction of client-side scripting. By the end of the Web's first decade, the focus of WebApps had shifted substantially. Improvements in technical infrastructure resulted in WebApps that were functionally very rich. In recent years, we have seen the emergence of concepts and technologies that continue this trend—such as Web 2.0, Ajax, and Web services. All place a strong emphasis on support for rich functionality and highly interactive applications (typified by WebApps such as blogs, wikis, and RSS-driven applications).

Because early WebApps focused primarily on information management and access, the focus of the design process (when one was applied),

---

1 One of the first forms of server-side functionality—Common Gateway Interface (CGI)—emerged in 1993 in the very early days of the Web.

practices, and models was quite naturally on information design. As the focus of WebApps has shifted toward increasingly complex functionality, design approaches have lagged behind. The challenge for WebE teams is to conduct functional design in a way that complements other design activities (e.g., interaction design and information design) in a seamless manner.

In some respects WebApp functional design is simpler than functional design for conventional applications. The functional design of WebApps is almost always component based and compartmentalized. This enables many functions to be designed as simple WebApp increments without too much concern for coupling among components.[2] Functional design leverages sophisticated languages that are well integrated with the Web environment (consider, for example, the strong relationship between JavaScript and HTML) and can draw upon advanced frameworks and environments (Chapter 14). When functional design works well, it can be as simple as adopting a particular framework and tuning the built-in functionality for the purposes of the WebApp to be constructed. For example, a good content management system (Chapter 16) might provide most of the functionality required to implement a rich product catalog as part of a WebApp.

However, in other respects, WebApp functional design can be much more complex than for conventional applications. The designer must consider the substantial constraints imposed by the Web infrastructure—such as a distributed model (which complicates aspects like information handling and user responsiveness), security issues, and the limited interface model inherent in Web browsers. It is also more difficult to achieve effective integration if the associated information architecture is complex.

In this chapter we examine WebApp functional design in an attempt to provide a pathway through this maze. We begin by considering the nature of WebApp functionality and how different types of functionality within a WebApp should be handled. This leads to the description of a process for designing the functional components of a WebApp. We then move on to consider an overall functional architecture for WebApps and how it might be developed. We finish by considering various aspects of the detailed functional design.

The Nature of WebApp Functionality

The scale, complexity, and type of functionality that is incorporated into a WebApp can vary significantly. As a consequence, the WebE team's approach to functional design must be tuned to the types of functionality that have been requested by

---

2 It's important to note, however, that *coupling*—a qualitative measure of the degree to which components are connected to one another—may still be a concern in functionally complex WebApps.

stakeholders and identified as part of the communication activity (Chapter 4). Before we discuss how to perform functional design, it's worth considering the different types of WebApp functionality that are likely to be encountered. To illustrate this let us consider some examples.

What Are Typical Examples of Functionality?

A WebApp function can be something as simple as implementing a pull-down menu or as complex as performing the sophisticated calculations required to support a business workflow. To illustrate the spectrum of functional complexity, consider a few examples:

Example 1: Client-side interaction support. WebApps often incorporate client-side functionality aimed at providing support for user navigation and information access (see Figure 11.1a). The most common examples of these are drop-down menus, rollovers, and image preloading.

Example 2: Client-side information management. WebApps sometimes implement complex client-side manipulation of information (see Figure 11.1b). Examples include browser-based interfaces to an underlying functional application, and applications involving complex information manipulation, including preloading of data and Ajax applications.

Example 3: Server-side content handling. WebApps can incorporate server-side functionality to manage dynamic and rapidly changing content (see Figure 11.1c). Examples here would be discussion boards, wikis, and sites presenting content from live events (e.g., news sites, sports sites).

Example 4: Server-side management of large data sets. WebApps can use server-side functionality to manage large complex data sets (see Figure 11.1d). Examples include product catalogs, document repositories, libraries, and personnel lists.

Example 5: Process and/or workflow support. WebApps often implement a specific computational or transformational process that supports procedural data entry, transaction management, or business workflows (see Figure 11.1e). Examples include online shopping, enrollment processes, and online surveys.

Can Functionality Be Categorized?

The examples we have just discussed illustrate the diversity of WebApp functionality, but examples alone do not provide sufficient guidance for designing this functionality. As a first step in our discussion of functional design, we'll establish categories of functionality, understand the attributes of each category, and then consider how each is addressed as part of the design process. WebApp function-

FIGURE 11.1

Examples of different WebApp functionality: (a) Drop-down menus as an example of client-side information access support (**www.smh.com.au**). (b) Image zooming and scrolling as an example of client-side manipulation of data (**maps.google.com**). (c) Live score updates as an example of functionality to handle dynamic content (**www.wimbledon.org**). (d) Searching a product repository as an example of managing large data sets (**www.amazon.com**). (e) A workflow process as an example of WebApp process support (**www.amazon.com**).

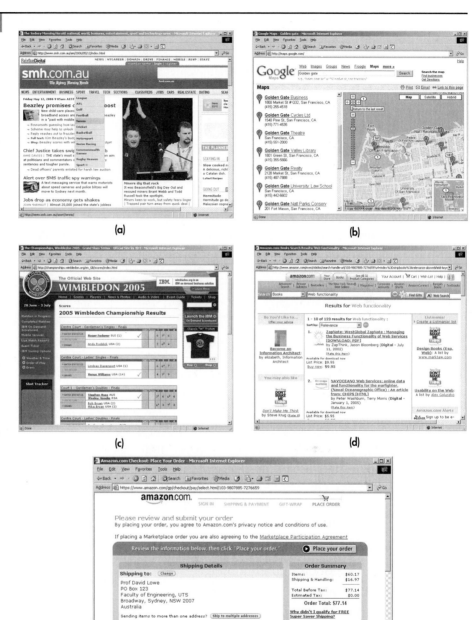

ality can be classified into six main categories that are summarized in Table 11.1 (along with a brief example for each from **SafeHomeAssured.com**).

It should be noted that the User-Level Functionality category does not imply client-side functionality (i.e., implemented "close" to the user). Similarly, the Application-Level Functionality category does not imply server-side functionality. Where and how the functionality is implemented is essentially an issue that is addressed when the functional architecture is designed. These two broad groupings relate to the *intent* of the functionality—and hence, *when* (rather than *how* or *where*) you should be considering it.

For example, with **SafeHomeAssured.com,** the formatting of the product information for presentation to the user would be considered as category 1B (User Information Support) but may well occur within a content management system (CMS) on the server. Conversely, logging the user's actions in interacting with the application (including not only which links are selected, but also where the mouse is moved) is considered category 2A (Application Interaction Support) but might be tracked by client-side scripting.

It is also useful to note that these categories, while broadly orthogonal, are not completely independent. Indeed, in many cases there will be different ways of viewing the same functionality. To illustrate this, consider a **SafeHomeAssured. com** function that provides live data updates from an active security sensor. We could implement the live updates through some user-level functionality that periodically causes the client to request an update that is then dynamically generated (on request) from the underlying data repository. Conversely, we could conceive of this as an application-level issue where a back-end process regularly regenerates the sensor pages from an underlying data stream. In this particular case, it should be seen as both. The regular updating of the *available* information to reflect the current sensor data is an application-level functionality. The repeated refreshing of the *displayed* information is a user-level functionality.

Is It Always Possible to Distinguish Between Information and Function?

Often, the boundary between the information and functional domains is blurred. Consider a WebApp information architecture that has included breadcrumbs (Chapter 10) in the design in order to provide support for users to maintain their orientation within the information space. The functional designer might decide to implement this particular characteristic of the information architecture by adding some code to the Web server that automatically generates and adds breadcrumbs for every page that is delivered. In this case the functional design is being driven by a particular need in the information design.

Table 11.1 WEBAPP FUNCTIONALITY CATEGORIES

Group 1: User-Level (External) Functionality. These categories include functionality that directly affects users' experience of the WebApp and is usually directly perceivable by them.

Category 1A: User Interaction Support. This category of functionality includes anything that affects the way in which a user might directly interact with the WebApp and encompasses the following: dynamically adapting the access mechanisms (e.g., highlighting a link when the mouse is positioned over it), facilitating access to navigation mechanisms (e.g., drop-down menus), adaptation (online or off-line, personal or global) of the navigational structures and available options, and providing global navigation options (e.g., a site main menu) and location support (e.g., breadcrumbs).

SafeHomeAssured.com example: As was shown in Figure 9.4, a user applies a set of tools to draw a layout of the floor space. This particular increment will require very sophisticated drawing support, such as the ability to drag and drop items from the drawing toolbox.

Category 1B: User Information Support. This category covers any functionality that affects the nature of the information and/or how it is presented to the user and includes the following: content and presentation adaptation, live or dynamic content updating, user modification of content, and providing global contextual information (e.g., functionality to automatically include a site banner or enforce particular style sheets).

SafeHomeAssured.com example: Presentation to the user of live sensor data for security monitoring (see Figure 9.8).

Category 1C: User Task Support. This includes any functionality that supports, guides, or controls the user in achieving specific tasks. The most common examples are searching and workflow management (e.g., handling the workflow path being followed by a user, including the various options and exceptions), but it also encompasses the following: generation of trails and breadcrumbs, dynamic checking and feedback on user-provided information, login mechanisms, and access control.

SafeHomeAssured.com example: Product order management.

Group 2: Application-Level (Internal) Functionality. These categories relate to functionality that is necessary to support the WebApp, but which will only be visible to users as a second-order effect.

Category 2A: Application Interaction Support. This category covers the functionality that is necessary to manage and maintain the interaction mechanisms but not to directly control the specific elements with which a user interacts. This will encompass, for example, tracking and recording of the interactions by particular users (so that subsequent evaluation and adaptation can occur). Other aspects include the following: search index generation and maintenance, usage logging and analysis, and monitoring for broken links and other potential interaction faults.

SafeHomeAssured.com example: Profiling of users based on their product history.

Category 2B: Application Information Support. This encompasses any application-level management of information. This includes the following: development and maintenance of content management systems (CMS), database maintenance, and monitoring for content expiration or style discrepancies.

SafeHomeAssured.com example: Background monitoring of customers' security sensors during times they are not logged in.

Category 2C: Application Task Support. This covers the internal WebApp support for overall user tasks. This includes aspects such as gateways to other applications (such as payment systems within an e-commerce WebApp); user authentication; and batch, off-line, or time-critical task processing (such as processing of submitted orders or monitoring of an online auction progress).

SafeHomeAssured.com example: Batch processing of customer orders.

The reverse can also occur (though less commonly). As a simple example consider a particular workflow that incorporates a sequence of steps. Each of these steps is then implemented as a set of pages in a navigational pathway. In this case the information design is being driven by a particular need in the functional design.

What this tells you is that the information and functional designs are deeply interwoven and may need to be carried out in parallel. This will be discussed in more detail in the following section.

Functional Design in the Design Process

Functional design is not a discrete task that is performed at just one point in the design process. Rather, it is interwoven with other design activities. The functional categorization presented in the preceding section, "The Nature of WebApp Functionality," gives us a way of focusing on different aspects of the desired functionality and looking at where they are addressed in the design process.

Taking a broad view of WebApp design, there is a major split between user-level functionality and application-level functionality. *User-level functionality* is the expression of the WebApp capabilities that support users in achieving their goals. *Application-level functionality* represents a lower-level design of internal functionality that may not be directly visible to users (except in terms of second-order effects). Given these definitions, it is reasonable to state that user-level functionality is more tightly coupled to the core WebApp requirements and the consequent analysis. Application-level functionality is more deeply embedded within the structure of the WebApp and will often emerge out of the progressive design of the user-level functionality.

Referring to Figure 11.2, the outer layers represent the progressive specification of the WebApp. The inner layers relate to the design. The aspect of design that is the closest expression of the requirements is the interaction design, a task that captures the way in which a user interacts with the application. The interaction (interface) design has both information and functional elements, and often precipitates specific information design and the functional design tasks. Both information design and functional design can progress in parallel and often occur iteratively. The user-level functional aspects respond to the designed interactions and determine how these will be achieved. The application-level functional design provides the internal support for achieving user functionality. Hence, application-level functional design will typically follow, and respond to, the user-level functional design.

What Are the Elements of a Functional Design Process?

The elements of a functional design process are shown in Figure 11.3. Referring to the figure, the functional design commences with the design of the user functionality, derived from a definition of user goals (documented as plain language state-

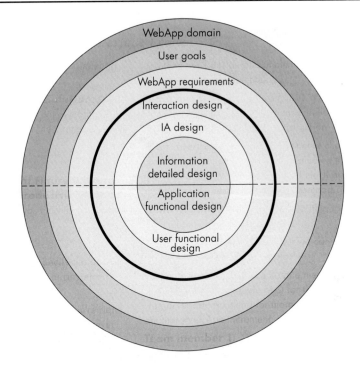

ments and/or use cases during the communication activity). User functionality is represented as both the interaction model (UML sequence and/or state diagrams) and the functional model (UML activity diagrams).

The user functionality design is developed in parallel with the information architecture to ensure that they are consistent. In essence you begin by considering both the analysis model (Chapter 7) and the initial information architecture (Chapter 10) and then examining how functionality affects the following:

- The user's interaction with the application
- The information that is presented
- The user tasks that are conducted

The user functionality design will be combined with the information design to create a functional architecture. A *functional architecture* is a representation of the functional domain of the WebApp and describes the key functional components in the WebApp and how these components interact with each other. Given its central role, we'll discuss the functional architecture in considerable detail later in this chapter in the section "Functional Architecture."

The application functionality design defines the internal support functionality for the WebApp. It usually follows from the user functionality and will also affect the functional architecture.

FIGURE 11.3

WebApp functional design process.

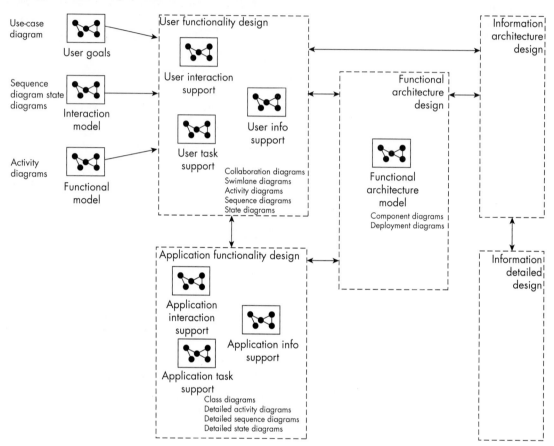

How Much Functional Design Is Enough?

Like all other design tasks, the formality and breadth of functional design will depend on the nature of the WebApp. A large WebApp with complex functionality that is deeply woven into the organization's business processes will typically require the full set of functional design modeling tasks shown in Figure 11.3.[3] Conversely, a smaller WebApp that only supplements an organization's business operations will require much less formal design. In such a case, functional design might be limited to sequence diagrams for the user functionality and a component diagram for the functional architecture.

---

3   This is particularly true when the WebApp is a key business interface to potential and actual customers.

For **SafeHomeAssured.com,** different increments will require quite different levels of functional design. The first WebApp increment (related to the company and its products) will have very little functional complexity—probably being limited to some content management for the product database—and hence the functional design would be minimal. For increment 6 (related to the control and monitoring of sensors), the functionality will be much more complex, and hence the design will be much more detailed.

How Would Initial Functional Design Be Conducted for SafeHomeAssured.com?

SafeHomeAssured.com has an interesting mix of information-focused and functionally focused components. In the initial communication activity (Chapter 4), we identified an initial set of informational and applicative goals for **SafeHomeAssured.com** reproduced in part here:

- To provide users with requested product specs.
- To provide tools that will enable users to represent the layout of a "space" (i.e., house, office/retail space) that is to be protected.
- To make customized recommendations about security and monitoring products that can be used within the user space.
- To enable users to obtain a quote for product cost.
- To allow users to place an order for security hardware.
- To allow users to control monitoring equipment (e.g., cameras, microphones) within their space.
- To enable users to "sign up" for monitoring services.
- To allow monitoring customers to query the monitoring database about their account activity.

These goals were then refined into the following list of functions to be performed:

- Provide product quotation
- Process security system order
- Process user data
- Create user profile
- Draw user space layout
- Recommend security system for layout
- Process monitoring order
- Get and display account info
- Get and display monitoring info
- Customer service functions (to be defined later)
- Tech support functions (to be defined later)

Ultimately these functions are elaborated into a set of use cases that capture the key user information and functional interactions.

As we noted earlier, the first **SafeHomeAssured.com** increment is predominantly information focused (Chapter 4), but subsequent increments begin to introduce increasingly complex functionality. Let's consider increment 2, which covers the following usage scenarios or use cases.

Card No.	Card Name
2	Download product specs.
3	Get info that is customized to my user category.
4	Look up a specific sensor.

During analysis modeling, the WebE team developed simple content and interaction models for this increment, but decided that the functionality was so simple that a separate functional model was not really necessary (especially since much of the functionality in this case would be quite clear from the sequence diagram of the interaction model).

Design in this case would commence with the information architecture, given that the three usage scenarios all relate to access to information. However, once a draft information architecture has been developed, the team would be able to ask and answer the following questions:

Q: Is there any required functionality that affects the user interaction with the application?

A: For scenario 4, users browse the product catalog by drilling down through product categories. The scenario indicates that the users select a particular category from a list of all categories. They are then provided with a list of subcategories. When they select a subcategory, all products in that category are listed, allowing a specific product to then be selected. This is shown in the wireframe in Figure 11.4.

Q: Is there any required functionality that affects the information that is presented?

A: For scenario 3, the products that are presented are customized to the user category (e.g., *guest, registered user,* or *homeowner*). The domain model developed previously shows that certain products are available only to registered users, and certain information (such as price) changes depending upon the user class. Functionality is required to support content adaptation.

Q: Is there any required functionality that affects the user tasks being carried out?

A: Accessing products requires search support.

Some aspects of the initial functional design for these user functions can be performed immediately, but other aspects of these functions will be performed in conjunction with, or will influence, the development of the overall functional architecture. For example, the functionality associated with changing the subcategory list when a category is selected, and changing the product list when a subcategory is chosen, will require client-side functionality. This can be designed immediately, or more likely, could be extracted from an existing JavaScript code library for this type of functionality. However, the functionality will also require appropriate server-side functionality to generate the product lists and build the resultant client page. This is where you start making general architectural decisions.

Our discussion in this section illustrates that some aspects of the functional design will be straightforward due, at least in part, to the inherent structures and technologies imposed by the broader Web architecture. Other aspects, however, will need deeper consideration and require the development of an overall functional architecture.

Example wire-
frame for **Safe-
HomeAssured.
com** product
browsing.

Functional Architecture

A functional architecture is a representation of the functional domain of the
WebApp. The architectural representation answers two key questions:

- How do we partition the functionality into components that have clearly
  defined roles and interfaces?

- Where does each functional component exist, and what does it interact with?

In other words, the functional architecture decomposes the WebApp into constituent functional components.

What Does a Functional Architecture Look Like?

There are many ways of modeling and documenting functional architectures[4]; however, because most WebApps are highly modular, a good baseline model is a UML component diagram [OMG04]. This diagram indicates how the WebApp would be organized into a set of main system *components* and represents the connections between these components.[5]

Figure 11.5 presents a preliminary functional architecture for increment 2 of **SafeHomeAssured.com.** Note that the *location* of the functional components describes where the functional components are executed, rather than where they are stored (or even generated, if the functionality is dynamically created). In this architecture the decision has been made to dynamically generate the product information pages (including the intermediate category pages). This occurs because the actual content is dependent upon the user class. In this particular architecture, the generation of the product access, category, and product information pages (which would have been designed as part of the information architecture) are created dynamically by the *dynamic page compilation* component. This in turn will use either the *search result generation* or the *product page generation* component to create the page content, and the *product menu generation* component to create the associated menus and other navigation aids (such as breadcrumbs). A back-end component, *search indexer,* will be responsible for generation of the search indexes.

Note that this architectural model has also been extended to show the relationship to the information architecture.[6] For example, the *dynamic page compilation* component is responsible for creating the *product access* page and all subpages below this in the information hierarchy. When the IA is modified, we can see what functional components are likely to be affected, and vice versa.

How Do We Develop the Functional Architecture?

The obvious place to initiate the functional design is to consider both the WebApp analysis model (along with any specifications that accompany it) and the initial information architecture. We have already noted that it is possible to identify the functionality that exists in each of the categories listed in Table 11.1. Each scenario or part of a scenario (such as *Customize product content depending upon user type*) can be decomposed into the following generic scenario component categories:

---

4   We recommend you examine [Bas03]. This is an excellent overall introduction to software architectures and will give you a good understanding of many of the architectural issues that a Web engineer needs to consider.
5   See the quick introduction to UML 2 component diagrams on the Agile Modeling site at **www.agilemodeling.com/artifacts/componentDiagram.htm.** (accessed August 7, 2007).
6   This means that this diagram is no longer a *strictly UML compliant* component diagram, but in the interest of demonstrating the relationship between the information and functional architectures, we believe that this is appropriate.

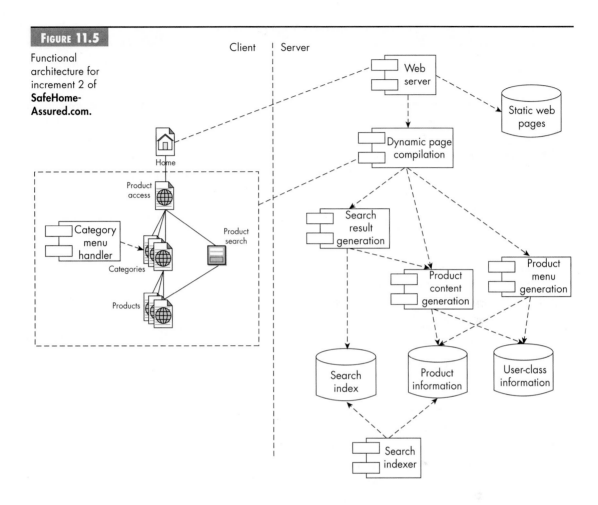

FIGURE 11.5

Functional architecture for increment 2 of **SafeHome-Assured.com.**

- *Information selection* (i.e., functionality associated with the identification and/or selection of information to be presented to the user)

- *Information compilation* (i.e., functionality associated with merging information together into a composite to be presented to the user)

- *Information processing* (i.e., the analysis or calculation of data)

- *System interaction* (i.e., functionality associated with interactions with other systems external to the WebApp)

We then consider whether the specific scenario component should be invoked dynamically on user request, dynamically on event initiation, or manually. Finally, we perform a clustering, amalgamation, and refinement of the architecture components. As an example, consider the sidebar discussion associated with the development of a functional architecture for **SafeHomeAssured.com.**

SAFEHOME

SafeHome

Functional Architecture Modeling

The scene: SafeHomeAssured.com WebE team meeting room after the initial development of the IA for the second increment (product access)

The players: The WebE team leader and the team member who has taken on the role of system architect

The conversation:

Team leader: Okay, so we have a relatively clear IA for the second increment. What are your thoughts on how we tie this in with the functionality that's needed?

System architect: Well, I've been thinking about the general functional architecture. If this were a simple, small product catalog, we'd manage it as just static pages. Even if the catalog was bigger, we could still just stick all the product information in a single database with an extra table that links products into one or more categories. We'd then access the products through a simple script that dynamically generates the intermediate pages, as well as the product pages. This would be pretty easy, since the client already has all the product information in a couple of databases that we can merge. But . . .

Team leader: So, what's the complication?

System architect: Well, in this case we need to adapt the product content based on who the user is.

Knowing the user type is pretty easy—we can just use the Web server session variable that gets set when they log in—but the tricky part is actually adapting the content as well as the other aspects.

Team leader: What do you mean?

System architect: Actually, we can still extract the content dynamically; it's just that there's a bit of extra functionality associated with first adapting the content to modify things like prices. Remember that marketing said that certain users get an automatic discount on the standard prices. We also have to make sure we only link to and allow access to pages that are okay for that user category.

Team leader (pointing at the diagram that was shown in Figure 11.5): Okay, so in your sketch here . . . the *product content generation* component is about creating the right product information for the user, the *product menu generation* component creates the structures and links to available products, and the dynamic page *compilation* component puts them together . . .

System architect: Yeah, you've got it, and the *compilation* component also does all the housekeeping stuff like adding the right banners and footers as well.

[They continue to discuss the diagram, including how the search functionality is integrated into the architecture.]

A number of other factors, in addition to those discussed in the sidebar, can also affect the design of the functional architecture. For example, allowing multiple administrative users to manage and update content might indicate that the use of a CMS is appropriate. This suggests, or even imposes, a particular shape to at least part of the functional architecture (e.g., the CMS might facilitate automated content adaptation).

What About Functionality for Exception Handling?

Because a major factor in the functional design is often the handling of exceptions, it is important to design functionality that enables the system to cope with unusual circumstances. For most increments in **SafeHomeAssured.com,** this is not a major issue, but exception handling must still be considered. For example, product information is assessed within the *dynamic page compilation* component. This component generates *SafeHome* product access pages and also generates the intermediate category pages that form the navigational pathway to the products (as defined in the information architecture). This allows these intermediate pages to be generated in a way that ensures that they contain links only to those products that are available to the current user. Consider the following two HTML fragments for the same *security cameras* category page:

Web page: Security Camera Category (for Guests)

```
. . .
<a href="/products/genprod.exe?type=prod&prod-id=3467"><div class="Product">Camera Model XF67</div></a>
<a href="/products/genprod.exe?type=prod&prod-id=3470"><div class="Product">Camera Model XQ99</div></a>
. . .
```

Web page: Security Camera Category (for Account Holder)

```
. . .
<a href="/products/genprod.exe?type=prod&prod-id=3467"><div class="Product">Camera Model XF67</div></a>
<a href="/products/genprod.exe?type=prod&prod-id=3468"><div class="Product">Camera Model XF69</div></a>
<a href="/products/genprod.exe?type=prod&prod-id=3470"><div class="Product">Camera Model XQ99</div></a>
. . .
```

The *dynamic page compilation* component has excluded (from the list provided for guests) one of the security camera products (*Model XF69*) that is available only for account holders. However—and this is the key point—what if the URL for that product information (or rather, for dynamically generating that product information) was e-mailed by an account holder to a guest? That is, what happens if a guest directly entered the URL:

www.safehomeassured.com/products/genprod.exe?type=prod&prod-id=3469

If the **SafeHomeAssured.com** WebApp is designed to control access to products by relying on the *product menu generation* component,[7] there would be an easy way for users to bypass this control. To avoid this problem, the *dynamic page compilation* component must also check appropriate accesses and reply with a suitable error message page when necessary. This is an example of ensuring that the functional architecture addresses possible exceptions and doesn't create "functional loopholes."

---

7 The *product menu generation* component would create links to those products that are available for a specific user.

Overall, exception handling is a relatively straightforward design issue for simple informational WebApps. It becomes much more complex when a WebApp has complex workflows in which the sequencing of events can be compromised or lead to situations that are difficult to handle. Consider, for example, the following scenario in an online hotel WebApp. A user wishes to book a hotel room for a particular night. The user enters a date, and the WebApp checks availability and finds that one room is available. This is communicated to the user, who then requests that the room be booked and provides payment details. The WebApp confirms the booking.

This workflow seems simple enough. But what would have happened if between checking for room availability (only one was available) and asking to make the booking, someone else booked that room? If the workflow was poorly designed, the WebApp may not have checked availability again upon payment. The room might then be double-booked! Issues such as these are exacerbated in the Web environment due to the distributed nature of WebApps. In the next section, "Detailed Functional Design," we briefly examine how this can be handled through the use of state diagram models.

In theory, the functional architecture can be designed prior to the selection of underpinning technology (and then used to drive the technology selection). In practice, this is rarely the case. There is a strong interplay between the technology frameworks and the architecture that is adopted—since the frameworks impose certain constraints and support certain approaches. We will look at these issues in more detail in Chapter 14.

Can Architectural Patterns Be Used During Functional Design?

Patterns are discussed in detail in Chapter 13. However, one particular pattern—*model-view-controller*—for WebApp functional architectures is so common that it is worth discussing briefly here.

Jacyntho and his colleagues [Jac02] suggest a three-layer design architecture that decouples an application interface from navigation and from application behavior. They argue that keeping interface, application, and navigation separate simplifies implementation and enhances reuse. The *model-view-controller* (MVC) architecture [Kra88] is one of a number of suggested WebApp infrastructure models that decouples the user interface from the WebApp functionality and informational content. The **Model** part of the MVC architecture (sometimes referred to as the "**Model** object") contains all application-specific content and processing logic, including all content objects, access to external data and information sources, and all processing functionalities that are application specific. In other words, this is essentially the content, as well as any metadata, navigational structures, user profiles, and so on.

The **View** part of the MVC architecture contains all interface-specific functions and enables the presentation of content and processing logic, including all content objects, access to external data and information sources, and all processing functionalities required by the end user.

The **Controller** part of the MVC architecture manages access to and manipulation of the **Model** and the **View.** It also coordinates the flow of data between them. In a WebApp, the controller monitors user interaction and, based on this, takes data from the **Model** and uses this to update or construct the **View.** A schematic representation of the MVC architecture is shown in Figure 11.6.

Referring to the figure, user requests or data are handled by the **Controller.** The **Controller** also selects the **View** object that is applicable based on the user request. Once the type of request is determined, a behavior request is transmitted to the **Model,** which implements the functionality or retrieves the content required to accommodate the request. The **Model** object can access data stored in a corporate database, as part of a local data store or as a collection of independent files. The data developed by the **Model** must be formatted and organized by the appropriate **View** object and then transmitted from the application server back to the client-based browser for display on the customer's machine.

If you compare Figure 11.5 with Figure 11.6, you will notice that the functional architecture that was developed for increment 2 of **SafeHomeAssured.com** has

---

FIGURE 11.6

The MVC architecture.
Source: Adapted from [Jac02].

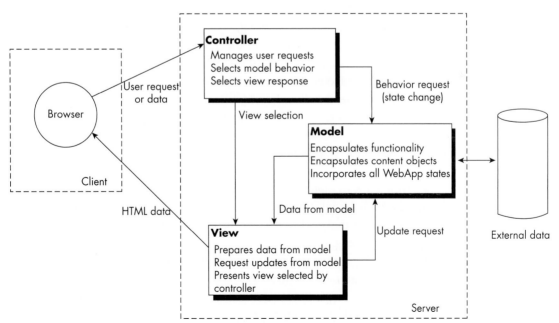

strong similarities to the MVC model, though the **View** and **Control** aspects are intertwined.

In many cases, a WebApp functional architecture is defined within the context of the development environment in which the application is to be implemented (e.g., ASP.net, JWAA, or J2EE). If you have further interest, see [Fow03] for a discussion of development environments and their role in the design of Web application architectures.

Detailed Functional Design

Because the WebE process is incremental and WebApp construction usually makes heavy use of component-based development, detailed functional design results in few formal models or detailed documentation. When modeling is required, it borrows heavily from conventional functional design approaches such as UML [OMG04] [Pil05]. UML provides a number of design representations that are useful for the functional designer (e.g., sequence diagrams, state diagrams), but it does not provide good integration with detailed information design. However, both WAE and WebML (informational design approaches discussed in Chapter 10) can be extended to the functional domain.

How Can WAE Modeling Be Used for Detailed Design?

WAE establishes a set of extensions to UML that facilitate the modeling of WebApp low-level design [Con99]. In Chapter 10, we illustrated the use of WAE with an example for **SafeHomeAssured.com** shown in Figure 10.11. WAE is particularly suited to modeling the client-server interactions that are typical of WebApps.

Figure 11.7 shows the main icons used to represent objects within a WAE model. By combining these icons, it becomes possible to represent complex interactions between data objects, functional objects, and presentation objects—as well as to indicate where the interaction between these objects occurs. The analysis view was illustrated in Chapter 10. The logical view describes the conceptual elements in the WebApp, whereas the physical view shows how this maps to actual implementation components.

Referring back to Figure 10.11, you can see that it captures both information structure and functional processing, but doesn't show the specific design of the logical components that enable this mixing of information and function. Figure 11.8 shows the logical design that is derived from Figure 10.11 and highlights the way in which functionality leads to information, and vice versa.

WAE models are useful when exploring the functional-information boundary, but in general they would be a rather cumbersome approach for undertaking the detailed functional design of an entire WebApp. We recommend limiting their use

FIGURE 11.7

WAE model key notation.

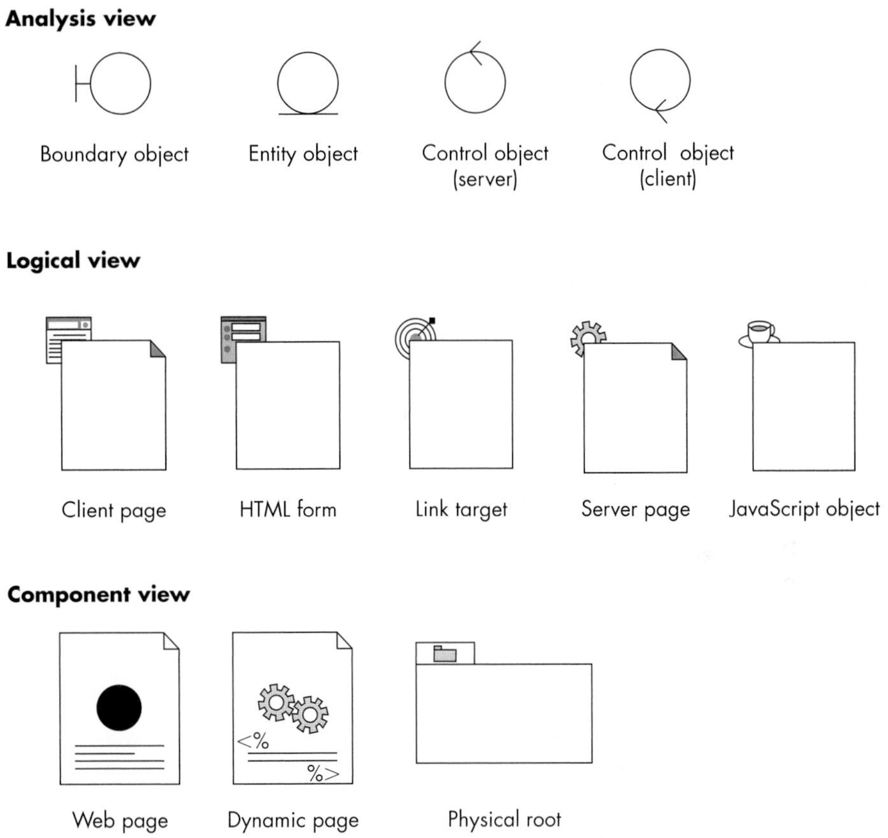

Analysis view

Boundary object   Entity object   Control object (server)   Control object (client)

Logical view

Client page   HTML form   Link target   Server page   JavaScript object

Component view

Web page   Dynamic page   Physical root

to quick drafts for the purpose of exploring particular interactions.[8] Keeping a WAE model up to date and synchronized with the constructed system would not (except in rare cases) provide any significant benefit during the development process.

Why Is WebML Appropriate for Workflow Modeling?

If you are developing workflow-oriented applications, we recommend the adaptation of WebML for more effective workflow support [Bra03] [Bra06]. Many WebApps are used to provide a front-end interface to organizational processes that have a defined sequence of steps. Examples are abundant, but some simple ones include the payment process in e-commerce applications (e.g., select the items, confirm the order, provide payment details, confirm payment), event or travel ticketing

8 It's worthwhile to become familiar enough with the notation to be able to sketch out (on a whiteboard) specific detailed designs for review by the WebE team.

FIGURE 11.8

Derivation of detailed information and functional designs from the WAE model (from Figure 10.11).

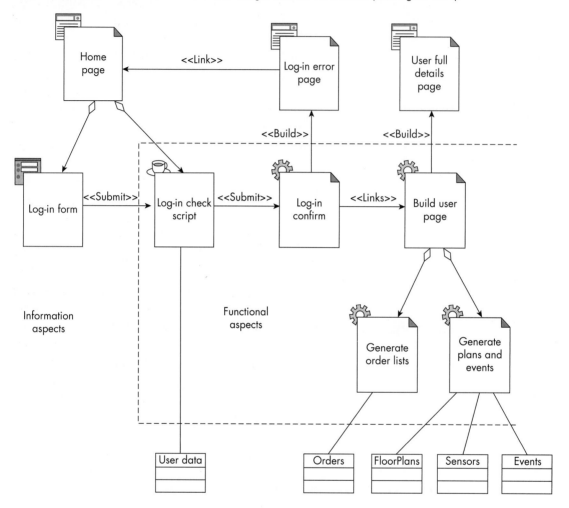

(e.g., select the event or travel route, select date and time, select seating, confirm payment), online auctions, application submissions, and so forth—the list is long.

WebML has been adapted [Bra06] to model workflow-oriented applications. Business workflows[9] are modeled, and then these processes are mapped into a

---

9   There are many ways to model business workflows. The one used in the adaptation of WebML is called BPMN (Business Process Management Notation) [Whi04a][Whi04b] and is based on modeling events, tasks, artifacts, and decision points. Details on BPMN can be found at the Object Management Group's BPMN site, **www.bpmn.org/**.

WebML design model that has been extended to support more effective modeling of the process. The modeling approach represents different cases or scenarios (e.g., a particular instance of a loan application) that will be encountered as the process is applied. Each case will go through various activities or process steps that might occur at different times or by different people. These process steps can be modeled using WebML. For example, the process of managing a specific loan application would include the following steps: (1) an initial submission of the application by a customer, (2) validation by a loan manager, (3) completion of credit checks by a bank employee, and (4) final approval (or rejection) by an authorized loan approver.

A WebML hypertext design model for the workflows associated with the processing of a loan request is illustrated in Figure 11.9. Referring to the figure, a number of workflow paths can be seen. For example, in the workflow at the top of the figure the loan manager is initially presented with a list of *LoanRequest* cases that are currently assigned to the *PreliminaryValidation* activity (upper left-hand box). If a particular *LoanRequest* case is selected, the workflow session commences [i.e., the *Start* icon (with the triangle)], and the manager is presented with the relevant details of the *LoanRequest* case, as well as a form to be completed (i.e., *Data Entry* within the *Preliminary validation page*). If the case is invalid ("*Not valid*"), then this particular activity ends [workflow points to the *End* icon (with the square and the black dot in the upper left-hand corner)] and the particular *LoanRequest* case is terminated, ending any further processing steps required for this case. If the manager confirms that the *LoanRequest* case is valid, the details of the *LoanRequest* case are modified (i.e., the *Modify* icon) and the case is assigned to the next two activities in the process (i.e., *JobCheck* and *FinancialCheck*). This activity then ends, but the particular case is obviously not terminated since further process activities are pending (represented by the *End* icon with the large black dot in the center).

A WebML model, like the one shown in Figure 11.9, can provide substantial benefit when modeling reasonably complex workflows. It enables the designers to uncover errors, omissions, or inconsistencies before finalizing the functional architecture for the WebApp. As we have already discussed, the WebML modeling approach is overkill for simple functionality such as that typical of increment 2 of **SafeHomeAssured.com** (where the functionality is almost entirely triggered by user browsing events and there is little process or "history" between events or interactions between users). However, where the WebApp has functionality that is distributed in time or between multiple users,[10] WebML modeling is recommended.

---

10 For example, if one user submits a request that must then be handled by another user (or class of users), then there is benefit in adopting the approach to modeling process cases and separate activities that form part of a composite process.

FIGURE 11.9

Example application of WebML to business workflow modeling for a loan request process.
Source: From WebML training materials. Reproduced with permission of Marco Brambilla, Politecnico di Milano.

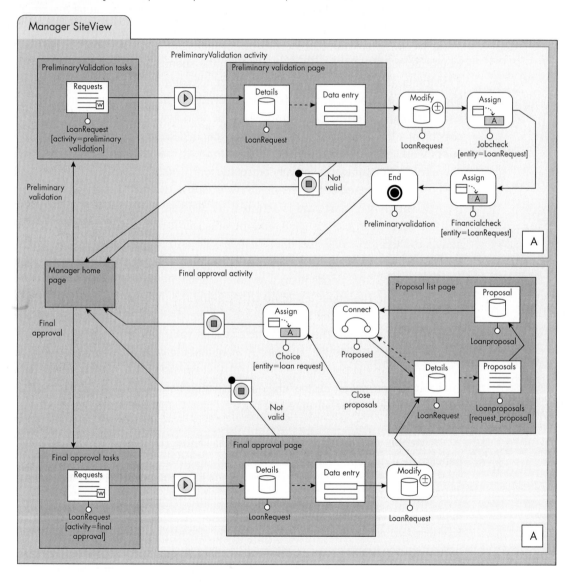

For **SafeHomeAssured.com,** any WebApp increment that involves asynchronous interaction between a user and the WebApp would be a candidate for modeling using WebML. For example, increment 4 of **SafeHomeAssured.com** includes the scenario *Get recommendations for sensor layout for my space.* If a user enters a layout and the WebApp immediately generates a recommendation, an associated workflow is not required and a simple functional component can be designed. Conversely, if the layout recommendations need to be manually created by a **SafeHomeAssured. com** employee (or even checked prior to release to the customer), then an appropriate workflow should be included for managing the requests for recommendations. Even if the recommendation can be generated automatically, but the processing effort required means it cannot be done on the fly (and instead the request needs to be placed in a queue before the recommendation is generated automatically), a workflow needs to be designed for returning the result to the customer once it has been generated.

An excellent source of more information on WebML, including the extensions for modeling of processes and workflows, can be found at the WebML.org website at **www.webml.org.**

State Modeling

As WebApps grow more complex, it is likely that you will have to accommodate interacting processes, particularly with multiple simultaneous users (or at least multiple users whose interactions with the Web servers are interleaved). A significant issue in the design of WebApps is ensuring that the state of the underlying information is correctly preserved when we have complex interacting processes.

In an earlier example, we discussed an online hotel booking application. Given that interacting processes are the norm in this WebApp, the potential for overbooking of the hotel (or indicating that a room was available and then having to indicate that it wasn't) is a significant design concern. Effective design for situations like this can be managed through the use of *state modeling.*

A *state* is an externally observable mode of behavior. External *stimuli* cause *transitions* between states. A *state model* represents the behavior of a WebApp by depicting its states and the events that cause the WebApp to change state. In addition, a state model indicates what actions (e.g., process activation) are taken as a consequence of a particular event. State models are created using *state diagrams.*

State diagrams allow a designer to represent WebApp behavior. They are particularly useful when different behaviors can be triggered by a variety of different events or in situations in which current WebApp processing is dependent on previous

FIGURE 11.10

Example state diagram for **SafeHomeAssured.com.**

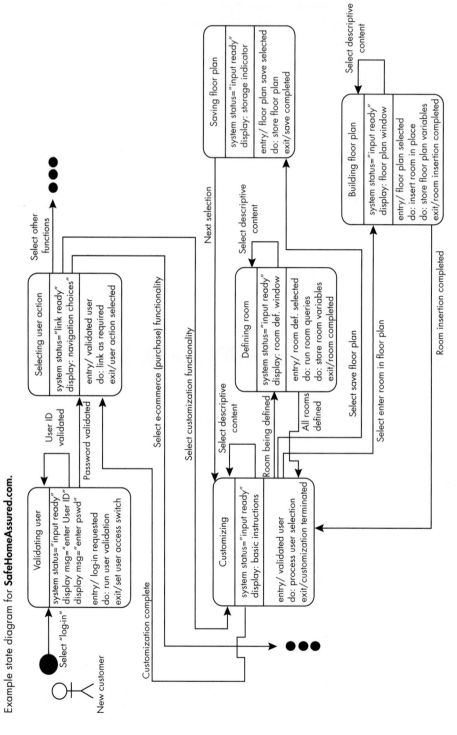

actions of one or more users, especially when the response for one user will be affected by what other users do.[11]

Figure 11.10 illustrates a state diagram for *new customer interaction* for **SafeHomeAssured.com.** In this diagram six externally observable states (represented by rounded rectangles) are identified. The state diagram indicates the events that are required to move the customer from one state to another state, the information that is displayed as a state is entered, the processing that occurs within a state, and the exit condition that allows a transition to occur.

The behavior of **SafeHomeAssured.com** as observed by users is largely independent of what other users are doing, with the exception of customers and **SafeHome-Assured.com** employees who interact during home monitoring. Consider a situation in which a customer has signed up for monitoring services. The **SafeHomeAssured.com** monitoring software may automatically monitor the cameras (via image-processing algorithms) and other sensors in the customer's house and identify anomalous situations such as:

1. The security system is *armed,* and an entrance sensor indicates a security breach of less than x seconds. This might occur when a homeowner enters the home without first disarming the security system. An audible alert should remind the homeowner to disarm the system within a given time interval.

2. The security system is *armed,* and a sensor indicates a possible security breach of greater than x seconds on an entrance or greater than y seconds on any other sensor. This might indicate a true security breach.

3. A sensor within the security system indicates a possible fire or other emergency situation.

In case 1 the event should be logged but no further action taken. In case 2 **SafeHomeAssured.com** should initiate its security breach process. This might involve a **SafeHomeAssured.com** employee being alerted and informed (via the relevant workflow) of the possible breach. The employee can then view the breach information (such as the video footage or the location of a tripped sensor), as well as information on who the customer has indicated should be alerted in the event of a breach (e.g., police or private security). The workflow system might queue the possible breach for action, and if not acted upon within 60 seconds, it escalates the breach to a *critical* status. In case 3 the process is slightly different and involves both immediate contact of emergency services and an attempt by **SafeHomeAssured.com** to contact the homeowner to alert him or her to the danger.

---

11 For example, the availability of a hotel room depends upon whether other users have already booked rooms.

These scenarios immediately raise questions as to how long a breach should be tracked and what happens if the breach persists (e.g., a sensor has failed). Answers may have been derived during the communication activity or as an analysis model is created, but some elements are likely to have been unresolved until the detailed design.

Where We've Been . . . Where We're Going

Today, many WebApps incorporate rich dynamic content, adaptation and personalization for individual users, powerful interactivity, and intricate workflows and process support. All this has led to an increasingly complex interplay between the content that underpins most WebApps and the functionality that brings that content to life and makes it accessible and useful.

In this chapter we have looked at how to design the functionality that enables the current generation of WebApps. This functional design does not occur in isolation but has strong connections to the analysis model, the information design, and the selection of the technologies that are being used to implement the designs. Some of the key messages in this chapter were not about the specific notations or methods, but rather about how we weave these analysis and design elements together.

The functional architecture is strongly influenced by the information architecture. WAE provides a vehicle for considering how we weave detailed navigation paths together with the functionality required to generate the pages in a path. WebML allows a designer to model complex process workflows in a manner that will lead to more effective functional design.

Now that we've examined both information design and functional design, the next step is to see how these come together in the actual technical design and WebApp construction. In Chapter 12 we consider the tasks and technology required to transform a design into a working WebApp.

References

[Bas03]   Bass, L., P. Clements, and R. Kazman, *Software Architecture in Practice,* 2nd ed., Addison-Wesley Professional, 2003.

[Bra03]   Brambilla, M., S. Ceri, S. Comai, P. Fraternali, and I. Manolescu, "Specification and Design of Workflow-Driven Hypertexts," *Journal of Web Engineering (JWE)* vol. 1, no. 2, April 2003, pp. 163–182.

[Bra06]   Brambilla, M., S. Ceri, P. Fraternali, and I. Manolescu, "Process Modeling in Web Applications," *ACM Transactions on Software Engineering and Methodology (TOSEM)* vol. 15, no. 4, 2006, pp. 360–409.

[Cer00] Ceri, S., P. Fraternali, and A. Bongio, "Web Modeling Language (WebML): A Modeling Language for Designing Web Sites," *Proceedings of WWW9 Conference,* Amsterdam, 2000, pp. 137–157.

[Cer02] Ceri, S., P. Fraternali, A. Bongio, M. Brambilla, S. Comai, and M. Matera, *Designing Data-Intensive Web Applications,* Morgan Kaufman, 2002.

[Con99] Conallen, J., *Building Web Applications with UML,* Addison-Wesley Object Technology Series: Addison-Wesley, 1999, p. 336.

[Fow03] Fowler, M., et al., *Patterns of Enterprise Application Architecture,* Addison-Wesley, 2003.

[Jac02] Jacyntho, D., D. Schwabe, and G. Rossi, "An Architecture for Structuring Complex Web Applications," 2002, **www2002.org/CDROM/alternate/478/** (accessed August 7, 2007).

[Kra88] Krasner, G., and S. Pope, "A Cookbook for Using the Model-View Controller User Interface Paradigm in Smalltalk-80," *Journal of Object-Oriented Programming* vol. 1, no. 3, 1988, pp. 26–49.

[Low03] Lowe, D., and B. Henderson-Sellers, "Characterising Web Systems: Merging Information and Functional Architectures," in V. K. Murthy and N. Shi (eds.), *Architectural Issues of Web-Enabled Electronic Business,* Idea Group Publishing, 2003.

[OMG04] Object Management Group (OMG), "UML 2.0 OCL Specification," 2004, **www.omg.org/cgi-bin/doc?ptc/2003-10-14** (accessed August 7, 2007).

[Pil05] Pilone, D., and N. Pitman, *UML 2.0 in a Nutshell,* O'Reilly, 2005.

[Whi04a] White, S., "Business Processing Modeling Notation (BPMN), Version 1.0," 2004, **www.bpmn.org** (accessed August 7, 2007).

[Whi04b] White, S., "Process Modeling Notations and Workflow Patterns," IBM Corporation BPTrends, 2004, **www.bptrends.com/** (accessed August 7, 2007).

12

CONSTRUCTION AND DEPLOYMENT

R egardless of the type of WebApp that has to be built or the process (or lack of process) that is used to build it, a WebE team must eventually construct an application using the design as a guide and available technologies as a tool set. The team must also deploy the WebApp across as many environments as are required (and a few more that no one considers until the last minute). In the context of the WebE process presented in Chapter 3 (Figure 3.2), a WebApp is engineered as a series of increments. The last two activities in the WebE process are:

Construction. WebE tools and technology are applied to construct the WebApp that has been modeled. Once the WebApp increment has been constructed, a series of rapid tests are conducted to ensure that errors in design (i.e., content, architecture, interface, navigation) are uncovered. Additional testing addresses other WebApp characteristics.

Deployment. The WebApp is configured for its operational environment, it is then delivered to end users, and an evaluation period commences. Evaluation feedback is presented to the WebE team, and the increment is modified as required.

Construction builds all informational and functional components that must be delivered for a WebApp increment. The activity involves code generation and testing. Because of its overall importance to the WebE process and to the quality perceived by an end user, testing is considered separately in Chapter 15.

Deployment occurs after a WebApp increment has been verified by the WebE team and includes the tasks that are necessary to install the WebApp in each required environment.

It's reasonable to ask why construction and deployment are considered together in the same chapter. Although these two activities are conceptually distinct, the distributed nature of the Web, coupled with the incremental nature of the WebE process, causes them to be deeply intertwined. Once components that define an increment have been constructed (coded and tested), each can be deployed immediately, providing benefit to stakeholders as rapidly as possible.

It is even possible to define an individual component as a WebApp increment, allowing individual components to be progressively deployed.

Although this may not always be a good thing to do,[1] it does provide significant flexibility and can be a powerful tool if handled appropriately. Indeed, an ongoing process of content updating, editorial changes, interface tuning, and related tasks can result in a much more organic evolution of the WebApp and a blurring of the boundary between construction and deployment.

In order to maintain agility during the WebE process, component-level design is not generally conducted as part of informational design (Chapter 10) or functional design (Chapter 11).[2] Detailed component-level design is usually postponed until the construction activity begins. It is less formal and is conducted in conjunction with code generation and testing. Formal consideration of component design tends to be restricted to issues such as selection, adaptation, and management of components.

In this chapter we begin by looking at the construction and deployment activities as well as the environments that are used as these activities are conducted. We will then examine specific construction and deployment tasks and recommendations for good practice. Finally, we move on to a consideration of components and how their development and management becomes an integral part of construction and deployment activities.

Construction and Deployment within the WebE Process

Figure 12.1 depicts the WebE process with the construction and deployment activities highlighted. Key WebE actions associated with these activities are also shown. The figure has been modified slightly from the version presented in earlier chapters to emphasize iteration between construction and deployment.

What Is the Interplay Between Construction and Deployment?

Although the overall process cycle is repeated for each WebApp increment, there is also significant iteration and interplay directly between construction and deployment for a particular increment. In some cases, a minor issue is identified as a consequence of the construction or deployment, and this requires a quick pass through other WebE activities (e.g., modeling). Sometimes this inner iterative path (shown in the figure) will be intentional and planned, and on other occasions it may be serendipitous or simply a consequence of the developmental sequencing.

---

1   How many times do you encounter websites with frustrating dead ends that lead to "under construction" pages, or pages with sloppy editing that have been released before being carefully checked?
2   The modeling that occurs during those design activities focuses on high-level architectural issues.

FIGURE 12.1

Construction
and deployment
in the WebE
process flow.

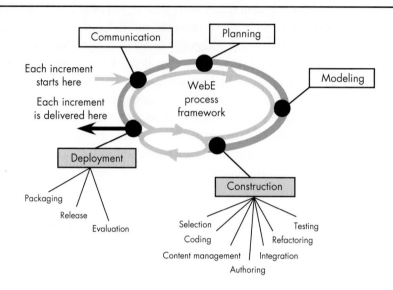

For example, increment 2 of **SafeHomeAssured.com** provides product informa-tion to the user, including the ability to look up information on particular sensors. The increment also customizes the information for particular classes of users. The functional architecture that was discussed in Chapter 11 (see Figure 11.5) includes components that perform *product content generation* (i.e., extraction of the re-quested content for a particular page) and *dynamic page compilation* (i.e., dynami-cally putting the content, headers, footers, menus, and any supporting interaction scripting together into the resultant page). Although the design for increment 2 may have been done as a cohesive whole, construction might begin by creating a version of content generation that provides relevant content but has not yet imple-mented the functionality to adapt this to particular users. If this "cut-down" version of the increment's functionality is acceptable to the client, then this intermediate construction could be deployed (i.e., made available to users) while the additional functionality is coded.

Now, let's consider a situation in which it is necessary to do a quick loop back through the whole WebE process. Assume that increment 2 has now been deployed and a final review of the increment is conducted (by all interested stakeholders). The reviewers encounter the following situation:

1. A user is browsing for product information in a specific category.

2. The category does not contain any products that are available to that user.

It is unclear whether this is the desired functionality (*does the client want the user to know about the existence of a category even if the user doesn't have access to any products in that category?*) or simply an oversight. A quick check with the appropriate stakeholder (i.e., reinitiation of the communication activity) indicates that it's all right for the user to know about the category, but that the category should include some text that informs the user that only existing **SafeHomeAssured.com** customers have access to those products. The WebE team checks that this is still consistent with the current design (i.e., the modeling activity) and then implements and releases the change. All this can be accomplished within a few hours.

These examples illustrate the way in which deployment and construction can be interwoven in order to enable a more rapid and responsive WebE process.

What Role Do Deployment Environments Play?

WebE-related technologies and how they impact WebApp development are considered in detail in Chapter 14. However, it's worthwhile noting that WebE development environments do have a significant effect on when and how various WebApp increments and their related components are constructed and deployed.

In very simple WebApps that are not mission-critical, it may be acceptable to have a single developer create local content (e.g., edited on a local machine without the content being hosted on a server). The content is then published to the production server for immediate access by users. This is shown in Figure 12.2a. However, for more complex WebApps (where it is crucial that WebApp quality is ensured prior to release), a more complex development environment becomes appropriate. Consider Figure 12.2b, which shows a possible development environment containing four distinct server types:

Development servers. Developers and authors use these servers to perform all authoring and unit-level testing.[3] These servers are, in effect, *sandboxes* in which the developers can create, manipulate, and test their own WebApp components. In some cases developers may have their own local environment containing a copy of all, or some relevant subset of, the WebApp components, as well as appropriate development tools [e.g., editors, integrated development environments (IDEs), reference material, profilers]. Typically, this development configuration would not be the same as the staging or production servers.

Test server. Once developers complete the unit-level testing of their components, they can integrate them for verification within the full WebApp environment. Typically, the test servers would not have development tools installed because they might interfere with the valid testing of the WebApp.

---

3   In this context, *unit-level testing* implies an organized attempt to uncover errors in an informational or functional component prior to its publication as part of an increment.

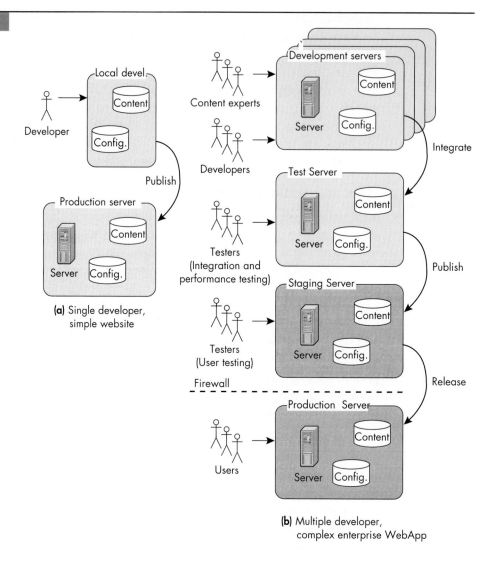

FIGURE 12.2

WebApp development environments.

(a) Single developer, simple website

(b) Multiple developer, complex enterprise WebApp

Both integration and performance testing (Chapter 15) are performed on this server.

Staging server. This server is intended to provide a mirror of the full production environment so that comprehensive user testing of the WebApp can occur without having to release the WebApp to the production server and hence the full user population. This server should be as close to the production environment as possible, including operating system(s), support applications, hardware, drivers, clustering, and so forth.

> **Production server.** When the WebApp is ready to be released for use by all users, it is placed on this server. It is crucial that changes are not released to this server until they are thoroughly tested on the staging server.

The actual environment to be adopted for a particular WebApp project will depend on the scale of the project, the number of developers and stakeholders, and the business criticality of the WebApp. In many cases, the four different servers outlined previously might be collapsed into three servers (development, staging, production) or even two servers (development, production). In some cases the WebE team can use a single networked development environment. In other cases, different Web engineers might each operate from different development servers. The production "server" (and therefore also the staging server) might involve a cluster of computers to support load balancing. In some cases you we might have a development and a test server that are logically distinct, but run on the same physical server. Despite these variations, the basic principles[4] remain the same:

- Keep the development environment and the production environment separate. Do *not* develop directly on the servers that are accessible to your users!

- Provide the developers with an environment that facilitates their productivity.

- Where possible, undertake testing in the same environment that your users will see.

Note that the particular development and production environments should be integrated with the functional architecture. For example, if a content management system (CMS) is adopted (Chapter 16), then the way in which the CMS is used by developers to create, integrate, and publish components will need careful consideration.

The following sidebar presents a discussion of the deployment environment for **SafeHomeAssured.com.**

---

4   For worthwhile discussions of some of these issues, try the following (some of these are specific to particular technologies, but the general principles will still apply in broader cases):
- Phillip Greenspun, "Using CVS for Web Development," **http://philip.greenspun.com/wtr/cvs.html** (accessed August 13, 2007).
- InformIT, "Approaches to Content Management," **www.informit.com/articles/article.aspx?p=23469** (accessed August 13, 2007).
- IBM WebSphere Developer Technical Journal, "The Ideal WebSphere Development Environment," **www-128.ibm.com/developerworks/websphere/techjournal/0312_beaton/beaton.html** (accessed August 13, 2007).
- Dell Power Solutions, "Keys to Successful Deployment of .NET Applications," **www.dell.com/content/topics/global.aspx/power/en/ps2q03se_jamison?c=us&cs=555&l=en&s=biz** (accessed August 13, 2007).

SafeHome

Deployment Environments

The scene: SafeHomeAssured. com WebE team meeting room as the team discusses the deployment environment during initial project planning

The players: The WebE team leader and the WebE technical manager

The conversation:

Team leader: Well, we know that the client has their own production server with a managed hosting provider, and they have arranged both for us to have access to install any Web servers, databases, application servers, and any other applications that might be necessary and for us to have a remote access for increment release cycles.

Technical manager: Yep—they've said all the documentation on this should be in our hands in the next day or so. As soon as we get it I'll go through it and make sure we have access sorted out.

Team leader: Great—but the real issue is deciding what we need at our end.

Technical manager: Well, I assume our normal environment would work. In other words, I'll develop an image of the development environment, with our normal development tools and any others that are relevant for this project, and image this on to each of the developers' computers. I'll also set up a staging server for the testing. I don't think we'll need a separate test server, since the project isn't too big, and the staging server should be able to handle the normal testing load—and everyone has ready access to it.

Team leader: OK—that seems to make sense. Can we have that set up by the end of the week? We need to check it all out and make sure that all the connections work.

Construction

The construction activity encompasses a set of selection, coding, authoring, integration, refactoring, and testing actions that lead to an operational WebApp that is ready for delivery to end users. *Selection* involves the identification of relevant preexisting components (or objects within components) that can be reused within the proposed design. *Coding* covers the adaptation of existing components or creation of new components and may involve the direct creation of HTML or scripting-language source code or the automatic generation of code using an intermediate design representation of the component to be built.

Content management (Chapter 16) involves the creation, migration, and structuring of content. This encompasses content creation, implementation of database schemas, or conversion of legacy content into, say, XML. *Authoring* involves the integration of raw content with the graphic design (layout) and the mapping of the content into the screens and pages. It might also include implementation of style sheets. *Integration* comprises the linking of the code, content, and presentation into the final components to be released. *Refactoring* is an iterative action that "polishes" the implemented components to improve their structure and clarity and remove redundant code. And finally, *testing* involves the verification that the various components and objects are correct.

Is There a Generic Set of Construction Tasks?

In the early days of the Web, developers avoided the delineation of specific tasks for building WebApps. After all, they argued that a WebApp "evolves organically," and defining specific tasks was "old school." It just wasn't possible to be agile if a set of tasks was defined. True? Well, no, we don't think so.

What would happen if you tried to build a house organically? If you refused to define a reasonable task sequence? There's a reason that construction tasks are defined—they help the builder to manage the project effectively and avoid errors. For example, when a house is built, the foundation must be laid, the house must be framed, the roof must be built and sealed, windows must be installed, rough electrical wiring must be run, rough plumbing must be installed, . . . the list is long. But what if—in the interest of agility—a builder decided to paint the walls before windows were installed? Sounds reasonable at first, until you consider what might happen if it rained. There's a reason for a task sequence. It is important to note that many construction tasks can be conducted in parallel. Other tasks can be applied iteratively, and a few may have to be repeated when mistakes are made.

The set of construction tasks for WebApps is somewhat shorter than the analogous task set for building a house, but the challenge of WebApp construction is equally complex and probably nowhere nearly as well understood. Web engineers do not build from a set of static blueprints. Rather, they build applications from a design that must be refined and adapted as work progresses. At each step, they must test the work that they have completed and then integrate their work with other components of the WebApp. A good reference for tasks in software construction is [Fir01], and this has been extended into the Web domain in [Hen02] and [Hai01]. The specific set of tasks will depend upon the nature of the WebApp. For example, the need for the task *Build site map* would depend upon whether the information design included a site map. Nevertheless, the next sidebar lists a sample set of tasks that are specific to the construction activity for WebApps.

What Is *Refactoring* and How Should It Be Applied?

Once a component has been built, it is evaluated to determine its conformance to the design and its effectiveness within the WebApp architecture. As a consequence of this evaluation, the component is "polished" to improve its structure and clarity and to remove or modify redundant or inefficient code. This is termed *refactoring*. Fowler [Fow99] describes refactoring in the following way:

> Refactoring is the process of changing a software system in such a way that it does not alter the external behavior of the code yet improves its internal structure. It is a

Sample Construction Task Set

Foundation tasks: These tasks involve establishing the foundation for the effective implementation of the WebApp. This ensures consistency and maintainability.

Implement brand identity components.
Build evaluation and design products.
    Build white sites,[5] skeleton sites,[6] and wireframes.
    Prototype the human interface.

Architecture tasks: These tasks focus on the construction of the overall WebApp structure.

Implement website architecture and infrastructure.
    Review architectural design.
    Code and test components that enable the WebApp architecture.
    Acquire reusable architectural patterns.
    Test the infrastructure to ensure interface integrity.
Choose an appropriate component framework.
    Evaluate the potential component frameworks.
    Screen the candidate list of component frameworks.

Low-level tasks: These tasks emphasize the construction of the constituent functional and information components of the WebApp.

Build functional components.
    Review component-level design.
    Create a set of unit tests for the component.
    Code component data structures and interface.
    Code internal algorithms and related processing functions.
    Review code as it is written.
        Look for correctness.
        Ensure that coding standards have been maintained.
        Ensure that the code is self-documenting.
Manage content.
    Implement content management.
    Author content.
    Integrate content with user interface.
Create navigation support.
    Create navigation maps.
    Create breadcrumb support mechanisms.
Undertake unit testing of WebApp components.

Integration tasks: These tasks involve the overall construction of the WebApp.

Integrate components.
Implement content management strategy.
Implement personalization strategy.

---

disciplined way to clean up code that minimizes the chances of introducing bugs. In essence when you refactor you are improving the design of the code after it has been written.

Refactoring is a key element in many agile methodologies, including Extreme Programming.[7] This is primarily because agile methods argue against "looking ahead." That is, most agile methods suggest that the WebE team should *not* try to build some design feature into a WebApp increment that one or more members of the team "know" will be required later (in another increment). If careful design plan-

---

5 A *white site* is an implemented system that to the user will look superficially complete but will lack some or most of the underlying functionality and content.

6 A *skeleton site* is one that contains all primary information structure and functional components but lacks the implementation of the key interface components.

7 See the ExtremeProgramming.org website, **www.extremeprogramming.org/rules/refactor.html,** for a discussion on the role of refactoring in XP.

ning has not occurred, this restriction could lead to construction work performed on the current increment that may result in significant changes to the design or architecture that was established for an earlier increment.

When WebApps are refactored, the existing design is examined for redundancy, unused design elements, inefficient or unnecessary algorithms, poorly constructed or inappropriate content and data structures, or any other design failure that can be corrected to yield a better design. For example, a first design iteration might yield a component that exhibits low cohesion (i.e., it performs three functions that have only a limited relationship to one another). The designer may decide that the component should be refactored into three separate components, each exhibiting higher cohesion. The result will be WebApps that are easier to integrate, easier to test, and easier to maintain.[8]

For WebApps, refactoring can involve polishing the functional components, but it can also involve polishing the user interaction. For example, with **SafeHome-Assured.com** when you we complete increments 1, 2, and 3, you have an interface that makes available product information and ordering, but not any of the details of the monitoring layouts or services. When you add increment 4, the relevant menu options are added, but this might also require refactoring to tidy up the overall menu structures.

Construction Principles and Concepts

A set of fundamental principles and concepts allows a WebE team to create maintainable, testable WebApps. The principles and concepts that guide the construction task are closely aligned to programming style, programming languages, and programming methods. However, there are a number of Web-specific fundamental principles that are useful to keep in mind during the construction activity.

Preparation principles. Before you create a single Web page or write one line of code, be sure you:

- Understand the problem you're trying to solve.

- Understand basic WebApp design principles and concepts.

- Pick a language that meets the needs of the component to be built and the environment in which it will operate.

---

8 For more information on refactoring, begin with the classic text in this area by Martin Fowler [Fow99]. You could also take a look at the "What Is Refactoring" page on the Cunningham & Cunningham, Inc., site, **http://c2.com/cgi/wiki?WhatIsRefactoring** and the Refactoring Home Page, **www.refactoring.com/.** For some simple examples, see the Perl.com site at **www.perl.com/pub/a/2003/10/09/refactoring.html.**

- Select an environment that provides tools that will make your work easier.
- Create a set of unit tests that will be applied once the component you create is completed.

Selection principles. As you select existing, reusable components and objects, be sure you:

- Take into account the constraints of the technical environment.
- Match the components to the information and functional environments.
- Consider the skills and knowledge of both the developers and likely maintainers.
- Consider issues of IP (intellectual property), the proprietary nature of the components, and whether they are portable.

Coding principles. As you begin writing code, be sure you:

- Write code that is self-documenting.
- Constrain your algorithms by following structured programming [Boh00] practices.
- Select data structures that will meet the needs of the design.
- Understand the functional architecture and create interfaces that are consistent with it.
- Keep conditional logic as simple as possible and ensure it is testable.
- Adopt coding styles that aid in readability (e.g., select meaningful identifier names and follow other local coding standards). A wide variety of links to coding standards can be found at the Literate Programmer website, **www.literateprogramming.com/fpstyle.html.**

More books have been written about programming (coding) and the principles and concepts that guide it than about any other topic in the software engineering process. Books on the subject include early works on programming style [Ker78], practical software construction [McC93], programming pearls [Ben99], the art of programming [Knu98], pragmatic programming issues [Hun99], and many, many others. Although all these have been written for conventional software, the guidance they provide applies equally to WebApps.

Content management. As content is managed, be sure you:

- Select data structures that will meet the needs of the design.
- Understand the information architecture and create content and navigational structures that are consistent with it.

- Ensure consistency in the formats and data structures.
- Avoid reliance on proprietary data formats.
- Treat your content as publishable material—not as software.

Authoring principles: As you create Web pages (or templates for pages), be sure you:

- Continually consider issues of usability.
- Remember to address issues of accessibility.
- Understand how your users *will* react, not how *you want* them to react.
- Learn from competitors.

Like coding, a substantial amount has been written about content management and Web authoring styles. A good starting point is the W3C website, **www. w3.org/TR/webarch/#app-principles.** Another source of useful information is Jakob Nielsen's usability website, **www.useit.com,** and an excellent text on managing content is [McG01].

Integration principles. As you integrate your components and objects, be sure you:

- Keep backups—preferably in some form of version control system. You need to be able to rewind the WebApp to earlier versions.
- Look for component interface mismatches or inconsistencies.
- Take the opportunity to identify components that need refactoring.

Refactoring principles. As you refactor your WebApp, be sure you:

- Understand common refactorings (see the list of example refactorings on the *Refactoring Home Page* at **www.refactoring.com/catalog/index.html**).
- Refactor often, and in small steps, when the opportunity arises (but don't change unnecessarily—see the section on not changing things if they are working on the Cunningham & Cunningham, Inc., website at **http://c2.com/cgi/wiki?IfItIsWorkingDontChange**).
- Make sure the implementation communicates the design in an obvious way.

Testing principles. After you've completed your first components, be sure you:

- Conduct a pain walkthrough.
- Perform unit tests and correct errors you've uncovered.
- Select tests that are most likely to locate errors rather a to hide them.

Chapter 15 considers WebApp testing in detail.

Deployment

The deployment activity encompasses three actions: packaging, release, and evaluation. Because WebApp development is incremental in nature, deployment happens not once, but a number of times as the WebApp moves toward completion. The release of components can be accomplished in a very fine-grained manner by releasing new components from the staging server to the production server after the individual components have been tested. For example, it may be appropriate to release corrections to content or functionality, important new items to an evolving list, or new content or functionality that is being demanded "now" by users of the deployed WebApp. However, in many cases, this approach may be ill advised.

If many small, ongoing changes are made, users could become confused and the likelihood of integration errors and unintended side effects would grow. In most cases, it is better to *package* a group of changes and *release* them as a set (except where a change is correcting a damaging error).

Each package-release cycle provides end users with an operational WebApp increment that provides usable functions and features. Each evaluation cycle provides the WebApp team with important guidance that results in modifications to the content, functions, features, and approach taken for the next increment.

Is There a Generic Set of Deployment Tasks?

Many deployment tasks for WebApps are similar to those for the deployment of conventional software and information systems. But others are specific to the Web domain. For example, *packaging* for conventional software systems might involve creation of installation functionality that can be distributed on the appropriate media to those who will be "installing" the application. For WebApps, packaging focuses on identifying the set of components to release to the production server and the guidelines for when and how this release might occur.[9]

Because the new WebApp functionality or content will be available immediately to all relevant users, the release action must also consider the following issues:

- How will the changes be communicated or announced?

- How will users be guided through the use of complex content or functionality?

- Should a special feedback mechanism be provided for reports of errors or other issues related to the new content or functionality?

- Should changed content be indexed in search engines?

---

9   For example, does the production server need to be taken off-line temporarily for the release? Is it better to do the release during a quiet usage period?

When deployment occurs for a heavily used WebApp, the impact of the new content and functionality will be instantaneous. It is critically important to establish a quality assurance approach that helps to avoid the instantaneous negative impact of a "bad" increment.

A generic set of tasks for deployment is shown in the sidebar. It should be noted that many of the subtasks associated with *Determine release set, Determine release process, Support planning,* and *Establish evaluation processes* are initiated as part of the *planning* activity that is conducted earlier in the WebE process.

Sample Deployment Task Set

Deployment planning: These tasks focus on planning the deployment.
Determine release set.
Identify new components for release.
Confirm component configurations are appropriate.
Confirm release set with customer.
Determine release process.
  Plan release schedule and timing.
  Plan communication of changes.
  Establish fault contingency planning.
Support planning.
  Plan internal support mechanisms.
  Establish support channels.
  Undertake internal support training.

Establish problem-logging procedures.
Deployment execution: These tasks cover the actual deployment.
Establish evaluation processes.
  Plan evaluation processes.
  Plan user tracking.
  Establish user feedback mechanisms.
  Create problem log.
  Create problem-logging mechanisms.
  Analyze evaluation data.
Release components.
  Confirm successful release.
Carry out change communication tasks.
Conduct ongoing support.

The release of a new WebApp increment can involve (possibly significant) changes to business processes. It is often this element of change that is most problematic and often least understood or managed within WebApp development and deployment. A detailed discussion of business process reengineering and workflow modification is beyond the scope of this book. If you have further interest, take the time to examine two excellent books on this topic, [Har03] and [Sha01].

What Deployment Principles Should Guide the WebE Team?

The deployment of a WebApp increment represents an important milestone for any Web engineering project. Smooth deployment of a WebApp provides content and functionality and immediate benefits to end users. But if deployment is poorly planned, rife with errors, and inefficiently performed, end users experience only aggravation and frustration. In order to ensure that a smooth deployment will occur, a number of key principles should be followed as the team prepares to deliver an increment:

Principle 1: Customer expectations for the WebApp increment must be managed.   Too often, the customer expects more than the team has promised to deliver, and disappointment occurs immediately. This results in feedback that is not productive and ruins team morale. In her book on managing expectations, Naomi Karten [Kar94] states: "The starting point for managing expectations is to become more conscientious about what you communicate and how." She suggests that a developer must be careful about sending the customer conflicting messages (e.g., promising more than you can reasonably deliver in the time frame provided or delivering more than you promise for one software increment and then less than promised for the next). Agile development approaches and access to the staging server can help here. Agile approaches will facilitate incremental delivery of content and functionality, providing the client with earlier feedback on the WebApp, and hence supporting management of the client expectations. The use of a staging server allows demonstration of each increment to the client prior to its public release, and hence earlier refinement.

Principle 2: A complete delivery package should be assembled and tested. Again, the use of the staging server can be invaluable for demonstrating content and functionality for a particular WebApp increment. It also allows the increment to be thoroughly beta-tested with actual users and in all likely operating environments (different hardware, different browser configurations and network bandwidths, and different security settings).

Principle 3: A support regime must be established before the WebApp is delivered.   End users expect responsiveness and accurate information when a question or problem arises. If support is ad hoc, or worse, nonexistent, customers will rapidly become dissatisfied. Support should be planned, support processes and responses should be prepared, and appropriate record-keeping mechanisms should be established so that the WebE team can conduct a categorical assessment of the kinds of support requested.

   As an example, if the **SafeHomeAssured.com** WebApp includes a form-based query for more information, then before this is released the team should ensure that there are suitable business processes for **SafeHomeAssured.com** employees to respond to the submitted queries.

Principle 4: Buggy WebApps should be fixed first, delivered later.   Under time pressure, some WebApp developers will deliver low-quality increments with "under construction" notices and warnings to the customer that bugs "will be fixed in the next release." This is a mistake. There's a saying in the software business: "Customers will forget you delivered a high-quality product a few days late, but they will never forget the problems that a low-quality product caused them. The WebApp reminds them every day."

The delivered WebApp provides benefits for the end user, but it also provides useful feedback for the WebE team. As the increment is put into use, end users should be encouraged to comment on features and functions, ease of use, reliability, and any other characteristics that are appropriate. Feedback should be collected and recorded by the development team and used to: (1) make immediate modifications to the delivered increment (if required), (2) define changes to be incorporated into the next planned increment, (3) make necessary design modifications to accommodate changes, and (4) revise the plan (including the delivery schedule) for the next increment to reflect the changes. Acquisition of feedback for WebApps is relatively simple because developers can implement sophisticated logging and tracking mechanisms to analyze user behaviors.

How Are Version Control and CMS Used?

We discuss version control and CMSs in detail in Chapter 16. However, both have important roles to play during the construction and deployment activities. A brief overview is worthwhile at this point.

In the first chapter of this book, we argued that change, often rapid and sometimes profound, is a key driver for all Web engineering projects. It would follow that the management of change is crucial to the successful construction and deployment of the WebApp as a whole and each increment as it is released. Both version control and a CMS are change management tools. They provide the following generic benefits [Dar00]:

- Ensure that published content is correct and consistent with other content.
- Control and track changes to content including the implementation of mechanisms that enforce who may make a change.
- Verify that the correct version of a function has been implemented and that the version corresponds properly to versions of related functions.
- Enable the WebE team to rebuild a WebApp rapidly if the system fails or crashes.
- Allow the team to roll back to a previous version if serious unforeseen errors are encountered in the most recent version.

As the size and complexity of a WebApp grows, the need for comprehensive version control and a robust CMS at every stage of construction and deployment also grows. In essence, version control and CMS act as a "governor" when the team

SafeHome

Content Management

The scene: An emergency meeting of the **SafeHomeAssured.com** WebE team in the meeting room, 15 minutes after the deployment of increment 5, *Monitoring Services*

The players: The WebE team leader and other members of the WebE team

The conversation:

Team leader: So, what you're telling me is that we have a problem.

Team member 1: Yeah, a big one. We tested the new increment thoroughly on the testing and staging servers and it worked fine, but we've just discovered a real problem now that it's on the production server and has been released to the public.

Team leader: That's what you said on the phone before. Explain the problem!

Team member 2: Well, we're still not quite sure why, but there seems to be some sort of strange interplay between the new process that allows existing customers to order new monitoring services. The result is sometimes when someone places a new order to include monitoring a new sensor, occasionally it will stop the monitoring of all other sensors for that person. We don't know why yet, but the whole team is busy trying to debug it. We should have it cracked soon.

Team leader: Look, this is pretty serious. Because we've been advertising the release of this new functionality, we've got a lot of customers wanting to try it out—and you can imagine the lawsuits if someone is burgled while we were supposed to be monitoring their house—and we weren't because of this flaw. I don't think we have any choice but to remove this increment, until we know that we have it fixed.

Team member 1: Well, we can remove the new increment and go back to the version we had beforehand really quickly—in the next 5 minutes—simply by triggering a re-upload of the previous version of the full system from the content management system. Are you sure you want to do that? Won't the customers wonder why the new functionality has suddenly disappeared?

Team leader: Yeah, it won't be good PR, but I've spoken to management and they agree; it's better to do this than risk the problems this new increment could cause. I want you to arrange to have the WebApp wound back to the version prior to release of the current increment. Now!

Team member 1: Okay—it'll be done within 5 minutes.

attempts to make many rapid changes. By slowing things down just a bit, they improve WebApp quality and help the WebE team to avoid costly errors.

Construction and the Use of Components

Component-level design often occurs as part of the construction activity, after the overall functional and information architectures have been established. As core WebApp components are designed, the intent is to translate the design model into an operational WebApp increment. The level of abstraction of the WebApp design models is still relatively high, and the abstraction level of the operational WebApp is low. The translation can be challenging, opening the door to the introduction of subtle errors that are difficult to find and correct in later stages of the WebE process. In a famous lecture, Edsger Dijkstra, a major contributor to our understanding of conventional software design, stated [Dij72]:

> Software seems to be different from many other products, where as a rule, higher quality implies a higher price. Those who want really reliable software will discover that they must find a means of avoiding the majority of bugs to start with, and as a result, the programming process will become cheaper . . . effective programmers . . . should not waste their time debugging—they should not introduce bugs to start with.

Although these words were spoken many years ago, they remain true today. When the design model is translated into source code, Web pages, CMS content, or link structures, we continue to follow a set of design principles that not only perform the translation but also do not "introduce bugs to start with."

What Is a Generic Component?

Stated in a general fashion, a component is a modular building block for a computer-based system. More formally, the OMG Unified Modeling Language (UML) Specification [OMG04] defines a component as ". . . a modular, deployable, and replaceable part of a system that encapsulates implementation and exposes a set of interfaces." When this concept is applied to WebApps, a component can refer to a functional building block, but also a content building block (e.g., a collection of Web pages and other associated content elements such as style sheets and presentation templates, or a database schema that captures a generic domain model).

As we discussed in Chapter 10, the functional architecture can be described in terms of the components that are used for constructing the WebApp and the ways in which these components are interconnected. Because components reside within the WebApp architecture, they often communicate and collaborate with other components and with other entities (e.g., other systems, devices, people) that exist outside the boundaries of the WebApp.

The true meaning of the term *component* will differ depending on the point of view of the developer who uses it. In the subsections that follow, we examine two important views of what a component is and how it is used as design modeling proceeds.

How Is an Object-Oriented Component Defined?

In the context of object-oriented software engineering (e.g., [Let06], [Bru04]), a component contains a set of collaborating classes. Each class within a component has been fully elaborated to include all attributes and operations that are relevant to its implementation. As part of the design elaboration, all interfaces that enable the classes to communicate and collaborate with other design classes must also be defined.

To illustrate this process of design *elaboration,* consider the **ProductMenu-Generation** component in the functional architecture shown in Figure 11.5. This component is responsible for generating DHTML code (i.e., HTML fragments, as well as required JavaScript modules and CSS style sheets) that can be used in the dynamic creation of Web pages and provides the navigational elements for those pages. Figure 12.3 shows an object-oriented design for this component.

OO-based design of the **ProductMenuGeneration** component from **SafeHomeAssured.com:** (a) Component showing the interfaces. (b) Component design.

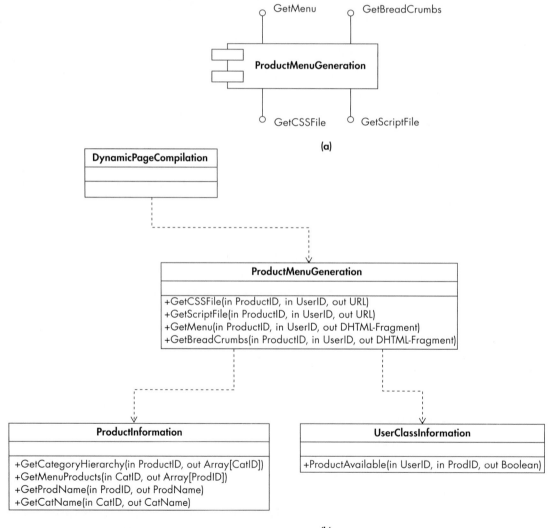

(a)

(b)

The component provides methods for determining the URL of the CSS style sheet and the JavaScript file that need to be included into the overall composite page and that contain the relevant style and scripting information to support the navigation elements. The methods are passed to the current user and product IDs so that any appropriate customization can occur.

The component also provides two further methods that return the DHTML fragments (to be embedded into the resultant product page) for the product menu and the navigational breadcrumbs. Again, these functions are passed to the relevant product ID, but also the user ID, so that the menu and other page-based representations can be customized so that they don't provide links to the products that are not available to that user.

The **ProductMenuGeneration** component would be used by the **Dynamic-PageCompilation** component to obtain the necessary navigation components, which would then be embedded into the overall DHTML page to be passed to the client browser.

This design task results in a detailed design (an elaboration) of the components being developed. It is applied to every component defined as part of the architectural design. Once the components are elaborated, each attribute, operation, and interface is specified; the data structures appropriate for each attribute are identified, and the algorithmic detail required to implement the processing logic associated with each operation is designed. Finally, the mechanisms required to implement the interface are designed. For OO software, this may encompass the description of all messaging that is required to effect communication between objects within the system.

Conventional OO class diagram models don't cope well with Web content objects (pages, style sheets, XML content, etc.) because content objects do not encapsulate operations (except where there is embedded JavaScripting). However, there is no reason why they can't be modeled in the same way as functional classes [Con02].

How Is a Conventional Component Defined?

In the context of conventional software engineering, a component is a functional element of a program that incorporates processing logic, the internal data structures that are required to implement the processing logic, and an interface that enables the component to be invoked and data to be passed to it. A traditional component, also called a *module,* resides within the software architecture and serves one of three important roles: (1) a control component that coordinates the invocation of all other problem domain components, (2) a problem domain component that implements a complete or partial function that is required by the customer, or (3) an infrastructure component that is responsible for functions that support the processing required in the problem domain. In a WebApp we can extend this to include, (4) a content component that represents available content—either as static Web pages and other flat files, or in some structured form like XML or database content.

What Are the Characteristics of a "Good" Component?

Four basic design principles for good components have been widely adopted in object-oriented software engineering and are equally applicable to WebApp component-level design. The underlying motivation for the application of these principles is to create WebApp designs that are more amenable to change and to reduce the propagation of side effects when changes do occur. These principles [Mar00] can be used to guide the designer as each WebApp component is developed.

Principle 1: A designer should specify a WebApp component in a way that allows it to be extended (within the information or functional domain that it addresses) without the need to make internal (content, code, or logic) modifications to the component itself.   To accomplish this, the designer creates abstractions that serve as a buffer between the actual required component characteristics and likely extensions.

This may seem to go against the agile philosophy of not trying to predict future enhancements, but we believe that it is an appropriate compromise. We are not arguing that functionality or information that *might* be relevant in a later iteration should be designed based on a hunch. Rather, you should ensure that your designs are extensible.

For example, assume that the **SafeHomeAssured.com** remote Web-based monitoring functionality makes use of a **Detector** class that must check the status of each type of security sensor. It is likely that as time passes, the number and types of security sensors will grow. If internal processing logic is implemented as a sequence of *if-then-else* constructs, each addressing a different sensor type, the addition of a new sensor type will require additional internal processing logic (still another *if-then-else*). This is a violation of the first principle.

One way to accommodate the first principle for the **Detector** class is illustrated in Figure 12.4. The sensor interface presents a consistent view of sensors to the **Detector** component. If a new type of sensor is added, no change is required for the **Detector** class (component). The first principle is accommodated. Similarly, when we design navigational structures or page templates, they should cope with new content without requiring changes. Consider the *Product catalog browsing* function in **SafeHomeAssured.com.** As new products are added, the templates used in the product dynamic page compilation should remain unchanged.

FIGURE 12.4

Designing for
extensibility:
following the
first component
design principle.

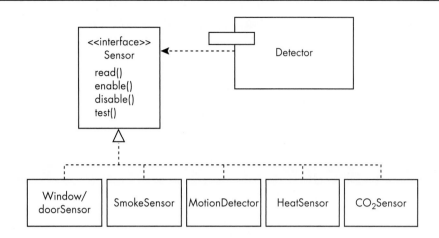

Principle 2: A component that uses a base class should continue to function properly if a class derived from the base class is passed to the component instead. This demands that any class derived from a base class[10] must honor any implied contract between the base class and the components that use it. In the context of this discussion, a "contract" is a precondition that must be true before the component uses a base class and a postcondition that should be true after the component uses a base class. When a designer creates derived classes, they must also conform to the pre- and postconditions. In the context of WebApps, this tells us that if content X is meaningful to a user when included in a given Web page, then it should be meaningful when included in another page within the same navigational hierarchy.

For **SafeHomeAssured.com,** if the product content generation component is able to generate a relevant page fragment for a specified general product, then it should also be able to do so for any specialized product that contains additional details.

Principle 3: The more a component depends on other concrete components (rather than on abstractions such as an interface), the more difficult it will be to extend. For example, if we want to create a set of Web pages to have a similar look and feel, the overall aesthetic (look and feel) should be captured as a separate presentation component (e.g., a style sheet) rather than being embedded into the individual pages. This would enable the look and feel to be much more readily modified.

---

10 A *base class* is a general class from which other *derived classes* can be created. For example, if **Car** is a base class, then **Coupe** and **Sedan** are derived classes. In general, derived classes inherit the attributes of the base class.

Principle 4: The designer should create a specialized interface to serve each major category of clients.   Only those operations that are relevant to a particular category of clients should be specified in the interface for that client. If multiple clients require the same operations, they should be specified in each of the specialized interfaces. For WebApps, this means that content, functionality, or links should be made available to a particular user only when that user is authorized to use them. It will (usually) just frustrate users if they see some WebApp component but find that they cannot access it.

Component-Level Design Guidelines[11]

As WebApp component-level design proceeds, a set of pragmatic design guidelines can be applied in addition to the principles we just discussed. These guidelines apply to components, their interfaces, and the dependencies and inheritance characteristics that have an impact on the resultant design. Ambler [Amb02] suggests the following guidelines:

Components.   Naming conventions should be established for components that are specified as part of the architectural models and then refined and elaborated as part of the component-level design. Architectural component names should be drawn from the problem domain and should have meaning to all stakeholders who view the architectural models. Often these names will emerge during the design of the WebApp information architecture or during the underlying domain modeling. For example, with **SafeHomeAssured.com** the class name **FloorPlan** is meaningful to everyone reading it regardless of their technical background.

On the other hand, infrastructure components or elaborated component-level classes should be named to reflect implementation-specific meaning. For example, if in implementing the product search in **SafeHomeAssured.com,** the search results are stored in an array, then **ProductResultArray** might be an appropriate name.

It is also worthwhile to use stereotypes[12] to help identify the nature of components at the detailed design level. For example, <<infrastructure>> might be used to identify an infrastructure component, <<database>> could be used to identify a database that services one or more design classes or the entire system, and <<table>> can be used to identify a table within a database. Figure 12.5 illustrates a good set of stereotypes, taken from WAE, to use for the information components in a WebApp.

---

11 This section makes reference to UML concepts and terminology. If you are unfamiliar with UML, we advise you to review a UML tutorial. A good list of UML tutorials is available at the Object Management Group website at **www.uml.org/#Links-Tutorials.**

12 A *stereotype* is an "extensibility mechanism" [Aro02] within UML that allows a Web engineer to define a special modeling element whose semantics are custom defined. In UML, stereotypes are represented in double angle brackets (e.g., <<stereotype>>).

FIGURE 12.5

Example subset of WAE class stereotypes.
Source: Adapted from [Con02].

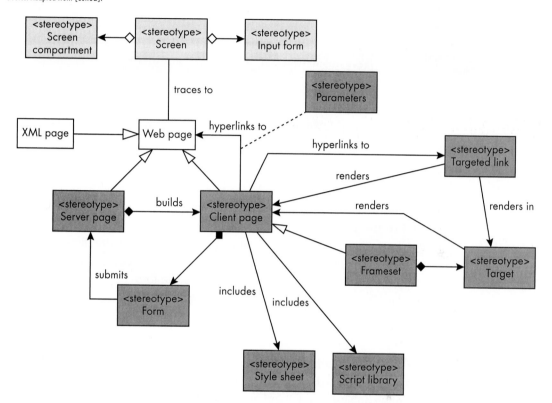

Interfaces. Interfaces provide important information about communication and collaboration (as well as helping you to achieve the first component design principle discussed in the last subsection, "What Are the Characteristics of a "Good" Component?"). However, unfettered representation of interfaces tends to complicate component diagrams. Ambler [Amb02] recommends that (1) a simpler "lollipop" representation of an interface should be used in lieu of the more formal UML box and dashed arrow approach, when diagrams grow complex, (2) for consistency, interfaces should flow from the left-hand side of the component box, and (3) only those interfaces that are relevant to the component under consideration should be shown, even if other interfaces are available. These recommendations are intended to simplify the visual nature of UML component diagrams.

Dependencies and inheritance. For improved readability, it is a good idea to model dependencies from left to right and inheritance from bottom (derived classes) to top (base classes). In addition, component interdependencies should be represented via interfaces, rather than by representation of a component-to-component dependency. Similarly, with information architectures, the navigation flow should be reflected in a left-to-right, or top-to-bottom, representation in the associated diagrams.

Component Design Steps

Earlier in this chapter we noted that component-level design is elaborative in nature (i.e., it is about taking a broad abstract architectural design and elaborating it to obtain the design detail). As a designer, you must transform information from analysis and architectural models into a design representation that provides sufficient detail to guide construction tasks. The following steps represent a typical task set for component-level design, when it is applied for WebApps.

Step 1. Identify all information and functional design classes that correspond to the problem domain.   Using the analysis and architectural models for information and functionality (Chapters 7, 10, and 11) identify the specific content and detailed functional components that are to be used in constructing each WebApp page. For information components, this is a form of detailed slice design discussed in Chapter 10. Considering the **SafeHomeAssured.com** WebApp, an example of a functional component might be a **Camera** class that corresponds to a particular security sensor.

Step 2. Identify all information interaction and functional design classes that correspond to the infrastructure domain.   These classes are not described in the analysis model and are often missing from the functional architecture models, but they must be described at this point. Classes and components in this category include client interaction components such as list boxes and menu roll-overs (often available as reusable components), operating system components, content and data management components, and others.

In **SafeHomeAssured.com,** an example of an information interaction class would be the design of the roll-overs for the main menu at the top of each page—to be designed for implementation on the client (and hence most likely in JavaScript). An example of a functional design class is the **SearchResultGeneration** class.

Step 3. Elaborate all design classes that are not acquired as reusable components.   Elaboration requires that all interfaces, attributes, and operations necessary to implement the class be described in detail. Design heuristics (e.g., component cohesion and coupling) must be considered as this task is conducted. An example of this is shown in Figure 12.6, which illustrates the elaboration of the **SearchResultGeneration** class.

SafeHome-
Assured.com
Search-
Result-
Generation
class.

SearchResultGeneration
+CreateSearchList (SearchTerms: String): HTMLFragment() +CreateSearchItem (ID: Integer): HTMLFragment() +QueryIndex (SearchTerms: String): Array of ID() +GetIndexItem (ID: Integer): ProductDetails()

SafeHomeAssured.com **SearchResultGeneration** collaboration diagram.

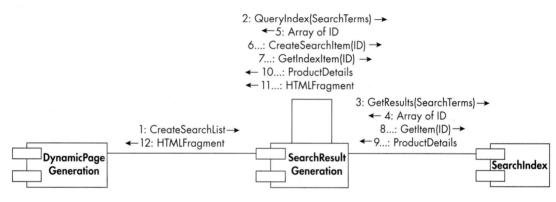

Step 4a. Specify message details when classes or components collaborate. The analysis model makes use of a collaboration diagram to show how analysis classes collaborate with one another. As component-level design proceeds, it is sometimes useful to show the details of these collaborations by specifying the structure of messages that are passed between objects within a system. Although this design activity is optional, it can be used as a precursor to the specification of interfaces that show how components within the system communicate and collaborate. Figure 12.7 shows a collaboration diagram illustrating the sequence of calls that occur in the generation of a set of search results.

Step 4b. Identify appropriate interfaces for each component. Within the context of component-level design, a UML interface is a group of externally visible (i.e., public) operations. Stated more formally, an interface is the equivalent of an abstract class that provides a controlled connection between design classes. In essence, the content that is exposed and/or the operations that are available are defined for the design class. Every operation within the abstract class (the interface) should be cohesive; that is, it should exhibit processing that focuses on one limited function or subfunction, or one information view.

Step 4c. Elaborate attributes and define data types and data structures required to implement them.   In general, data structures and types used to define attributes are defined within the context of the language that is to be used for implementation. In the **SafeHomeAssured.com** examples used earlier, this would include determining the data structures used to manage the array of IDs returned when querying the search index.

Step 4d. Describe processing flow within each functional component in detail.   This may be accomplished using a combination of a programming language (e.g., Java) and a natural language (e.g., English) to create a pseudocode or with a UML activity diagram. In the **SafeHomeAssured.com** example for the *Create-SearchList()* method, the WebApp component designer might define the following processing flow:

```
call QueryIndex (SearchTerms) result = ArrayIDs
For each ID in ArrayIDs
        Call CreateSearchItem(ID) result = HTMLFragment
        Append HTMLFragment to QueryFragment
Return QueryFragment
```

Step 5. Describe which data are to be persistent data (Web pages, databases, etc.) and which are to be dynamically constructed.   Databases and files normally transcend the design description of an individual component. In most cases, these persistent data stores are initially specified as part of architectural design. In **SafeHomeAssured.com** the designer would define users' orders to be persistent. In addition, the designer would probably also want to record things such as their **search queries,** so that users could subsequently personalize their experience.

Step 6. Develop and elaborate behavioral representations for a class or component.   UML state diagrams are used as part of the analysis model to represent the externally observable behavior of the system and the more localized behavior of individual analysis classes. During component-level design, it is sometimes necessary to model the behavior of a design class.

Step 7. Elaborate deployment diagrams to provide additional implementation detail.   UML deployment diagrams are used as part of architectural design and are represented in descriptor form. In this form, major system functions (often represented as subsystems) are represented within the context of the computing environment that will house them. In **SafeHomeAssured.com** the product catalog sits on a separate database server, which runs on a different server from the Web server. This then raises issues such as: Where does the implementation of the database index generation occur? Where does the **SearchResultGeneration** component described earlier exist?

Step 8. Factor every component-level design representation and always consider alternatives. Throughout this book we have emphasized that design is an iterative process. The first component-level model you create will not be as complete, consistent, or accurate as the *n*th iteration you apply to the model. It is essential to *refactor* as design work is conducted.

In addition, you should not suffer from tunnel vision. There are always alternative design solutions, and the best designers consider all (or most) of them before settling on the final design model. You should develop design alternatives and consider each carefully.

Where We've Been . . . Where We're Going

Construction and deployment are the culmination of one, and possibly many, iterations through the WebE process. After thorough communication, thoughtful planning, and detailed engineering modeling, the WebE team constructs and deploys a WebApp increment. The result is an operational increment that is available to the end users.

Construction and deployment are WebE activities that draw everything together. But they do not occur in isolation. Much of WebApp construction and deployment is deeply interwoven with the particular technologies, tools, and languages that are used in during construction. And each of these WebE technologies is diverse and evolving very rapidly.

The construction activity encompasses selection, coding, authoring, integration, refactoring, and testing actions. When completed, these actions (and the WebE tasks that are defined for each) lead to an operational WebApp that is ready for delivery to end users.

Component-level design often occurs in parallel with the construction activity. Design and implementation are guided by a set of simple principles. Once these actions are completed, the resulting WebApp component is refactored to improve the delivered end product.

The deployment activity encompasses three actions: packaging, release, and evaluation. Because Web engineering is incremental in nature, deployment happens not once, but a number of times as the WebApp moves toward completion. Like construction, a set of principles can be applied to guide the deployment.

Construction is a component-based activity. Well-designed components (whether acquired from a third party or developed by the WebE team) exhibit four key characteristics that result in a WebApp that can be easily maintained. A distinct set of design and construction steps can guide a Web engineer during the construction activity.

The unrelenting demand for rapid construction and deployment can force WebApp developers to take shortcuts. There is nothing wrong with trying to be agile, but if shortcuts lead to errors and end-user dissatisfaction, the "need for speed" becomes counterproductive.

A WebE team should establish an effective environment to support development before it commences. Such an environment uses test servers and staging servers to allow effective evaluation of rapidly developed changes before they are incrementally released. And if a mistake is made, the environment will allow a rollback to a previous version of the deployed WebApp as quickly as possible.

In Chapters 13 and 14 we examine ways in which Web engineers can increase their development productivity. In Chapter 13 we look at design patterns and consider how these can take some of the guesswork out of the design process by leveraging preexisting knowledge and solutions. In Chapter 14 we take a quick look at the range of technologies that are available to developers, and how these can be most effectively leveraged. Basically, we'll examine how to use cutting edge technology most effectively, without getting cut on those sharp edges!

References

[Amb02] Ambler, S., "UML Component Diagramming Guidelines," 2002, **www.modelingstyle.info/** (accessed November 18, 2006).

[Aro02] Arolow, J., and I. Neustadt, *UML and the Unified Process,* Addison-Wesley, 2002.

[Ben99] Bentley, J., *Programming Pearls,* Addison-Wesley, 1999.

[Boh00] Bohl, M., and M. Rynn, *Tools for Structured Design: An Introduction to Programming Logic,* 5th ed., Prentice-Hall, 2000.

[Bru04] Bruegge, B., and A. Dutoit, *Object-Oriented Software Engineering: Using UML, Patterns and Java,* 2nd ed., Prentice-Hall, 2004.

[Con02] Conallen, J., *Building Web Applications with UML,* 2nd ed., Addison-Wesley Object Technology Series: Addison-Wesley, 2002, p. 336.

[Dar99] Dart, S., "Change Management: Containing the Web Crisis," *Proc. Software Configuration Management Symposium,* Toulouse, France, 1999, **www.perforce.com/perforce/conf99/dart.html** (accessed August 13, 2007).

[Dar00] Dart, S., *Configuration Management: The Missing Link in Web Engineering,* Artech House Publishers, November 2000.

[Dij72] Dijkstra, E. W., "The Humble Programmer," *Communications of the ACM* vol. 15, no. 10, 1972, pp. 859–866. Turing Award lecture. Also available at **www.cs.utexas.edu/users/EWD/ewd03xx/EWD340.PDF** (accessed August 13, 2007).

[Fir01] Firesmith, D. G., and B. Henderson-Sellers, *The OPEN Process Framework: An Introduction,* Addison-Wesley, 2001.

[Fow99] Fowler, M., K. Beck, J. Brant, W. Opdyke, and D. Roberts, *Refactoring: Improving the Design of Existing Code,* Addison Wesley, 1999.

[Hai01] Haire, B, B. Henderson-Sellers, and D. Lowe, "Supporting Web Development in the OPEN Process: Additional Tasks," *COMPSAC'2001: International Computer Software and Applications Conference,* IEEE Computer Society Press, Chicago, 2001.

[Hai02] Haire, B., D. Lowe, and B. Henderson-Sellers, "Supporting Web Development in the OPEN Process: Additional Roles and Techniques," in Z. Bellahsene, D. Patel, and C. Rolland (eds.), *Proc. Object-Oriented Information Systems,* Montpellier, France, 2002, vol. LNCS 2425, Springer-Verlag, Berlin, pp. 82–94.

[Har03] Harmon, P., *Business Process Change: A Manager's Guide to Improving, Redesigning, and Automating Processes,* Morgan Kaufmann Series in Data Management Systems, 2003, Morgan Kaufmann Publishers Inc.

[Hen01] Henderson-Sellers, B., B. Haire, and D. Lowe, "Adding Web Support to OPEN," *Journal of Object Oriented Programming* vol. 14, no. 3, 2001, pp. 34–38.

[Hen02] Henderson-Sellers, B., D. Lowe, and B. Haire, "OPEN Process Support for Web Development," *Annals of Software Engineering* vol. 13, 2002, pp. 163–202, **http://manta.cs.vt.edu/ase** (accessed August 13, 2007).

[Hun99] Hunt, A., D. Thomas, and W. Cunningham, *The Pragmatic Programmer,* Addison-Wesley, 1999.

[Kar94] Karten, N., *Managing Expectations,* Dorset House, 1994.

[Ker78] Kernighan, B., and P. Plauger, *The Elements of Programming Style,* 2nd ed., McGraw-Hill, 1978.

[Knu98] Knuth, D., *The Art of Computer Programming,* 3 volumes, Addison-Wesley, 1998.

[Let06] Lethbridge, T., and R. Laganiere, *Object-Oriented Software Engineering: Practical Software Development Using UML and Java,* McGraw-Hill, 2005.

[Mar00] Martin, R., "Design Principles and Design Patterns," **www.objectmentor.com,** 2000 (accessed August 13, 2007).

[McC93] McConnell, S., *Code Complete,* Microsoft Press, 1993.

[McG01] McGovern, G., and R. Norton, *Content Critical: Gaining Competitive Advantage Through High-Quality Web Content,* 2001, Financial Times Prentice Hall.

[OMG04] Object Management Group (OMG), *UML 2.0 OCL Specification,* 2004, **www.omg.org/cgi-bin/doc?ptc/2003-10-14** (accessed August 13, 2007).

[Pil05] Pilone, D., and N. Pitman, *UML 2.0 in a Nutshell,* O'Reilly, 2005.

[Sha01] Sharp, A., and P. McDermott, *Workflow Modeling: Tools for Process Improvement and Application Development,* Artech House, 2001.

13

DESIGN PATTERNS

It's all about speed, said a young WebApp developer, as he sat drinking his third cup of coffee. "We've got to crank out this website in less than 3 weeks, and that doesn't give us much time for what you call a *process.*"

The young man was only partially correct—speed is paramount, especially once the construction activity begins. But an agile WebE process allows a WebE team to create the engine that generates speed. If you want to get it out the door quickly, you can't reject the notion of a process.

In a speed-oriented environment, a Web engineer cannot afford the time to reinvent the wheel. Reinvention wastes time, and worse, a new "wheel" may not be as good as one that was invented previously. If a reasonable solution already exists and is available, it should be used.

It makes sense for Web engineers to leverage the work of others who have already solved similar problems. This can be achieved by the strategic use of *patterns.* Brad Appleton [App98] defines a *design pattern* in the following manner: "A pattern is a named nugget of insight which conveys the essence of a proven solution to a recurring problem within a certain context amidst competing concerns."

Stated in another way, a pattern is a way of capturing a description of a particular problem and a good solution to that problem. This information is documented in a predictable way using a template and is available to be used over and over again. But a good pattern provides more than a problem description and a solution. It also provides Web engineers with insight into both of these and enables them to be certain that the pattern is appropriate to the current need.

In this chapter we look at what patterns are and how you can make most effective use of them. We'll illustrate this by looking at some of the most common patterns.

Patterns: Understanding the Concept

The concept of a design pattern has its origins in work by Christopher Alexander, an architect who became interested in using pattern languages to represent design knowledge. He described patterns in the following way [Ale77]: "Each pattern describes a problem which occurs over and over again in our environment, and then describes the core of the solution to that problem, in such a way that you can use this solution a million times over, without ever doing it the same way twice."

The implication of Alexander's definition is that each developer can interpret and adapt the pattern to the specific problem that must be solved. The pattern remains unchanged, but the implementation is targeted at the immediate need. Time is saved because a proven solution that suits the problem being addressed is identified and described. And solution identification and description are usually far more time consuming than the physical construction of the solution.

What Exactly Is a Pattern?

The word *pattern* has many interpretations, but for most people it will bring to mind the concept of something that is representative of a given class. However, in Web engineering it has a more precise meaning.

A seminal book on software patterns by Gamma et al. [Gam95] introduced a language for describing patterns for software design. In this book, the authors stated:

> [Y]ou'll find recurring patterns of classes and communicating objects in many object-oriented systems. These patterns solve specific design problems and make object-oriented design more flexible, elegant, and ultimately reusable. They help designers reuse successful designs by basing new designs on prior experience. A designer who is familiar with such patterns can apply them immediately to design problems without having to rediscover them.

A key aspect of patterns is that they don't just show a particular solution, or even a template for a class of solutions. Rather, they provide a mapping from a class of problems to a class of solutions. The intent of each design pattern is to provide a description that enables a designer to determine (1) whether the pattern is applicable to the current work, (2) whether the pattern can be reused (hence, saving design time), and (3) whether the pattern can serve as a guide for developing a similar, but functionally or structurally different pattern. A good pattern should allow WebApp developers (who may not be experts) to take advantage of the expertise of others. As long as you can understand enough about a problem to be able to recognize a relevantpattern, you can then use the pattern to guide the development of a particular fragment of the solution.

Patterns can vary enormously in scale, focus, and applicability. One pattern might describe the type of solution to use (e.g., a set of radio buttons) for a single fragment of an interaction (e.g., uniquely selecting one item from a small set of five or fewer items). Another pattern might broadly describe the entire structure of an application (e.g., a matrix navigation structure). A pattern might focus on solving a problem of interaction, navigation, functionality, presentation, or some other aspect of the problem.

A pattern should also provide sufficient detail to determine the circumstances under which it might be applied. To illustrate, consider the problem of selecting uniquely one item from a small set of five or fewer items. Two possible solutions might be (1) to use a set of radio buttons, or (2) to use a drop-down list. Which solution is better? In order to answer, you must understand more about the problem. If it's important for all options to be available (visible) at the same time (and all the time), then radio buttons are important. If the range of options changes dynamically, and only the current selection needs to be visible, then a drop-down list might be more appropriate. Although this is a relatively trivial example, it highlights that even simple design decisions can involve knowledge that might not be immediately available or might be overlooked. Good patterns provide enough information to help developers make good design choices![1]

What Does a Pattern Look Like?

Mature engineering disciplines make use of thousands of design patterns. These patterns describe frequently encountered problems in mechanical, electrical, chemical, civil, automotive, aeronautical, biomedical, and many other engineering disciplines and propose proven solutions to those problems. All design patterns can be described using the template [Mai03] shown in the sidebar.

INFO

Design Pattern Template

Pattern name. Describes the essence of the pattern in a short but expressive name

Intent. Describes the pattern and what it does

Also-known-as. Lists any synonyms for the pattern

Motivation. Provides an example of the problem

Applicability. Notes specific design situations in which the pattern is applicable

Structure. Describes the classes that are required to implement the pattern

Participants. Describes the responsibilities of the classes that are required to implement the pattern

Collaborations. Describes how the participants collaborate to carry out their responsibilities

Consequences. Describes the "design forces" that affect the pattern and the potential trade-offs that must be considered when the pattern is implemented

Related patterns. Cross-references related design patterns

A description of the design pattern may also consider a set of design forces. *Design forces* describe nonfunctional requirements (e.g., ease of maintainability,

---

1   For more discussion of patterns, a good starting point is the Wikipedia page **http://en.wikipedia. org/wiki/Design_pattern_(computer_science)**.

portability) associated with the application domain in which the pattern is to be applied. In addition, forces define the constraints that may restrict the manner in which the design is to be implemented. In essence, design forces describe the environment and conditions that must exist to make the design pattern applicable (e.g., a given interface pattern might only be appropriate when users already have particular domain knowledge). The pattern characteristics (structure, participants, and collaborations) should also indicate the attributes of the design that may be adjusted to enable the pattern to accommodate a variety of problems. These attributes represent characteristics of the design that can be searched (e.g., via a database) so that an appropriate pattern can be found. Finally, guidance associated with the use of a design pattern provides an indication of the ramifications of design decisions.

The names of design patterns should be chosen with care. One of the key technical problems in software reuse is the inability to find existing reusable patterns when hundreds or thousands of candidate patterns exist. The search for the "right" pattern is aided immeasurably by a meaningful pattern name.

WebApp Patterns: Design Focus and Granularity

Although there are many different types of patterns and many different ways they can be categorized, we will examine pattern categories by focusing on two dimensions: the design focus of the pattern and the level of granularity of consideration. *Design focus* identifies which aspect of the design model is relevant (e.g., information architecture, navigation, interaction). *Granularity* identifies the level of abstraction that is being considered (e.g., does the pattern apply to the entire WebApp, a single Web page, a subsystem, or an individual WebApp component?).

How Is Design Focus Used to Identify Patterns?

In earlier chapters on design in Web engineering, we discussed a variety of different levels of design. Stated another way, our design focus becomes narrower as we move further into WebApp design. The problems (and solutions) you encounter when designing an information architecture are different from the problems (and solutions) that are encountered when performing interface design. Therefore, it should come as no surprise that patterns for WebApp design can be developed for different levels of design focus so that you can address the unique problems (and related solutions) that are encountered at each level. Design patterns can be categorized in the following manner:

- **Information architecture patterns** relate to the overall structure of the information space and the ways in which users will interact with the information.

- **Navigation patterns** define navigation link structures, such as hierarchies, rings, and tours.

- **Interaction patterns** contribute to the design of the user interface. Patterns in this category address how the interface informs the user of the consequences of a specific action, how a user expands content based on usage context and user desires, how to best describe the destination that is implied by a link, and how to inform the user about the status of an ongoing interaction, and interface-related issues.

- **Presentation patterns** assist in the presentation of content to the user via the interface. Patterns in this category address how to organize user interface control functions for better usability, how to show the relationship between an interface action and the content objects it affects, and how to establish effective content hierarchies.

- **Functional patterns** define the workflows, behaviors, processing, communications, and other algorithmic elements within a WebApp.

In most cases, it would be fruitless to explore the collection of information architecture patterns when a problem in interaction design is encountered. You would examine interaction patterns, because that is the design focus that is relevant to the work being performed.

Why Is Granularity an Important Characteristic of a Pattern?

When a problem involves "big picture" issues, we attempt to develop solutions (and use relevant patterns) that focus on the big picture. Conversely, when the focus is very narrow (e.g., uniquely selecting one item from a small set of five or fewer items), the solution (and the corresponding pattern) is targeted quite narrowly. In terms of the level of granularity, patterns can be described at the following levels:

- **WebApp.** This level of abstraction will typically relate to *architectural patterns* that define the overall structure of the application, indicate the relationships among different components or increments, and define the rules for specifying relationships among the elements (pages, packages, components, subsystems) of the architecture.

- **Page/screen/subsystem.** These *design patterns* address a specific element of the design such as an aggregation of components to solve some design problem, relationships among elements on a page, or the mechanisms for effecting component-to-component communication. An example might be the *broadsheet* pattern[2] for the layout of a WebApp home page.

---

2   A *broadsheet* pattern addresses the problem of laying out a variety of different content in a readable and accessible way. A proposed solution is to represent the content as if it were a newspaper broadsheet (the front page of a newspaper), with multiple columns, masthead titles,

- **Component.** *Component patterns* relate to individual small-scale elements of a WebApp. Examples include individual interaction elements (e.g. radio buttons, text blocks), navigation items (e.g., how you might format links), or functional elements (e.g., specific algorithms).

It is also possible to define the relevance of different patterns to different classes of applications or domains. For example, a collection of patterns (at different levels of design focus and granularity) might be particularly relevant to e-business WebApps.

Pattern Repositories

Most Web engineers recognize that patterns are a useful tool. However, they face a major problem in finding an existing pattern that is a good fit for the problem they need to solve. Stated more specifically, you'll need some mechanism that will enable you to look up a pattern in an effective way. The mechanism must provide a means for describing the characteristics of the problem, the design focus, the granularity required, and the WebApp domain. From this description, the mechanism should provide candidate patterns that might be applicable. A pattern repository provides such a mechanism.

What Is a Pattern Repository?

A *pattern repository* is an organized collection of proven patterns that may be of use to a WebE team. In essence, it is a database that enables you to implement the mechanism discussed in the preceding paragraph.

A pattern repository grows and evolves as time passes. A good WebE team will establish a process for capturing new patterns as they are identified. Patterns are proposed and submitted to the repository and are reviewed by others, who critique the pattern and comment on its applicability and quality. In some cases, a pattern evolves as reviewers suggest additions or deletions to make it more effective.

What Patterns Sources Are Available for Web Engineers?

There are a number of excellent sources of information on patterns that are relevant to WebApp development. Table 13.1 includes a list of useful starting resources—though additional resources are constantly appearing (and existing resources sometimes disappear).

---

and feature text that might link to more detail elsewhere. See the *White Hat Web Design and SEO Optimization Services* site **www.white-hat-web-design.co.uk/articles/newspaper.php** for a discussion and the *UTS Union Ltd* site **www.utsunion.uts.edu.au/** for an example.

TABLE 13.1   WEBAPP DESIGN PATTERN REPOSITORIES AND INFORMATION SOURCES

A   Web Design Patterns by Martijn van Welie
www.welie.com/patterns/

B   Improving Web Information Systems with Navigational Patterns
www8.org/w8-papers/5b-hypertext-media/improving/improving.html

C   Hypermedia Design Patterns Repository
www.designpattern.lu.unisi.ch/

D   IAWiki
http://iawiki.net/WebsitePatterns

E   IBM Patterns for e-Business
www-128.ibm.com/developerworks/patterns/

F   Patterns for Personal Web Sites
www.rdrop.com/~half/Creations/Writings/Web.patterns/index.html

G   Designing Interfaces: Patterns for Effective Interaction Design
http://designinginterfaces.com/

H   WebPatterns
http://webpatterns.org/

I   The Interaction Design Patterns Page
www.visi.com/~snowfall/InteractionPatterns.html

J   InteractionPatterns by Tom Erickson
www.pliant.org/personal/Tom_Erickson/InteractionPatterns.html

K   Improving Web Information Systems with Navigational Patterns
www8.org/w8-papers/5b-hypertext-media/improving/improving.html

L   An HTML 2.0 Pattern Language
www.anamorph.com/docs/patterns/default.html

M   Common Ground—A Pattern Language for HCI Design
www.mit.edu/~jtidwell/interaction_patterns.html

N   Indexing Pattern Language
www.cs.brown.edu/~rms/InformationStructures/Indexing/Overview.html

Can a WebE Team Create Its Own Set of Patterns?

Some pattern experts argue that it's difficult to create your own patterns because you will be influenced by your own solutions. A pattern should represent best practice and be able to be described in a way that supports its reuse in the context of other problems. It is sometimes difficult for developers to be impartial when evaluating their own solutions because they often feel that their own solutions are the best possible. In reality, they are just the best that they were able to identify. Nevertheless, best practice suggests that it's reasonable to create a local patterns repository in an attempt to capture and retain the expertise of your Web engineers—

especially when your company relies on the expertise of particular individuals who may move on to other endeavors.

The simplest form of patterns repository can be a spreadsheet that includes the key fields outlined in the design pattern template described in the Design Pattern Template sidebar earlier in this chapter. A slightly more complex version might be a database with a front end that supports validation of fields, meta-data tagging, and other functionality. An alternative that you might like to consider—and which is more in keeping with the development of WebApps—is an Intranet-based wiki that would allow editing and evolution of patterns.[3] Regardless of the particular form that a patterns repository might take, the real challenge is not in the design of the repository but rather in the design of the *processes* by which the patterns are captured and then used.

Patterns are about capturing expertise and then reusing that expertise across many WebE projects. Therefore, in order for patterns to work in your environment, a sustainable process should be implemented and high-level management support must be in evidence.

SAFEHOME

Establishing a Patterns Repository

The scene: Senior staff meeting in the WebE team meeting room— 2 years *before* commencing the **SafeHomeAssured.com** project

The players: Chief technical officer (CTO) and senior project managers

The conversation:

CTO (chairing the meeting): Okay, so that covers the main agenda items for the meeting. Are there any other topics that anyone wants to discuss?

Project manager 1: Well, I did have one thing that has come out of this last project that I think could help us address some of the quality problems that we were discussing earlier.

CTO (getting interested): Go on . . .

Project manager 1: One of the problems I keep finding with my developers is that they come across

problems and then spend ages developing solutions, only to discover the time wasn't well spent.

Project manager 2: I'm not sure I understand— do you mean that they developed unnecessary solutions?

Project manager 1: No, that's not it at all. Most of the time the solutions are fine—and we definitely needed to create them. What I mean is that, now that I've been here for a while, I'm starting to see the same sorts of designs being developed—especially since I've started specializing on these remote equipment monitoring WebApps that we've been doing more of. Many of our developers haven't been here as long—and so they haven't got experience. They keep reinventing the wheel.

CTO: Yeah, but isn't that why we have the project team meetings, and open-plan offices, and that sort of

(continued)

---

3   For a typical example, see the Information Architecture Wiki site at **www.iawiki.net.**

stuff—to share ideas about how you might approach problems—just so that you don't spend a whole lot of time redoing something that someone else has already done?

Project manager 1: Sure—and that works some of the time. But sometimes the person who did it originally has moved on, or forgotten, or just doesn't make the connection. And this doesn't help us share knowledge between the different teams. What I think we really need is a collection of common problems, and the answers we've already developed.

Project manager 3: Oh—you mean a pattern repository. The last place I worked at had one of those, and it worked really well. At the end of each project, all the developers had to spend a short amount of time adding any patterns they could identify into the collection—it was basically just a simple WebApp someone threw together with a few forms and a simple search interface.

CTO: Patterns? Repository? Explain.

Project manager 3: [Explains the concepts.]

CTO: But doesn't creating the repository and adding to it take up valuable time? Who did you bill it to?

Project manager 3: It did take time—but it ended up saving much more. And we didn't bill it to anyone. Or rather, we billed it against an internal account that had been set up—and then whenever a developer used a pattern that was in the system, he or she indicated how much time using the pattern might have saved.

CTO: OK—it sounds interesting. How about you come back to the meeting next week with a concrete proposal about how we might manage it.

A pattern repository will only be useful (and used!) if it contains a wide variety of problem descriptions and their solutions. For this to occur, an organization must commit money and support to ensure that Web engineers are given time to add their expertise to the repository on an ongoing basis. In other words, the repository and the process needed to make it grow should be integrated into the organizational culture. And it helps if there is someone who is willing to champion the idea.

How Do We Find and Use Patterns?

Getting information into a repository is only half the battle. It won't be of any use unless patterns can then be found when they are needed. As analysis and design progress, a WebE team can examine the emerging WebApp models[4] to see whether or not aspects of the problem being described might be covered by one or more patterns. Possible patterns might be identified in one of two ways:

1. Based on the characteristics of the problem at hand, a repository is searched and one or more candidate patterns emerge.

2. Patterns in the repository are browsed in a more general fashion in the hope of finding a pattern that matches the problem at hand.

---

4   WebApp models are discussed at length in Chapters 6 through 11.

Once a candidate pattern has been found, the information contained within the pattern template is evaluated by asking the following questions:

- Is the pattern appropriate for the WebApp domain? That is, is the context appropriate?
- Is the pattern indeed appropriate for the design focus and granularity of the problem?
- Can the pattern be used without making any trade-offs or compromises that are incompatible with the current WebApp design?
- Can the pattern be used without making any trade-offs or compromises that are incompatible with other elements of the design?

If each of these questions is answered in the affirmative, the team should proceed to evaluate the pattern in greater detail.

SafeHome

Applying Patterns

The scene: Informal discussion at the desk of a **SafeHome-Assured.com** designer during the development of increment 6, *Sensor control*

The players: WebApp designer and **SafeHome-Assured.com** chief system architect

The conversation:

System architect: How is the design of the camera control interface coming along?

WebApp designer: Not too bad—I've built most of the underlying code to connect to the actual sensors without too many problems. I've also started thinking about the interface for the users to actually move, pan, and zoom the cameras from a remote Web page, but I'm not sure I've got it right yet.

System architect: So, what have you come up with?

WebApp designer: Well, the requirements are that the camera control needs to be highly interactive—as the user moves the control, the camera should move as soon as possible. So I was thinking of having a set of buttons laid out like a normal camera, and when the user clicks them it controls the camera.

System architect: Hmmm. Yeah, that would work, but I'm not sure it's right. For each click of a control you need to wait for the whole client-server communication to occur, and so you won't get a good sense of quick feedback.

WebApp designer: That's what I thought—and why I wasn't very happy with the approach, but I'm not sure how else I might do it.

System architect: Well, why not just use the *interactive device control* pattern!

WebApp designer: Uhmmm—what's that? I haven't heard of it.

System architect: It's basically a pattern for exactly the problem you're describing. If you look it up in our patterns database, you'll find the details. The solution it proposes is basically to create a control connection to the server with the device, through which control commands can be sent. That way you don't need to send normal HTTP requests. And the pattern even shows how you can implement this using some simple Ajax techniques. You have a simple client-side JavaScript that communicates directly with the server and sends the commands as soon as the user does anything.

(continued)

Example Patterns

To illustrate the range of patterns that can be applied to WebApp design and to provide an aggregation of the various patterns sources, we have provided a set of example patterns that can be used during Web engineering work. For each broad category we also consider a concrete example that applies to **SafeHomeAssured.com.** In the following tables, the letter in the source column refers to the information sources listed in Table 13.1.

Is It Possible to Define Patterns That Address Problems at the Business Level?

As we have already noted, patterns can be developed at any level of abstraction. *Business-level patterns* relate to the overall WebApp and how stakeholders might use the WebApp. In general they describe broad approaches that would typically be considered during the modeling activity—analysis and early design stages. See Table 13.2.

As an example, consider **SafeHomeAssured.com** increment 3, *Product quotes and processing product orders* where the functionality to support users placing orders for products is developed.

Since Interaction Is Pervasive, There Must Be Many Interaction Patterns. True?

Absolutely! Many *interaction patterns* have been published and all focus on supporting user interaction with WebApps. This is a very broad area and can include general user experience, as well as the design of user interface look and feel, layout, and interaction support. Interaction patterns can also address how the WebApp interface is structured and used, including detailed interaction support and functionality (e.g., searching or indexing) to support the user interaction. See Table 13.3.

TABLE 13.2   EXAMPLE BUSINESS-LEVEL PATTERNS

Pattern Category (Pattern Name)	Source*	Brief Description
Business Patterns Collaboration (user to user) Information aggregation (user to data) Extended enterprise (business to business) Self-service (user to business)	E	These patterns describe different forms of stakeholder interactions: users interacting with other users (such as in auction sites), users interacting with businesses (such as in e-commerce applications), and actions between businesses (such as with supply chain management applications).
Integration Patterns Access integration Application integration	E	These patterns describe combinations of the business patterns that can be used to integrate multiple applications, multiple modes of access, and multiple sources of information to build one seamless application.
Composite Patterns Account access e-Commerce e-Marketplace Portal	E	These describe the combination of business patterns and integration patterns to provide overall solutions that perform complex business functions. A typical example might be an e-commerce pattern that links a self-service pattern (describing the user engagement) and an information aggregation pattern (for access to catalogs, etc.) with an application integration pattern.
e-Commerce Booking process Case study Login Newsletter Premium content lock Product advisor Product comparison Product configurator Purchase process Registration Shopping cart Store locator Testimonials Virtual product display	A	These patterns describe specific examples of e-commerce applications, looking at different ways in which the interaction between users and the enterprise can be supported.
Site Types Artist site Automotive site Branded promo site Campaign site Commerce site Community site Corporate site Multinational site Museum site My site News site Portal Web-based application	A	These are patterns describing domain-specific WebApps, highlighting the broad content, structure, navigation, and functionality required within that application domain.

*See Table 13.1.

SAFEHOME

Selecting a Business Pattern

The scene: Initial discussions at the commencement of design of increment 3, *Product quotes and processing product orders*

The players: WebApp designer and **SafeHome-Assured.com** chief system architect

The conversation:

WebApp designer: I started to do some initial thinking about increment 3 yesterday, but thought I would bounce some ideas off you before I got too far along.

System architect: Okay, what have you come up with?

WebApp designer: Like you said, there's no sense reinventing a solution for a problem that's already been solved. So I thought I would see what I could find that might suit our product quotes and ordering system. We've already roughly spec'd out the requirements on cards 5 [*Get a product quote*] and 8 [*Place a product order*] and done some work on the pricing models and payment types our stakeholders will accept. I thought a good place to start looking at

possible solutions might be the IBM e-business patterns site you showed me. Here, let me bring it up on the screen. See, this is clearly a self-service application—but what type is it?

[The designer proceeds to access the following page:

www-128.ibm.com/developerworks/patterns/u2b/ select-application-topology.html.]

System architect: Hmmm, a lot of different possibilities.

WebApp designer: Yep, but see this table at the top? It helps us find a suitable pattern. In this case the key drivers seem to be fairly clear—the client is keen to improve both organizational efficiency and keep the application complexity as simple as possible. That seems to indicate that the *customized presentation to host* is the right pattern. It basically involves providing a presentation layer over the top of their existing ordering system, rather than trying to redo the whole thing from scratch.

[The designer and architect continue to discuss the details of the proposed architecture, using the pattern as a basis for exploring design issues.]

As an example, **SafeHomeAssured.com** increment 2 allows a user to search for information on a particular sensor. The detailed analysis of this particular use case indicates that it would be appropriate to include a search engine. Since searching is a very common problem, it should come as no surprise that there are many search-related patterns. Looking at the patterns in Table 13.3, we find the following patterns, and the associated problems that they solve:

Advanced search. Users must find a specific item in a large collection of items.

Help wizard. Users need help on a certain topic related to the site or when they need to find a specific page on the site.

Search area. Users must find a page.

Search tips. Users need to know how to control the search engine.

Search results. Users have to process a list of search results.

TABLE 13.3 EXAMPLE INTERACTION PATTERNS

Pattern Category (Pattern Name)	Source*	Brief Description
User Experiences Community building Fun Information seeking Learning Shopping	A	These patterns define the broad purpose of the WebApp and the forms of user interaction that should occur in supporting that purpose. For example, a site that has the purpose of community building should support users in collecting and sharing information. The pattern describes how this can be achieved through mechanisms such as forums and recommendations.
Searching Advanced search FAQ Help wizard Search area Search tips Search results Simple search Site index Site map Topic pages	A	There are a wide range of different purposes and approaches to searching. These patterns describe solutions that are appropriate to different search contexts.
Interface Layout Active reference Behavioral grouping Behavior anticipation Here I am Index navigation Information factoring Information-interaction coupling Information-interaction decoupling Information on demand Process feedback Selectable key words Selectable search space Simple search interface	C	Interface and layout patterns describe approaches to designing the arrangement of the actual objects on each Web page. This is typically a visual communication issue and affects the way in which users relate to the page. For example, these patterns address issues such as providing information about the current status of navigation (e.g., trails), and providing the user with information on the consequence of activating an interface object (e.g., where will this link lead me?).
Organizing the Page Card stack Center stage Closable panels Diagonal balance Liquid layout Movable panels Responsive disclosure Responsive enabling Titled sections Visual framework	G	These patterns are similar to the preceding, describing the arrangement of the Web page and how this arrangement addresses specific problems. For example, card stacks (e.g., tabs) solve the problem of how to arrange content into groups when a single page would be too overcrowded.
Commands and Actions Action panel Command history Multilevel undo Progress indicator Smart menu items	G	These patterns relate to specific interface components and how to design them for maximum ease of use. Usually this relates to supporting effective feedback to users on the progress or availability of functionality.

TABLE 13.3   (CONTINUED)

Pattern Category (Pattern Name)	Source*	Brief Description
Getting Input from Users Drop-down chooser Fill in the blanks Forgiving format Good defaults Illustrated choices Input hints Input prompt	G	These patterns relate specifically to user provision of information and how this can be best supported under different circumstances.

*See Table 13.1.

For **SafeHomeAssured.com** the number of products is not particularly large, and each has a relatively simple categorization, so an advanced search or a search wizard is probably not necessary. Similarly, the search is simple enough not to require search tips. The description of the **search box,** however, is given (in part) as shown in the sidebar:

EXAMPLE PATTERN

Simple Search: The Search Box Pattern

Problem: Users need to find an item or specific information.

Use when: Any website that already has primary navigation. Users may want to search for an item in a category. Users may want to further specify a query.

Solution: Offer a search

The search interface

Offer search functionality consisting of a search label, a key word field, a filter if applicable, and a "Go" button. Pressing the return key has the same function as selecting the Go button. Also provide Search Tips and examples in a separate page. A link to that page is placed next to the search functionality. The edit box for the search term is large enough to accommodate three typical user queries (typically around 20 characters). If

the number of filters is more than two, use a combo box for filter selection, otherwise a radio button.

Search — editbox — for/in — filter — Go button

or just . . .

— editbox — Go button

Presenting search results

The search results are presented on a new page with a clear label containing at least "Search results" or similar. The search function is repeated in the top part of the page with the entered key words so that the users know what the key words were.

Etc.

*From **www.welie.com/patterns/showPattern. php?patternID=search.**

The pattern goes on to describe substantial details about how the search results are accessed, presented, matched, and so on. Based on this, the **SafeHomeAssured.com**

Example **Safe-HomeAssured. com** search functionality. (a) Search widget. (b) Search results.

Product search: Camera   Go Help

(a)

Search Results: Your search for <Camera> returned 13 results.

Items 1 to 10 (Page 1 2)

Item	Description	Rank
1	Camera Model XYZ123: *This camera is Lorem ipsum dolor sit amet, consectetur adipisicing elit, sed do eiusmod tempor incididunt ut labore et dolore magna aliqua. Ut enim ad minim veniam, quis nostrud exercitation ullamco laboris nisi ut aliquip.*	10.0
2	Camera Model XYZ128: *This camera is Lorem ipsum dolor sit amet, consectetur adipisicing elit, sed do eiusmod tempor incididunt ut labore et dolore magna aliqua. Ut enim ad minim veniam, quis nostrud exercitation ullamco laboris nisi ut aliquip.*	10.0
3	Camera Model ABC456: *This camera is Lorem ipsum dolor sit amet, consectetur adipisicing elit, sed do eiusmod tempor incididunt ut labore et dolore magna aliqua. Ut enim ad minim veniam, quis nostrud exercitation ullamco laboris nisi ut aliquip.*	9.81
4	Camera Mount for XYZ123: *This camera mount is Lorem ipsum dolor sit amet, consectetur adipisicing elit, sed do eiusmod tempor incididunt ut labore et dolore magna aliqua. Ut enim ad minim veniam, quis nostrud exercitation ullamco laboris nisi ut aliquip.*	8.34
5	Camera Network Interface QWE872: *This camera interface is Lorem ipsum dolor sit amet, consectetur adipisicing elit, sed do eiusmod tempor incididunt ut labore et dolore magna aliqua. Ut enim ad minim veniam, quis nostrud exercitation ullamco laboris nisi ut aliquip.*	6.23

...

(b)

WebE team can put together the search widget shown in Figure 13.1a, and which is included in the header of all pages. When a search is performed, the results appear as shown in Figure 13.1b.

What Navigation Patterns Are Available?

The success of a WebApp is often predicated on the ease with which a user can move within the information space. As a WebE team begins the design, a broad array of navigation problems can arise. The problem may be as simple as the ordering of content as the navigation path is traversed or as complex as the layout of a comprehensive navigation structure. Navigation patterns address these and other problems that relate to the organization of the content as expressed in the navigation structures of the WebApp. See Table 13.4.

As an example that illustrates a situation in which a navigation pattern might be useful, consider **SafeHomeAssured.com** increment 6. The WebE team has to implement support for a registered user to control and monitor various sensors within the user's space. In this case, the developers realize that a user may want to select and view different sensors in quick succession. In a case such as this, having to repeatedly navigate back to a selection of sensors would be cumbersome.

TABLE 13.4   EXAMPLE NAVIGATION PATTERNS

Pattern Category (Pattern Name)	Source*	Guided Tour
Navigation Patterns Active reference Landmark News Node in context Set-based navigation Shopping basket	B	These are general patterns that describe the arrangement of the content that is appropriate within different contexts. For example, the *News* pattern describes a structure where the most recent news content is linked (usually with a brief summary) directly from the home or main page, and older content is available through a structured archive.
Structure Navigation Collection center Complex entity Guided tour Hybrid collection Index navigation Navigation context Navigation strategy News Node as a navigation view Opportunistic linking Selectable search engine Set-based navigation Structured answer	C	These patterns are similar to the preceding and focus on different arrangements of content to suit different purposes. For example, the *Guided tour* pattern addresses the problem of assisting users to gain a structured overview when they do not have a specific target in mind. Conversely, the *Opportunistic Linking* pattern describes a solution to the problem of keeping a user engaged by providing link suggestions as the user moves through the information space.
Navigation Bread crumbs Directory Doormat navigation Double tab Faceted navigation Fly-out menu Headerless menu Icon menu Image browser Main navigation Map navigator Meta navigation Minesweeping Overlay menu Repeated menu Retractable menu Scrolling menu Shortcut box Split navigation Teaser menu Trail menu	A	Rather than describing specific navigation structures, these patterns describe mechanisms for accessing and understanding that structure. Although most of the specific mechanisms will be familiar to most designers (and indeed users), the specific problems being addressed may not be so obvious. As an example, the *Minesweeper* pattern involves dynamic presentation of content summaries (and usually links to further information) only when the user moves the mouse over trigger points (i.e., the user can "hunt" for interesting content). This pattern is inappropriate when the user is looking for specific information, but can provide a very effective means of engaging users in exploratory or fun sites (or subsites).
Getting Around Animated transition Clear entry points Color-coded sections Global navigation	G	These patterns describe aspects of the interface that relate to an understanding of the navigation structure and options that are available.

(continued)

TABLE 13.4 (CONTINUED)

Pattern Category (Pattern Name)	Source*	Guided Tour
Organizing the Content Extras on demand Intriguing branches One-window drill-down Two-panel selector Wizard	G	These patterns highlight specific instances of navigational options rather than a general structure. For example, the *Intriguing Branches* pattern describes embedding links directly throughout content rather than as a separate structure, as a solution to provide contextual navigation (a good example of this is a wiki).

*See Table 13.1.

A much simpler mechanism is described by the *Two Panel Selector* panel described in the sidebar (presented only in part):

EXAMPLE PATTERN

*Quick Selection: The Two-Panel Selector Pattern**

What: Put two side-by-side panels on the interface. In the first, show a set of items that the user can select at will; in the other, show the content of the selected item.

Use when: You're presenting a list of objects, categories, or even actions. Messages in a mailbox, sections of a website, songs or images in a library, database records, files—all are good candidates. Each item has interesting content associated with it, such as the text of an e-mail message or details about a file's size or date. You want users to see the overall structure of the list, but you also want users to walk through the items at their own pace, in an order of their choosing.

Physically, the display you work with is large enough to show two separate panels at once. Very small cell phone displays cannot cope with this pattern, but a screen such as the Blackberry's or iPhone's can.

Why: The Two-Panel Selector is a learned convention, but an extremely common and powerful one. People quickly learn that they're supposed to select an item in one panel to see its contents in the other. They might learn it from their e-mail clients, from Windows Explorer, or from websites; whatever the case, they apply the concept to other applications that look similar.

When both panels are visible side by side, users can quickly shift their attention back and forth, looking now at the overall structure of the list ("How many more unread e-mail messages do I have?"), and now at an object's details ("What does this email say?"). This tight integration has several advantages over other physical structures, such as two separate windows or One-Window Drilldown.

. . .

How: Place the selectable list on the top or left panel, and the details panel below it or to its right. This takes advantage of the visual flow that most users who read left-to-right languages expect. (Try reversing it for right-to-left language speakers.)

When the user selects an item, immediately show its contents or details in the second panel. Selection should be done with a single click. But while you're at it, give the user a way to change selection from the keyboard, particularly with the arrow keys. This reduces both the physical effort and the time required for browsing and contributes to keyboard-only usability.

Make the selected item visually obvious . . . .

*From the Designing Interfaces website at
http://designinginterfaces.com/Two-Panel_Selector.

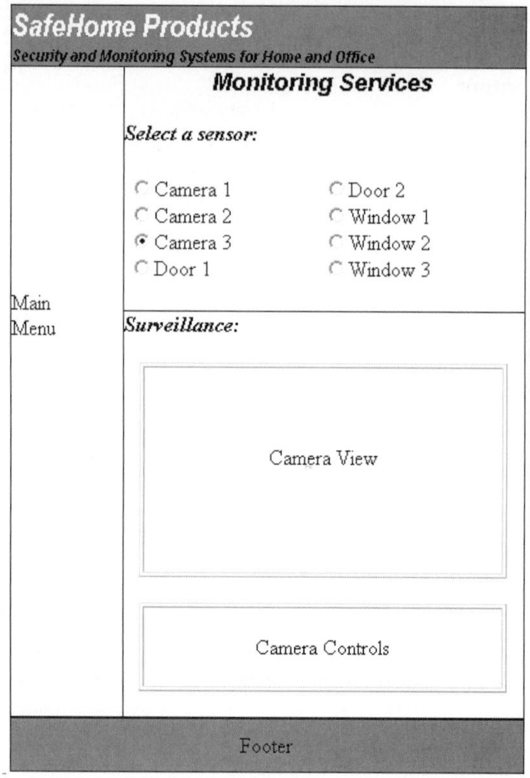

FIGURE 13.2

Example naviga-
tion design
for the sensor
monitoring
functionality.

The **SafeHomeAssured.com** WebE team put together the navigation design shown in
Figure 13.2.

Where Do Content and Presentation Patterns Fit In?

The WebE team uses business patterns to help address overall design issues that
relate to the WebApp's use within a business context. The team uses interaction
and navigation patterns to establish communication with the WebApp and to move
through the information space. Finally, it applies content and presentation patterns
to specify the content within the WebApp and organize the content to support Web-
App objectives. See Table 13.5.

Consider again the example of the selection and monitoring of sensors from
the previous section, "What Navigation Patterns Are Available?" After this increment has been constructed, the **SafeHomeAssured.com** team conducts some usability
tests and discovers that the users found it awkward to know quickly which sensor
to select (using the top pane of radio buttons shown in Figure 13.2). Reconsidering
this aspect of the design, the designer finds the *Map Navigator* pattern described in
the sidebar.

Providing a Navigational Contest: The Map Navigator Pattern*

Problem: Users need to find a location of choice on a map.

Use when: The site has the possibility to search for a special location. For example, a corporate site or e-commerce site may have a store locator to allow users to find a physical store. In other cases, such as a website that allows people to find arbitrary destinations, users will see their search results as positions on a map.

Solution: Show a map with the points of interest and provide navigation links in all corners.

The map is displayed with the points of interest (POIs) in the center of the image. Mark different POIs using different flags or colors, and provide a legend explaining them. If there is only one POI, provide the exact details of that POI. When there are multiple POIs, *minesweeping* [another pattern] can be used to display details of the POI as the user moves the mouse over it.

Users can move their "window" on the map by selecting any of the navigation links in the corners. The page will reload and show a slightly different portion of the map. Add zooming, and indicate the scale of the map. Many people may want to print the map so that they can take it with them, so a printer-friendly page must be available.

Why: We know maps from the real world, and we are comfortable with seeing them on the Web. The navigation features are not ideal on the Web since they require reloading of the page, but this will not lead to usability problems.

. . .

*From Welie.com interaction design patterns website at **www.welie.com/patterns/showPattern. php?patternID=map-navigator**).

TABLE 13.5 EXAMPLE CONTENT AND PRESENTATION PATTERNS

Pattern Category (Pattern Name)	Source*	Brief Description
Basic Page Types Article page Blog page Contact page Event calendar Form Guest book Home page Input error message Printer-friendly page Processing page Product page	A	These patterns describe specific components of WebApps and the content that might be appropriate to include in supporting those components. For example, an *Event Calendar* (which might be used in a community site, such as a local sports club) provides not only lists of events, but typically would support this with a date selector time line showing when events are scheduled, and (for sites with many events) support for categorization and filtering.
Showing Complex Data Cascading lists Jump to item Overview plus detail Row striping Sortable table Tree table	G	These patterns describe particular ways of presenting content to users. For example, the *Overview Plus Detail* pattern shows a section of content, but also includes an indication of where it is positioned within an abstraction or summary of the full content. The most common use is when a user drills down into detail, such as with map data or content that can be represented spatially.
Making It Look Good Corner treatments Deep background Few hues, many values	G	This is a small sample of specific graphic design patterns. Note that in general, however, graphic design issues are normally expressed as design heuristics or guidelines (see, for example, Jakob Nielsen's usability website at **www.useit.com**) rather than patterns that link specific problems with solutions.

*See Table 13.1.

FIGURE 13.3

Revised version
of the navigation
design for the
sensor monitor-
ing functionality.

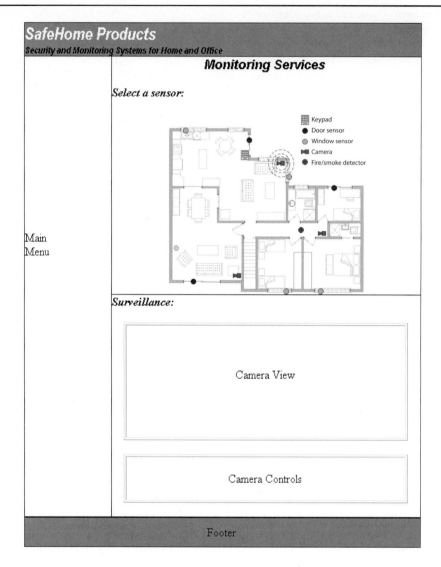

The result of applying this pattern to a minor redesign of the sensor selection and monitoring is shown in Figure 13.3.

Where We've Been . . . Where We're Going

Given the rapidly changing nature of the Web and the complexity of designing effective WebApps, using the best design solution at the right time is a challenge for Web engineers. Anything that can help you to ensure that solutions are appropriate and reflect best practice is to be encouraged—and this is exactly what patterns attempt to achieve.

Patterns capture the knowledge of experts and provide developers with a way to record their hard-earned experience. Once they are cataloged in a repository, patterns make that knowledge available to others. In this chapter we have discussed only a small subset of all patterns that are available for Web engineers. You can begin your search for appropriate patterns using the websites listed in Table 13.1 or the other tables contained within this chapter, or you can work within your organization to develop an in-house repository. Regardless of your approach, your organization will avoid reinventing the wheel every time you encounter a design problem.

In Chapter 14, we will round off our consideration of the construction of WebApps with a look at the technologies, tools, and environments that actually allow Web engineers to implement the engineering models that we have spent most of this book discussing.

References

[Ale77] Alexander, C., *A Pattern Language: Towns, Buildings, Construction,* Oxford University Press, 1977.

[Amb02] Ambler, S., "UML Component Diagramming Guidelines," 2002, **www.modelingstyle.info/** (accessed November 18, 2006).

[App98] Appleton, B., "Patterns and Software: Essential Concepts and Terminology," 1998, **www.cmcrossroads.com/bradapp/docs/patterns-intro.html** (accessed August 13, 2007).

[Ber98] Bernstein, M., "Patterns in Hypertext," *Proc. 9th ACM Conf. Hypertext,* ACM Press, 1998, pp. 21–29.

[Bus96] Buschmann, F., et al., *Pattern-Oriented Software Architecture,* Wiley, 1996.

[Fow03] Fowler, M., et al., *Patterns of Enterprise Application Architecture,* Addison-Wesley, 2003.

[Gam95] Gamma, E., et al., *Design Patterns,* Addison-Wesley, 1995.

[Gar97] Garrido, A., G. Rossi, and D. Schwabe, "Patterns Systems for Hypermedia," 1997, **www.inf.puc-rio.br/~schwabe/papers/PloP97.pdf** (accessed August 13, 2007).

[Ger00] German, D., and D. Cowan, "Toward a Unified Catalog of Hypermedia Design Patterns," *Proc. 33rd Hawaii Intl. Conf. on System Sciences,* IEEE, vol. 6, Maui, Hawaii, June 2000, **www.turingmachine.org/~dmg/research/papers/dmg_hicss2000.pdf** (accessed August 13, 2007).

[Mai03] Maioriello, J., "What Are Design Patterns and Do I Need Them?" developer.com, 2003, **www.developer.com/design/article.php/1474561** (accessed August 13, 2007).

[Per99] Perzel, K., and D. Kane, "Usability Patterns for Applications on the World Wide Web," 1999, **http://jerry.cs.uiuc.edu/~plop/plop99/proceedings/Kane/perzel_kane.pdf** (accessed August 13, 2007).

14

TECHNOLOGIES AND TOOLS

Writing about Web engineering technologies is a lot like trying to stand on a railway platform and recognize the people inside a fast-moving train. You know they're in there, but the train is moving so fast that it's really hard to identify the occupants of one car before they're replaced by the occupants of the next.

New tools and Web technologies are changing very rapidly. In reality, by the time you read this chapter, there will be an entirely different technology and tools landscape. As a Web engineer, you'll be asked to evaluate and apply languages, tools, frameworks, and environments that don't exist as we write this chapter.

For example, at this point in time, technologies to support Web 2.0 (such as Ajax and RSS) are the subject of much discussion, but by the time you read this chapter it is likely other technologies[1] will have come into focus. In this chapter we discuss the current state of Web technologies in an effort to illustrate WebE approaches and possibilities. There are two main categories of technologies that we'll discuss:

1. **Implementation tools.** Includes technologies as diverse as Web application servers, content management systems, file-sharing systems, and security management

2. **Development tools.** Includes design modeling, issue tracking, and application testing

In some cases the boundary between these two categories will be blurred. For example, a design tool may be integrated into the content management system.

General Issues

Prior to discussing specific technologies, there are several important general issues that are worth considering. The first focuses on the need to compartmentalize WebApp capabilities and the tools that allow us to

---

1 Although speculating about what technologies might emerge in the future is fraught with danger, this won't stop us trying! Possible technologies that might be significant in the near future (which could be the present by the time you read this) include: the mainstreaming of semantic Web technologies, the increasing emergence of Web services, and the emergence of tools that facilitate automatic adaptation to different user clients and help in the development of context-aware applications.

achieve those capabilities. The second addresses the origin of the tools we use: Are they developed by an open community of developers and users or are they provided by a single commercial vendor? The third issue considers the impact of the WebApp category on the types of tools and technologies that can be used to develop the WebApp.

How Does Separation of Concerns Impact Tools and Technologies?

The principle of *separation of concerns*[2] argues that a conceptualization of a problem or solution should be broken down into unique components that focus on specific aspects while minimizing the interaction between the components. In software engineering jargon, singular focus is often referred to as the *cohesiveness* of a component, and component interaction is referred to as the *coupling* between components. We always strive to increase cohesion and decrease coupling. The result is a system that is simpler to understand and maintain.

For WebApps, separation of concerns usually means compartmentalizing the following WebApp components:

- Content storage
- Content adaptation
- Presentation
- Presentation adaptation
- Content structuring and navigation
- Functionality (e.g., search and workflow management)

Many application frameworks will adopt some form of separation of concerns similar to the preceding. For example, content management systems (Chapter 16) will usually separate content storage (stored as *content objects*) from the presentation of the content (stored as *presentation templates*). Even the underlying technologies themselves have gradually evolved toward increasing separation of concerns. The very earliest Web technology, HTML, embedded both presentation and navigation directly into the content, leading to substantial maintenance challenges. Subsequent technologies worked to separate these elements: XML represents content, CSS represents presentation formatting, and XLink represents link structures. By emphasizing separation of concerns with these newer technologies, the ability to maintain (i.e., correct, adapt, and enhance) existing WebApps is greatly enhanced.

Recalling the MVC (model-view-controller) framework presented in Chapter 11, we see another example of separation of concerns. MVC defines a framework

---

2   A good starting point for further information on separation of concerns is the Wikipedia article on *separation of concerns* at **http://en.wikipedia.org/wiki/Separation_of_concerns** (accessed August 13, 2007).

that decouples content and navigation (*model*) from both the application interface (*view*) and the functional manipulation of the model (*controller*). Many implementation technologies have adapted MVC or a variant of it.

Which Technology—Open Source or Proprietary?

As you evaluate the technology and tools landscape, the choice between open source and proprietary tools can become a significant issue. Wikipedia[3] defines *open source* in the following way:

> **Open source** describes practices in production and development that promote access to the end product's sources [source code]. Some consider it as a philosophy, and others consider it as a pragmatic methodology. Before *open source* became widely adopted, developers and producers used a variety of phrases to describe the concept; the term *open source* gained popularity with the rise of the Internet and its enabling of diverse production models, communication paths, and interactive communities. Subsequently, open source software became the most prominent face of open source.

In contrast with open source, proprietary tools and technologies are developed by a single vendor who generally does not make the source code available to end users or others.

Open source tools (e.g., the Apache Web server and the *Eclipse* development environment) have the advantage of broad-based development, extensibility, and rapid evolution and improvement. The evolution of open source tools is market driven in the truest sense of the word, and the community of end users has a feeling of ownership that is often missing when proprietary tools are used. Defects within open source tools are discovered relatively quickly, resulting in commendable product quality. The community development atmosphere, however, can create problems when support is required.

Proprietary tools often have the advantage of improved support (or at least accountability for the support) and a clearer release cycle. Such tools are often packaged more effectively and are often easier for nontechnologists to implement within their organization.

In general, the choice between open source and proprietary WebE technology and tools should be based on your answers to the following questions:

- Does the tool meet the capabilities that are required and the functionality that is to be deployed?
- Are the reported quality and extensibility adequate for your needs?

---

3 http://en.wikipedia.org/wiki/Open_source.

- Does the evolutionary direction predicted for the tool meet your needs today and in the future?
- Does the tool have adequate support facilities, online documentation, and help?
- Does the cost of the tool fall within your project or organizational budget?

Once you've established answers to these questions, your team can debate whether open source or proprietary technologies are right for you.

SafeHome

Open Source versus Proprietary

The scene: The **SafeHome-Assured.com** meeting room, during the initial discussions on the development of increment 2

The players: The WebE team leader and the WebE technical manager

The conversation:

WebE team leader: Okay, so we're agreed then that the logical way to store the content is to simply leave it in the existing database formats that the stakeholders use, rather than trying to map it into XML. This will allow them to continue to leverage their existing processes for updating the content. The next question is how we access this database from within the relevant WebApp components. I was assuming we would probably use an off-the-shelf proprietary database server like SQL Manager. What do you think?

WebE technical manager: Well, yes, we could, but given the nature of the project, I thought an open source solution might be better. Something like MySQL or Ingres.

WebE team leader: Why? Functionally it's all fairly simple. Wouldn't one of the proprietary database servers be easier to set up quickly straight out of the box?

WebE technical manager: Yes, but marketing has already indicated that they believe ongoing changes and evolution are likely, and they don't want to be locked into a particular platform, and generally the open source products will give us much more flexibility in adapting to other products and environments.

WebE team leader: Hmm—good point. How about you document some of this, and I'll discuss it with marketing before we commit to a final decision?

What Is the Impact of Application Categories on WebE Technology?

In Chapter 1, we discussed a wide array of WebApp categories—informational, download, customizable, interaction, user-input, transaction-oriented, service-oriented, portals, database access, and data warehousing. In most cases, the WebApp category will help define the types of WebE technologies that can be applied.

Early WebApps were informational. That is, they provided the end user with hypermedia-based content in a static unidirectional flow. When they included functionality, it was largely intended to change the flow of control or the nature of the content or its presentation.

In recent years, WebApps have evolved to include much more complex bidirectional engagement with users. These WebApps have often been collectively referred to as Web 2.0. Examples that are typical of this class of application are

- **Folksonomies.** WebApps that support the collaborative generation of content provision and categorization aimed at supporting information retrieval (e.g., *Flickr,* **www.flickr.com**)

- **Mashups.** WebApps comprising combinations of multiple information sources to provide synergistic outcomes (see *programmableweb* at **www.programmableweb.com** for a long list of examples)

- **Social networking.** WebApps that focus on constructing rich connections between users (e.g., see the *Social Networking Site* list on Wikipedia at **en.wikipedia.org/wiki/Social_networking_sites**)

- **Wikis.** WebApps that allow users to add, remove, and edit common content, thereby supporting community construction of WebApps (e.g., see *Wikipedia* at **www.wikipedia.com**).

Even more recently, WebApps have used a mix of client-side interface technologies and server-side functionality to create applications that mimic the rich interactivity more typically associated with desktop applications. Examples include *Writely* (now *Google Docs*), a WebApp-based word processor; *Kiko* (**www.kiko.com**), a calendar WebApp; and *Box* (**www.box.net**), an online file storage WebApp.

As the overall sophistication, degree of interactivity, breadth of functionality, and scope of content increase for WebApps, Web technologies must keep pace. Web technologies have evolved to create applications that progressively remove the limitations (for both user and maintainer) that have historically limited the global impact of WebApps.

Implementation Tools and Technologies

It is very easy, as a novice WebApp developer (or in some cases, even an experienced Web engineer) to become overwhelmed by the huge number of Web application technologies and the rapid pace of change. Consider the following representative list of standards and technologies selected at random—all of which are potentially useful in the implementation of a WebApp. This is just a tiny percentage of the available platforms and tools.[4]

---

4   As we noted in the introduction to this chapter, by the time you read this, some of the technologies listed will have disappeared and many new ones (not listed) will have emerged.

> . . ., Ajax, ASP, ColdFusion, Communique, CSS, DOM, Eclipse, Gnutella, GRDDL, Hibernate, HTML, InkML, J2EE, JavaScript, JBoss, Jigsaw, Joomla!, JSP, Kerberos, Lasso, Mambo, MathML, Maven, OWL, PHP, PICS, Plone, PNG, RDF, Rhythmyx, Scarab, Shale, Shibboleth, SMIL, SOAP/XMLP, SPARQL, Struts, SVG, SVN, TeamSite, Tomcat, Torque, Turbine, Vignette, WebLogic, WebSphere, XForms, XHTML, XLink, XML, XPath, XPointer, XSL and XSLT, Zope, . . .

How can a Web engineer keep abreast of such a rich set of technologies? The short answer is to avoid trying to become expert in every technology and instead work to understand the broad classes of technologies that are available. Investigate specific instances of tools and technologies only when necessary.

What Are Application Frameworks?

An *application framework* is a set of libraries and/or components that are used to implement the basic structure of an application. The framework provides both an underlying architecture and substantial amounts of code to support this architecture. For WebApps, this often includes mechanisms for managing content, interfacing with access control systems and databases, managing user sessions, and the handling of presentation and styles.

WebApp frameworks cover a broad spectrum of applications. Simple frameworks have a single primary purpose, such as page generation from database content. Complex frameworks address a variety of features and needs. Many of the more sophisticated frameworks are based on common architectural models such as the model-view-controller (MVC) model that was briefly discussed earlier in this chapter and in Chapter 11. A good example of an MVC-based framework is Apache Struts, which is used in the creation of Java Web applications. It supports clear separation of concerns and allows different developers (graphic designers, content experts, coders) to manage relevant sections of the application.

Frameworks are usually based on a single primary implementation language. For example, Struts[5] is Java based, FuseBox[6] is based on PHP, Zope[7] is based on Python, and Catalyst[8] is based on Perl.

Typically, when an application framework is used, it will need to be selected early in the design process, because it will affect the overall design architecture that is adopted. It then influences the overall design and will guide the WebE team as it makes specific implementation decisions.

---

5 http://struts.apache.org/.
6 www.fusebox.org/.
7 www.zope.org/.
8 www.catalystframework.org/.

A good starting point for further information on Web application frameworks can be found on Wikipedia at **http://en.wikipedia.org/wiki/Web_application_frameworks.**

How Are Content Management Systems and Version Control Technologies Applied?

Rich and varied content is the core feature of almost all Web applications. This content is generated and/or managed by diverse users, and the same content will often be used in diverse ways by different categories of users. A *content management system* (CMS)[9] supports the management, editing, conversion, and updating of content within Web-based systems.

The functionality supported by content management systems is very diverse (see CMS matrix at **www.cmsmatrix.org/**), and different content management systems support different capabilities:

- Presentation templates, themes, and skins
- Monitoring, statistics, and content tracking
- Content staging and deployment
- Security management to authenticate users and control access for both editing and viewing specified content
- Support for diverse applications: wikis, discussion forums, guest books, event calendaring, FAQs, etc.

More sophisticated CMSs provide version control capabilities (Chapter 16), enabling the WebE team to track changes to content and allowing the state of an application to be "wound back" to a previous version of the content. For more information on CMSs see the list of systems on *Wikipedia* at **en.wikipedia.org/wiki/List_of_content_management_systems** and the list on *CMS Watch* at **www.cmswatch.com.**

What If a Search Capability Must Be Provided with Our WebApp?

Many tools support search capabilities within WebApps. The simplest of these provides an indexer that generates an index of site content and a search tool that queries the indexes. More advanced search tools provide customization of the search, configuration of the indexing strategies, and tools to support analysis of the search logs.

Unlike application frameworks, and to a lesser extent content management systems, search engine functionality is relatively well defined and doesn't have much effect on the architecture of the application. For this reason, it is usually rea-

---

9 Content management systems (CMS) are discussed in more detail in Chapter 16.

sonable to defer decisions on the specific search tool until late in the development process except where the search functionality is particularly complex or unique. More information on search tools can be found at **www.searchtools.com** and at **www. searchenginewatch.com.**

Development Tools and Technologies

There are hundreds of software development tools that can be adapted to Web engineering work, and an almost equally wide range of tools that have been created to support the implementation of Web-based systems. Most of these Web engineering tools, however, tend to focus on low-level implementation issues. There are very few tools or technologies that have been created to support the earlier activities in the Web engineering process (such as communication, requirements gathering, analysis, and design modeling) or the broader project aspects (e.g., project management, testing, issue tracking).

Many of the tools that do exist for Web engineering have been adapted from tools that were originally developed for conventional software applications. Often this adaptation is a little cumbersome or has limited consideration of the specific characteristics of WebApps (e.g., see the comments on issue tracking later in this chapter in the subsection "Are There Tools That Can Assist with the Management of the WebE Process?"). In other cases, the tools have been developed as research prototypes, have not yet been fully adapted for full commercial-strength usage, and are not particularly robust.

However, a wide variety of Web engineering tools do exist. We'll examine some of these tool categories in the sections that follow.

Can I Acquire Tools That Will Help Me with the Modeling Activity?

Although there are numerous tools available for the modeling and design of conventional software, only a few tools have been developed specifically for modeling WebApps. The most common tools are those that integrate some element of application modeling into the actual implementation tools. For example, both Microsoft *FrontPage* and Adobe *Dreamweaver*—two of the leading Web design and publishing tools—each provide a powerful page-level design tool, but higher-level structural modeling tools provided by Microsoft and Adobe are more limited. Both allow the designer to graphically create and edit a site-map view that shows the basic WebApp structure, but the models have relatively limited levels of sophistication in terms of representing elements such as functional workflows, and almost no ability to model business processes, use cases, or usage scenarios. Other tools— especially those aimed at code generation—usually suffer similar limitations.

One example of a Web-focused modeling tool that goes part way to providing richer modeling is *WebRatio*.[10] Although WebRatio does not provide anywhere near the implementation richness of more commercial tools, it does provide much better support for the modeling and documentation of application content, front-end interfaces, and most especially, the navigational structures required within an application. The tool also partially automates the generation of project documentation and application code from the designs—though as with most tools supporting automatic application generation, the resultant application code will typically require considerable tuning.

Jochen Rode [Rod05] provides an interesting discussion of Web-focused tools in the modeling area, addressing their limitations and strengths.

Are There Testing Tools That Focus Specifically on WebApps?

A large number of tools have been developed to support the testing of WebApps. Several good sources of information on these tools are available at

- *Software QA/Test Resource Center:* **www.softwareqatest.com/ qatweb1.html**
- *Web Test Tools Directory:* **www.webtesttools.com/**
- *Applied Testing and Technology:* **www.aptest.com/resources.html**

As you scan through the many testing tools referenced at these sites, you'll notice that the vast majority of the tools focus on testing of an implemented WebApp, and there are relatively few tools that address evaluation or testing of a WebApp's specification or designs. Testing tools can be divided into the following categories:

- Language validation tools (e.g., HTML checks, validation of XML content against a schema, referential checks of database content)
- Navigation validation (e.g., checking that links are valid, testing of page reachability)
- Performance and load testing (e.g., server latency, stress testing)
- Platform and environment evaluation (e.g., testing of WebApp integrity across multiple browsers and versions, platforms)
- Functional testing (e.g., validation of client-side JavaScript, server-side components)
- Usage analysis (e.g., analysis of access logs, search queries)

---

10 See **www.webratio.com/** for more information on WebRatio.

Many of these tools can be used either statically by applying them to an implemented WebApp prior to release or dynamically by ongoing automated analysis of the operating WebApp. For example, there are many test tools that can be configured to automatically crawl the WebApp pages that are visible to a client, looking for particular errors such as broken links, expired content, or designs that are not consistent with a given template.

Are There Tools That Can Assist with the Management of the WebE Process?

It would be wonderful if a suite of tools existed to support Web project management, gathering and formulation of WebApp requirements, project scoping and cost estimation, issue tracking, and quality assurance. To date, however, there are very few tools that directly support the Web engineering process.

Most WebApp developers use a combination of more general software project management tools (e.g., Microsoft *Project*) and customized tools of their own making. Consider, the example shown in Figure 14.1 of a Microsoft *Excel* spreadsheet used by the **SafeHomeAssured.com** team to track issues that emerge during the development. In this example, the development team is small enough and cohesive

FIGURE 14.1

Example issue tracking in **SafeHomeAssured.com** using an Excel issue tracking spreadsheet.

	Issue ID	Added By	Date	Status	Type	Keywords	Description	Assigned to	Resolution
Project: SHA									
3.13		JimH	3/8/06	Pending	Requirement (Usage)	credit card, order, validation	What happens if the credit card details are declined when finalising the order?	RogerP	
3.14		JimH	4/8/06	Closed	Design	credit card, order, validation	Should we validate that the format of a supplied credit card number is valid on the client-side before submitting them for checking?	DavidL	Definitely! Trying to process an order with an invalid card number costs SHA money! There is no point in submitting an obviously invalid card number. (see Item 3.16)
3.15		RogerP	4/8/06	Closed	Requirement	order, cancellation	Have realised that we have not previously considered at all the possibility that a user might want to cancel an order after it has been submitted. Is this an issue?	DavidL	Discussed this with client (email ref: JS-5/8/06) and they indicated that this might be nice to have, but could be ignored in the current implementation.
3.16		JimH	6/8/06	Opened	Design	credit card, order, validation	Need to know what are the valid formats for a credit card?		
Increment 4: Sensor Layouts									
4.1		RogerP	5/8/06	Opened	Requirement	sensors, layout	Is there a limit to the number of sensors which can be included in a layout?		
Increment 5: Monitoring Services									
Increment 6: Sensor Control and Monitoring									
Increment 7: Account Management									

enough that a lightweight approach such as this would be sufficient to achieve the desired outcome of tracking issues that emerge and how they are subsequently dealt with.

Although the paucity of Web engineering process support tools is unfortunate, to some extent it is understandable given the agile approach that dominates most WebApp development. Many tools require significant overhead in terms of setup and maintenance and will therefore often impose development overheads that can conflict with agility if it is not managed carefully. For example, given the rapid evolution of the detailed navigational design of most WebApps, a formal model of that design, captured in a design tool, can become quite difficult to maintain.

Where We've Been. . . Where We're Going

In this chapter we provided a brief overview of the technologies and tools that can be applied to the development of WebApps. The vast majority of tools available to Web developers focus on the construction of WebApps. To date, relatively few tools support either the modeling of WebApps or the development process itself.

Three important issues should be considered as you examine technologies and tools that may be of use for Web engineering work. The first—separation of concerns—focuses on the need to compartmentalize WebApp capabilities and the tools that allow you to achieve those capabilities. The second addresses the origin of the tools you will use—are they developed by an open community of developers and users or are they provided by a single commercial source? The third issue considers how a specific WebApp category might dictate the types of tools and technologies that can be used.

Broad categories of WebE technologies that are applicable to all types of WebApps include application frameworks, content management systems, and search capabilities. Development technologies encompass modeling and testing tools, as well as process support.

The real challenge for a WebApp developer is determining the level of formal modeling, testing, and process support that is appropriate. We would like to see the emergence of tools that are lightweight and integrate into an agile methodology seamlessly, and yet do not lead to calcification of the specification or design. Unfortunately these tools do not yet exist.

Reference

[Rod05] Rode, J., "Web Application Development by Nonprogrammers," Virginia Polytechnic Institute, PhD dissertation, 2005, **http://scholar.lib.vt.edu/theses/available/etd-07062005-152028/unrestricted/dissertation.pdf** (accessed August 13, 2007).

TESTING WEBAPPS

There is an urgency that always pervades the Web engineering process. As communication, planning, modeling, and construction are conducted, stakeholders—concerned about competition from other Web-Apps, coerced by business pressure, and worried that they'll miss a market window—press to get the WebApp online. As a consequence, technical activities that often occur late in the WebE process, such as WebApp testing, are sometimes given short shrift. This can be a catastrophic mistake. To avoid it, your WebE team must ensure that each WebE work product exhibits high quality. Wallace and his colleagues [Wal03] note this when they state:

> Testing shouldn't wait until the project is finished. Start testing before you write one line of code. Test constantly and effectively, and you will develop a much more durable Web site.

Since analysis and design models cannot be tested in the classical sense, your Web engineering team should conduct pair walkthroughs (Chapter 5) as well as executable tests. The intent is to uncover and correct errors before the WebApp is made available to its end users.

Testing Concepts

Testing is the process of exercising a WebApp with the intent of finding (and ultimately correcting) errors. In fact, because Web-based systems and applications reside on a network and interoperate with many different operating systems, browsers [or other interface devices such as set-top boxes, personal digital assistants (PDAs), and mobile phones], hardware platforms, communications protocols, and "backroom" applications, the search for errors represents a significant challenge for Web engineers.

To understand the objectives of testing within a Web engineering context, we must consider the many dimensions of WebApp quality.[1] In the context of this discussion, we consider quality dimensions that are particularly relevant in any discussion of testing for WebE work. We also consider the nature of the errors that are encountered as a consequence of testing, and the testing strategy that is applied to uncover these errors.

---

1   WebApp quality has been considered in Chapter 5.

What Are the "Dimensions" of Quality?

Quality is incorporated into a WebApp as a consequence of good analysis and design. The quality of complex, application-critical components can be assessed by conducting a pair walkthrough (Chapter 5). This review approach assesses various elements of the design model as they are created. But some components may not undergo pair walkthrough.[2] Rather, a sequence of testing steps designed to uncover errors and other quality problems is applied. Reviews and testing examine one or more of the following quality dimensions [Mil00]:

- *Content* is evaluated at both a syntactic and semantic level. At the syntactic level, spelling, punctuation, and grammar are assessed for text-based documents. At a semantic level, correctness (of information presented), consistency (across the entire content object and related objects), and lack of ambiguity are all assessed.

- *Function* is tested to uncover errors that indicate lack of conformance to stakeholder requirements. Each WebApp function is assessed for correctness, instability, and general conformance to appropriate implementation standards (e.g., Java or XML language standards).

- *Structure* is assessed to ensure that it properly delivers WebApp content and function, is extensible, and can be supported as new content or functionality is added.

- *Usability* is tested to ensure that each category of user is supported by the interface and can learn and apply all required navigation syntax and semantics.

- *Navigability* is tested to ensure that all navigation syntax and semantics are exercised to uncover any navigation errors (e.g., dead links, improper links, erroneous links).

- *Performance* is tested under a variety of operating conditions, configurations, and loading to ensure that the system is responsive to user interaction and handles extreme loading without unacceptable operational degradation.

- *Compatibility* is tested by executing the WebApp in a variety of different host configurations on both the client and server sides. The intent is to find errors that are specific to a unique host configuration.

- *Interoperability* is tested to ensure that the WebApp properly interfaces with other applications and/or databases.

---

2 In an ideal world, reviews would be conducted for every informational and functional component. But in reality, the WebE team rarely has the resources or time to do this. In some cases, only critical components are reviewed prior to coding, particularly if the "pair programming" approach is not used.

- *Security* is tested by assessing potential vulnerabilities and attempting to exploit each. Any successful penetration attempt is deemed a security failure.

A strategy and tactics for WebApp testing has been developed to exercise each of these quality dimensions and is discussed later in this chapter in the subsection "What Testing Strategy Should We Apply?".

What Types of Errors Occur Within a WebApp Environment?

We have already noted that the primary intent of WebApp testing is to uncover errors (and correct them). Errors encountered as a consequence of successful WebApp testing have a number of unique characteristics [Ngu00] that can have a profound impact on testing and error discovery.

Many types of WebApp tests uncover problems that are first evidenced on the client side (i.e., via an interface implemented on a specific browser, PDA, or mobile phone). Therefore, you often see a symptom of the error, not the error itself.

A WebApp is implemented in a number of different configurations and within different environments. Therefore, it may be difficult or impossible to reproduce an error outside the environment in which the error was originally encountered.

Although some errors are the result of incorrect design or improper coding (in HTML, client-side scripting, server-side programming, or other programming aspects), many errors can be traced to the WebApp configuration. Those errors that are design related can be difficult to trace across three architectural layers—the client, the server, and the network itself. Some errors are due to the *static operating environment* (i.e., the specific configuration in which testing is conducted), while others are attributable to the dynamic operating environment (i.e., instantaneous resource loading or time-related errors).

These attributes suggest that environment plays an important role in the diagnosis of all errors uncovered during the WebE process. In some situations (e.g., content testing), the site of the error is obvious, but in many other types of WebApp testing (e.g., navigation testing, performance testing, security testing) the underlying cause of the error may be considerably more difficult to determine.

What Testing Strategy Should We Apply?

The strategy for WebApp testing adopts basic principles for all software testing and applies a strategy and tactics that are often used for object-oriented systems. The following steps summarize the approach:

1. The content model for the WebApp is reviewed to uncover errors.
2. The interface model is reviewed to ensure that all use cases have been accommodated.

3. The design model for the WebApp is reviewed to uncover navigation errors.

4. The user interface is tested to uncover errors in presentation and/or navigation mechanics.

5. Selected functional components are unit tested.

6. Navigation throughout the architecture is tested.

7. The WebApp is implemented in a variety of different environmental configurations and is tested for compatibility with each configuration.

8. Security tests are conducted in an attempt to exploit vulnerabilities in the WebApp or within its environment.

9. Performance tests are conducted.

10. The WebApp is tested by a controlled and monitored population of end users. The results of their interaction with the system are evaluated for content and navigation errors, usability concerns, compatibility concerns, and WebApp reliability and performance.

Because many WebApps evolve continuously, the testing process is an ongoing activity conducted by Web support staff that use regression tests derived from the tests developed when the WebApp was first engineered.

How Much Test Planning Is Necessary?

The use of the word *planning* (in any context) is anathema to some Web developers. As we noted in earlier chapters, these developers just jump straight into construction—hoping that a killer WebApp will emerge. A Web engineer recognizes that planning establishes a road map for all work that follows. It's worth the effort. In their book on WebApp testing, Splaine and Jaskiel [Spl01] state:

> Except for the simplest of Web sites, it quickly becomes apparent that some sort of test planning is needed. All too often, the initial number of bugs found from ad hoc testing is large enough that not all of them are fixed the first time they're detected. This puts an additional burden on people who test Web sites and applications. Not only must they conjure up imaginative new tests, but they must also remember how previous tests were executed in order to reliably re-test the Web site/application and ensure that known bugs have been removed and that no new bugs have been introduced.

Two questions for every Web engineer are: how do we "conjure up imaginative new tests," and what should those tests focus on? The answers to these questions are contained within a test plan.

A WebE test plan identifies: (1) the testing tasks to be applied as testing commences, (2) the work products to be produced as each testing task is executed, and (3) the manner in which the results of testing are evaluated, recorded, and reused

SafeHome

Establishing a Testing Philosophy

The scene: SafeHomeAssured.com team leader's office

The players: Team leader and two members of the WebE team as the delivery date for increment 2, *Detailed product information and downloads,* approaches

The conversation:

Team member 1: Things are going well. All the product content is in place, with appropriate navigation links to everything.

Team leader: Excellent. When do we start testing?

Team member 1: Testing? Well, we didn't. I mean, there's not a lot to test.

Team member 2: It's sort of like the first increment, mostly content and display. We didn't do a whole lot of testing for increment 1.

Team leader: But we did review all the content carefully, no?

[Both team members nod.]

Team leader: And we did make sure that all the many links worked, even if they pointed to dummy pages. Right?

[Both team members nod.]

Team leader: So we did content and navigation testing, did we not? And this increment is considerably more complex. We've got a variety of different content with a variety of different links.

Team member 1: So you want us to do . . . what, exactly?

Team leader: Spend an hour planning this and then tell me how you're going to "test" the increment. In this case, that might mean a combination of reviews and actual tests, say of all navigation links, of downloads to be sure that they work without problems, of the interface to ensure that it'll be clear to users. You might even do a few performance tests to be sure that the downloads don't take forever . . . things like that.

Team member 2: As far as reviews go, we've been conducting pair walkthroughs as we developed the increment and . . .

Team leader (interrupting): That's terrific, and it should make things go very smoothly, but in this case, I think we should broaden the reviews to include a few more sets of eyes, just in case.

Team member 1: All right. We can do that. So basically, you want us to be sure that all the stuff in increment 2 works.

Team leader: Actually no. What I want you guys to do is to find as many errors in increment 2 as you possibly can, before you deliver it to end users.

Team member 2 (looking mildly confused): But I thought our job was to prove that it works.

Team leader (smiling): Someone once said something about testing that's worth remembering. "Testing can show the presence of bugs, but it can't guarantee their absence." Your job is to find as many bugs as you can . . . before your users find them for you.

when regression testing is conducted. In some cases, the test plan is integrated with the project plan. For very large or complex WebApps, the test plan can be a separate document.

The Testing Process—An Overview

The testing process for Web engineering begins with tests that exercise content and interface functionality that is immediately visible to end users. As testing proceeds, aspects of the information and functional architecture and navigation are exercised. The user may or may not be cognizant of these WebApp elements. Finally, the focus shifts to tests that exercise technological capabilities that are not always apparent to end users—WebApp infrastructure and installation and implementation issues.

Figure 15.1 juxtaposes the WebApp testing process with a design pyramid that describes key design actions. Note that as the testing flow proceeds from left to right and top to bottom, user-visible elements of the WebApp design (top elements of the pyramid) are tested first, followed by infrastructure design elements.

Content testing (and reviews) attempts to uncover errors in the content that is present as a part of virtually every WebApp. This testing activity is similar in many respects to copyediting for a written document. In fact, the development time for a large WebApp might include (or contract) the services of a professional copy editor to uncover typographical errors, grammatical mistakes, errors in content consistency, errors in graphical representations, and cross-referencing errors. In addition to examining static content for errors, this testing step also considers dynamic content derived from data maintained as part of a database system that has been

FIGURE 15.1

The testing process.

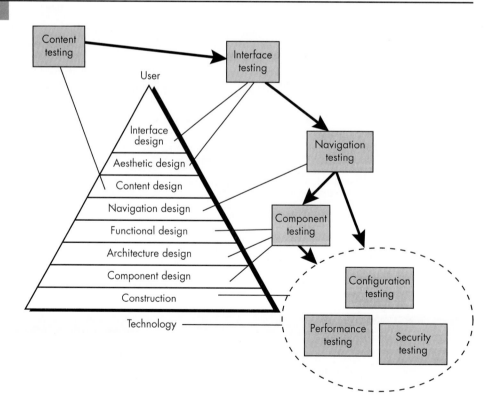

integrated with the WebApp. In many cases this form of testing (like many of the others) may also need to continue on an ongoing basis as new content is added during the life of the WepApp. For example, with **SafeHomeAssured.com,** it would be expected that new products are continuously being added to CPI's product catalog—and the content for these will need to be checked.

Interface testing exercises interaction mechanisms and validates aesthetic aspects of the user interface. The intent is to uncover errors that result from poorly implemented interaction mechanisms or omissions, inconsistencies, or ambiguities that have been introduced into the interface inadvertently.

Navigation testing applies use cases, derived as part of the analysis modeling, in the design of test cases that exercise each usage scenario against the navigation design. Navigation mechanisms (e.g., menu bars) implemented within the interface layout are tested against use cases and navigation pathways to ensure that any errors that impede completion of a use case are identified and corrected.

Component testing exercises content and functional units within the WebApp. The "unit" of choice within the content architecture is the Web page. Each Web page encapsulates content, navigation links, and processing elements (forms, scripts, applets). A *unit* within the WebApp functional architecture may be a defined functional component that provides service directly to an end user or an infrastructure component that enables the WebApp to perform all its capabilities. Each functional component is tested in much the same way as an individual module is tested in conventional software. In most cases, tests are black-box oriented.[3] However, if processing is complex, white-box tests[4] may also be used. In addition to functional testing, database capabilities are also exercised.

As the WebApp architecture is constructed, navigation and component testing are used as *integration tests.* The strategy for integration testing depends on the content and WebApp architectures that have been chosen (Chapter 10). If the content architecture has been designed with a linear, grid, or simple hierarchical structure, it is possible to test Web pages while they are integrated in a top-down or bottom-up manner. However, if a mixed hierarchy or network (Web) architecture is used, integration testing is similar to an approach used for object-oriented systems. *Thread-based testing*[5] can be used to integrate the set of Web pages (a navigation pathway may be used to define the appropriate set) required to respond to a user event. Each thread is integrated and tested individually. *Regression testing* is

---

3   A black-box test is designed without knowledge of the internals of a component. Only information that passes through the interface to the component is used to design the test.
4   White-box testing techniques make use of the internal structure of the component. For functional components, this implies knowledge of internal processing logic.
5   Thread-based testing integrates a set of content or functional components (or Web pages) that are required to respond to one use case or navigation pathway.

applied to ensure that no side effects occur. *Cluster testing* integrates a set of collaborating pages (determined by examining the use cases and navigation pathways). Test cases are derived to uncover errors in the collaborations.

Each element of the WebApp architecture is unit tested to the extent possible. For example, in an MVC architecture (Chapter 10) the model, view, and controller components are each tested individually. Upon integration, the flow of control and data across each of these elements is assessed in detail.

Configuration testing attempts to uncover errors that are specific to a particular client or server environment. A cross-reference matrix that defines all probable[6] operating systems, browsers,[7] hardware platforms, and communications protocols is created. Tests are then conducted to uncover errors associated with each possible configuration.

Security testing incorporates a series of tests designed to exploit vulnerabilities in the WebApp and its environment. The intent is to demonstrate that a security breach is possible.

Performance testing encompasses a series of tests that are designed to assess: (1) how WebApp response time and reliability are affected by increased user traffic and/or functional complexity, (2) which WebApp components are responsible for

---

TASKS

WebApp Testing

1. Review stakeholder requirements.
   - Identify key user goals and objectives.
   - Review use cases for each user category.
2. Establish priorities to ensure that each user goal and objective will be adequately tested.
3. Define the WebApp testing strategy by describing the types of tests that will be conducted.
4. Develop a test plan.
   - Define a test schedule, and assign responsibilities for each test.
   - Specify automated tools for testing.
   - Define acceptance criteria for each class of test.
   - Specify defect-tracking mechanisms.
   - Define problem-reporting mechanisms.
5. Perform unit tests.
   - Review content for syntax and semantics errors.
   - Review content for proper clearances and permissions.
   - Test interface mechanisms for correct operation.
   - Test each component (e.g., script) to ensure proper function.
6. Perform integration tests.
   - Test interface semantics against use cases.
   - Conduct navigation tests.
7. Perform configuration tests.
   - Assess client-side configuration compatibility.
   - Assess server-side configurations.
8. Conduct performance tests.
9. Conduct security tests.

---

6 The mission-criticality of the WebApp coupled with the probability that a specific aspect of the environment will be encountered dictates whether that aspect will be tested or not.
7 Browsers are notorious for implementing their own subtly different "standard" interpretations of HTML and JavaScript.

performance degradation and what usage characteristics cause degradation to occur, and (3) how performance degradation impacts overall WebApp objectives and requirements.

Content Testing

Faults in WebApp content can be as trivial as minor typographical errors or as significant as incorrect information, improper organization, or violation of intellectual property laws. Content testing attempts to uncover these and many other problems before the user encounters them.

Content testing combines both reviews and the generation of executable test cases. Reviews are applied to uncover semantic errors in content. Executable testing is used to uncover content errors that can be traced to dynamically derived content that is driven by data acquired from one or more databases.

What Are the Objectives of Content Testing?

Content testing has three important objectives: (1) to uncover syntactic errors (e.g., typos, grammar mistakes) in text-based documents, graphical representations, and other media, (2) to uncover semantic errors (i.e., errors in the accuracy or completeness of information) in any content object presented as navigation occurs, and (3) to find errors in the organization or structure of content that is presented to the end user.

To accomplish the first objective, automated spelling and grammar checkers may be used. However, many syntactic errors evade detection by such tools and must be discovered by a human reviewer (tester). As we noted in the preceding section, copyediting is the single best approach for finding syntactic errors.

Semantic testing focuses on the information presented within each content object. The reviewer (tester) must answer the following questions:

- Is the information up to date and factually accurate?
- Is the information concise and to the point?
- Is the layout of the content object easy for the user to understand?
- Can information embedded within a content object be found easily?
- Have proper references been provided for all information derived from other sources?
- Is the information presented consistent internally and consistent with information presented in other content objects?
- Can the content be interpreted as being offensive or misleading, or does it open the door to litigation?

- Does the content infringe on existing copyrights or trademarks?
- Does the content contain internal links that supplement existing content? Are the links correct?
- Does the aesthetic style of the content conflict with the aesthetic style of the interface?

Obtaining answers to each of these questions for a large WebApp (containing hundreds of content objects) can be a daunting task. However, failure to uncover semantic errors will shake the user's faith in the WebApp and can lead to failure of the Web-based application.

During content testing, the structure and organization of the content architecture is tested to ensure that required content is presented to the end user in the proper order and relationships. For example, the **SafeHomeAssured.com** WebApp presents a variety of information about sensors that are used as part of security and surveillance products. Content objects provide descriptive information, technical specifications, a photographic representation, and related information. Tests of the **SafeHomeAssured.com** content architecture strive to uncover errors in the presentation of this information (e.g., a description of sensor X is presented with a photo of sensor Y).

How Is Database Testing Used to Validate Content?

Modern WebApps do much more than present static content objects. In many application domains, WebApps interface with sophisticated database management systems and build dynamic content objects that are created in real time using the data acquired from a database.

For example, a financial services WebApp can produce complex text-based, tabular and graphical information about a specific equity (e.g., a stock, bond, or mutual fund). The composite content object that presents this information is created dynamically after the user has made a request for information about the specific equity. To accomplish this, the following steps are required: (1) a large equities database is queried, (2) relevant data are extracted from the database, (3) the extracted data must be organized as a content object, and (4) this content object (representing customized information requested by an end user) is transmitted to the client environment for display. Errors can and do occur as a consequence of each of these steps. The objective of database testing is to uncover these errors. However, database testing for WebApps is complicated by a variety of factors:

1. **The original client-side request for information is rarely presented in the form [e.g., structured query language (SQL)] that can be input to a database management system (DBMS).** Therefore, tests should be

designed to uncover errors made in translating the user's request into a form that can be processed by the DBMS.

2. **The database may be remote to the server that houses the WebApp.** Therefore, tests that uncover errors in communication between the WebApp and the remote database must be developed.[8]

3. **Raw data acquired from the database must be transmitted to the WebApp server and properly formatted for subsequent transmittal to the client.** Therefore, tests that demonstrate the validity of the raw data received by the WebApp server must be developed, and additional tests that demonstrate the validity of the transformations applied to the raw data to create valid content objects must also be created.

4. **The dynamic content object(s) must be transmitted to the client in a form that can be displayed to the end user.** Therefore, a series of tests must be designed to: (1) uncover errors in the content object format, and (2) test compatibility with different client environmental configurations.

Considering these four factors, test case design methods should be applied for each of the "layers of interaction" [Ngu01] noted in Figure 15.2. Testing should ensure that: (1) valid information is passed between the client and server from the interface layer, (2) the WebApp processes scripts correctly and properly extracts or formats user data, (3) user data are passed correctly to a server-side data transformation function that formats appropriate queries (e.g., SQL), and (4) queries are passed to the data management layer[9] that communicates with database access routines (potentially located on another machine).

Data transformation, data management, and the database access layers shown in Figure 15.2 are often constructed with reusable components that have been validated separately and as a package. If this is the case, WebApp testing focuses on the design of test cases to exercise the interactions between the client layer and the first two server layers (WebApp and data transformation) shown in the figure.

The user interface layer is tested to ensure that HTML scripts are properly constructed for each user query and properly transmitted to the server side. The WebApp layer on the server side is tested to ensure that user data are properly extracted from HTML scripts and properly transmitted to the data transformation layer on the server side. The data transformation functions are tested to ensure that a correct SQL is created and passed to appropriate data management components.

8 These tests can become complex when distributed databases are encountered or when access to a data warehouse is required.
9 The data management layer typically incorporates an SQL call-level interface (SQL-CLI) such as Microsoft OLE/ADO or Java Database Connectivity (JDBC).

FIGURE 15.2

Layers of
interaction.

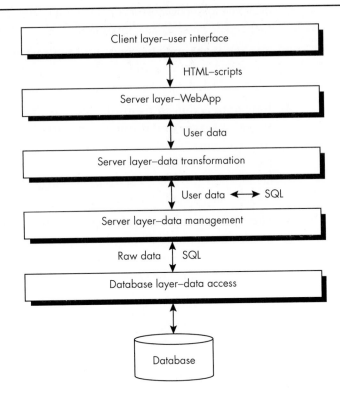

A detailed discussion of the underlying technology that must be understood
to adequately design these database tests is beyond the scope of this book. If you
have additional interest and/or a need in this area, please see [Sce02], [Ngu01], and
[Bro01].

User Interface Testing

Verification and validation of a WebApp user interface occurs at three distinct points
in the WebE process. During communication (Chapter 4) and modeling (Chapter 7),
the interface model is reviewed to ensure that it conforms to customer requirements
and to other elements of the analysis model. During design (Chapter 9), the interface
design model is reviewed to ensure that generic quality criteria established for all
user interfaces have been achieved and that application-specific interface design
issues have been properly addressed. During testing, the focus shifts to the execution of application-specific aspects of user interaction as they are manifested by
interface syntax and semantics. In addition, testing provides a final assessment of
usability.

Is There a Viable Interface Testing Strategy?

The overall strategy for interface testing is to: (1) uncover errors related to specific interface mechanisms (e.g., errors in the proper execution of a menu link or the way data are entered in a form), and (2) uncover errors in the way the interface implements the semantics of navigation, WebApp functionality, or content display. To accomplish this strategy, a number of tactical steps are initiated:

- **Interface features are tested to ensure that design rules, aesthetics, and related visual content are available to the user without error.** Features include type fonts, the use of color, frames, images, borders, tables, and related interface features that are generated as WebApp execution proceeds.

- **Individual interface mechanisms are tested in a manner that is analogous to unit testing.** For example, tests are designed to exercise all forms, client-side scripting, dynamic HTML, scripts, streaming content, and application-specific interface mechanisms (e.g., a shopping cart for an e-commerce application). In many cases, testing can focus exclusively on one of these mechanisms (the "unit") to the exclusion of other interface features and functions.

- **Each interface mechanism is tested within the context of a use case or navigation pathway for a specific user category.** This testing approach is analogous to integration testing in that tests are conducted as interface mechanisms are integrated to allow a use case or navigation pathway to be executed.

- **The complete interface is tested against selected use cases and navigation pathways to uncover errors in the semantics of the interface.** The purpose of these tests is to demonstrate conformance to specific use-case or navigation pathway semantics. It is at this stage that a series of usability tests are conducted.

- **The interface is tested within a variety of environments (e.g., operating systems, browsers) to ensure that it will be compatible.** In actuality, this series of tests can also be considered to be part of configuration testing.

How Do We Test Specific Interface Mechanisms?

When a user interacts with a WebApp, the interaction occurs through one or more interface mechanisms. These mechanisms include [Spl01]:

- **Links.** Navigation mechanisms that link the user to some other content object or function.

- **Forms.** A structured document containing blank fields that are filled in by the user. The data contained in the fields are used as input to one or more WebApp functions.

- **Client-side scripting.** A list of programmed commands in a scripting language (e.g., JavaScript) that handle information input via forms or other user interactions.

- **Dynamic HTML.** Provides access to content objects that are manipulated on the client side using scripting or cascading style sheets (CSSs).

- **Client-side pop-up windows.** Small windows that pop up without user interaction.[10] These windows can be content oriented and may require some form of user interaction.

- **Server-side scripts.** Server-side scripts implement methods that allow a Web server to interact dynamically with users (e.g., a WebApp that contains forms may use a CGI script, servlet or ASP script to process the data contained in a form once it is submitted by the user).

- **Streaming and push content.** *Streaming content* is encountered when material (usually audio or video) is downloaded in a manner that allows it to be displayed while it is still being downloaded (rather than having to wait for the entire content to be downloaded). *Push content* is encountered when content objects are downloaded automatically from the server side rather than waiting for a request from the client side.

- **Cookies.** A block of data sent by the server and stored by a browser as a consequence of a specific user interaction. The content of the data is WebApp-specific (e.g., user identification data or a list of items that have been selected for purchase by the user).

- **Application-specific interface mechanisms.** Include one or more "macro" interface mechanisms such as a shopping cart, credit card processing, or a shipping cost calculator.

In the paragraphs that follow, we present a brief overview of testing considerations for each interface mechanism.

Links.   Each navigation link is tested to ensure that the proper content object or function is reached.[11] You can build a list of all links associated with the interface layout (e.g., menu bars, index items) and then execute each individually. In addition, links within each content object must be exercised to uncover bad URLs or links to improper content objects or functions. Finally, links to external WebApps

---

10 Pop-ups have become pervasive and are a major irritant to some users. They should be used judiciously.

11 These tests can be performed as part of either interface or navigation testing.

should be tested for accuracy and also evaluated to determine the risk that they will become invalid over time.

Forms.   At a macroscopic level, tests are performed to ensure that: (1) labels correctly identify fields within the form and that mandatory fields are identified visually for the user, (2) the server receives all information contained within the form and that no data are lost in the transmission between client and server, (3) appropriate defaults are used when the user does not select from a pull-down menu or set of buttons, (4) browser functions (e.g., the back arrow) do not corrupt data entered in a form, and (5) scripts that perform error checking on entered data work properly and provide meaningful error messages.

At a more targeted level, tests should ensure that: (1) form fields have the proper width and data types, (2) the form establishes appropriate safeguards that preclude the user from entering text strings longer than some predefined maximum, (3) all appropriate options for pull-down menus are specified and ordered in a way that is meaningful to the end user, (4) browser "auto-fill" features do not lead to data input errors, and (5) the tab key (or some other key) initiates proper movement between form fields.

Client-side scripting.   Black-box tests are conducted to uncover any errors in processing as the script is executed. These tests are often coupled with forms testing, because script input is often derived from data provided as part of forms processing. A compatibility test should be conducted to ensure that the scripting language that has been chosen will work properly in the environmental configurations that support the WebApp. In addition to testing the script itself, Splaine and Jaskiel [Spl01] suggest that "you should ensure that your company's [WebApp] standards state the preferred language and version of scripting language to be used for client-side (and server-side) scripting."

Dynamic HTML.   Each Web page that contains dynamic HTML is executed to ensure that the dynamic display is correct. In addition, a compatibility test should be conducted to ensure that the dynamic HTML works properly in the environmental configurations that support the WebApp.

Pop-up windows.   A series of tests ensure that: (1) the pop-up is properly sized and positioned, (2) the pop-up does not cover the original WebApp window, (3) the aesthetic design of the pop-up is consistent with the aesthetic design of the interface, and (4) scroll bars and other control mechanisms appended to the pop-up are properly located and function as required.

Server-side scripts.   Black-box tests are conducted with an emphasis on data integrity (as data are passed to the Server-side script) and script processing once validated data have been received. In addition, performance testing can be conducted to ensure that the server-side configuration can accommodate the processing demands of multiple invocations of the scripts [Spl01].

Push content.   Tests should show that the user can request and restrict push content as necessary and that the timing of the content delivery is appropriate.

Streaming content.   Tests should demonstrate that streaming data are up to date, properly displayed, can be suspended without error, and can be restarted without difficulty.

Cookies.   Both server-side and client-side testing are required. On the server side, tests should ensure that a cookie is properly constructed (contains correct data) and properly transmitted to the client side when specific content or functionality is requested. In addition, the proper persistence of the cookie is tested to ensure that its expiration date is correct. On the client side, tests determine whether the WebApp properly attaches existing cookies to a specific request (sent to the server).

Application-specific interface mechanisms.   Tests conform to a checklist of functionality and features that are defined by the interface mechanism. For example, Splaine and Jaskiel [Spl01] suggest the following checklist for shopping cart functionality defined for an e-commerce application:

- Test the minimum and maximum number of items that can be placed in the shopping cart. Also test just above and just below the maximum and minimum.
- Test a checkout request for an empty shopping cart.
- Test proper deletion of an item from the shopping cart.
- Test to determine whether a purchase empties the cart of its contents.
- Test to determine the persistence of shopping cart contents (this should be specified as part of customer requirements).
- Test to determine whether the WebApp can recall shopping cart contents at some future date (assuming that no purchase was made).

A WebE team can develop an interface testing checklist based on these guidelines, but adapted to the particular functionality being tested. The checklist is used to guide the team as tests are designed and executed.

How Do We Test Interface Semantics?

Once each interface mechanism has been unit tested, the focus of interface testing changes to a consideration of interface semantics. Interface semantics testing "evaluates how well the design takes care of users, offers clear direction, delivers feedback, and maintains consistency of language and approach." [Ngu01]

A thorough review of the interface design model can provide partial answers to the questions implied by the preceding paragraph. However, each use-case scenario (for each user category) should be tested once the WebApp has been implemented. In essence, a use case becomes the input for the design of a testing sequence. The intent of the testing sequence is to uncover errors that will preclude a user from achieving the objective associated with the use case.

As each use case is tested, the Web engineering team maintains a checklist to ensure that every menu item has been exercised at least one time and that every embedded link within a content object has been used. In addition, the test series should include improper menu selection and link usage. The intent is to determine whether the WebApp provides effective error handling and recovery.

Usability Testing

Usability testing[12] is similar to interface semantics testing (discussed in the preceding section, "User Interface Testing") in the sense that it also evaluates the degree to which users can interact effectively with the WebApp and the degree to which the WebApp guides users' actions, provides meaningful feedback, and enforces a consistent interaction approach. Rather than focusing intently on the semantics of some interactive objective, usability reviews and tests are designed to determine the degree to which the WebApp interface makes the user's life easy.[13]

The WebE team can design usability tests, but it is the end users who conduct the tests. The following sequence of steps is applied [Spl01]:

- Define a set of usability testing categories and identify goals for each.
- Design tests that will enable each goal to be evaluated.
- Select participants who will conduct the tests.
- Log the details of the participants' interaction with the WebApp while testing is conducted.
- Develop a mechanism for assessing the usability of the WebApp.

Usability testing can occur at a variety of different levels of abstraction: (1) the usability of a specific interface mechanism (e.g., a form) can be assessed, (2) the usability of a complete Web page (encompassing interface mechanisms, data objects, and related functions) can be evaluated, or (3) the usability of the complete WebApp can be considered.

---

12 A worthwhile guide to usability testing can be found at **www.ahref.com/guides/design/199806/0615jef.html.**
13 The term *user-friendly* is often used in this context. The problem, of course, is that one user's perception of a "friendly" interface may be radically different from another's.

The first step in usability testing is to identify a set of usability categories and establish testing objectives for each category. The following test categories and objectives (written in the form of a question) illustrate this approach: [14]

Interactivity. Are interaction mechanisms (e.g., pull-down menus, buttons, pointers) easy to understand and use?

Layout. Are navigation mechanisms, content, and functions placed in a manner that allows the user to find them quickly?

Readability. Is text well written and understandable? [15] Are graphic representations intuitive and easy to understand?

Aesthetics. Do the layout, color, typeface, and related characteristics lead to ease of use? Do users "feel comfortable" with the look and feel of the WebApp?

Display characteristics. Does the WebApp make optimal use of screen size and resolution?

Time sensitivity. Can important features, functions, and content be used or acquired in a timely manner?

Personalization. Does the WebApp appropriately tailor itself to the specific needs of different user categories or individual users?

Accessibility. Is the WebApp accessible to people with disabilities?

Within each of these categories, a series of tests is designed. In some cases, the "test" may be a visual review of a Web page. In other cases interface semantics tests may be executed again, but in this instance usability concerns are paramount.

As an example, consider usability assessment for interaction and interface mechanisms. Constantine and Lockwood [Con99] suggest that the following interface features should be reviewed and tested for usability: animation, buttons, color, control, dialogue, fields, forms, frames, graphics, labels, links, menus, messages, navigation, pages, selectors, text, and tool bars. As each feature is assessed, it is graded on a qualitative scale by the users who are doing the testing. Figure 15.3 depicts a possible set of assessment "grades" that can be selected by users. These grades are applied to each feature individually, to a complete Web page, or to the WebApp as a whole.

---

14 For additional usability questions, see the "Usability" sidebar.
15 The FOG Readability Index and others may be used to provide a quantitative assessment of readability (see **http://en.wikipedia.org/wiki/Readability_test** for more information).

Usability

Constantine [Con95] argues that usability is not derived from aesthetics, state-of-the-art interaction mechanisms, or built-in interface intelligence. Rather, it occurs when the architecture of the interface fits the needs of the people who will be using it.

The only way to determine whether "usability" exists within a system you are building is to conduct usability assessment or testing. Watch users interact with the system, and answer the following questions [Con95]:

- Is the system usable without continual help or instruction?
- Do the rules of interaction help a knowledgeable user to work efficiently?
- Do interaction mechanisms become more flexible as users become more knowledgeable?
- Has the system been tuned to the physical and social environment in which it will be used?
- Are users aware of the state of the system? Do users know where they are at all times?

- Is the interface structured in a logical and consistent manner?
- Are interaction mechanisms, icons, and procedures consistent across the interface?
- Does the interaction anticipate errors and help the user correct them?
- Is the interface tolerant of errors that are made?
- Is the interaction simple?

If each of these questions is answered "yes," it is likely that usability has been achieved. Any answers of "no" probably indicate an aspect requiring attention.

Among the many measurable benefits derived from a usable system are [Don99]: increased sales and customer satisfaction, competitive advantage, better reviews in the media, better word of mouth, reduced support costs, improved end-user productivity, reduced training costs, reduced documentation costs, and reduced likelihood of litigation from unhappy customers.

FIGURE 15.3

Qualitative assessment of usability.

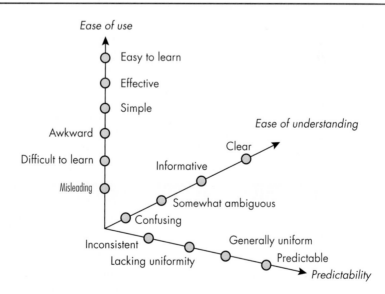

SafeHome

Interface and Usability Testing

The scene: The Web engineering area at CPI Corporation

The players: Two members of the **SafeHome-Assured.com** team working as a pair, who are evaluating the results of interface and usability testing for **SafeHomeAssured.com,** increment 4, *Space layout and security system design*

The conversation:

Team member 1 (looking glum): Man, the interface tests went okay, but we crashed and burned in the usability tests.

Team member 2 (looking equally glum): Yeah, look at the user rating for increment 4. We get an average of 2 out of a possible 5. I've spent some time talking to users who participated, and it doesn't look good.

Team member 1: You know, I was a bit worried that they'd have trouble figuring out how to build the layout [looking at a live interface that is equivalent to Figure 9.4] and they did.

Team member 2: Using it seemed pretty obvious to me.

Team member 1: That, my friend, doesn't matter; it's *not* obvious to them. Look at these comments:

"Couldn't figure out how to get started."

"This is too hard, way too hard."

"It's not easy to erase my mistakes as I lay out the space. And this thing leads to way too many mistakes!"

"I tried to save my layout but couldn't figure out how to retrieve it later."

"This sucks!"

Team member 2 (wincing): Ouch! At least all the links, functionality, and underlying infrastructure work fine.

Team member 1 (laughing ruefully): That's true, but the users hate it, so we're screwed.

Team member 2: Maybe not. It looks like the majority of the problems go to complexity, and I suspect that a lot of that is because the users aren't used to doing stuff like this, so it's not at all intuitive for them. The functionality is inherently complex because of what the users are doing, so we can't really solve the problem by making it simpler. What if we help them understand it by building in an animated tutorial that shows how to do all the key drawing and layout management functions? We could also have 10 or 12 predefined floor plans—you know, for common house designs—so that the user won't have to do a layout.

Team member 1: Those ideas might help, but we have to run it by users first, *before* we do the work. And we'll also have to get an extension for the deployment date for this increment.

Team member 2: Man, I'm not happy about this.

Team member 1: You'd be a lot less happy if we released it to the world and we got thousands of comments like these [waiving the sheet of paper with usability testing comments], rather than a few dozen.

Team member 2: (sighing) I suppose. Let's go . . . we've got work to do.

Compatibility Testing

WebApps must operate within environments that differ from one another. Different computers, display devices, operating systems, browsers, and network connection speeds can have a significant influence on WebApp operation. Each computing configuration can result in differences in client-side processing speeds, display resolution, and connection speeds. Operating system vagaries may cause

WebApp processing issues. Different browsers sometimes produce slightly differ-ent results, regardless of the degree of HTML, CSS, and JavaScript standardization within the WebApp. Required plug-ins may or may not be readily available for a particular configuration.

In some cases, small compatibility issues present no significant problems, but in others, serious errors can be encountered. The most common problem aris-ing from compatibility issues is poor usability. This can arise from the following: download speeds may become unacceptable, lack of a required plug-in may make content unavailable, browser differences can change page layout dramatically, font styles may be altered and become illegible, or forms may be improperly organized. *Compatibility testing* strives to uncover these problems before the WebApp goes online.

The first step in compatibility testing is to define a set of "commonly encoun-tered" client-side computing configurations and their variants. In essence, a tree structure is created, identifying each computing platform, typical display devices, the operating systems supported on the platform, the browsers available, the likely Internet connection speeds, and similar information. Next, the WebE team derives a series of compatibility validation tests, derived from existing interface tests, navi-gation tests, performance tests, and security tests. The intent of these tests is to un-cover errors or execution problems that can be traced to configuration differences.

Component-Level Testing

Component-level testing, also called *function testing*, focuses on a set of tests that at-tempt to uncover errors in WebApp functions. Each WebApp function is a software module (implemented in one of a variety of programming or scripting languages) and can be tested using black-box (and, in some cases, white-box) techniques.

Component-level test cases are often driven by forms-level input. Once forms data are defined, the user selects a button or other control mechanism to initiate execution. The following test case design methods [Pre05] are typical:

- **Equivalence partitioning.** The input domain of the function is divided into input categories or classes from which test cases are derived. The input form is assessed to determine what classes of data are relevant for the function. Test cases for each class of input are derived and executed, while other classes of input are held constant. For example, an e-commerce application may implement a function that computes shipping charges. Among a variety of shipping information provided via a form is the user's postal code. Test cases are designed in an attempt to uncover errors in postal code process-ing by specifying postal code values that might uncover different classes of errors (e.g., an incomplete postal code, a correct postal code, a nonexistent postal code, an erroneous postal code format).

- **Boundary value analysis.** Forms data are tested at their boundaries. For example, a shipping calculation function requests the maximum number of days required for product delivery. A minimum of 2 days and a maximum of 14 are noted on the form. However, boundary value tests might input values of 0, 1, 2, 13, 14, and 15 to determine how the function (and associated error processing) reacts to data at and outside the boundaries of valid input.[16]

- **Path testing.** If the logical complexity of the function is high,[17] path testing (a white-box test case design method) can be used to ensure that every independent processing path in the component has been exercised.

In addition to these test case design methods, a technique called *forced error testing* [Ngu01] is used to derive test cases that purposely drive the WebApp component into an error condition. The purpose is to uncover errors that occur during error handling (e.g., incorrect or nonexistent error messages, WebApp failure as a consequence of the error, erroneous output driven by erroneous input, side effects that are related to component processing).

Each component-level test case specifies all input values and the expected output to be provided by the component. The actual output produced as a consequence of the test is recorded for future reference during support and maintenance.

In many situations, the correct execution of a WebApp function is tied to proper interfacing with a database that may be external to the WebApp. Therefore, database testing becomes an integral part of the component-testing regime. Hower [How97] discusses this when he writes:

> Database-driven Web sites can involve a complex interaction among Web browsers, operating systems, plug-in applications, communications protocols, Web servers, databases, [scripting language] programs . . ., security enhancements, and firewalls. Such complexity makes it impossible to test every possible dependency and everything that could go wrong with a site. The typical Web site development project will also be on an aggressive schedule, so the best testing approach will employ risk analysis to determine where to focus testing efforts. Risk analysis should include consideration of how closely the test environment will match the real production environment. Will the test scenarios closely mimic real-life users, Internet connections, modems, communications, hardware, clients, loads, data, database table sizes, and so on? Will the differences be significant? Ideally, the test and production environments will be the

---

16   In this case, a better input design might eliminate potential errors. The maximum number of days could be selected from a pull-down menu, precluding the user from specifying out-of-bounds input (though error checking would still be needed to handle invalid values passed directly in a URL).

17   The logical complexity can be determined by computing the cyclomatic complexity of the algorithm. See [Pre05] for additional details.

same, but budget constraints often prevent this, and the risk is that the differences may distort test results and make certain types of testing irrelevant. Other typical considerations in risk analysis include:

- Which functionality in the Web site is most critical to its purpose?
- Which areas of the site require the heaviest database interaction?
- Which aspects of the site's CGI, applets, ActiveX components, and so on are most complex?
- What types of problems would cause the most complaints or the worst publicity?
- What areas of the site will be the most popular?
- What aspects of the site have the highest security risks?

Each of the risk-related issues discussed by Hower should be considered when designing test cases for WebApp components and related database functions.

Navigation Testing

A user travels through a WebApp in much the same way as a visitor walks through a store or museum. There are many pathways that can be taken, many stops that can be made, many things to learn and look at, activities to initiate, and decisions to make. As we have already discussed, this navigation process is predictable in the sense that visitors have a set of objectives when they arrive. At the same time, the navigation process can be unpredictable because visitors, influenced by something they see or learn, may choose a path or initiate an action that is not typical for the original objective. The job of navigation testing is: (1) to ensure that the mechanisms that allow the WebApp user to travel through the WebApp are all functional, and (2) to validate that each navigation objective can be achieved by the appropriate user category.

How Do We Test Navigation Syntax?

The first phase of navigation testing actually begins during interface testing. Navigation mechanisms are tested to ensure that each performs its intended function. Each of the following navigation mechanisms should be tested [Spl01]:

- **Navigation links.** These mechanisms include internal links within the WebApp, external links to other WebApps, and anchors within a specific Web page. Each link should be tested to ensure that proper content or functionality is reached when the link is chosen.
- **Redirects.** These links come into play when a user requests a nonexistent URL or selects a link whose destination has been removed or whose name has changed. A message is displayed for the user, and navigation is redirected to another page (e.g., the home page). To test redirects, you should

request incorrect internal links or external URLs and assess how the WebApp handles these requests.

- **Bookmarks.** Although bookmarks are a browser function, the WebApp should be tested to ensure that a meaningful page title can be extracted as the bookmark is created and that dynamic pages are bookmarked appropriately.

- **Frames and framesets.** Each frame contains the content of a specific Web page; a frameset contains multiple frames and enables the display of multiple Web pages at the same time. Because it is possible to nest frames and framesets within one another, these navigation and display mechanisms should be tested for correct content, proper layout and sizing, download performance, and browser compatibility.

- **Site maps.** A site map provides a complete table of contents for all Web pages. Each site map entry should be tested to ensure that the link takes the user to the proper content or functionality.

- **Internal search engines.** Complex WebApps often contain hundreds or even thousands of content objects. An internal (local) search engine allows the user to perform a key word search within the WebApp to find needed content. Search engine testing validates the accuracy and completeness of the search, the error-handling properties of the search engine, and advanced search features (e.g., the use of Boolean operators in the search field).

Some of the tests noted can be performed by automated tools (e.g., link checking), while others are designed and executed manually. The intent throughout is to ensure that errors in navigation mechanics are found before the WebApp goes online.

How Do We Test Navigation Semantics?

As navigation design is conducted, you create "a set of information and related navigation structures that collaborate in the fulfillment of a subset of related user requirements" [Cac02]. These are sometimes referred to as *navigation semantic units* (NSUs) and are defined by a set of navigation paths (called "ways of navigating") that connect navigation nodes (e.g., Web pages, content objects, or functionality). Taken as a whole, each NSU allows a user to achieve specific requirements defined by one or more use cases for a user category. Navigation testing exercises each NSU to ensure that these requirements can be achieved. As each NSU is tested, the WebE team must answer the following questions:

- Is the NSU achieved in its entirety without error?
- Is every *navigation node* (a destination defined for an NSU) reachable within the context of the navigation paths defined for the NSU?

- If the NSU can be achieved using more than one navigation path, has every relevant path been tested?

- If guidance is provided by the user interface to assist in navigation, are directions correct and understandable as navigation proceeds?

- Is there a mechanism (other than the browser back arrow) for returning to the preceding navigation node and to the beginning of the navigation path?

- Do mechanisms for navigation within a large navigation node (e.g., anchor point links for a long Web page) work properly?

- If a function is to be executed at a node and the user chooses not to provide input, can the remainder of the NSU be completed?

- If a function is executed at a node and an error in function processing occurs, can the NSU be completed?

- Is there a way to discontinue the navigation before all nodes have been reached, but then return to where the navigation was discontinued and proceed from there?

- Is every node reachable from the site map? Are node names meaningful to end users?

- If a node within an NSU is reached from some external source, is it possible to process to the next node on the navigation path? Is it possible to return to the previous node on the navigation path?

- Do users understand their location within the content architecture as the NSU is executed?

Navigation testing, like interface and usability testing, should be conducted by as many different constituencies as possible. Early stages of testing are conducted by Web engineers, but later stages should be conducted by other project stakeholders, an independent testing team, and ultimately, by nontechnical users. The intent is to exercise WebApp navigation thoroughly.

SafeHome

Navigation Testing

The scene: The Web engineering area at CPI Corporation

The players: Two members of the **SafeHome-Assured.com** team working as a pair, who are

planning navigation testing for **SafeHomeAssured.com,** increment 4, *Space layout and security system design*

(continued)

SafeHome (continued)

The conversation:

Team member 1: There really isn't much navigation for this increment. Basically, most of it is functionality associated with creating the space layout and then getting recommendations for monitoring equipment placement.

Team member 2: There's always navigation. Look, we've got to test all the links associated with the layout [looking at a live interface that is equivalent to Figure 9.4] and the new links to the animated tutorial and the predefined floor plans [approved as a consequence of feedback from interface and usability testing].

Team member 1: So what do we need to do?

Team member 2: We'll have to design tests for the navigation syntax and semantics. Each of the links implies an NSU—a navigation semantic unit. For example, the link "edit layout" [see Figure 9.4] implies a specific set of navigation paths and nodes.

Team member 1: Okay, so what you're saying is that to edit the layout we have to retrieve it from a data store, and to do that we'll need to input its name and then regenerate it.

Team member 2: We'll also need to test error handling associated with the retrieval. For example, what if a user specifies the wrong name?

Team member 1: And part of the navigation path might also consider what happens if the user forgets the name. I forgot what we designed. Do we list all

filenames under this user? Anyway, we have to test error handling.

Team member 2 (thinking for a moment): What about this. We're in the middle of creating a layout and the user decides to initiate another NSU.

Team member 1: What do you mean, another NSU?

Team member 2: Well, suppose I want to get a product spec for a monitoring device that is recommended as part of increment 4 and I use the navigation link "Product specs."

Team member 1: But that NSU has already been tested as part of increment 2 [*Detailed product information and downloads*].

Team member 2: I know, but this is a different context. We've got to be sure that we don't lose the layout being created while the user navigates to the product spec. Also we have to be sure that there's a way to return to the layout and that there are no errors when we do return.

Team member 1: But it'll take forever if we test every possible NSU. I really don't think . . .

Team member 2 (interrupting): We only test the NSUs that are highly likely to be invoked in this context and those that might have some form of interaction with the same content objects, not every possible NSU.

Team member 1 (smiling): I feel better, but not much.

Configuration Testing

Configuration variability and instability are important factors that make Web engineering a challenge. Hardware, operating system(s), browsers, storage capacity, network communication speeds, and a variety of other client-side factors are difficult to predict for each user. In addition, the configuration for a given user can change [e.g., operating system (OS) updates, new Internet service provider (ISP), and connection speeds] on a regular basis. The result can be a client-side environment that is prone to errors that are both subtle and significant. One user's impression of the WebApp and the manner in which that user interacts with it can differ significantly from another user's experience, if both users are not working within the same client-side configuration.

The job of configuration testing is not to exercise every possible client-side configuration. Rather, it is to test a set of probable client-side and server-side configurations to ensure that the user experience will be the same on all of them and to isolate errors that may be specific to a particular configuration.

How Do We Test the Server Side?

On the server side, configuration test cases are designed to verify that the projected server configuration [i.e., WebApp server, database server, operating system(s), firewall software, concurrent applications] can support the WebApp without error. In essence, the WebApp is installed within the server-side environment and tested to uncover errors as it operates.

As server-side configuration tests are designed, you should consider each component of the server configuration. Among the questions that need to be asked and answered during server-side configuration testing are:

- Is the WebApp fully compatible with the server OS?
- Are system files, directories, and related system data created correctly when the WebApp is operational?
- Do system security measures (e.g., firewalls or encryption) allow the WebApp to execute and service users without interference or performance degradation?
- Has the WebApp been tested with the distributed server configuration[18] (if one exists) that has been chosen?
- Is the WebApp properly integrated with database software? Is the WebApp sensitive to different versions of database software?
- Do server-side WebApp scripts execute properly?
- Have system administrator errors been examined for their effect on WebApp operations?
- If proxy servers are used, have differences in their configuration been addressed with on-site testing?

---

18 For example, a separate application server and database server may be used. Communication between the two machines occurs across a network connection. What happens if this connection fails?

How Do We Test the Client Side?

On the client side, configuration tests focus more heavily on WebApp compatibility with configurations that contain one or more permutations of the following components [Ngu01]:

- **Hardware.** CPU, memory, storage, and printing devices
- **Operating systems.** Linux, Macintosh OS, Microsoft Windows, a mobile-based OS
- **Browser software.** FireFox, Internet Explorer, Safari, Mozilla/Netscape, Opera, and others
- **User interface components.** Active X, Java applets, and others
- **Plug-ins.** QuickTime, RealPlayer, and many others
- **Connectivity.** Cable, DSL, regular modem, industry-grade connectivity (e.g., T1 lines)

In addition to these components, other variables include networking software, the vagaries of the ISP, and applications running concurrently on the client machine.

To design client-side configuration tests, the Web engineering team must reduce the number of configuration variables to a manageable number.[19] To accomplish this, each user category is assessed to determine the likely configurations to be encountered within the category. In addition, industry market share data may be used to predict the most likely combinations of components. The WebApp is then tested within these environments.

Security and Performance Testing

Both security and performance testing address the three distinct elements of the WebApp infrastructure—the server-side environment that provides the gateway to Internet users, the network communication pathway between the server and the client machine, and the client-side environment that provides the end user with a direct interface to the WebApp. But there, the similarity ends. Security testing focuses on unauthorized access to WebApp content and functionality along with other systems that cooperate with the WebApp on the server side. Performance testing focuses on the operating characteristics of the WebApp and on whether those operating characteristics meet the needs of end users.

---

19 Running tests on every possible combination of configuration components is far too time consuming, if not impossible.

How Do We Determine if the WebApp Is Secure?

WebApp security is a complex subject that must be fully understood before effective security testing can be accomplished.[20] WebApps and the client-side and server-side environments in which they are housed represent an attractive target for external hackers, disgruntled employees, dishonest competitors, and anyone else who wishes to steal sensitive information, maliciously modify content, degrade performance, disable functionality, or embarrass a person, organization, or business.

Security tests are designed to probe vulnerabilities of the client-side environment, the network communications that occur as data are passed from client to server and back again, and the server-side environment. Each of these domains can be attacked, and it is the job of the security tester to uncover weaknesses that can be exploited by those with the intent to do so.

On the client side, vulnerabilities can often be traced to preexisting bugs in browsers, e-mail programs, or communication software. Nguyen [Ngu01] describes a typical security hole:

> One of the commonly mentioned bugs is Buffer Overflow, which allows malicious code to be executed on the client machine. For example, entering a URL into a browser that is much longer than the buffer size allocated for the URL will cause a memory overwrite (buffer overflow) error if the browser does not have error detection code to validate the length of the input URL. A seasoned hacker can cleverly exploit this bug by writing a long URL with code to be executed that can cause the browser to crash or alter security setting (from high to low), or, at worst, to corrupt user data.

Another potential vulnerability on the client side is unauthorized access to cookies placed within the browser. Websites created with malicious intent can acquire information contained within legitimate cookies and use this information in ways that jeopardize the user's privacy, or worse, set the stage for identity theft.

Data communicated between the client and the server are vulnerable to *spoofing*. Spoofing occurs when one end of the communication pathway is subverted by an entity with malicious intent. For example, a user can be spoofed by a malicious website that appears to be the legitimate WebApp server (identical look and feel). The intent is to steal passwords, proprietary information, or credit card data.

On the server side, vulnerabilities include denial-of-service attacks and malicious scripts that can be passed along to the client side or used to disable server operations. In addition, server-side databases can be accessed without authorization (data theft).

---

20 Books by Andrews and Whittaker [And06], Galbraith et al [GN03], McClure and his colleagues [McC03], and Garfinkel and Spafford [Gar02] provide useful information about the subject.

To protect against these (and many other) vulnerabilities, one or more of the following security elements is implemented [Ngu01]:

- **Firewalls.** A filtering mechanism that is a combination of hardware and software that examines each incoming packet of information to ensure that it is coming from a legitimate source, blocking any data that are suspect.

- **Authentication.** A verification mechanism that validates the identity of all clients and servers, allowing communication to occur only when both sides are verified.

- **Encryption.** An encoding mechanism that protects sensitive data by modifying it in a way that makes it impossible to read by those with malicious intent. Encryption is strengthened by using *digital certificates* that allow the client to verify the destination to which the data are transmitted.

- **Authorization.** A filtering mechanism that allows access to the client or server environment only by those individuals with appropriate authorization codes (e.g., user ID and password).

Security tests should be designed to probe each of these security technologies in an effort to uncover security holes that can be exploited by those with malicious intent.

The actual design of security tests requires in-depth knowledge of the inner workings of each security element and a comprehensive understanding of a full range of networking technologies. If the WebApp is business-critical, maintains sensitive data, or is a likely target of hackers, it's a good idea to outsource security testing to a vendor that specializes in it.

SafeHome

Preparing for Security Testing

The scene: The Web engineering meeting room at CPI Corporation

The players: The team leader, two representatives from the marketing department, and a few members of the **SafeHomeAssured.com** team discussing the need for security testing after the communication activity commences

The conversation:

Team leader: It's apparent based on the results of requirements gathering that we've got some privacy

and security issues that must be addressed for **Safe-HomeAssured.com.**

Marketing rep 1: Yeah, I really like the home video monitoring capability, but could you imagine what would happen if someone hacked into our system and invaded the privacy of one of our customers. It'd be a disaster and a major lawsuit!

Team leader (nodding): Video isn't the only issue. We need to protect the customer from unauthorized access to any feature of the system. Things like a burglar hacking into the system and disabling a customer's security system, or accessing their account information . . .

Team member 1: You're both right. Here's what I think we can do to design the system so that . . .

Team leader (interrupting): Whoa! We're getting ahead of ourselves. Before we design anything, we've got to understand the security issues that **SafeHomeAssured.com** presents.

Marketing rep 2: We budgeted money for a security consultant.

Team leader: Good. I want to get the consultant involved right now, and I want one whose firm not only consults but will do full-scale security testing once the WebApp is built.

Team member 2: If they tell us what tests they're going to conduct, we can be sure to design the WebApp in a way that addresses the tests. Sort of a crib sheet.

Marketing rep 1: That's true, but I think you should also get their advice on how we need to design this WebApp to make it attack-proof.

Team member 1: There's no WebApp that's "attack-proof," only WebApps that are very secure.

Team leader (ticking off points on his fingers): That's true . . . we need to protect the data that moves from the server to the client side, we need to protect all content that the site delivers, we need to encrypt passwords and other account info, we need to protect the customer from dishonest employees of CPI, we need . . .

Marketing rep 2 (interrupting): We need a list of all those things and more to give to the security consultant.

Team member 2: And then we need to know the kinds of testing that they're going to perform . . . in detail!

Team leader (looking at everyone present): Each of you work up a list and e-mail it to me by tomorrow at 9:00 a.m. I'll do a composite, and then we'll contact a few security consulting and testing firms and go from there.

Team member 1: Are we going to be doing any security testing?

Team leader: I'm sure you will, but the heavy lifting is best left to professionals.

How Should We Test WebApp Performance?

Nothing is more frustrating than a WebApp that takes minutes to load content when competitive sites download similar content in seconds. Nothing is more aggravating than trying to log in to a WebApp and receiving a "server busy" message, with the suggestion that you try again later. Nothing is more disconcerting than a WebApp that responds instantly in some situations and then seems to go into an infinite wait-state in other situations. All of these occurrences happen on the Web every day, and all of them are performance-related.

Performance testing is used to uncover performance problems that can result from lack of server-side resources, inappropriate network bandwidth, inadequate database capabilities, faulty or weak operating system capabilities, poorly designed WebApp functionality, and other hardware or software issues that can lead to degraded client-server performance. The intent is twofold: (1) to understand how the system responds as *loading* increases (i.e., number of users, number of transactions, or overall data volume), and (2) to collect metrics that will lead to design modifications to improve performance.

What Are the Objectives of Performance Testing?

Performance tests are designed to simulate real-world loading situations. As the number of simultaneous WebApp users grows, or the number of online transactions increases, or the amount of data (downloaded or uploaded) increases, performance testing will help answer the following questions:

- Does the server response time degrade to a point where it is noticeable and unacceptable?
- At what point (in terms of users, transactions, or data loading) does performance become unacceptable?
- What system components are responsible for performance degradation?
- What is the average response time for users under a variety of loading conditions?
- Does performance degradation have an impact on system security?
- Is WebApp reliability or accuracy affected as the load on the system grows?
- What happens when loads that are greater than maximum server capacity are applied?
- What is the impact of poor performance on company revenues?

To develop answers to these questions, two different performance tests are conducted: (1) *load testing*—real-world loading is tested at a variety of load levels and in a variety of combinations, and (2) *stress testing*—loading is increased to the breaking point to determine how much capacity the WebApp environment can handle. Each of these testing strategies is considered in the subsections that follow.

How Does Load Testing Assess Performance?

The intent of load testing is to determine how the WebApp and its server-side environment will respond to various loading conditions. As testing proceeds, permutations to the following variables define a set of test conditions:

N, the number of concurrent users

T, the number of online transactions per unit of time

D, the data load processed by the server per transaction

In every case, these variables are defined within normal operating bounds of the system. As each test condition is run, one or more of the following measures are collected: average user response, average time to download a standardized unit of data, or average time to process a transaction. The WebE team examines these measures to determine whether a precipitous decrease in performance can be traced to a specific combination of N, T, and D.

Load testing can also be used to assess recommended connection speeds for users of the WebApp. Overall throughput P is computed in the following manner:

$$P = N \times T \times D$$

As an example, consider a popular sports news site. At any given time, 4000 concurrent users submit a request (a transaction T) once every 30 seconds on average. Each transaction requires the WebApp to download a news article that averages 12 kbytes in length. Therefore,

> $N = 4000$ users
> $T = 0.033$ transactions per second per user
> $D = 12$ kbyte per transaction

and throughput can be calculated as

$$P = 4000 \times 0.033 \times 12 \approx 1600 \text{ kbyte/s}$$

The network connection for the server would therefore have to support this average data rate and should be tested to ensure that it does.

How Does Stress Testing Assess Performance?

Stress testing is a continuation of load testing, but in this instance the variables, N, T, and D are forced to meet and then exceed operational limits. The intent of these tests is to answer each of the following questions:

- Does the system degrade "gently" or does the server shut down as capacity is exceeded?
- Does server software generate "server not available" messages? More generally, are users aware that they cannot reach the server?
- Does the server queue requests for resources and empty the queue once capacity demands diminish?
- Are transactions lost as capacity is exceeded?
- Is data integrity affected as capacity is exceeded?
- What values of N, T, and D force the server environment to fail? How does failure manifest itself? Are automated notifications sent to technical support staff at the server site?
- If the system does fail, how long will it take to come back online?

- Are certain WebApp functions (e.g., compute intensive functionality, data streaming capabilities) discontinued as capacity reaches the 80 or 90 percent level?

A variation of stress testing is sometimes referred to as *spike/bounce testing* [Spl01]. In this testing regime, the load is spiked to capacity, then lowered quickly to normal operating conditions, and then spiked again. By bouncing system loading, testers can determine how well the server can marshal resources to meet very high demand and then release them when normal conditions reappear (so that they are ready for the next spike).

SafeHome

Preparing for Performance Testing

The scene: The Web engineering meeting room at CPI Corporation

The players: The team leader and two members of the **SafeHomeAssured.com** team discussing the need for performance testing prior to the modeling activity for increment 6, *Online control of monitoring equipment*

The conversation:

Team leader: Marketing is really enthusiastic about the video monitoring capability that we're building into this increment for **SafeHomeAssured.com.**

Team member 1 (sighing): There are a lot of design issues for this and testing issues as well.

Team member 2: I worked on a project that had online video streaming in my last job. We've got to establish an environment at the customer site that allows us to stream video from monitoring cameras. That means having a box that establishes the right encoding option based on the number of frames per second we're transmitting, targeting the video stream to our servers—maybe to a customer-specific Web-page—so that access can be controlled, and then . . .

Team member 1 (interrupting): There's some proprietary technology that might help us. The one I'm thinking about sends a Java applet in front of the video stream that decodes the video at the client's Java-enabled browser—no plug-ins or other configuration issues. I think we should . . .

Team member 2 (interrupting): Yeah—and I'm sure I saw something that set up a direct video connection from the client browser to the actual camera, bypassing the server, so that there was no real load hit at all except when the page was first loaded.

Team leader (interrupting): We have a lot of design work to do on this one, and I don't want to do it here. Before we break, I want to talk about performance testing for this increment.

Team member 1: Hard to do that without a solid design concept.

Team member 2: Well, there are some fundamental questions that performance testing will have to address: How will server response degrade as the number of users accessing video grows? We'll use a classic *N-T-D* analysis [see the preceding subsection "How Does Load Testing Assess Performance?"] to get a handle on required throughput. Stuff like that.

Team member 1: We'll also need to determine whether any performance degradation has an impact on system security. Given the privacy aspects of this, that's critical.

Team leader: We'll need to do a series of stress tests, the implication being we'll need to have a complete testing environment set up with streaming video from a number of locations, access from a variety of PCs, and so on.

SAFEHOME (CONTINUED)

Team member 1: Whoa. You're right! I don't think we factored any of that into our time estimate for this increment.

Team leader (shaking his head): Unfortunately we didn't. I'll go talk with marketing and renegotiate the deployment date for this increment.

Team member 2: They won't buy it.

Team leader: Yeah, they will. If they don't give us more time, we can't test performance. We won't know

how the system will look to end users. And if we don't know how it will perform, we can't guarantee that users will be happy with it. And if they're not happy, we lose business, get a bad rep, and lose revenue over the long haul.

Team member 2: All because we don't performance test?

Team leader (smiling): That's my story, and I'm sticking to it.

TOOLS

Taxonomy for WebApp Testing

In his paper on the testing of e-commerce systems, Lam [Lam01] presents a useful taxonomy of automated tools that have direct applicability for testing in a Web engineering context. We have appended representative tools in each category.[21]

Configuration and content management tools manage version and change control of WebApp content objects and functional components:
Representative tools:
A comprehensive list is provided at Dave Eaton's website at **www.daveeaton.com/scm/CMTools. html.**

Database performance tools measure database performance, such as the time to perform selected database queries. These tools facilitate database optimization.
Representative tool:
BMC Software (**www.bmc.com**)

Debuggers are typical programming tools that find and resolve software defects in the code. They are part of most modern application development environments.
Representative tools:
Accelerated Technology
(**www.acceleratedtechnology.com**)

IBM VisualAge Environment (**www.ibm.com**)
JDebugTool (**www.debugtools.com**)

Defect management systems record defects and track their status and resolution. Some include reporting tools to provide management information on defect spread and defect resolution rates.
Representative tools:
EXCEL Quickbugs (**www.excelsoftware.com**)
McCabe TRUETrack (**www.mccabe.com**)
Rational ClearQuest (**www.rational.com**)

Network monitoring tools watch the level of network traffic. They are useful for identifying network bottlenecks and testing the link between front- and back-end systems.
Representative tools:
A comprehensive list is provided at the Stanford Linear Accelerator Center at **www.slac.stanford. edu/xorg/nmtf/nmtf-tools.html.**

Regression testing tools store test cases and test data and can reapply the test cases after successive software changes.
Representative tools:
Compuware QARun (**www.compuware.com/ products/qacenter/qarun**)
Rational VisualTest (**www.rational.com**)
Seque Software (**www.seque.com**)

(continued)

---

21 Tools noted here do not represent an endorsement, but rather a sampling of tools in this category. In addition, tool names are registered trademarks of the companies noted.

Site monitoring tools monitor a site's performance, often from a user's perspective. Use them to compile statistics such as end-to-end response time and throughput, and to periodically check a site's availability.
Representative tool:
Keynote Systems (**www.keynote.com**)

Stress tools help developers explore system behavior under high levels of operational usage and find a system's breakpoints.
Representative tools:
Mercury Interactive (**www.merc-int.com**)
Scapa Technologies (**www.scapatech.com**)

System resource monitors are part of most OS server and Web server software; they monitor resources such as disk space, CPU usage, and memory.
Representative tools:
Successful Hosting.com (**www.successfulhosting. com**)
Quest Software Foglight (**www.quest.com**)

Test data generation tools assist users in generating test data.
Representative tools:

A comprehensive list is provided at the Software QA/Test Resource Center at **www.softwareqatest.com/qatweb1.html.**

Test result comparators help compare the results of one set of testing to that of another set. Use them to check that code changes have not introduced adverse changes in system behavior.
Representative tools:
A useful list is provided at the Applied Testing and Technology website at **www.aptest.com/ resources.html.**

Transaction monitors measure the performance of high-volume transaction processing systems.
Representative tools:
QuotiumPro (**www.quotium.com**)
Software Research eValid (**www.soft.com/eValid/ index.html**)

Website security tools help detect potential security problems. You can often set up security probing and monitoring tools to run on a scheduled basis.
Representative tools:
A comprehensive list is provided Timberline Technologies at **www.timberlinetechnologies. com/products/www.html.**

Where We've Been . . . Where We're Going

The goal of WebApp testing is to exercise each of the many dimensions of WebApp quality with the intent of finding errors or uncovering issues that may lead to quality failures. Testing focuses on content, function, structure, usability, navigability, performance, compatibility, interoperability, capacity, and security. Testing incorporates reviews that occur as the WebApp is designed and tests that are conducted once the WebApp has been implemented.

The WebApp testing strategy exercises each quality dimension by initially examining "units" of content, functionality, or navigation. Once individual units have been validated, the focus shifts to tests that exercise the WebApp as a whole. To accomplish this, many tests are derived from the user's perspective and are driven by information contained in usage scenarios (use cases). A Web engineering test plan is developed and identifies testing steps, work products (e.g., test cases), and mechanisms for the evaluation of test results. The testing process encompasses seven different types of testing.

Content testing (and reviews) focus on various categories of content. The intent is to uncover both semantic and syntactic errors that affect the accuracy of content or the manner in which it is presented to the end user. Interface testing exercises interaction mechanisms that enable a user to communicate with the WebApp and validates aesthetic aspects of the interface. The intent is to uncover errors that result from poorly implemented interaction mechanisms, or omissions, inconsistencies, or ambiguities in interface semantics.

Navigation testing applies use cases, derived as part of the analysis activity, in the design of test cases that exercise each usage scenario against the navigation design. Navigation mechanisms are tested to ensure that any errors impeding completion of a use case are identified and corrected. Component testing exercises content and functional units within the WebApp. Each Web page encapsulates content, navigation links, and processing elements that form a "unit" within the WebApp architecture. These units must be tested.

Configuration testing attempts to uncover errors and/or compatibility problems that are specific to a particular client or server environment. Tests are then conducted to uncover errors associated with each possible configuration. Security testing incorporates a series of tests designed to exploit vulnerabilities in the WebApp and its environment. The intent is to find security holes. Performance testing encompasses a series of tests that are designed to assess WebApp response time and reliability as demands on server-side resource capacity increase.

In Chapter 16, we examine another quality assurance mechanism—change and content management. As we discussed in Chapter 1, change is constant when WebApps are built and maintained. It is for this reason that specialized techniques must be developed to manage changes to WebApp content and function.

References

[And06] Andrews, M., and J. Whittaker, *How to Break Web Software: Functional and Security Testing of Web Applications and Web Services,* Addison-Wesley, 2006.

[Bro01] Brown, B., *Oracle9i Web Development,* 2nd ed., McGraw-Hill, 2001.

[Cac02] Cachero, C., et al., "Conceptual Navigation Analysis: A Device and Platform Independent Navigation Specification," *Proc. 2nd Intl. Workshop on Web-Oriented Technology,* June 2002, **www.dsic.upv.es/~west/iwwost02/papers/cachero.pdf.** (accessed August 13, 2007).

[Con95] Constantine, L., "What Do Users Want? Engineering Usability in Software," *Windows Tech Journal,* December 1995, **www.foruse.com.** (accessed August 13, 2007).

[Con99] Constantine, L., and L. Lockwood, *Software for Use,* Addison-Wesley, 1999. See also **www.foruse.com/** (accessed August 13, 2007).

[Don99] Donahue, G., S. Weinschenck, and J. Nowicki, "Usability Is Good Business," Compuware Corp., July 1999, **www.compuware.com.** (accessed August 13, 2007).

[Gal03] Galbraith, B. et al, *Professional Web Services Security,* Wrox Press, 2003.

[Gar02] Garfinkel, S., and G. Spafford, *Web Security, Privacy and Commerce,* O'Reilly, 2002.

[How97] Hower, R., "Beyond Broken Links," *Internet Systems,* 1997, **http://portal.acm. org/citation.cfm?id=265138** (accessed August 13, 2007).

[Lam01] Lam, W., "Testing E-Commerce Systems: A Practical Guide," *IEEE IT Pro,* March/April 2001, pp. 19–28.

[McC03] McClure, S., S. Shah, and S. Shah, *Hacking Exposed: Attacks and Defense,* Addison-Wesley, 2003.

[Mil00] Miller, E., "WebSite Testing," 2000, **www.soft.com/eValid/Technology/White. Papers/website.testing.html** (accessed August 13, 2007).

[Ngu00] Nguyen, H., "Testing Web-based Applications," *Software Testing and Quality Engineering* May/June 2000, **www.stqemagazine.com** (accessed August 13, 2007).

[Ngu01] Nguyen, H., *Testing Applications on the Web,* Wiley, 2001.

[Pre05] Pressman, R. S., *Software Engineering: A Practitioner's Approach,* 6th ed., McGraw-Hill, 2005.

[Sce02] Sceppa, D., *Microsoft ADO.NET,* Microsoft Press, 2002.

[Spl01] Splaine, S., and S. Jaskiel, *The Web Testing Handbook,* STQE Publishing, 2001.

[Wal03] Wallace, D., I. Raggett, and J. Aufgang, *Extreme Programming for Web Projects,* Addison Wesley Professional, 2003.

CHANGE AND CONTENT MANAGEMENT

Change management procedures and a content management system work in conjunction with one another. Together, they help ensure that: (1) all requested changes to WebApp content and functionality are managed in a way that does not disrupt the Web engineering process or corrupt the quality of the WebApp itself, and (2) all WebApp content is properly collected, structured, and presented to the end user who requests it.

To keep the WebE process flowing smoothly, change must be managed in a way that does not devour resources when they are needed to model, construct, and deploy an important WebApp increment. To maintain quality, each WebApp object that is changed must be managed to ensure that the change is made correctly, recorded for future reference, and does not conflict with other changes that have already been made.

Content management collects, manages, and publishes all content that is seen by each end-user category, including content (and functions) that have undergone change. A *content management system* incorporates automated tools with a process that ensures that content is correctly structured and presented based on an end-user request.

Change

Although we all tend to believe the propaganda that argues "everything is changing," the reality is that most things don't. The core elements of every business are the same today as they were a century ago—we need to create, market, and sell our products; service our customers; empower our employees; and invest the company's profits to help it grow. But at the same time, we see profound changes to the technology that supports the core elements of the business, the nature of the products that we develop, and the demographics of our customer base. The very way we do business is changing. Since Web-based systems have evolved into a technology that supports the core elements of a business, we have to expect that WebApp requirements will change as the Web-based system is engineered and after it has been deployed.

What Are the Attributes of a "Change"?

In the context of Web engineering, a "change" has a number of important attributes:

- A *description* that explains the nature of the change from the point of view of the stakeholder(s) affected by the change
- An *impact* that describes how the change will manifest itself externally (what end users will see) and how it will affect the internal content and functionality of the WebApp
- A *target* that defines the specific WebApp objects (both content and functionality) that will be changed
- An *implementation pathway* that describes the technical aspects of how the change will be made
- A *history* that records when the change was requested, assessed, and implemented and what WebApp content and functionality was affected

Changes and the attributes that describe them are relatively easy to manage for small projects. But things become more complicated as the size of the Web engineering effort grows. The number of content objects and functions grows significantly, and the interrelationships among these WebApp elements become more complex. The number of people working on the project increases, and the likelihood of two people making changes that conflict with one another (without the other person's knowledge) also grows. Hence, the effort expended on the management of change is directly proportional to the size and criticality of the WebApp that is being changed.

Why Are Changes Requested?

Earlier in the book (Chapter 5) we discussed some of the reasons that changes occur. To recapitulate: (1) nontechnical stakeholders may have an afterthought[1] about the WebApp in general or the increment that is currently being developed in particular, (2) and users may request different modes of interaction or demand different functions or content, or (3) Web engineers may learn that unexpected modifications are required to achieve WebApp requirements or to improve the WebApp infrastructure. In addition, the business environment may change, leading to new business rules and requirements.

---

1   The afterthought may be precipitated by new business requirements (e.g., the demographics of the projected market are different from those originally defined), new or modified content or functions (e.g., the content that was originally to be presented is not the content that is now desired), changes in management (e.g., a new executive manager "wants to go another way"), to name just a few.

What Elements of the WebApp Change?

The "why" of changes provides us with an understanding of motivation, but it tells us nothing about "what" actually changes. In the most general sense, WebApp content changes. When used in this context, *content* means any information that is used to construct a WebApp and includes: (1) *text* in both structured and unstructured formats, (2) *images* represented as photos, graphic representations, line drawings, and illustrations, (3) *audio,* such as voice recordings, music, and natural and synthesized sounds, (4) *motion,* such as video and animation, (5) *navigation mechanisms,* such as buttons, links, and menus, (6) *input mechanisms,* such as pull-down menus, forms, and button selections, (7) *data,* such as files or databases that serve the WebApp, (8) *client-based functions* such as scripts that perform data processing on the client side, and (9) *server-based functions* that implement server-side processing.

Every request for change ultimately leads to modifications in one or more of the content categories noted. For example, let's assume that after the sixth increment of the **SafeHomeAssured.com** WebApp (online control of security monitoring equipment) has been implemented, end-user feedback indicates a need for easier manipulation of video and audio information. Changes to the user interface for monitoring will be required. At the same time, a new generation of inexpensive, miniature, wireless high-definition (HD) video cameras now makes it possible to place video in every room and acquire a high-quality video signal. However, changes will be required to control software at the customer site, to control functions within the WebApp, and to control the user interface itself. A wide array of content objects and WebApp functions will require change. One of the challenges for the WebE team is to ensure that: (1) only the content that requires change is changed, (2) a change to one content object will not have a negative impact on another, and (3) old versions of the WebApp (e.g., that support older camera technology) will work properly with any server-based functionality that has been changed.

Change Management for Web Engineering

Throughout this book we have discussed the special nature of Web applications and the Web engineering process that is required to build them. Web engineering uses an iterative, incremental process model that applies many principles derived from agile software development. Using this approach, an engineering team often develops a WebApp increment in a very short time period using a customer-driven approach. Subsequent increments add additional content and functionality, and each is likely to implement changes that lead to enhanced content, better usability, improved aesthetics, better navigation, enhanced performance, and stronger security. Therefore, in the agile world of Web engineering, change is viewed somewhat differently.

Recalling the words of Ivar Jacobson [Jac02]:

> An agile team is a nimble team able to appropriately respond to changes. Change is what software development is very much about. Changes in the software being built, changes to the team members, changes because of new technology, changes of all kinds that may have an impact on the product they build or the project that creates the product. Support for changes should be built-in everything we do in software, something we embrace because it is the heart and soul of software.

Jacobson suggests that Web engineers must embrace change, and yet, a typical agile team eschews all things that appear to be process-heavy, bureaucratic, and formal. This, of course, leads us to a number of fundamental questions that are addressed in the subsections that follow.

Why Do We Need Change Management?

As WebApps become increasingly important to business survival and growth, the need for change management grows. Why? Because without effective controls, improper changes to a WebApp (recall that *immediacy* and *continuous evolution* are the dominant attributes of many WebApps) can lead to unauthorized posting of new product information, erroneous or poorly tested functionality that frustrates visitors to a website, security holes that jeopardize internal company systems, and other economically unpleasant or even disastrous consequences.

What Issues Should We Consider?   As a WebE team prepares to develop its strategy for change management, four issues [Dar99] should be considered:

> **Content.** A typical WebApp contains a vast array of content—text, graphics, applets, scripts, audio and video files, forms, active page elements, tables, streaming data, functions, and many others. The challenge is to organize this sea of content into a rational set of *configuration objects.*[2] Once configuration objects have been identified, we then establish appropriate *configuration control mechanisms* for these objects. One approach is to model the WebApp content by representing the relationships between objects and the specialized properties of each object.[3] The nature (static or dynamic) of each object and its projected longevity (e.g., temporary, fixed existence, or permanent object) are examples of properties that are required to establish an effective approach to change management. For example, if a content item is

---

2   The term *configuration* refers to all elements of the WebApp. A *configuration object* is a named part of the WebApp (e.g., **SpaceLayout**), has a set of attributes that can be used to describe it, and can be interconnected with other objects (e.g., **SpaceLayout** is "connected" to **Walls, Doors** and **Windows** objects).

3   Software engineering methods can be used for particularly complex WebApps. These methods include data modeling (e.g., [Car01] and [Sim05]) and/or UML models.

changed hourly, it has temporary longevity. The control mechanisms for this item would be different (less formal) from those applied for a forms component that is a permanent object.

People. Because a significant percentage of WebApp development continues to be conducted in an ad hoc manner, any person involved in the WebApp can (and often does) create content. Many content creators have no technical background and are completely unaware of the need for change management. As a consequence, the WebApp can—if not managed effectively—change in an uncontrolled fashion.[4] Therefore, the WebE team must establish change management mechanisms that are acceptable not only to technical people, but also to nontechnical developers of content.

Scalability. The techniques and controls applied to small WebApps do not scale upward well. It is not uncommon for a simple WebApp to grow significantly as interconnections with existing information systems, databases, data warehouses, and portal gateways are implemented. As size and complexity grow, small changes can have far-reaching and unintended effects that can be problematic. Therefore, the rigor of change control mechanisms should be directly proportional to application scale.

Politics. Who "owns" a WebApp? This question is argued in companies large and small, and its answer has a significant impact on the management and control activities associated with Web engineering. In some instances Web developers are housed outside the IT organization, creating potential communication difficulties. Dart [Dar99] suggests the following questions to help understand the politics associated with Web engineering:

- Who assumes responsibility for the accuracy of the information on the website?
- Who ensures that quality control processes have been followed before information is published to the site?
- Who is responsible for making changes?
- Who assumes the cost of change?

The answers to these questions help determine the people within an organization (the key stakeholders) who must adopt a change management process for WebApps.

---

4   It's reasonable to argue that certain types of WebApps can and should be allowed to grow organically. For example, a website that exhibits various art forms (e.g., short stories, film, visuals) created by contributors could allow such content to be posted and changed without control. The dynamic nature of the site might be one of its strengths. However, WebApps that deliver content and function providing specific services or critical information cannot afford the luxury of organic growth and uncontrolled change.

Change management for Web engineering is still immature, but a new generation of tools that are specifically designed for Web engineering has emerged over the past few years. These tools provide functionality that helps to address the following issues [Dar99]:

- How to create a change management process that is nimble enough to accommodate the immediacy and continuous evolution of WebApps
- How to best introduce change management concepts and tools to developers who are completely unfamiliar with the technology
- How to provide support for distributed WebApp development teams
- How to provide control in a quasi-publishing environment where content changes on a near-continuous basis
- How to attain the granularity required to control a large array of configuration objects
- How to incorporate configuration management functionality into existing WebE tools
- How to manage changes to objects that contain links to other objects

The WebE team should select a tool set that provides change management support and at the same time provides meaningful the preceding solutions for issues.

What Is the Basic Change Management Activity? At its core, the change management activity is straightforward, but the execution of the process can pose problems in the fast-paced world of Web engineering. The key is to manage change in a disciplined way while at the same time remaining agile. Easy to say—not always easy to do!

Change management is an "umbrella activity" that is applied throughout the WebE process. It encompasses five actions: identification, change control, version control, auditing, and status reporting. We'll examine each briefly in the following subsections.

How Should We Identify the Objects That Will Change?

Elements of the WebApp configuration must be identified and named. The implication is that a content item that is to be managed must be identified in some unique way. The names of some content items are obvious. For example, the **SafeHomeAssured.com** WebApp contains product specifications for all security hardware (e.g., sensors, video cameras, control panels). Each product specification is composed of one or more of the following content items: a text-based description, a photograph, a schematic diagram or other graphical image representing connectivity or interfacing issues, a video segment providing installation instructions. A content object that we identify generically as **ProductSpecification** can be represented as a collection of named items:

ProductSpecification = Text + Photo + Schematic + Video

However, in order to manage changes to WebApp content, we must identify specific content. CPI Corporation now offers a new miniature HD video camera as part of its home monitoring suite of products. The wireless camera can be controlled remotely (e.g., on/off, pan, zoom, focus) via the Internet and transmits HD video images to the user via the **SafeHomeAssured.com** WebApp.

The camera model number is HDV485. Hence, it would seem reasonable to name all content associated with the product specification for the camera using the format **PS-HDV485-<type>** where **<type>** is TXT, PHOTO, SCH, or VID. To illustrate, the descriptive text and photo for the camera would be identified as PS-HDV485TXT.html, and PS-HDV485PHOTO.jpg, respectively. The content name provides worthwhile identifying information.

How Should We Control a Change That Is about to Be Made?

The basic approach to change control has been discussed in Chapter 5. To review, each requested change is categorized into one of four classes:

Class 1. A content or function change that corrects an error or enhances local content or functionality

Class 2. A content or function change that has an impact on other content objects or functional components within the increment

Class 3. A content or function change that has a broad impact across a WebApp (e.g., major extension of functionality, significant enhancement or reduction in content, major required changes in navigation)

Class 4. A major design change (e.g., a change in interface design or navigation approach) that will be immediately noticeable to one or more categories of end users

Once the requested change has been categorized, it can be assessed according to the algorithm shown in Figure 5.7, reproduced here as Figure 16.1.

Referring to the figure, class 1 and 2 changes are treated informally and are handled in an agile manner. For a class 1 change, you should evaluate the impact of the change on the configuration objects that will be affected, but no external review or documentation is required. The content object to be changed can

Managing
changes for
WebApps.

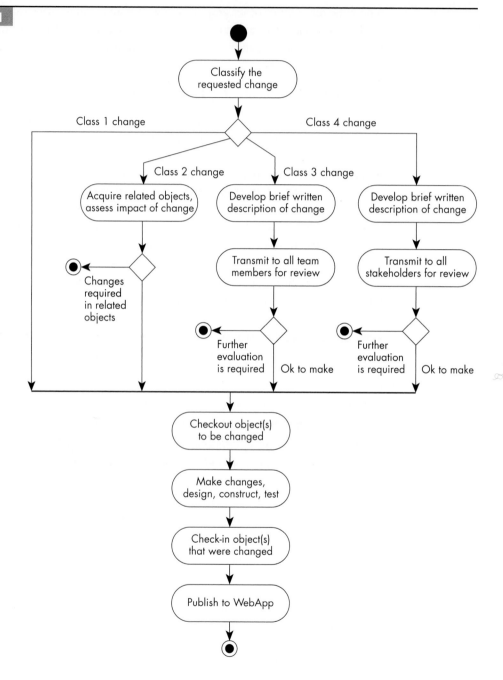

be "checked out" of the project database,[5] the change is made, and appropriate quality assurance activities are applied. The object is then "checked in" to the database, and appropriate version control mechanisms are used to create the next version of the software.

These version control mechanisms, integrated within the change control process, implement two important elements of change management—access control and synchronization control. *Access control* governs which Web engineers (or other stakeholders) have the authority to access and modify a particular content object. *Synchronization control* helps to ensure that parallel changes, performed by two different people, don't overwrite one another.

For class 2 changes, it is incumbent on you to review the impact of the change on related objects (or to ask other developers responsible for those objects to do so). If the change can be made without requiring significant changes to other objects, modification occurs without additional review or documentation. If substantive changes are required, further evaluation and planning are necessary.

Class 3 and 4 changes are also treated in an agile manner, but some descriptive documentation and more formal review procedures are required. A *change description*—describing the change and providing a brief assessment of its impact—is developed for class 3 changes. The description is distributed to all members of the WebE team (including other stakeholders who have interest) who review it to better assess its impact. A change description is also developed for class 4 changes, but in this case, the review is conducted by all stakeholders.

SafeHome

Managing a Change

The scene: SafeHomeAssured.com team leader's office

The players: Team leader and two members of the WebE team as the delivery date for increment 6, *Online control of monitoring equipment,* approaches

The conversation:

Team leader: I just got a call from marketing. They want to make a change prior to the release of this increment.

Team member 1 (cursing under his breath): You have got to be kidding. We've already been delayed because of design and then security testing issues, and I'm not sure we can make the delivery date as is.

Team member 2 (shrugging her shoulders in resignation): What's the change?

Team leader: Basically, they've conducted additional focus groups, and they've found that people

(continued)

---

5 The *project database,* also called a *repository,* contains all named content objects and is often part of a content management system, discussed later in this chapter in the section "Content Management."

SafeHome (continued)

love the idea of monitoring their house remotely, but are scared that someone within CPI will have the capability to monitor them . . . sort of a big brother thing.

Team member 1 (interrupting): But we've addressed that in the design by . . .

Team leader (raising his hand): I know, but they're worried about how visible that will be to the users. They want something that's obvious and foolproof for the end user. [He explains a new option that will provide a biometric log-in specific only to the end user and modification to the interface design that will accommodate the log-in.]

Team member 2: That's hardware and software! Class 4 change for sure.

Team member 1 (frowning): And if it's class 4, we'll need to develop a full change description, discuss impact, get review by all stakeholders . . .

Team leader: And in this case, postpone any action until this increment is released as is. We'll release this biometric functionality as a new increment, say increment 6a, or as part of increment 7.

Team member 1: That means modifying the overall schedule and the estimates and delivery date for increment 7, no matter which strategy we adopt.

Team member 2: No one ever said that change is free. Marketing is going to learn that real quick.

Team leader: I think they already understand, but we'll see.

Team member 1 (thinking a moment): You know, since we're making changes, there's some functionality associated with camera control that I'd really like to refactor. It's class 1, and I think we can add it when we make the bigger mods.

Team leader (smiling): You've got to be kidding.

How Do We Manage Different Versions of a WebApp or Its Components?

Although only a single version of a WebApp is made available to end users, other versions may exist. An older version may be archived for historical purposes. A new version, containing different aesthetics, content, and functionality (along with new navigation pathways) may be under development.

A version control system implements or is directly integrated with four major capabilities: (1) a *project database* (repository) that stores all relevant content objects, (2) a *version management* capability that stores all versions of a content object (or enables any version to be constructed using differences from past versions), (3) a *make facility* that enables you to collect all relevant content objects and construct a specific version of the WebApp. In addition, version control and change control systems often implement (4) an *issues tracking* (also called *bug tracking*) capability that enables the team to record and track the status of all outstanding issues associated with each configuration object.

A number of different automated approaches to version control have been proposed. The primary difference in approaches is the sophistication of the attributes that are used to construct specific versions of a system and the mechanics of the process for construction.

How Can a WebE Team Ensure That a Change Has Been Properly Implemented?

The answer is twofold: (1) conduct pair walkthroughs, and (2) perform a change management audit.

The pair walkthrough (presented in Chapter 5) focuses on the technical correctness of the content object that has been modified. The reviewers assess the object to determine consistency with other content, detect omissions, or uncover potential side effects. A pair walkthrough should be conducted for all but the most trivial changes.

An *audit* complements the pair walkthrough by assessing a content object for characteristics that are generally not considered during the walkthrough. The audit asks and answers the following questions:

1. Have any extra modifications been incorporated in addition to those alterations that relate to the requested change?
2. Has a pair walkthrough been conducted to assess technical correctness?
3. Has the WebE process been followed, and have local Web engineering standards been properly applied?
4. Has the change been "highlighted" in the source code? Have the change date and change author been specified? Do the attributes of the content object reflect the change?
5. Have change management procedures for noting the change, recording it, and reporting it been followed?
6. Have all related objects been properly updated?

In some cases, the audit questions are asked as part of a pair walkthrough. However, when change management is a formal activity, the audit is conducted separately by a quality assurance group. Such formal audits also ensure that the correct objects have been incorporated into a specific increment and that all documentation is up to date and consistent with the version that has been built.

How Do We Let Stakeholders Know What Changes Have Been Made?

Status reporting is a change management task that answers the following questions: (1) What happened? (2) Who did it? (3) When did it happen? (4) What else will be affected?

Status reporting plays a vital role in the success of a large WebApp project. When many people are involved, it is likely that "the left hand may not know what the right hand is doing." Two developers may attempt to modify the same content object with different and conflicting intents. A WebE team may spend weeks building a WebApp increment to conform to an obsolete business requirement. The person who would recognize serious side effects for a proposed change is not aware that the change is being made. Status reporting can help to eliminate these problems by improving communication among all people involved.

Each of the core change management tasks described in the preceding sections must be streamlined to make it as "lean" as possible. At the same time, change must be managed so that it does not lead to chaos, and versions must be controlled so that a high-quality WebApp is available to its end users.

Content Management

In his encyclopedic treatment of the subject, Bob Boiko [Boi05] states that "content management is about gaining control over the creation and distribution of information and functionality." *Content management* is related to change management in the sense that a content management system establishes a process (supported by appropriate tools) that acquires existing information (from a broad array of WebApp objects), structures it in a way that enables it to be presented to an end user, and then provides it to the client-side environment for display.

How Is a Content Management System Used?

A *content management system* (CMS) can be used whenever a WebApp has significant content to be produced and published.[6] The most common use of a CMS occurs when a dynamic WebApp is built. Dynamic WebApps create Web pages on the fly. That is, the user typically queries the WebApp requesting specific information. The WebApp queries a database, manipulates and formats the information accordingly, and presents it to the user.

As a representative example, consider the **SafeHomeAssured.com** feature that allows an end user to design the floor plan layout (a **SpaceLayout**) for the space to be secured. Once **Walls, Doors,** and **Windows** are specified, the end user can indicate requirements for specialized monitoring hardware (e.g., video cameras, microphones). **SafeHomeAssured.com** then executes internal functions to select appropriate security sensors (e.g., a sensor appropriate for a window of type A), searches a database for specific information about the sensors (e.g., installation requirements, pricing), and then collects and configures this information into a content template. The resultant Web page is built on the server side and passed to

---

6   When used in this context, the term *published* refers to the retrieval, formatting, and presentation of content for the end user.

FIGURE 16.2

Content manage-
ment system.

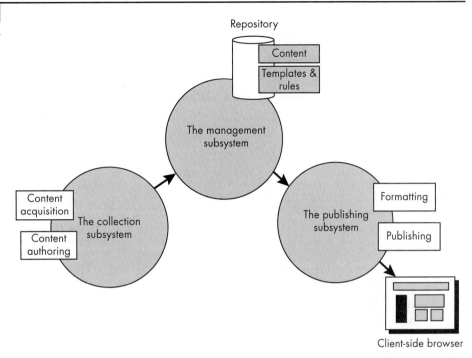

the client-side browser for examination by the end user. A generic representation
of this is shown in Figure 16.2.

What Are the Major Elements of a CMS?

In the most general sense, a CMS "configures" content for the end user by invoking
three integrated subsystems: a collection subsystem, a management subsystem,
and a publishing subsystem [Boi05].

The collection subsystem. Content is derived from data and other nonnu-
merical information that must be created or acquired by a content developer. The
collection subsystem encompasses all actions required to create and/or acquire
content, and the technical functions that are necessary to convert content into a
form that can be represented by a markup language (e.g., HTML, XML) and to organize content into packets that can be displayed effectively on the client side.

Content creation and acquisition (often called *authoring*) commonly occurs in
parallel with other Web engineering activities and is often conducted by nontechnical content developers. This activity combines elements of creativity and research
and is supported by specialized and generic tools that enable the content author
to characterize content in a manner that can be standardized for use within the
WebApp.

For example, employees of CPI Corporation who write SafeHome product specs and develop schematics need to know little or nothing about Web engineering and the **SafeHomeAssured.com** WebApp. In many cases, the product specs exist in electronic form before the WebE project commences. However, new product specifications can be added at any time and changes to the existing specifications may occur on a relatively frequent basis. The *SafeHome* product specifications should be placed in a database (or simple file management system) so that each can be acquired when needed.

Once content exists, it must be retrieved from its storage place and converted to conform to the requirements of a CMS. The conversion involves stripping raw content of any unnecessary information (e.g., redundant graphical representations) and formatting the content using a markup language (e.g., HTML, XML) that can be processed by browser software. The content is then mapped into an information structure that will enable it to be managed and published.

The management subsystem.   Once content has been authored, acquired, and converted, it must be stored in a repository, cataloged for subsequent acquisition and use, and labeled to define: (1) current status (e.g., is the content object complete or in development?), (2) the appropriate version of the content object, and (3) related content objects. Therefore, the *management subsystem* implements a repository that encompasses the following elements:

- **Content database.** The information structure that has been established to store all content objects

- **Database capabilities.** Functions that enable the CMS to search for specific content objects (or categories of objects), store and retrieve objects, and manage the file structure that has been established for the content

- **Change management functions.** The functional elements and associated workflow that support content object identification, version control, change control, change auditing, and reporting

In addition to these elements, the management subsystem implements an administration function that encompasses the metadata and rules that control the overall structure of the content and the manner in which it is supported.

A management subsystem that might be implemented for **SafeHomeAssured.com** could span a broad range of complexity. A simple flat file system could be created. The file would contain a directory for all *SafeHome* sensors, control panels, and monitoring equipment with pointers to all related products and all related content. For example, a file entry for the HDV485 video camera would have pointers to the text specification, photograph, schematic diagram, installation instructions, oper-

FIGURE 16.3

A CMS
repository.

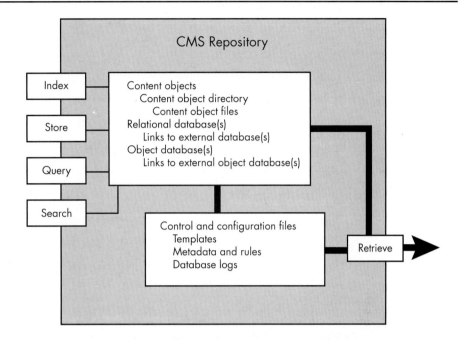

ating instructions, and related *SafeHome* products. At the other end of the complexity spectrum, the WebE team could build a sophisticated **SafeHomeAssured.com**
repository[7] that contains all relevant information for all *SafeHome* products, all information saved by end users (e.g., orders, account information, a named space
layout), and "control and configuration files" [Boi05] for organizing and publishing
content for the **SafeHomeAssured.com** end user. A schematic representation of a CMS
repository is presented in Figure 16.3.

Control and configuration files represent a set of "rules" that are defined by the
WebE team for the processing of user input and for the formatting and publication
of WebApp content. For example, the **SafeHomeAssured.com** WebE team might define
a template for order entry that would include a standardized method (e.g., standardized forms) for identifying customers, defining the product(s) to be purchased, specifying the mode of payment, selecting the shipping options (if required), and so forth.
Another template might be defined to format a bill of materials for all sensors, control panels, and monitoring devices that the WebApp recommends for purchase.

---

7   A repository encompasses one or more linked databases, file systems, and related data struc-
    tures that contain WebApp content objects and the metadata required for the management
    of the content objects.

The publishing subsystem. Content must be extracted from the repository, converted to a form that is amenable to publication, and formatted so that it can be transmitted to client-side browsers. The publishing subsystem usually accomplishes these tasks using a series of templates. Each *template* is a function that builds a publication using one of three different components [Boi05]:

- **Static elements.** Text, graphics, media, and scripts that require no further processing are transmitted directly to the client side.

- **Publication services.** Provide function calls to specific retrieval and formatting services that personalize content (using predefined rules), perform data conversion, and build appropriate navigation links.

- **External services.** Provide access to external corporate information infrastructure such as enterprise data or backroom applications.

A content management system that encompasses each of these subsystems is appropriate for major Web engineering projects. However, the basic philosophy and functionality associated with a CMS are applicable to all dynamic WebApps. Extensive lists of free, open source, and commercially available CMS software can be found on the *CMS Matrix* site at **www.cmsmatrix.org/** and on *Wikipedia* at **http://en.wikipedia.org/wiki/List_of_content_management_systems.**

Criteria for Implementing a CMS

The question is not whether you'll need to manage content—that's a given. Regardless of its size, complexity, or focus, content must be managed for every WebApp. The real question is the degree of formality that you'll need to apply as content is managed and whether an actual CMS will be required.[8]

Although we've provided only an outline of a typical CMS, it should be obvious that the software required to support content management is relatively complex. In addition, the effort required to create an appropriate repository, collect and identify content objects, manage all content, and ultimately publish to end users represents substantial work for the WebE team and other stakeholders.

Not every WebApp requires formal content management, and an even smaller number of WebApps justify the overhead of a comprehensive CMS. During the communication and planning activities that occur early in a Web engineering project, it is necessary to collect information (requirements) to determine the degree

---

8 Deciding which CMS (if any) will be right for your project can be a challenge. Before you make a decision, you might consider visiting the *Open Source CMS* website at **www.opensourcecms.com** where you'll be able to test-drive "some of the best PHP/MySQL based free and open source" CMS systems available.

of formality that must be applied for content management. As requirements are gathered (Chapter 4), it is important to determine a set of criteria that provide an indication of the need for formal content management and a CMS [Boi05]:

- **Content volume.** The number of categories (classes) of content objects and the approximate number of content objects within each class
- **Contributor population.** The number of content contributors who will create content that will be used by the WebApp, and the complexity of the permissions structures controlling their access to content modification
- **Change volume.** The frequency and amount of change that is likely for each class of content and for content objects themselves
- **Publication volume.** The number of "publications" that will be produced from the content that is managed within the WebApp

In the subsections that follow, we examine each of these criteria to understand how it might influence the way in which you perform content management.

How Does Volume Affect Content Management?

Let's assume you have responsibility for the construction and maintenance of a small-business website. The site manages no more than 100 content objects (e.g., descriptive information, product photos, a simple FAQ section, graphic images). Each of these content objects is stored as a separate named file.

In this situation, content management is easy. You know exactly where each content object is and what is contained within each file. There is no need for a formal content management approach. A CMS would be overkill.

Now let's consider a situation in which a larger business constructs an e-commerce WebApp. The business sells 800 products, divided into 10 different categories (classes), each with its own description, photograph, and related information. In addition, hundreds of generic content objects flesh out the site (e.g., a biography of the founder with her photograph). Well over 1000 content objects must be managed.

The degree of formality with which you manage this volume of content would have to increase. At a minimum, the WebE team would have to define file naming conventions, establish simple rules for the nature of specific types of content (e.g., a product description is generally limited to no more than 500 words), and establish guidelines for change management.

But would a CMS be necessary in this situation? To answer this question, we'll need additional information that can only be acquired by examining who contributes to the creation on content, how often content changes, and the ways in which content is presented to end users.

Does the Population of Content Creators Have an Effect on CMS?

As the number of content creators grows, a number of problems arise: (1) it becomes increasingly difficult to enforce consistency (in structure, in style, and in content) within a specific content class, (2) change management becomes more challenging because changes may arise from a number of uncoordinated sources, and (3) centralized content management becomes problematic because each content creator wants to own and control the content that she created. Each of these problems can be mitigated, but solutions require an increase in the formality with which content management is applied.

To illustrate this, consider a situation in which the CPI Corporation marketing department decides that it wants to create a "Do-it-Yourself Advice" section for the **SafeHomeAssured.com** WebApp. The intent of this advice section is to provide installation and usage advice from existing *SafeHome* customers.

The company solicits advice from 50 "expert" customers. Each is asked to provide advice on any topic (relevant to *SafeHome*) of his choosing. If no further guidance is provided to the experts, the WebE team would have an immediate content management problem. Each contribution would have its own format and style, there would be significant variations in length, and topic coverage would be spotty.

The **SafeHomeAssured.com** WebE team decides to mitigate these problems by increasing the level of change management formality. First, the team defines a class of content object that it calls **Advice.** All contributions to the "Do-it-Yourself Advice" section of the WebApp will be categorized as advice. More importantly, all content objects within the **Advice** class must conform to the following set of rules:

- All **Advice** objects must be in the form of a *question* followed by an *answer.*
- All questions must be a single sentence of less than 20 words.
- All answers must be less than 500 words and may contain links to diagrams or photos as well as links to other **Advice** objects.
- All **Advice** objects must be time and date stamped.
- All **Advice** objects must be submitted only by an expert with a predefined ID and password.
- Any other expert with a predefined ID and password can add an addendum to an **Advice** object. The addendum can be no more than 250 words in length.

These rules could be given to each expert customer and then enforced by the WebE team member who has responsibility for managing this content. If a more formal level of content management is desired, each **Advice** object could be submitted via an automated forms-based tool that enforces the rules automatically. The tool would name objects and store them in an **Advice** directory for easy access. By managing the **Advice** content in this way, content object consistency is improved significantly and change management is facilitated.

How Does the Change Volume Affect the Formality of Change Management?

As the number of content objects and content contributors grows, there is a high probability that the number of changes will also grow. Stated simply, there's more stuff that could change and more people who will think of reasons to change it!

Within the context of content management formality, change volume is composed of two different components [Boi05]: content object throughput and change frequency. *Content object throughput* is measured by considering how many content objects pass into or out of the repository (or other content storage mechanisms) for any reason. Stated mathematically, content object throughput T, is defined as:

$$T = Obj_{new} + Obj_{old} + Obj_{edit}$$

where

Obj_{new} = number of new content objects added over a predefined period of time (say, one month)

Obj_{old} = number of content objects that have become obsolete and are removed from the WebApp over a predefined period of time

Obj_{edit} = number of content objects that are changed (edited) in some way over a predefined period of time

As the content object throughput increases, the need for more formal methods of content management also increases.

Change frequency refers to the frequency with which the WebApp itself will change. That is, how often will aspects of the WebApp design be modified over a predefined time span? A substantive change to aesthetic design, content design, architecture design, navigation design, and component design invariably has some impact on WebApp content. As a consequence, you may have a need for more formal content management.

How Does Publication Volume Affect Content Management Formality?

Publication volume is measured by considering two factors: the number of publication types and the degree of publication customization. *Publication types* refer to the different structures and styles for presenting WebApp content. As the number of publication types grows, the need for a template-based approach to the creation of end-user content becomes more apparent. *Publication customization* refers to the degree to which end-user input affects the final content presented as part of a customization. A WebApp that produces dynamic Web pages in a format selected by the end user is a classic example of heavy publication customization.

For example, consider a situation in which CPI Corporation decides to extend the **SafeHomeAssured.com** WebApp to service not only retail customers but also original equipment manufacturers (OEMs), wholesale distributors, retail stores, other security firms, governmental agencies, and others. Each end-user category requires a different structure and style for *SafeHome* product information. The content objects used for retail sales remain unchanged, and some new content objects are added to meet the needs of distinct user types. However, all content objects (both old and new) must be custom-published for each user category.

As the publication volume and the degree of customization grow, it becomes increasingly difficult to manage the creation of each required publication. Therefore, automated tools (a CMS) are needed to create the range of publications demanded by different user categories.

SafeHome

Assessing the Need for a CMS

The scene: SafeHomeAssured. com team leader's office

The players: Team leader and members of the WebE team prior to the beginning of the modeling activity for increment 2, *Detailed product information and downloads*

The conversation:

Team leader: Now that we have a basic **SafeHomeAssured.com** informational site up and running, we've got to make a critical architectural decision. How do we manage *SafeHome* content?

Team member 1: Based on requirement gathering input so far, it looks like we'll have about 40 individual **SafeHome** components, each with a product spec, a photo, installation instructions, some with videos. We also have user-derived content.

Team member 2: Obviously, some components will be intimately related to other components, so we'll have links between them. The question is, do we "hard-wire" these links into the content . . . or do we establish them as part of a repository and then dynamically generate the links based on the user's needs? The user-derived content is also interrelated.

For example, the layout is related to the monitoring components that are chosen for it.

Team leader (musing): That's the core architectural question, isn't it? Do we implement a repository and a CMS?

Team member 3: The answer, whatever it is, goes way beyond this increment and will undoubtedly affect the entire WebApp across all increments we build.

Team leader: Thoughts?

Team member 1: Look, we can be sure of one thing . . . if *SafeHome* becomes a big hit, the WebApp will grow and content will expand. For example, I talked to one marketing person who wanted an "advice column" placed inside the product info and another stakeholder who wants to archive all video collected during online control and monitoring; that's increment 6, I think. Anyway, those features didn't make the cut, but they might be introduced later. So . . . I think we'll need a solid information architecture that's expandable. A good CMS can give us that.

Team member 2: I think we should keep it simple. Once we get in bed with a CMS, we're constrained to its architecture and limitations. If we implement our own database, we'll have flexibility.

Team member 1 (frowning): What we don't need is to reinvent the wheel.

Team member 3: Look, if we can find a repository structure that can meet our needs, I'm all for going that way. We've got plenty of work just building custom *SafeHome* features. We don't need to get bogged down implementing extensive data structures and data management functionality, particularly if capability already exists, and I think it does.

Team leader: This is a big decision, and debating it endlessly won't get us anywhere. Here's what I propose. [Looks at team member 1.] I want you to spend the next few days researching our options. I just read an interesting paper: "How to Evaluate a CMS system." I'll send you the URL [see the *Step Two Designs* website at **www.steptwo.com.au/papers/ kmc_evaluate/**]. If possible, come up with three to five candidate CMSs that meet our needs. We can test-drive each to check it out.

Team member 1 (looking wary): But . . . what exactly are our needs?

Team member 3: We can use the requirements we gathered to list them and then maybe extrapolate just a bit to cover future requests. The types of content

we'll manage, the complexity of the relationship is among content objects, the number of static versus dynamic content objects, the total project volume of content, the number of people who will contribute content, the number of content changes we're likely to see, that sort of stuff.

Team member 1 (looking at team member 3): Make me a list, would you?

Team member 3: Sure.

Team member 2 (addressing team member 3): Every one of the items you've just mentioned indicate a relatively small system. Less than 40 components. A content hierarchy that is not particularly complex. Relatively few dynamic objects. Only a few people who generate CPI content . . .

Team member 1 (interrupting): But potentially thousands of users will generate their own content— quotes, layouts, bills of material, not to mention dynamic content that is derived from monitoring features.

Team leader (raising her hand): Okay, stop. As the architect for this project, it's my opinion that we'll need a CMS. It may be that we can use a very simple implementation. Maybe not. Let's do some analysis and decide no later than Friday.

Where We've Been. . . Where We're Going

Because Web-based systems support the core elements of a business, their requirements will change as they are being built and after they have been deployed. When changes are requested, they are manifested in modifications to content objects—text, images, audio, video, navigation mechanisms, input mechanisms, data, and client- and server-based functions. Both changes and the content objects themselves must be managed.

The change management process encompasses five major actions: identification, change control, version control, auditing, and status reporting. A set of naming conventions is created for content objects during identification. Change control defines the criticality and impact of changes and establishes a process that enables changes to be made without confusion and error. Version control allows the WebE team to maintain multiple versions of a content object. Auditing is a quality assurance activity that helps to ensure that changes have been made correctly and that there are no unintended consequences. Finally, status reporting develops mechanisms for reporting what changes happened and when they occurred, who made the changes, and what other content objects have been affected.

Content management allows the WebE team to develop a process and a set of tools for the collection, management, and publication of all content objects associated with a WebApp. The collection subsystem establishes a basis for the creation and/or acquisition of content, and the technical functions that are necessary to convert and organize content into a form that can be delivered to end users. The management subsystem implements a content database and associated change management capabilities. The publishing subsystem allows content to be organized and structured into final form. The formality of a change management process and the system that supports it varies with the complexity and size of the WebApp that is to be deployed.

References

[Boi05]   Boiko, B., *Content Management Bible,* 2nd ed., Wiley, 2005.

[Car01]   Carlis, J., and J. Maguire, *Mastering Data Modeling,* Addison-Wesley, 2001.

[Dar99]   Dart, S., "Change Management: Containing the Web Crisis," *Proc. Software Configuration Management Symposium,* Toulouse, France, 1999, **www.perforce.com/perforce/conf99/dart.html** (accessed August 14, 2007).

[Dar91]   Dart, S., "Concepts in Configuration Management Systems," *Proc. Third International Workshop on Software Configuration Management,* ACM SIGSOFT, 1991, **www.sei.cmu.edu/legacy/scm/abstracts/abscm_concepts.html** (accessed August 14, 2007).

[Jac02]   Jacobson, I., "A Resounding 'Yes' to Agile Processes—But Also More," *Cutter IT Journal* vol. 15, no. 1, January 2002, pp. 18–24.

[Sim05]   Simsion, G., and G. Witts, *Data Modeling Essentials,* 3rd ed., Elsevier, 2005.

FUTURE DIRECTIONS

17

I n the first chapter of this book, we noted that "The Web has become an indispensable technology for business, commerce, communication, education, engineering, entertainment, finance, government, industry, media, medicine, politics, science, and transportation—to name just a few areas that impact your life." We argued that because the Web has become so important, it's only reasonable to engineer the WebApps that an ever-increasing percentage of the world's population uses every day in rich, diverse, and important ways.

But what of the future? Where is the Web going? How will users interact with a "new" Web, and how will this interaction change our lives, our work, and our world view? How will Web engineers respond to future Web directions, and what tools and technology will be available to help them?

To be honest, we can't answer any of these questions with any degree of certainty. If the evolution of the Web over the last decade has taught us anything, it is that the speed of change is amazing, the impact is difficult to overstate, and the nature of each killer WebApp that emerges is unexpected (at least until it does emerge, at which point we all realize how obvious it was). Nevertheless, in this final chapter we'll try to comment briefly on the questions that we just raised.

The Changing Nature of the Web and WebApps

A decade ago, the Web was a tool for disseminating information. An anointed few Webmasters created WebApps, and to a great extent, controlled the information space. Those days are over. Today's Web is egalitarian. The BBC [BBC06] noted that "Blogs, Wikis, social networking sites, file sharing services have transformed the Web . . ." The resultant explosion of Web content has provided enormous benefits to end users, but has also created many questions about content accuracy, legality, accessibility, and its overall worth. The BBC continues:

> But in this world of [content] sharing there are also hazards. As the web becomes even more deeply embedded in our lives, it will become a new battleground, and security issues threaten to erode the public's trust in the internet.

The Web [and WebApps] can be used to steal your identity, trick you into buying nonexistent goods or, more worrying, to threaten the very infrastructure of our society.

And so, like all transcendent technologies, the Web provides enormous benefit and also provides the basis for significant harm. Our job as users and Web engineers is to harness the former and work to restrict those who would try to achieve the latter.

How Will Delivery of Web-Based Content and Functionality Change?

CNET [CNE05] addresses this question directly when it states: "Instead of treating the Web just as a handy way to publish information, businesses need to start acting like software companies and encourage programmers to build services on top of their platforms . . ."

It's likely that Web content and functionality will evolve as more and more mash-up WebApps emerge. Stated simply, a *mash-up application* uses information provided by multiple commercial WebApps to provide a new amalgam of information and/or functionality. As a simple example, an independent WebApp developer might create a WebApp (e.g., **www.mywikimap.com**) that taps a commercial website (e.g., Google Maps) with a database that contains gasoline prices across the United States. The result is a mash-up that provides the location of all low-cost gas stations in your postal code.

In addition to the unique ability to combine content and functionality from multiple WebApps and create content and functions that can be more valuable than the sum of their parts, Web content will be delivered across multiple platforms so that continuous access can be achieved. Even today, users access WebApps via wireless computing devices that include notebook PCs, mobile phones, and PDAs. Access will become ubiquitous, opening up opportunities for content delivery that has value in real time. For example, you stand in front of a restaurant you've never been to before and want to find out how good it is. You access a "restaurant reviews" WebApp via your mobile phone, key in the name of the eatery, and check the reviews before you enter. If you don't like what you see, you ask for another recommendation in the vicinity.

How Will WebApps Change?

Conventional WebApps (Web 1.0) will continue to evolve as better and more robust content is coupled with increasingly more sophisticated functionality. The result provides us with WebApps such as Google Maps, a WebApp that couples a vast collection of graphical satellite imagery with sophisticated manipulation functionality. As mash-ups continue to grow in sophistication and power, Web 2.0 capability begins to emerge. WebApps will tap multiple interconnected databases and the services that make the data valuable to different user categories. This "aggregate web of connected data sources and services" takes WebApp capability to the next level by establishing a synergy between ostensibly disparate content and functionality.

To illustrate this, consider the preceding restaurant example. A further step in the development of the "restaurant reviews" WebApp would be for it to automatically know your location [by using data provided from the built-in global positioning system (GPS) receiver] and to transparently correlate this with map data and business registry information so that it can recognize that you are standing in front of a particular restaurant, and automatically provide you with relevant information (e.g., reviews, menu, pricing, alternatives) without the need for an explicit search on your part. It may even know your particular tastes and search for reviews of that restaurant by other people who have a history of having similar views.

What Will Web Engineers Have to Do to Accommodate These Changes?

As a new generation of WebApps evolve, it's likely that they will tap "an aggregate Web of data sources and services" [Coa06]. To build this new generation of WebApps, Tom Coates [Coa06] suggests a few top-level guidelines for Web developers. Jeremy Zawodny [Zaw06] extends Coates' guidelines (shown below in boldface type) with the following commentary:

> **Look to add value to the aggregate Web of data.** As a company with infrastructure that can scale to scan, retrieve, and analyze a significant portion of all the public on-line information in the world, think about how you can use those capabilities to improve the world. What can you do that someone looking at a much smaller set of the data cannot? What patterns can be found? What connections can be made? What can you simplify for people?
>
> **Build for normal users, developers, and machines.** Make whatever you build easy to use, easy to hack [in the open source sense], and make it emit useful data in a structured form. That means you need a usability geek, an API geek, and probably an XML/RSS/JSON geek.
>
> **Start designing with data, not pages.** Figure out what data is important, how it will be stored, represented, and transferred. Think about the generic services that one can build on top of that repository. Only then should you get the wireframe geeks and/or the photoshop geeks involved . . .
>
> **Identify your first order objects and make them addressable.** Figure out what your service is fundamentally about. If it's a social shopping application, you're probably dealing with people, items, and lists of items. Nail those before going farther. And make sure there's a way to access each object type from the outside world. That means there's a URL for fetching information about an item, a list, etc. These are the building blocks that you'll use to make more complex things later on. Hopefully others will too.

Use readable, reliable, and hackable URLs. If the URL is hard to read over the phone or wraps in email, you're not there yet. Simplicity and predictability rule here. Consider something like **http://socialshopping.com/item/12345.** You can guess what that URL does, can't you? You may not grasp how important this is, but don't let that stop you from worrying about it. This stuff really does matter. Look at how most URLs in del.icio.us are guessable and simple. Mimic that.

Correlate with external identifier schemes. Don't go inventing complete new ways to represent and/or structure things if there's already an established mechanism that'd work. Not only is such effort wasteful, it significantly lowers the chance that others will adopt it and help to strengthen the platform you're building. You *are* building a platform, whether you believe it or not.

Build list views and batch manipulation interfaces. Make it easy to see all items of a given type and make it possible to edit them as a group. *Flickr* does this when you upload a batch of photos. Search, in its many forms, is the classic example of a "list view."

Create parallel data services using standards. Developers (and the code they write) will want to consume your data. Do not make this an afterthought. Get your engineers thinking about how they might use the data and make sure they design the product to support those fantasies. Again, always default to using an existing standard or extending one when necessary. Look at how flexible RSS and Atom are. Don't re-invent the wheel.

Make your data as discoverable as possible. The names and attributes you use should be descriptive to users and developers, not merely a byproduct of the proprietary internal system upon which they're built. This means thinking like an outsider and doing a bit of extra work.

These guidelines can provide a simple philosophical foundation for the development of Web 2.0 WebApps.

Can the Web Serve as a Platform for Application Software?

Absolutely! In fact, Web-based applications are beginning to emerge and may eventually become a significant competitor for conventional packaged software. As we noted in Chapter 14, WebApps are already using a mix of client-side interface technologies and server-side functionality to create applications that mimic the rich interactivity of desktop applications. By making them Web-based, however, we can add aspects that are difficult in conventional desktop applications: improved sharing and collaboration, distributed storage and access of data, and faster evolution of the application.

As an example, consider *Writely* (**www.writely.com**), a WebApp-based word processor that has recently been acquired by Google. In beta test as we write this chapter, *Writely* provides a meaningful array of word processing functionality including an online editor, spell-check, and related functionality. It allows existing word processor documents to be uploaded and stored and can then download documents in popular formats. It provides a built-in revision history and enables "roll back" to any previous version of a document.

It's not clear whether a Web-based application like *Writely* will ultimately supplant desktop applications such as Microsoft *Word* or Corel *Wordperfect*, but the era of Web-based application software has begun.

Can the Future Web Be an OS?

As the Web becomes the platform for certain types of application software, it's reasonable to consider whether a "WebOS" may evolve in the near future and what such an "operating system" might look like. Jason Kottke [Kot05] suggests that a WebOS will have three components:

- A *Web browser and add-ons* that "becomes the primary application interface through which the user views content, performs services, and manages data on their local machine and on the Web, often without even knowing the difference."

- *WebApps* that have been enhanced to provide a better user interface and other capabilities that make them approach desktop applications.

- A *local Web server* (that complements the local operating system) that "handle[s] the data delivery and content display from the local machine to the browser. This local server will likely be highly optimized for its task, but would be capable of running locally installed Web applications (e.g. a local copy of Gmail and all its associated data)."

The browser and Web server would still be operating system specific (i.e., written for Windows, Mac OS, or Linux), but all WebApps would be developed for the WebOS in a machine-independent manner.

Kottke [Kot05] delineates a number of advantages that are inherent in a WebOS:

Compared to "standalone" Web apps and desktop apps, applications developed for this hypothetical platform have some powerful advantages. Because they run in a Web browser, these applications are cross platform (assuming that whoever develops such a system develops the local Web server part of it for Windows, OS X, Linux, your mobile phone, etc.), just like Web apps such as Gmail, Basecamp, and Salesforce.com. You don't need to be on a specific machine with a specific OS. You just need a browser + local Web server to access your favorite data and apps.

For application developers, the main advantage is that instead of writing two or more programs for multiple platforms (one for the Web, one for Windows, etc.), they can write one app that will run on any machine with the WebOS using the same code base ...

> You also get the advantages of locally run applications. You can use them when you're not connected to the Internet. There could be an icon in the Dock that fires up Gmail in your favorite browser. For applications using larger files like images, video, and audio, those files could be stored and manipulated locally instead of waiting for transfer over the Internet.

The manner in which a WebOS will evolve is still a bit hazy. Nicholas Carr [Car05] comments on other related trends: "Cost, security and reliability concerns will ultimately lead companies to demand even less local data and applications than Kottke imagines. The user devices will become ever thinner, as applications, data and even the user operating system resides in central servers."

How Will the "Semantic Web" Change Things?

There are billions of content objects residing within hundreds of millions of Web pages. In order to find the content you need, a string of cleverly chosen key words is fed to one or more search engines. The result is tens of thousands of "hits"—many completely unrelated to the content you desire.

The challenge for Web engineers (and for users) is to better understand what content resides on the Web, to be able to find it easily, to establish relationships among content objects automatically and seamlessly, and to extract knowledge from seemingly disparate content and data sources. The *semantic Web* has been proposed as a mechanism for assigning greater meaning to the content that resides on the Web.

The semantic Web applies a set of technologies that include a *Resource Description Framework* (RDF), a *Web Ontology Language* (OWL), and the *Extensible Markup Language* (XML). Wikipedia [Wik06] describes the interaction of these technologies in the following manner:

> These technologies are combined in order to provide descriptions that supplement or replace the content of Web documents. Thus, content may manifest as descriptive data stored in Web-accessible databases, or as markup within documents (particularly, in Extensible HTML (XHTML) interspersed with XML, or, more often, purely in XML, with layout/rendering cues stored separately). The machine-readable descriptions enable content managers to add meaning to the content, thereby facilitating automated information gathering and research by computers.

In essence, XML establishes the rules for document syntax, RDF provides mechanisms for specifying descriptive information, and OWL enables a content provider to create domain-specific vocabularies that allow users to extract the semantics of the content.

In 1999, Tim Berners-Lee [Ber99] tried to look into the future of a semantic Web when he stated: "I have a dream for the Web [in which computers] become capable of analyzing all the data on the Web—the content, links, and transactions between people and computers. A 'Semantic Web,' which should make this possible, has yet to emerge, but when it does, the day-to-day mechanisms of trade, bureaucracy and our daily lives will be handled by machines talking to machines. The 'intelligent agents' people have touted for ages will finally materialize." We're not there yet, but it's likely that Berners-Lee's vision will materialize over the next decade.

Evolving Web Technologies and Web 2.0

To this point, we've talked about the changing nature of the Web. Now we'll examine some specific technological elements of these changes and how they relate to current and future directions. We'll begin by looking at Web 2.0.

What Is Web 2.0?

Web 2.0 refers not to a particular technology, or even a set of technologies, but rather to a trend within the design of WebApps. Before discussing this in more detail, it might be worth digressing for a moment and discussing a bit of recent history.

When Tim Berners-Lee created the first Web browser in the early 1990s, it was not just a browser. Rather, it was a browser-editor. The intent, right from the very earliest development of the Web, was that users of the Web would also be active participants in the creation of content for the Web. As the Web emerged into the mainstream, this concept was lost (at least, in part). For many years, the Web was simply a passive information distribution channel through which authors created content and made it available, and users accessed and used this content.

Web 2.0 returns to Berners-Lee's initial philosophy and makes the Web much more participatory. The term *Web 2.0* was originally coined by Tim O'Reilly in 2004. In a 2005 article, O'Reilly writes [ORe05]:

> The bursting of the dot-com bubble in the fall of 2001 marked a turning point for the web. Many people concluded that the web was overhyped, when in fact bubbles and consequent shakeouts appear to be a common feature of all technological revolutions. Shakeouts typically mark the point at which an ascendant technology is ready to take its place at center stage. The pretenders are given the bum's rush, the real success stories show their strength, and there begins to be an understanding of what separates one from the other.
>
> The concept of "Web 2.0" began with a conference brainstorming session . . . Could it be that the dot-com collapse marked some kind of turning point for the web, such that a call to action such as "Web 2.0" might make sense? We agreed that it did, and so the Web 2.0 Conference was born.

In the year and a half since, the term "Web 2.0" has clearly taken hold, with more than 9.5 million citations in Google. But there's still a huge amount of disagreement about just what Web 2.0 means, with some people decrying it as a meaningless marketing buzzword, and others accepting it as the new conventional wisdom . . .

In our initial brainstorming, we formulated our sense of Web 2.0 by example:

Web 1.0	$\longrightarrow$	Web 2.0
DoubleClick	$\longrightarrow$	Google AdSense
Ofoto	$\longrightarrow$	Flickr
Akamai	$\longrightarrow$	BitTorrent
mp3.com	$\longrightarrow$	Napster
Britannica Online	$\longrightarrow$	Wikipedia
personal websites	$\longrightarrow$	blogging
evite	$\longrightarrow$	upcoming.org and EVDB
domain name speculation	$\longrightarrow$	search engine optimization
page views	$\longrightarrow$	cost per click
screen scraping	$\longrightarrow$	web services
publishing	$\longrightarrow$	participation
content management systems	$\longrightarrow$	wikis
directories (taxonomy)	$\longrightarrow$	tagging ("folksonomy")
stickiness	$\longrightarrow$	syndication

In the article, O'Reilly goes on to explain that Web 2.0 is not a particular set of technologies, but rather a broad set of principles and practices that reflect the way in which the Web is evolving. He summarizes in the following way:

Let's close, therefore, by summarizing what we believe to be the core competencies of Web 2.0 companies:

- Services, not packaged software, with cost-effective scalability
- Control over unique, hard-to-recreate data sources that get richer as more people use them
- Trusting users as co-developers
- Harnessing collective intelligence
- Leveraging the long tail through customer self-service
- Software above the level of a single device
- Lightweight user interfaces, development models, AND business models

Providing an all-encompassing definition of Web 2.0 will always be contentious. However, we would argue that Web 2.0 is about creating a more engaged, interactive, collective Web experience, where all users are able to be active, rather than passive participants.

What Technologies Support Web 2.0?

Web 2.0 is already emerging with a raft of well-established Web applications that exemplify its characteristics (e.g., Wikipedia, Blogger, Flickr, BitTorrent, YouTube—to name just a few of the better-known applications). We have already discussed (Chapter 14) some of the technologies that are central to these applications. The technologies enable WebApps to achieve an additional degree of active participation. In this section, we'll examine these technologies in light of the changing nature of the Web. The following list is intended to be illustrative rather than exhaustive:

Blogs and wikis. A *blog* (a shortened form of *Web log*) is a commentary or diary that allows a Web user to share personal information, observations, or experiences. The content typically evolves continuously and helps provide a degree of freshness and dynamism to many sites.

Blog support tools enable unsophisticated users to create their own blog with little effort, build and edit their blog entries, create an archive of entries over a period of months or years, and encourage interaction among users by enabling them to respond to or annotate blog content. From a design perspective, blogs can be used to add a communication channel into an otherwise static application and play a crucial role in establishing a social network. From a business perspective, they can become a powerful marketing tool.

A *wiki* is a website that supports user editing of the site content. The resultant collaborative authoring process can result in the emergence of sites that are developed communally, and hence can reflect a rich set of experiences and views. Wikis are often used either to support a specific team in some activity (e.g., as a project documentation tool) or as a way of supporting social networking. Possibly the best-known Wiki is **www.wikipedia.org.**[1]

Mash-ups. A *mash-up* is a hybrid Web application that integrates content from multiple (usually third-party) sources in order to provide a novel synergistic outcome. Mash-ups usually access the content-rich environment of major providers (such as Google, Amazon, and eBay) using a simple public interface. Even when there is no public interface, it is often possible to utilize third-party data through simple "screen-scraping" of the data available on websites. The rich interactivity of many mash-ups typifies the evolving direction of Web 2.0.[2]

---

1 See also the relevant blog entries on Wikipedia at **http://en.wikipedia.org/wiki/BLOG, www.ojr. org/ojr/images/blog_software_comparison.cfm**, **http://en.wikipedia.org/wiki/Wiki,** and the WikiMatrix website at **www.wikimatrix.org/** (all accessed August 14, 2007).
2 See also the mash-up entry on Wikipedia at **http://en.wikipedia.org/wiki/Mashup_(web_application_ hybrid)** and the Programmable Web website at **www.programmableweb.com/mashups** (both accessed August 14, 2007).

Ajax.   Another technology that contributes to rich interactivity is *Ajax*—or *Asynchronous JavaScript and XML*. Ajax is actually a set of complementary technologies that, when used together, can create highly interactive Web applications that feel more like a desktop application than a WebApp. The approach uses JavaScript to download XML data continuously in preparation for the potential use of that data. The result is a more responsive application. The best-known Ajax application is probably **maps.google.com.** Numerous Ajax tool kits[3] have emerged that make constructing Ajax applications much simpler.

Syndication.   *Syndication* makes a fragment of a WebApp available for inclusion elsewhere. For example, you might choose to embed a short one-line "latest news" item, a short "weather report" fragment, or a recent forum post, within a new WebApp. The use of syndicated content can benefit both the provider (through greater exposure) and the receiver (through access to richer content). There are numerous syndication technologies, but undoubtedly the best known is RSS (*Really Simple Syndication*). Basically, RSS is an XML data format for encapsulating content that can be syndicated. The RSS feed can then be used either to directly embed the feed content into another page, or it can be used by an aggregator to collect syndicated content together for users to view. The end result in both cases will be content that is more up to date and more relevant to specific users.[4]

Web services.   A *Web service* is a software component (possibly remote) that provides some defined functionality using a specified interface. A Web service might support something as simple as validating a telephone number to ensure it is in a correct format or as complex as processing a credit card payment. The Web services architecture allows Web services to register with a service broker and then allows clients to locate and then utilize relevant services. Indeed, complex WebApps can be built up by combining rich sets of services.

Figure 17.1 shows the collection of the standards and technologies that comprise the Web services architecture. *Web services description language* (WSDL) is used to describe Web service interfaces. SOAP is a protocol for communicating with Web services. A range of other related standards are then built on top of this. For example, WS-BPEL (*Web Services—Business Process Execution Language*) describes the state transition interactions that occur in business processes and how these map to Web service operations.

---

3   See also the Ajax entry on Wikipedia at **http://en.wikipedia.org/wiki/Ajax_(programming)** and the Ajax article on the dmoz Open Directory Project website at **http://dmoz.org/Computers/ Programming/Languages/JavaScript/AJAX/** (both accessed August 14, 2007).
4   See also: **http://en.wikipedia.org/wiki/Web_syndication** and **http://en.wikipedia.org/wiki/ RSS_(file_format)**.

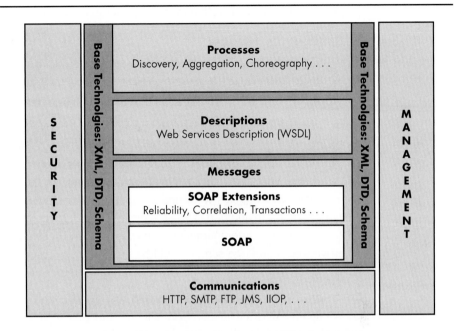

Strictly speaking, Web services do not focus on specific types of Web applications, but rather, define an architecture that supports the creation of applications. They do, however, facilitate the simpler implementation of rich applications. For example, many mash-ups are enabled by providers making their content available through a Web service.[5]

Metadata, ontologies, and folksonomies.   Effective use of content can be facilitated by using *metadata*—information *about* the content. The simplest form of metadata is information embedded directly into Web pages. A richer representation is possible using RDF (Resource Description Framework)—an XML format for making *statements* about *resources. Ontologies* (a representation of a domain that can be used as the basis of reasoning) can then be built on top of the RDF and can result in languages such as OWL (Web Ontology Language) that can be used to publish and share data that describes a particular domain.

So what is the likely impact of these technologies? They can be used to create highly structured information that can then be analyzed and processed in a variety of different ways. For example, FOAF (Friend of a Friend) is used to describe relationships between people. Information about each friend can be used to build adaptive applications that customize information based on who your friends are.

---

5   See also the description of Web services on Wikipedia at **http://en.wikipedia.org/wiki/Web_services** and on the World Wide Web Consortium site at **www.w3.org/2002/ws/** (both accessed on August 14, 2007).

A *folksonomy* is a collaboratively generated taxonomy, which uses user-generated tags and metadata to describe content (the labeling process is often referred to as *tagging*). This means that rather than having a single taxonomy, we end up with a rich multifaceted set of metadata. Because part of the metadata includes the author, users can identify subsets (created by selected individuals) that have categorized information in ways that make the most sense to them.[6]

VoIP.   *Voice over IP* (VoIP) enables the transmission of voice data over the Internet (rather than via conventional telephone networks). Today, VoIP is having a major impact on telecommunications through applications such as *Vonage* and *Skype*, and over time, it is also likely to have a major impact on the design of WebApps. For example, VoIP enables WebApps to support podcasting and rich customer service experiences. In addition, it will enable less obvious aspects such as automated switching between different media forms based on the delivery hardware (e.g., text when viewed on a large screen could be automatically converted to a VoIP voice stream when a mobile phone or PDA with limited screen space is being used).

Location-aware applications.   As GPS receivers become more common, it becomes increasingly feasible for Web clients to have available to them information on the location of the client. Once location is known, it is possible to develop Web-Apps so that the user experience can be appropriately customized to where the user is at the moment. Today, a limited version of this approach is used when a WebApp changes the advertizements that are presented, depending upon the location of the user inferred from the IP address. As Web access becomes more ubiquitous and users start accessing WebApps from a more diverse set of locations (and devices), everything from localized advertising ("If you're in the mood for a snack, visit Dom's bakery . . . you'll be passing us in less than a minute") to traffic warnings ("There is a traffic problem a quarter mile ahead"), to general assistance ("The nearest hospital is . . .").

These are only a few of many other emerging technologies that will play a part in the future of the Web.[7] Some will become a small part of the large and evolving Web landscape. Others are likely to be more crucial in fundamentally reshaping the Web.

---

6   See also information on RDF and ontologies on the World Wide Web Consortium website at **www.w3.org/RDF/** and **www.w3.org/2004/OWL/**, and on Wikipedia at **http://en.wikipedia.org/wiki/Ontology_(computer_science)** and **http://en.wikipedia.org/wiki/Folksonomy** (all accessed on August 14, 2007).
7   For an excellent discussion of the entire Web 2.0 landscape, visit the Web Design from Scratch site at **www.webdesignfromscratch.com/future-social-web-experience.cfm** (accessed August 14, 2007).

What Are Some Key Issues[8] That Should Be Considered as Technology Evolves?

Three key issues and a number of important questions must be considered as Web 2.0 evolves. The key issues are

Scalability. Web 2.0 technologies should have the ability to scale up to the level required for high-volume, mission-critical enterprise applications. Although scalability depends on the nature of the WebApp and the specific technologies being considered, most Web 2.0 technologies have been specifically designed to be distributed and scalable—and indications from many early Web 2.0 applications are that scalability is generally not a significant issue.

Interoperability. Web 2.0 technologies must be capable of being effectively integrated with existing legacy systems and databases. To date, many legacy applications are embedded within Web service wrappers. Many existing mash-ups have been achieved using this approach exclusively.

Applicability. Not every business has the opportunity to develop a new product or system as innovative and exciting as Google Maps. The question that arises is, What kinds of Web 2.0 technology should mainstream Fortune 2000 companies be thinking of for their customers? There are really several key elements of Web 2.0 that are essential for most companies. The first is *increased interactivity,* achieved through the adoption of technologies such as Ajax. Second, the strategic use of blogs and wikis can actively engage users and encourage them to participate. Third, more robust content that has been customized to be more relevant to users is an important business capability. RSS feeds might provide a key mechanism for this. And finally, consideration should be given to the way in which content is made available for use elsewhere—possibly through public access to relevant Web services.

In addition to scalability, interoperability, and applicability, two important questions should be answered:

- **What are the benefits, risks, and recommended practices for "opening up" access [via application programming interfaces (APIs)] to a company's current proprietary database and online functionality?** The benefits can include increased exposure for a company's products and services. For example, an online retailer might provide access to its catalog

---

8 For a set of interesting questions and issues, see the questions that were asked as part of a call for papers for Web 2.0; see the Cutter website at **www.cutter.com/content-and-analysis/journals-and-reports/cutter-it-journal/callforpapers01.html.** (accessed August 14, 2007).

and pricing, which could then encourage it to be included in aggregator sites that support product comparisons, potentially then leading to additional sales. The risks are that these comparisons could be damaging!

- **What are the benefits, risks, and recommended practices for allowing a company's customers to contribute "content" to the company's existing Web-based marketing material, product descriptions, and troubleshooting FAQs?** The benefits include excellent (or at least helpful) customer feedback, positive testimonials, useful sources of content, and more loyal customers. The downside can be negative views expressed about the company's products and services, and the cost of maintaining the systems to support the users' involvement.

What's Next for Web 2.0?

In order to understand how Web 2.0 will evolve over time, it's worth looking back at the evolution of the early Web (Web 1.0). As we noted earlier in this book, the Web began with very simple content-driven sites, evolved into WebApps that contained more complex information sources, and then adapted to the changing demands of users and corporate imperatives by adding in support for advanced functionality, such as in e-commerce applications. Web 2.0 technologies now enable added active participation of users into the utilization of content.

Referring to Figure 17.2, the next evolutionary step is to add the same degree of interactivity and user participation into the functional aspects of WebApps as currently exists with active content. Imagine being able to borrow someone else's filtering algorithms for use in a search engine, being able to upload your bill pay-

---

FIGURE 17.2

Evolution of
Web 2.0.

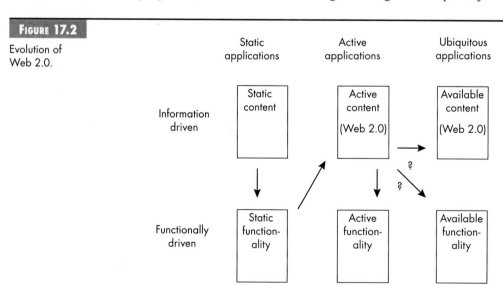

ment schedule to your online bank, or being able to participate in the collective creation of a new customized WebApp? All of this, and much more, will occur as Web 2.0 evolves, and you'll be able to do it wherever and whenever you wish!

One View of the Future

Prognostication is never easy, and efforts to predict the direction of the Web and its societal impact are suspect at best. Having said that, it's still fascinating to try to envision the "future" beyond Web 2.0.

In 2004, Robin Sloan [Slo06] developed a fictional short movie that provides a window into one possible future for the Web, the media, and each of us. We reproduce a transcript of the original movie below and urge you to see the updated version at **http://epic.makingithappen.co.uk/new-master1.html.**[9]

> In the year 2014 people have access to a breadth and depth of information unimaginable in an earlier age.
>
> Everyone contributes in some way.
>
> Everyone participates to create a living, breathing mediascape. However, the Press, as you know it, has ceased to exist. The Fourth Estate's fortunes have waned. 20th Century news organizations are an after-thought, a lonely remnant of a not too distant past.
>
> The road to 2014 began in the mid-20th Century.
>
> In 1989, Tim Berners-Lee, a computer scientist at the CERN particle physics laboratory in Switzerland, invents the World Wide Web.
>
> 1994 sees the founding of Amazon.com. Its young creator dreams of a store that sells everything. Amazon's model, which would come to set the standard for Internet sales, is built on automated personalized recommendations—a store that can make suggestions.
>
> In 1998, two Stanford programmers create Google. Their algorithm echoes the language of Amazon, it treats links as recommendations, and from that foundation powers the world's most effective search engine.
>
> In 1999, TiVo transforms television by unshackling it from the constraints of time—and commercials. Almost no one who tries it ever goes back.
>
> That year, a dot-com start-up named Pyra Labs unveils Blogger, a personal publishing tool.
>
> Friendster launches in 2002 and hundreds of thousands of young people rush to populate it with an incredibly detailed map of their lives, their interests and their social

---

9   This material is copyrighted by Robin Sloan and Matt Thomson and is reproduced with permission.

networks. Also in 2002, Google launches GoogleNews, a news portal. News organizations cry foul. GoogleNews is edited entirely by computers.

In 2003, Google buys Blogger. Google's plans are a mystery, but their interest in Blogger is not unreasonable.

2003 is the Year of the Blog.

2004 would be remembered as the year that everything began.

Reason Magazine sends subscribers an issue with a satellite photo of their houses on the cover and information custom-tailored to each subscriber inside.

Sony and Philips unveil the world's first mass-produced electronic paper.

Google unveils GMail, with a gigabyte of free space for every user.

Microsoft unveils Newsbot, a social news filter.

Amazon unveils A9, a search engine built on Google's technology that also incorporates Amazon's trademark recommendations.

And then, Google goes public.

Awash in new capital, the company makes a major acquisition. Google buys TiVo.

2005—In response to Google's recent moves, Microsoft buys Friendster.

2006—Google combines all of its services—TiVo, Blogger, GMail, GoogleNews and all of its searches into the Google Grid, a universal platform that provides a functionally limitless amount of storage space and bandwidth to store and share media of all kinds. Always online, accessible from anywhere. Each user selects her own level of privacy. She can store her content securely on the Google Grid, or publish it for all to see. It has never been easier for anyone, everyone to create as well as consume media.

2007—Microsoft responds to Google's mounting challenge with Newsbotster, a social news network and participatory journalism platform. Newsbotster ranks and sorts news, based on what each user's friends and colleagues are reading and viewing and it allows everyone to comment on what they see.

Sony's ePaper is cheaper than real paper this year. It's the medium of choice for Newsbotster.

2008 sees the alliance that will challenge Microsoft's ambitions. Google and Amazon join forces to form Googlezon. Google supplies the Google Grid and unparalled search technology. Amazon supplies the social recommendation engine and its huge commercial infrastructure. Together, they use their detailed knowledge of every user's social network, demographics, consumption habits and interests to provide total customization of content—and advertising.

The News Wars of 2010 are notable for the fact that no actual news organizations take part.

Googlezon finally checkmates Microsoft with features the software giant cannot match. Using a new algorithm, Googlezon's computers construct news stories dynamically, stripping sentences and facts from all content sources and recombining them. The computer writes a news story for every user.

In 2011, the slumbering Fourth Estate awakes to make its first and final stand. The New York Times Company sues Googlezon, claiming that the company's fact-stripping robots are a violation of copyright law. The case goes all the way to the Supreme Court, which on August 4, 2011 decides in favour of Googlezon.

On Sunday, March 9 2014, Googlezon unleashes EPIC.

Welcome to our world.

The "Evolving Personalized Information Construct" is the system by which our sprawling, chaotic mediascape is filtered, ordered and delivered. Everyone contributes now—from blog entries, to phone-cam images, to video reports, to full investigations. Many people get paid too—a tiny cut of Googlezon's immense advertising revenue, proportional to the popularity of their contributions.

EPIC produces a custom contents package for each user, using his choices, his consumption habits, his interests, his demographics, his social network—to shape the product.

A new generation of freelance editors has sprung up, people who sell their ability to connect, filter and prioritize the contents of EPIC.

We all subscribe to many Editors; EPIC allows us to mix and match their choices however we like. At its best, edited for the savviest readers, EPIC is a summary of the world—deeper, broader and more nuanced than anything ever available before.

Will any of this come to pass, and if it will, how far from Sloan's scenario will it be? Only time will tell. We believe, however, that there is at least one aspect of the likely future of the Web that this scenario hasn't captured. The future Web will be based not only on all of us playing a part in the creation and usage of rich complex content, but will also be based on all of us participating in the construction and usage of rich complex functionality. In the same way that Flickr allows users to share photos and YouTube allows users to share videos, we can imagine a site in the future that allows us to create, participate in, and share complex tasks—such as shared monitoring of security sensors in **SafeHomeAssured.com.**

The Changing Nature of Web Engineering

Technologies change, tools evolve, better methods emerge, and older ones fade away, but people remain the same. If we are to learn anything by observing the last half century, it's this—*most technology problems can be solved, but the people problems that are associated with the development and use of the technology present us with a continuing challenge.*

As Web engineering evolves over the next decade, our greatest challenges will remain the same:

- To recognize that stakeholder needs are paramount, but at the same time to understand that there are limits on how rapidly we can deliver high-quality, robust solutions.

- To refine a Web engineering process in a manner that allows it to be agile, adaptable, and effective, recognizing that the process should never get in the way of a good solution, but no process at all can often lead to a bad solution.

- To recognize that the nature of a desired WebApp solution will often evolve during the course of the development and that creating the right solution will often involve a complex interplay between new systems and changes to existing processes and behaviors—and that many of these changes won't become clear until the system is in place.

- To develop methods and techniques that give us better insight into the problem and a better feel for the Web-based solution, recognizing that methods and techniques are not a substitute for human communication and a meaningful understanding of the problem.

- To manage change in a way that satisfies the dynamic nature of the twenty-first century business environment, but at the same time avoiding the chaos that uncontrolled change can foster.

As Web engineers, we'll continue to work in the most dynamic and exciting technology area in the world today. Virtually everything and everybody in the modern world is connected to the Web in some way. It's our job to help ensure that the Web serves the world community in a way that makes life better for us all.

References

[BBC06] BBC News, "Building on the Future of the Web," May 22, 2006, **http://news.bbc.co.uk/2/hi/technology/4994570.stm** (accessed August 14, 2007).

[Ber99] Berners-Lee, T., *Weaving the Web,* Harper San Francisco, 1999.

[Car05] Carr, N., "Where's the OS?" August 24, 2005, **www.roughtype.com/archives/2005/08/jason_kottke_of.phpm** (accessed August 14, 2007).

[CNE05] CNET News.com, "From Web Page to Web Platform," August 16, 2005, **http://www.news.com/From+Web+page+to+Web+platform/2100-7345_3-5833940.html?tag=nl** (accessed August 14, 2007).

[Coa06] Coates, T., "My 'Future of Web Apps' Slides . . ." February 13, 2006, **www.plasticbag.org/archives/2006/02/my_future_of_web_apps_slides** (accessed August 14, 2007).

[Kot05]   Kotke, J., "GoogleOS? YahooOS? MozillaOS? WebOS?" August 23, 2005, **www.kottke.org/05/08/googleos-webos** (accessed August 14, 2007).

[ORe05]   O'Reilly, T., "What Is Web 2.0: Design Patterns and Business Models for the Next Generation of Software," September 30, 2005, **www.oreillynet.com/pub/ a/oreilly/tim/news/2005/09/30/what-is-web-20.html** (accessed August 14, 2007).

[Slo06]   Sloan, R., and M. Thomson, A video produced by the fictional "Museum of Media History," 2006, **http://epic.makingithappen.co.uk/new-master1.html.** (accessed August 14, 2007).

[Wik06]   Wikipedia, "Semantic Web," 2006, **http://en.wikipedia.org/wiki/Semantic_Web** (accessed August 14, 2007).

[Zaw06]   Zawodny, J., "Tom's Future of Web Apps, Translated for Product Managers," 2006, **http://jeremy.zawodny.com/blog/archives/006323.html** (accessed August 14, 2007).

Index